CONTENTS

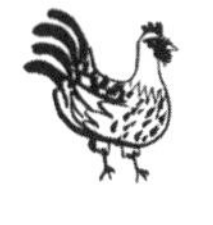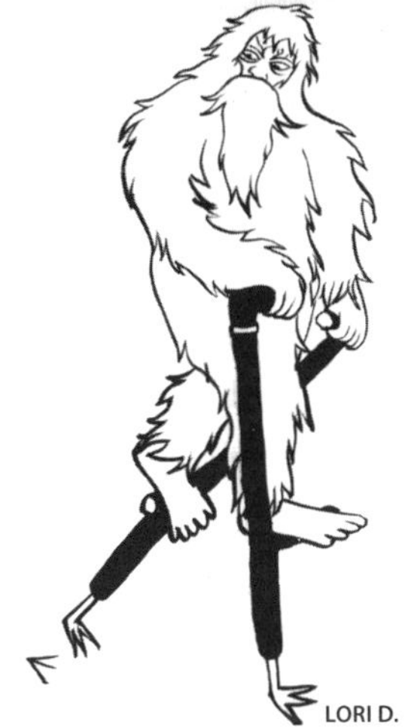

YETI BACK ISSUES

YETI ONE Harry Smith, Terry Riley, James Brown's Original Funky Divas, Alan Greenberg, Califone, Destroy All Monsters, Träd Gräs Och Stenar, Brad Johnson, Pita, Fennesz & Bauer, Robert Walser, Tae Won Yu (photographs), Jana Martin, "A Lo-Fi Metal Primer," Alphonse Allais, "Downtown 81," James Kochalka. On the CD: Iron & Wine (debut recording), Elliott Smith, Nobukazu Takemura, Harry Smith (debut release of his "field recordings"), Califone, Stereolab, L'Altra, Träd Gräs Och Stenar, Screamers, Turn On, Mice Parade, more. 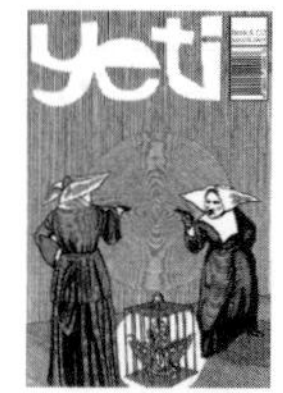

YETI TWO Alfred Jarry, Laura Cantrell, Aceyalone, Luc Sante ("The Birth of the Blues"), Richard Thompson, Trinie Dalton, Steffen Basho-Junghans, Amy Gerstler (poems + interview), Rachel Kushner, Brian Chippendale, Ben Katchor, Marcellus Hall. On the CD: Steffen Basho-Junghans, Shins, Keith Fullerton Whitman, Death Cab for Cutie, Califone, White Hassle, Pell Mell, Iron & Wine, Six Organs of Admittance, Takagi Masakatsu, Kill Me Tomorrow, Birdbrain, Carissa's Wierd, The Scene Is Now, more. 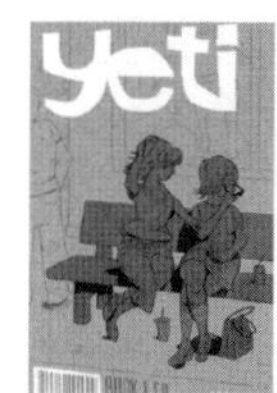

YETI THREE Unpublished William Burroughs interview, Devendra Banhart, Neko Case, Naomi Yang, R.J. Smith, Jason Miles, Michael Galinsky, Erik Davis, BloodNinja, Henry Flynt, Charles Peterson, "The Apes Guide to the Apes," Eileen Myles. On the CD: Devendra Banhart, Henry Flynt, Postal Service, Colin Meloy, Iron & Wine, Jolie Holland, I Rowboat, the Mad Scene, the Lights, Dan Melchior, Ian Nagoski, the Apes, the Robot Ate Me, Blues Goblins, Dream Lovers, Timesbold, Washington Phillips, KRMTX, more. 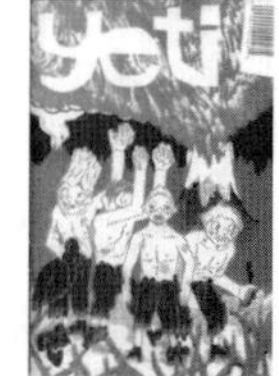

YETI FOUR Fred Tomaselli, Rev. Louis Overstreet, Stacey Levine, "How to sing along to 'Sweet Home Alabama'," Destroyer, Jana Martin, Peter Doyle, Octavia Butler, Sam Lipstyte, Will Sheff, Jason Miles, Melissa Dyne, Khaela Maricich, Peter Lamborn Wilson, Souled American, Vanessa Vaselka. On the CD: Destroyer, Califone, Bright, Okkervil River, Michael Hurley w/ Tara Jane O'Neil, Valet, Fly Ashtray, Plants, Rev. E.W. Clayborn, Theo Angell, the Blow, Souled American, Alela Diane, Somos Marquis Homos, more. 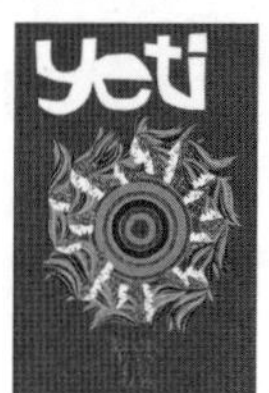

YETI BOOKS

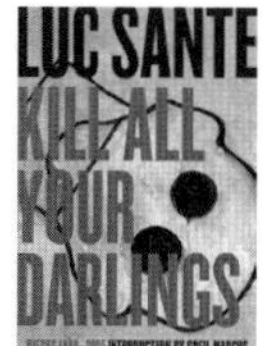

KILL ALL YOUR DARLINGS, by Luc Sante
Essays on music, art, photography, poetry, and life, from a brilliant critic with "burning passion and a prose style to die for" (William Gibson). Introduction by Greil Marcus.

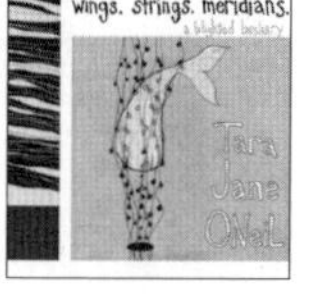

WINGS. STRINGS. MERIDIANS, by Tara Jane O'Neil
96 full-color pages of drawings and paintings, plus a 15-song CD of live tracks, four-track recordings, and film scores.

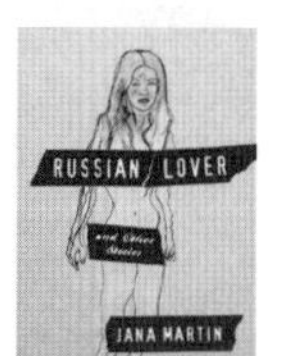

RUSSIAN LOVER AND OTHER STORIES, by Jana Martin
"Tough, funny stories from a writer wise enough to know that wisdom doesn't always come with experience." (Sam Lipsyte)

prices/ordering information at **yetipublishing.com**, where you'll also find the YETI blog and online group

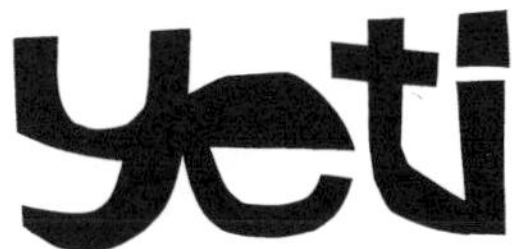

PUBLISHER & EDITOR
Mike McGonigal

MANAGING EDITOR
Steve Connell

CONTRIBUTING EDITOR
Fred Cisterna

COVER IMAGE
Saul Chernick
(adapted from his work
The Guardian, 2007,
ink on paper)

LAYOUT/DESIGN
Steve Connell

COPYEDITORS
Lily Hudson, Mara Reynolds
Katherine Spielmann

GRAPHICS GUY
Scott Nasburg

WEBMASTER
Marcus Estes

CD mastered by Tim Stollenwerk

CD manufactured by CDForge

Book printed in Canada
by Kromar Printing

THANKS to everyone who participated in the YETI program *Beneath the Underdog* at the 2007 Bumbershoot Festival in Seattle and the second YETI–curated Halleluwah Fest at Holocene in Portland

This issue is dedicated to the memory of
Ellen Hausler, Bengt Olsson, Prop Joe, and Charles Gocher

YETI is published 2 to 3 times a year by Yeti Publishing LLC

CONTACT US
PO Box 14806
Portland, OR 97293
yetipubs@gmail.com
yetipublishing.com

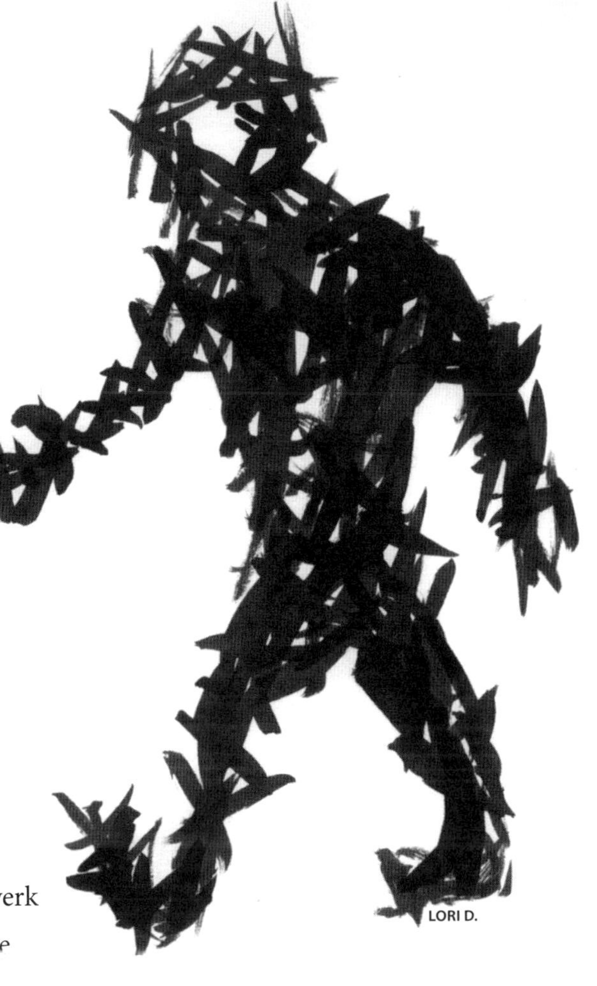

OF WOLVES AND VIBRANCY

A brief exploration of the marriage made in hell between folk music, dead cultures, myth, and highly technical modern extreme metal

by Scott Seward

ILLUSTRATION BY JASON TRAEGER

In my capacity as a custodian at a small island hospital off of the coast of New England, I have a host of duties to fulfill and I wear many hats. Many of these hats can be fairly smelly, and—given that I usually work by myself, and that the work itself tends to be somewhat mechanical and entirely physical—I find that I can be taken over and nearly overwhelmed at times by certain Proustian reveries triggered by the site-specific odors I come into contact with on a regular basis. Blood, urine, vomit, shit, freshly-mown grass, the salt-water spray from the harbor across the street, the oppressive, on hot days almost visible cloud surrounding the water-treatment plant out back, the cleansers and waxes, the iodine and ammonia, the food from the cafeteria, and even the thick, oil-streaked coffee that my Brazilian co-workers brew nightly in the break room far from prying eyes.

All of these smells, separately and in conjunction, have the power to intoxicate me, eliciting primal, nearly forgotten memories that go back as far as the cradle. And of course it's not just the smells. The sights and sounds of birth, death, and the various bodily humiliations visited upon us in between those two milestones, to which my position affords me a unique all-access pass, can fill my head with all manner of disorienting thoughts and connections that sometimes force sobering reflections about my own life and mortality upon me.

And then there are days when I simply dream of pie. Hot cherry pie.

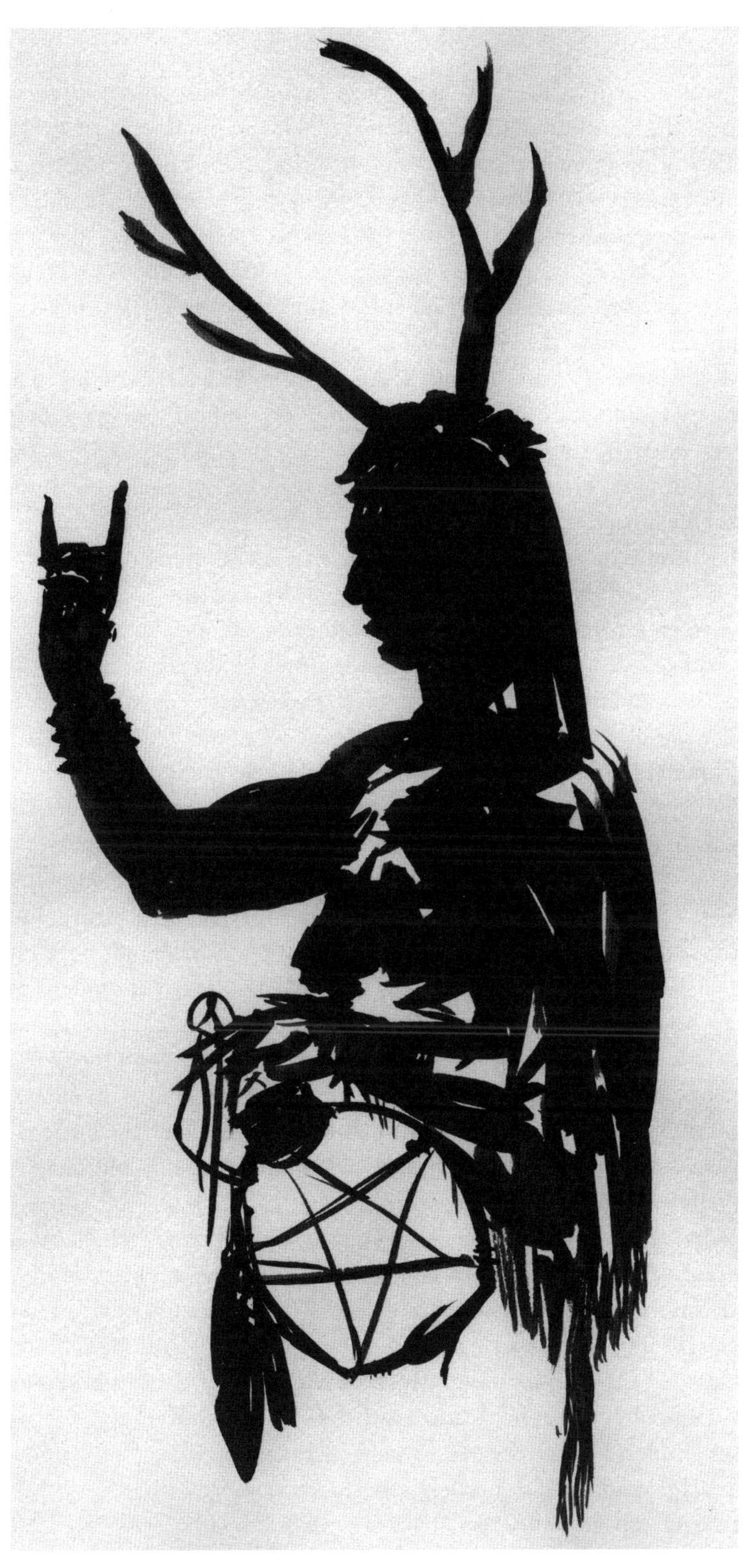

It might sound a little too cute if I were to say that all of this near-constant—occasionally alarming—stimulation provides inspirational and creative fodder for the writing about heavy metal I do every month for a metal magazine. But it would be true. And it might be a bit morbid if I were to say that a blood-streaked floor sometimes reminded me of what I love about metal. But that would be true too. I have an immediate, visceral reaction to the sounds of metal, as I do to the sight of blood, and both serve to connect me to the past via experience and memory and to the present via . . . what exactly?

With metal, I think it's that sense of immediacy and vitality that even mediocre examples of the genre can conjure up simply by virtue of hyperbole and that striving to be the most of something. The most base, or debased, or most grandiose, or most gloomy, or most triumphant. I respond strongly to unashamed displays of the will to power in most genres of any art. At the very least, I admire those who feel as if the infinite is within their grasp. No matter how misguided their central premise. Believing you are a bad-ass is half the battle when it comes to creating something compelling.

And as far as my reactions to blood . . . well, blood is blood. It's freaky and mysterious and hard to get out of carpets. Even a drop can send me swooning down the rabbit hole of scabby, incandescent childhood filth and fury.

If metal is the music that most accurately reflects my physical and mental reactions to my surroundings, then the metal I find myself attracted to, for reasons of empathy, sympathy, and love of moss-covered rocks in dark forests, is metal that makes the most of the past—the long ago and forgotten past, the past of myth, the past of runes, ruins, and revelry—and incorporates that past into a wholly modern form. I might say the same about rock music in general (I am a rockhead and love all its myriad guises), but modern extreme metal—the hard to grasp stuff, the nasty stuff, the stuff that doesn't reach out to include you, the stuff that lives in its own world away from the crowds, and that doesn't try too soothe even in its beauty—reminds me more of jazz or rap or tricky modern classical music, which demand that you crack codes before they will break bread with you and thus are more intriguing and captivating to a devourer of sound such as myself.

Rap and metal are close cousins. They rarely kiss, and when they do people often turn their heads away in embarrassment. And that's because they aren't third cousins—they live two houses down from one another and know each other well. They both have secret languages, worlds built from words and visions and fiery art filled with transcendent repetitions, monster beats, and often dour and dire predictions of harm and mishap. This, in a more general way, was jazz, too, once upon a time—dangerous, noisy, demanding, whispered about. Adored by underground Swedish hordes.

Metal and rap are still the danger sounds today, in a way that traditional and even alternative rock and roll—ever smarter, ever more bloodless and odorless—hardly ever is. There is ferment and experiment and the dedicated plowing of fertile fields in metal.

Of course, it's possible that my personality is simply better suited to the worlds that metal creates than those of other popular genres: tense, prone to delusions of grandeur, brooding storm clouds, fond of Vikings.

As I write this, I am on fire watch. The alarms are out in Wing Three and it is my job to spend the night at the hospital after my shift and search empty offices every hour for the sight of flames softly licking 'round bare wires or the acrid stench of smoke. For insurance purposes. I've set up camp on a couch in Acute Care. It's four a.m. and I'm blasting Orphaned Land's 2004 album *Mabool* on my headphones. I am hallucinating slightly as a result of the long day now turned to night.

Orphaned Land are from Israel and are beloved by Arabs and Jews alike. They combine their metal—which is already a combination of mid-tempo death metal and orthodox doom—with aching lyrical passages and harmonies (think of a combination of *Fiddler on the Roof* and *Jesus Christ Superstar*, if you dare), and high-spirited traditional Arabic and Israeli acoustic instrumentation, as well as a smattering of Yemenite chant and your general Old Testament-based vibe and charm.

Mabool is quite a ride. Like most compact discs, it's about twenty minutes too long, but even so, it's a striking artistic statement, and one that took all of seven years to make in between bouts of homeland insecurity and spilled blood and treasure. The acoustic folk elements are soldered seamlessly onto the electric metal chassis. Orphaned Land's metal tends to be fairly middle of the road, and even their death grunts are amiable. Not for them the extreme speed and aggression

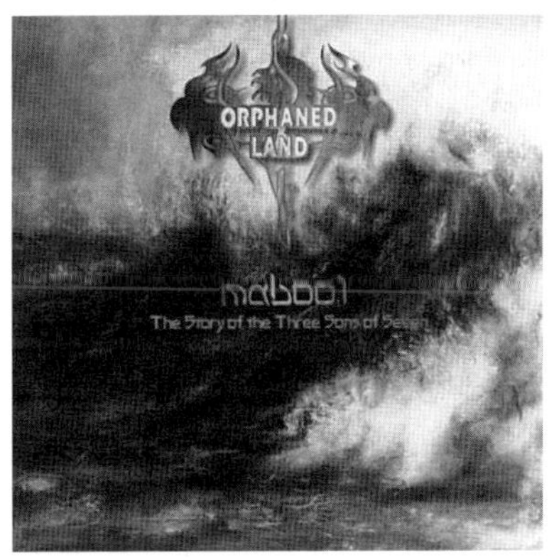

of, say, American death metal band Nile, the Ancient Egypt-obsessed brutes who leaven their bombastic pleas to Atum or Osiris with period-appropriate serpentine constructions played on Middle Eastern instruments. Nile's self-described "ithyphallic" metal shares some of the same mythological territory as extreme archeologists and Mesopotamia/Sumeria metal champs Melechesh and Absu, as well.

Even given Orphaned Land's relative placidness, though, *Mabool* is still an album you must give in to. Sink in to. When it comes to metal, it can be hard for literal-minded music fans to turn off their minds and float downstream. The social conditioning, the stigmas and stereotypes are so strong. I take heart in the fact that more people probably hate opera than meta (which is also a shame, and also partially vocal-based). Then there are the people who can never look beyond the juvenile and cartoonish aspects of some metal; to them the music will forever be monolithic, stupid, not worth bothering with.

The truth is, metal needs its puerile and unsavory elements to be as strong a form as it is. If you exclude the bad and the ugly from art and only focus on the good, then you are truly living in fairyland. Also, you are your grandmother. A song entitled "Strangled By Intestines" will not be to everyone's taste, but dig a little deeper and you will learn that its author, Joe Wolfe (of the group Heinous Killings), is revered by hundreds as one of the greatest low-tone goregrind vocalists of all time!

Orphaned Land has stopped whirling, and I am playing some Magane. Still no sign of fire in the building. The only thing I smell is the overripe scent of dying flowers in a vase of fetid yellow water, left on the table next to me by long-gone wishers of well. Magane are from Japan and make what they like to call Yomi metal. It is a blend of blackened death metal played with punkish zeal plus evocative strains of Gagaku (ancient Japanese court music) and Shinto chants and recitations. The band draws lyrical inspiration from the sacred Kojiki text when they're not shrieking about killing Christian pigs and drinking themselves to death. Shintoism!

Many camps of folk-metal lay great emphasis on the pre-everything world. Pre-Christian, pre-Roman, the supposedly anarchic wonderland of ice and snow before the invaders showed up. Metal has always been a great place for people who don't feel they belong in the world. And metal artists go to great lengths to create a home, a place, a life, a philosophy, a religion, out of the tools of their art. Or they go out of their way to trumpet the merits of their own small patch of soil.(Again with the rap comparisons. Speaking of which, you have no idea how members of the California Latino-American thrash-metal revival movement feel about the wrong people wearing high-top Reeboks. It ain't pretty.)

I can dig the sentiment. In the 1980s, I was a big admirer of British anarcho-punks like Crass and Flux Of Pink Indians, and the idea that some of these groups had punk-rock communes seemed so cool to me. In the states there was the Dischord house and the Better Youth Organization. Punk boy scouts, really. I would have looked for a like-minded place or cult myself at the time, but I've never been fond of gardening. Other than on an aesthetic basis, I can't say that I'm all that interested in Germanic neo-paganism, Odinism, heathenry, mysticism, Satanism, Celtic neo-Druidism, animism, shamanism, or ritual-based Asatru worship practices, but I admire their practitioners' pep and hand-crafted leatherware—and their music, of course.

To be honest, I'm not a huge fan of the real deal ancient folke consorts that dot the landscape of music festivals and renaissance faires. Too often they lack the fierceness and meatiness of music born from blood and fire and plague. Metal bagpipers usually trump the historically accurate but noticeably timid players in the traditional music camps. One listen to Finland's Korpiklaani, who rage like the Pogues after several years of weight-training, sends me instantly back to a time when trolls ruled the woods, in a way that all the progressive, well-meaning Breton flute toodlers in the world could never manage.

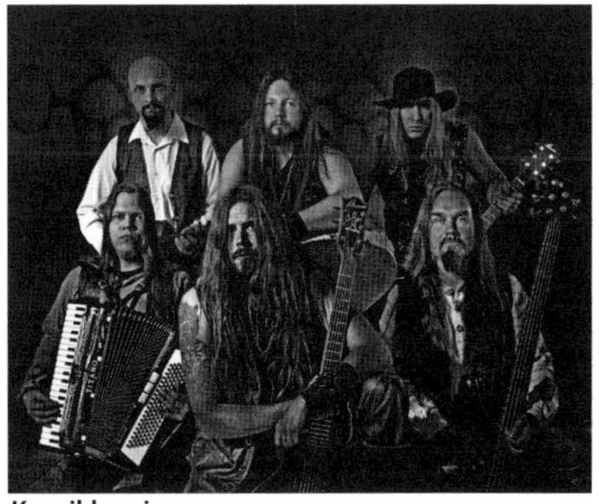
Korpiklaani

I also appreciate how *modern* Korpiklaani and other folk-metal artists are. They dream of the past, but they live in the here and now and make music that reflects that. The Viking folk-metal of Falkenbach, Tyr, Moonsorrow, Ensiferum, and Einherjer re-creates old Norse and Celtic battle rhythms and hymns with great liveliness and invention—they can also all play their heathen butts off—but they also never fail to bring new ideas to the world of metal and music through their deft use of modern recording techniques. Not unlike the brave—and oft derided—'70s progressive-rock titans of yore.

Tyr are from the remote Faroe Islands, equidistant between Iceland and Norway, whose fishing communities have never entirely lost the love or feel for their Viking and Celtic heritage. Tyr even sing some of their songs in Faroese, a language based on Old Norse and once outlawed by their Danish masters (the islands are now an "autonomous region" of Denmark).

Which brings me to my next point. The nationalism, neo-nationalism, and even national socialism of some modern metal bands is obviously problematic, though less so when you're listening to solo music for lute and are told that the artist is "Aryan-identified"... *If you say so.* Luckily, most of the best artists in the folk-metal and even current neo-folk world are simply avid tree-huggers, and while I might not want to ask some of them their views on immigration or rap music, that would probably also be the case with more than one of my favorite country performers.

Even a cursory glance through the interview section of *The Convivial Hermit* magazine—an excellent chronicle and repository for the wit and wisdom of scores of kindred spirits in the metal underground—will reveal more evidence of a longing to be left alone to create in peace than of overarching theories regarding the superiority of any one race. They are all like-minded souls who appreciate the efforts of others around the world and, through their art and fandom, probably have more contact with far-flung corners of the metal omniverse, and thus everywhere, than most provincial citizens ever will, myself included.

Being of the shut-in persuasion, I can appreciate the yokelism involved in writing impassioned opuses about the mountains and terrain right outside your door. I am all for forest-identified performers. Local color artists who may not stray far from the black and white paint on their palette, but who explore the possibilities of their limited repertoire to its fullest extent. I confess it can even make me a bit wistful. Or envious. My family has lived in New England for over four hundred years and I can't say that I know the land very well. Or that I feel I have a claim on it, or am a part of it. On the island I now call home, the pinkletink is supposedly the herald that announces the arrival of spring in our region. I'm still not sure whether the pinkletink is a bird, a flower, or a frog.

There is a tradition being passed down to young Nordic and Slavic and Asian and Russian misanthropes who are also one-man bands; they are honoring that tradition in their way and making something new and exciting out of it and learning about what makes their home unique. There is a freshness in even the most fumbling attempts to extract meaning from words and sounds and instruments that are, in some cases, thousands of years old. There is bravery in turning your back on modernity, even if only in song, and taking a walk in the woods.

I am currently writing this in Newton, Massachusetts. Don't ask me how I got here. I'm not a fan of the traffic patterns in the area, and the sprawl makes me grit my teeth. Familial warmth makes up for this, however. Not far from here is Brook Farm, that grand, doomed experiment in highbrow communal living where a few of my ancestors, as boys, learned to use a printing press and be Transcendental in every little way. In America, too—where dissatisfaction with modern life runs neck and neck with our ability to create new and often useless things to fill our lives with—there is purple mountain majestic metal that thrives on the arcane—and, apparently, bird-watching. One-man forest rangers such as Sapthuran, Blood of the Black Owl, and Celestiial.

Celestiial's debut, *Desolate North*, on the tiny Bindrune label, is a psychedelic mélange of ambient forest hush, bird sounds, gently strummed guitar, and muffled, tortured cries. It's a beautiful and unsettling journey. It would be practically New Age if it weren't for the whole tortured cry thing.

Blood of the Black Owl's main man—when he isn't harnessing masculine forest energy through funeral doom and wolf howls—has another group devoted to ritualistic drone-based pagan hypnotism. Ruhr Hunter celebrated its tenth anniversary with an elaborate box set that contains, along with a compact disc, moss and soil from the Pacific Northwest, ocean stones, crow feathers, mink bones and teeth, insects, branches, and white birch bark from the state of Maine! You know you want one.

And what did you do to commemorate Ruhr Hunter's tenth anniversary, hmmm? Plant a tree? Skin a mink?

So many of these bands and artists have been digging the nature scene for so long; they have years and years of sorrow, beauty, and brutality under their belts and are content for the most part to be ignored by everyone except the metal faithful.

None of this music is new, of course. Just new twists on old designs. And, in my eyes anyway, a certain perfection of a form.

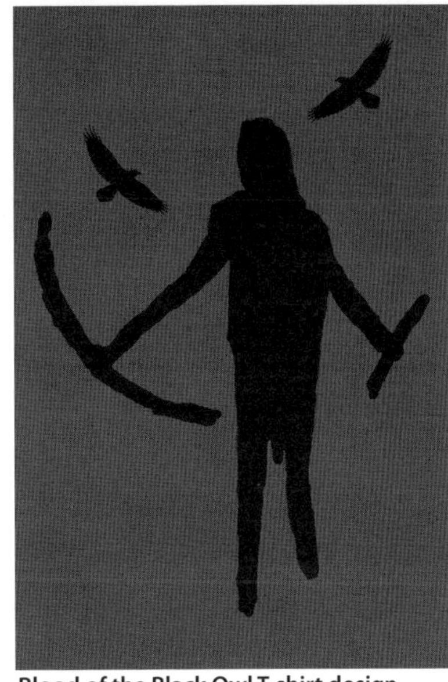
Blood of the Black Owl T-shirt design

It must also be understood that most of the new music I am so thrilled about is based on newer metal sub-genres such as technical death metal, funeral doom, black metal, and the like. Subgenres that came of age in the '90s. There is an all-encompassing synthesis occurring today in music that blurs the line between what is metal and what is . . . art-rock, prog, folk. All manner of genres are being assaulted by musicians who made their name with metal, but who are expanding their sounds so fast and furiously that new labels are being created daily by trainspotting weirdos working feverishly to keep up with new developments. It is a heady age.

So far I've avoided any discussion of the extremely popular and densely populated power metal/symphonic metal/progressive fantasy metal genres that have likewise been experiencing boom times in recent years.. This is not because of any distaste on my part for these hirsute, virtuoso, Beowulf-gobbling, steed-riding proponents of all that is metal. Nay, it is only that these sons and

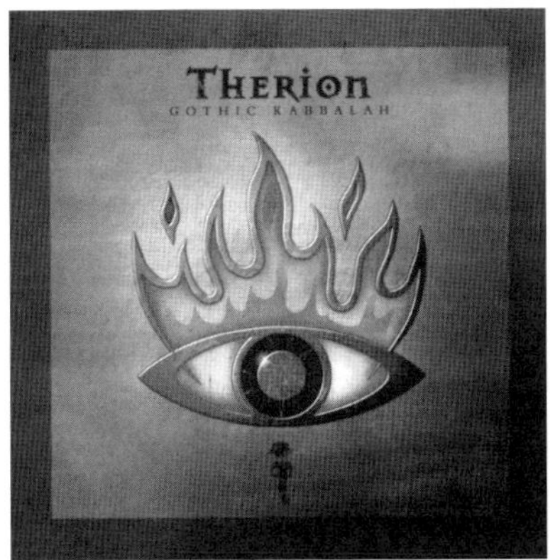

daughters of the almighty Iron Maiden deserve their own lengthy scrolls to record their many deeds of valor. Germany alone counts more minions devoted to the exploits of Hammerfall, Blind Guardian, and Iced Earth than you could shake a hobbit's walking stick at. God bless their obsessively melodramatic, triumphant hearts.

Have you heard the new Therion album? *Gothic Kabbalah*? It's a double-disc set devoted to the life and work of 17th-century mystic and runic scholar, Johannes Bureus. Yowza! Now we're talking. But as ineffably righteous as all that swordplay is, the art that truly stirs my senses lies closer to earth. And is of this earth, in its own weird way. Not that it doesn't also pay homage to what came before in the metallic realm. That is the honor and pleasure of all future metal musicians. Numerous folk-metal bands were inspired by the industrial neo-folk movement of the 1980s that involved people like Current 93, Death In June, Laibach, and Boyd Rice. Some of them, like morbid teens looking to shock, played with the totems and imagery of fascism and brown-shirt martialism.

The influence of industrial noise-rockers Swans, in their head trauma–inducing youth as well as their later apocalyptic folk-music-to-end-all-folk-music phase, can never be underestimated. But the roots of folk and fantasy and cryptic messages from beyond in metal are as old as metal itself. Even older. Born of comic books; sci-fi; horror movies; sword & sorcery epics; Poe; Lovecraft (especially Lovecraft); the British invasion of Kinks, Who, Them, Stones, Pretty Things, Beatles, Yardbirds; the garage rock that followed; ersatz-mystical sitar psychedelia; "Nights In White Satin"; "A Whiter Shade Of Pale"; fairytale psych; blues myth appropriations and misappropriations; Coven; Black Widow; Black Sabbath's iron man and wizard, and drug-dream fairies wearing boots (as a kid I was so perplexed by this song—a fairie wearing boots? How is that scary? What am I missing?); the folk revival; hippie folk; the folk-rock explosion; the progressive hard rock of High Tide, Hawkwind, and a thousand unwashed others from Magna Carta to Caravan to Gentle Giant to the Nice to Status Quo to Atomic Rooster to Jethro Tull to Lucifer's Friend.

And not least, of course, Led Zeppelin, who probably could have managed the whole "future of metal" thing by themselves (well, with a little help from Black Sabbath). Their unholy mix of hard proto-metal and exquisite UK folk is pretty much unmatched to this day. (That and their tight grooves and swing—two things that many people bemoan the lack of in current hard-ass bands).

Which brings us to the '80s and what would become the dominant sounds of today's modern extreme metal. The new wave of British heavy metal, second generation UK punk, American hardcore punk, Venom, Trouble, Bathory, Slayer, Hellhammer, Celtic Frost, Metallica, Sodom, Kreator, Mercyful Fate, Voivod, and others would invent the future of black metal, death metal, grindcore, and doom—and they did it with a smile.

All of which brings us, lastly, to wolves. The early '90s Norwegian

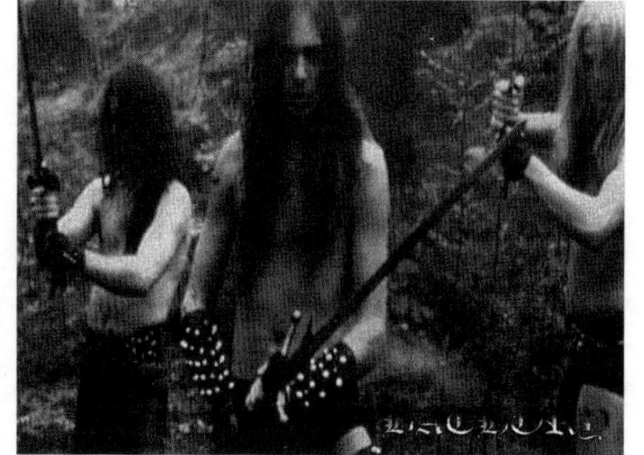

Bathory

explosion of black metal, that disharmonic din that tranformed a frosty, responsible nation seemingly overnight into a dark den for blasphemous church-burning nihilists, opened up the floodgates of creativity for a small group of outcasts and the metal world has never been the same. It certainly seemed as if death metal, which came into its own in the late '80s, would be metal's evolutionary success story for the '90s as well.

But black metal, so singlehandedly furious, more akin to the sounds of some avant-garde classical experiment in dissonant repetition and not so concerned at the time with death metal's extreme levels of technical prowess, would prove to be a do-it-yourself catalyst for many who had the fever but who lacked the flavor. Norway's Ulver were an early favorite, apart from the unholy trio of Darkthrone, Mayhem, and Emperor.

Ulver is the Norwegian word for "wolves," and the band's first three albums were a trilogy devoted to the concept of the wolf in man. Millions of people are at least subliminally aware of Ulver, since the poster for their lo-fi black-metal masterwork, *Nattens Madrigal*, was displayed for years on the wall of Anthony Soprano Jr's bedroom on the popular HBO drama *The Sopranos*. Pretty tricky of whoever put it there. The wolf in man, get it?

Ulver continue to confound and beguile audiences with everything from IDM and trip-hop-based soundtrack work, massively ambitious art rock, and other forays into the nether regions of experimental sound and vision. After the initial black metal albums they made their name with, they truly turned heads with a double-disc art-metal salute to William Blake's *The Marriage of Heaven and Hell*. They are quirky, to say the least. For our purposes it is the second album in their trilogy that is most important here. 1995's *Kveldssanger* is a neo-classical work of plainsong, cello, and guitar, and has enriched everyone it touches to this day. It seems like half or more of the tender spirits involved in the making of modern folk-metal—in whatever way,

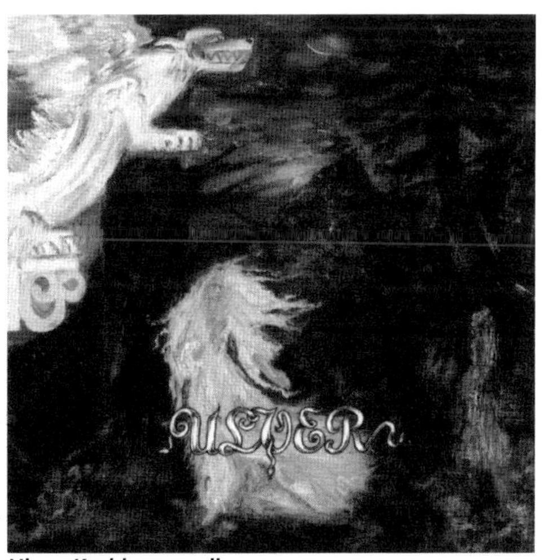

Ulver, *Kveldsanger* album cover

shape, or form that music comes in—have been possessed by Ulver's singular creation. And wolves have abounded ever since. Wolves, and woods, and ice, and snow, and more snow, and mountains, and blood, and wind, and gods, and even funny little trolls who drink too much beer in the Finnish forests. What a strange bunch. And yet how confident they are in their torment and fury and

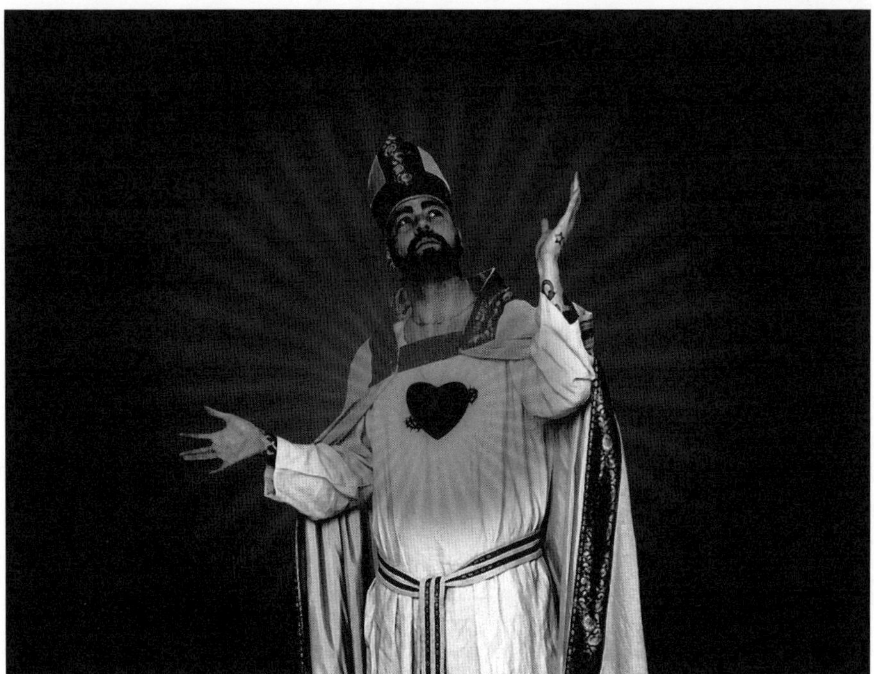

Ulver, still from their *It Is Not Sound* video, 2005

doubt and pride and growth and love of land and primitive ghosts.

I leave the last words to Ulver, from their 1999 *Metamorphosis* EP, an experiment in techno-derived wooziness with words by Rimbaud and wolves ever on the mind, naturally.

> Note: Ulver is obviously not a black metal band and does not wish to be stigmatized as such. We acknowledge the relation of part I & III of the trilogie (*Bergtatt* & *Nattens Madrigal*) to this culture, but stress that these endeavors were written as stepping stones rather than conclusions. We are proud of our former instincts, but wish to liken our association with said genre to that of the snake with Eve. An incentive to further frolic only. If this discourages you in any way, please have the courtesy to refrain from voicing superficial remarks regarding our music and/or personae. We are as unknown to you as we always were.

WORDS AND PICTURES
From the Pinakothek web log

by Luc Sante

I first thought of doing a blog a few years ago, when the mp3 blogs were new in the world and I was consuming dozens of them a day. Why not, I thought, make something similar, only with pictures instead of songs? After all, I have a visual archive that is as varied and deep as anybody's record collection. I put off doing it, though, because I felt shy about it, but probably even more because writing is my job, and I have people to support, and the idea of writing for nothing made me wince. And furthermore, writing doesn't come easy to me—every sentence is a stone carried up a mountain.

Then I dared myself to try. I did so tentatively and pseudonymously at first, until I was outed by Sasha Frere-Jones (I liked the first few enough that I couldn't help sending a few people the URL, coyly claiming it was the work of "a friend"). I've since come to realize that I've found my ideal form. I have revolving moods and a short attention span. If I were a musician I'd be turning out singles but having trouble with albums. And having a picture to work off— dissect, comment upon, contradict, employ as a shield, read like a palm, ride like a horse—sets me free. I can allow the picture to dictate the text, or use the picture as a pretext for worrying whatever's on my mind, or try to build a prose analogue to the picture. I'm having more real pleasure writing than I have in many years. Now if only this activity could pay my rent…

Luc Sante's Pinakothek blog can be found at http://ekotodi.blogspot.com/

MY DAD

This is my father as I never knew him, in jive-hepcat mode, sporting a Lester Young porkpie, Eisenhower jacket, skinny tie, sweater tucked in, high-water pants and white socks, and looking like he's about to launch into a dance routine. (He always did identify with Gene Kelly.) The picture was taken not long after the Liberation, in 1944 or '45, when he had successfully joined the Belgian army (in 1940 he had chased it all the way to Dunkirk to sign up, only to watch from the beach as the whole force sailed off to England). You can see that the truck belonged to his outfit, the 35th Fusiliers. They wore American uniforms and employed American ordnance, because none of their own had survived the war.

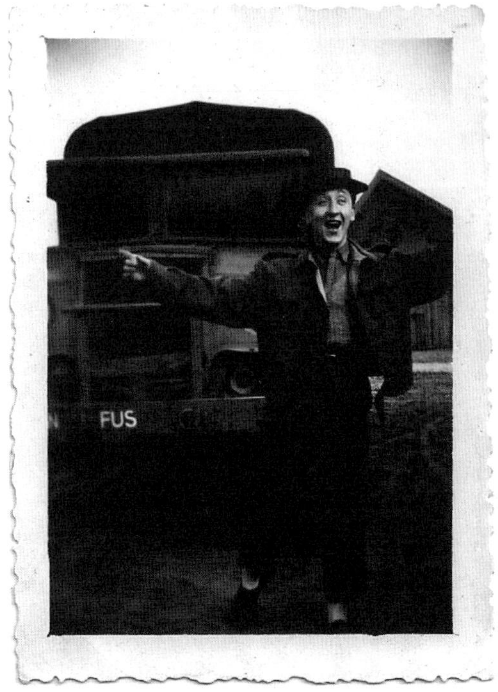

I found the picture just recently, among an overlooked trove of photos he kept in a tobacco tin painted with an alpine scene by one of the German POWs he was assigned to guard in a camp outside Mons. Most of the pictures date back to those postwar days, which might have been the happiest period of his life. In them he is always the shortest (he was 5' 2") and the most antic, always front and center, grinning wildly. I was born ten years later, and while I always knew my father as a wit, I never knew him as a kat; I saw him hold forth but never saw him cut up. He was beaten pretty badly by life—specifically by factory labor, financial insecurity, emigration and consequent alienation. In the last forty years of his life (he died in 2001), he essentially had no friends

The gaps between generations in my family are wide. At least two and as many as six of my great-great-grandparents (that's just *two* greats) were born in the eighteenth century. My grandfather was born in 1879, my father in 1921. I was born in 1954 and my son in 1999. My father in many ways remains a mystery to me. I intuited all kinds of stories in his past that he didn't want to tell me, presumably out of deference to my pious mother. I spent half my life hoping for some climactic old-age or possibly deathbed truth-telling, but instead he fell to Parkinson's and dementia and didn't speak at all in his last two or three years. At least I have photographs like this one, forensic evidence establishing the fact that my father had a youth. From me, in turn, my son will inherit mostly a pile of words.

SHILL

Just what is it that makes today's culture so different, so appealing? Anticipating Richard Hamilton by four years, Hank Williams first uttered the term *pop art* from the stage of the Grand Old Opry in 1952. Hank could see stretched out before him a future in which art would inextricably entwine with advertising. It was not an unappealing prospect, and Hank embraced it, envisioning museums filled with Brillo

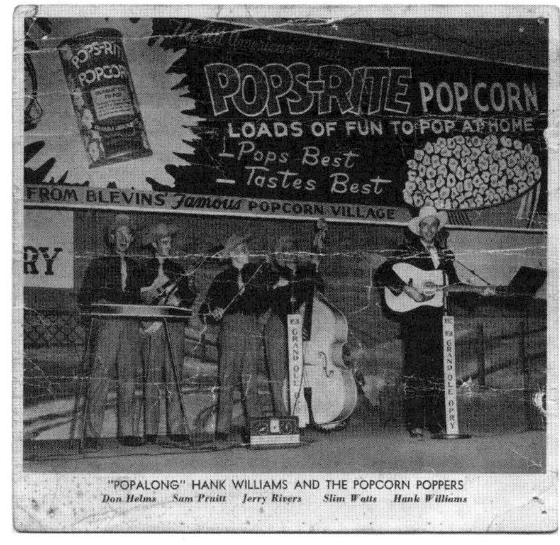

"POPALONG" HANK WILLIAMS AND THE POPCORN POPPERS
Don Helms   Sam Pruitt   Jerry Rivers   Slim Watts   Hank Williams

boxes and Ken-L-Ration labels and Goodyear Tires winged feet. He had always considered such works on a par with the output of the top European modernists, and all the more engaging because they had been devised by ordinary Americans without pretense, who got their hands dirty and enjoyed the song of the meadowlark at sunset.

He could imagine taking that song and fitting lyrics to it that would tell folks about Cities Service gasoline and Wheatena breakfast cereal, things he himself loved, and in return the gasoline people and the cereal people would put his name on a pump and his face on a box. It was all about people helping each other out, and it was also about the clean, uncluttered thrust of American imagery. He never quite understood why it was that when he visited a picture gallery, the paintings of streets never showed the Dr. Pepper signs and the Coppertone billboards and the barns were bereft of their Chew Mail Pouch in big letters. He thought it was a lot like pretending that people never had to go to the bathroom. It was like visiting somebody's house who had made a fortune running burlesque theaters and finding it full of plaster copies of Roman statues.

It was on the night of January 1, 1953 that he had his final vision. Racing from Knoxville to Canton, Ohio in the back of the big Cadillac, pumped full of morphine with a side of B12 to keep his eyes open, Hank kept sliding under the surface of this life, seeing things he didn't entirely understand. He seemed to be visiting the future. He saw people of all ages walking around with product names on their clothes. He saw a man with a beer label tattooed on his arm. He thought he understood that people were paying money to companies to help them spread their advertising. He saw movies that turned out to be commercials, and commercials that turned out to be movies. He saw what looked like advertisements but couldn't tell what products were being advertised.

He thought he understood that advertising and art had traded places in this future world, that advertising walked by itself and didn't stand for anything in particular. He understood that everything in life was a product, and probably always had been, and thought that now advertising was no longer about trying to get folks to buy products. It was more like hymns in church, which you sang not in order to believe but to stay on God's good side. He was trying to focus this thought when he died.

THE LIQUID DOLLAR

This is a drink ticket. It was currency at one time—actually it was better than the greenback equivalent, because it contained added value in the form of prestige. A drink was a drink, but a drink ticket was a badge of rank. If you wanted to impress a potential pickup, buying them a drink with a ticket carried more weight than flashing a roll. I'm amazed this ticket was never spent, and can only

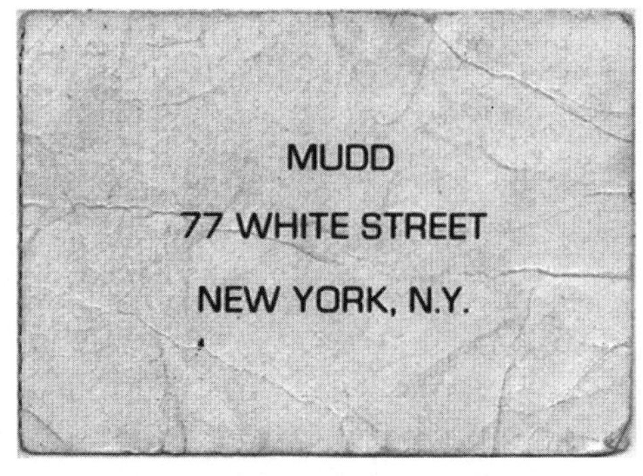

imagine it whiled away the years in some forgotten pocket until after the chance to redeem it had passed. Drink tickets were fought over, stolen, begged for, dubious promises made in exchange for. The drink ticket had a fixed value—it could be redeemed for one drink, top-shelf or well, beer or wine—but while it could generally be obtained for a line of blow, it wasn't necessarily self-evident whom you could perform this exchange with or under what circumstances. In any case, the blow-for-tix swap was probably less common than trades founded on sex, friendship, services rendered, or—above all—a brush of the wing of celebrity.

This drink ticket, issued probably in 1978 or '79, was a harbinger of the following decades. Velvet cordons were just coming in downtown; in the future lay VIP rooms, ultra-VIP rooms within VIP rooms, bottle clubs, memberships, and whatever crushing nonsense is currently on offer. At the time, my friends and I worked minimum-wage jobs, and most of us were paid in cash—not that we were in the black-economy sector, mind you; it was just cheaper for bosses than cutting checks, and it was understood that many of us wouldn't even have bank accounts. So the drink ticket provided an important lesson in economics as well as a glimpse into the future. We learned that not all dollars are of equal value. We learned that the better off you are, the more eager people will be to give you things. We learned that wealth has never been obtained through labor, or at least not through one's own labor. We learned that wealth envies celebrity more even than celebrity envies wealth—and this at a time when it was possible to be a bona fide celebrity and still be dead broke. This knowledge was lost on us, of course. A creature of today at large in the drink-ticket economy would set about brokering the stupid things.

NOWHERESVILLE

We are assembled here at the tomb of the unknown rockabilly band, somewhere on the shores of the Great American Sea. The rain is coming down slantwise, destroying our pompadours and making our string ties hang down like cooked spaghetti. We can barely hear the preacher over the torrent, but we know he is invoking the ghosts of all

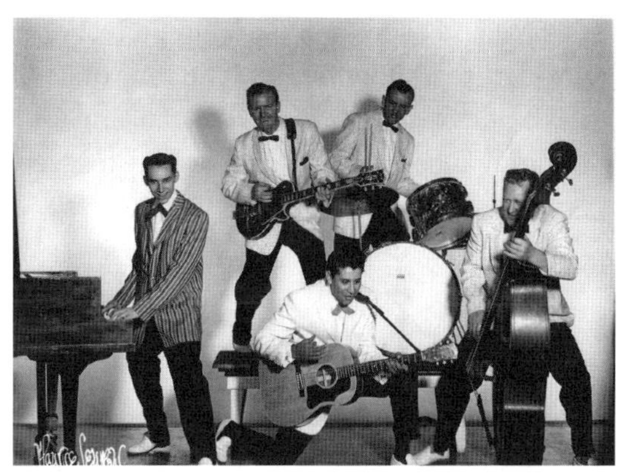

the failed bands from all the teenage campaigns of ages past—the doo-wop quintets who never settled on a name, the mod combos who couldn't afford matching suits, the psychedelic groups who slept through their one scheduled recording session, the punk outfits who lost key members to cough syrup or Jesus or manslaughter charges before they ever got a chance to play out. Their uneasy spirits stalk the land, infecting aspiring young players with fatal doubt, stalling the cars of talent scouts, shorting out amp connections, foreclosing on record stores.

And that is why we come here once a year to lay a wreath at the tomb of the unknown rockabilly band: to persuade them to rest, and lay off the young. But just have a look at them—they were never meant to be! They should never have tried occupying the same stage, and they should have left music to find its own way home. The piano player, with his incipient Mickey Mouse ears, was clearly destined for a career working with puppets. The twins on guitar and bass were natural-born casino greeters. The other guitarist has the fine tapered hands of a pest-control agent specializing in silverfish. And the drummer—he was meant as an example. What happened to him should have been shown to driver-safety classes in every high school in the country.

So that is perhaps the true meaning and significance of the unknown rockabilly band. There is a reason why they and their fellows trip up young musicians and dash hopes nurtured since childhood! They act out of kindness, based on their own sad experiences. They want to save the young from mediocrity and failure—or far worse, mediocrity and success. They are like Flannery O'Connor, who when asked whether she thought university programs discouraged too many writers, replied that they didn't discourage enough of them. But pop music has no university programs. At least not yet.

We should gaze upon the image of the unknown rockabilly band, captured in all their semblance of glory by Maurice Seymour of Chicago, and savor the fragile pantomimed ambition, the jackleg bravado, the rented instruments, the press-on smiles. We should earnestly thank them that they favored us with stage fright and bad haircuts and imperfect pitch at the right time and saved us from a lifetime of bitter regret if not one of endless lawsuits. One day, when all music is made by combinations of small and unassuming oblong boxes, the unknown rockabilly band will at last be able to sleep.

JESUS PUNK

About ten years ago I found myself in a large antique store in Berea, Kentucky. As readers of this blog might suppose, I'm a veteran ragpicker, but antiques tend to leave me frosty. I made my way through three floors of the usual glass, china, old toys, rugs, without much interest and without seeing much that would indicate the store was 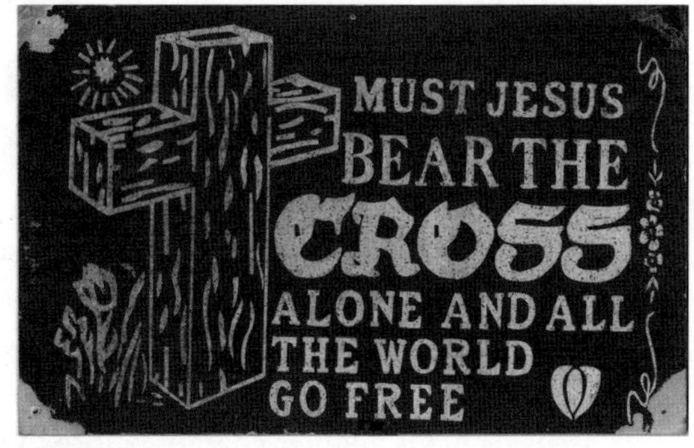

not in, say, Litchfield County, Connecticut. Then, in a corner of the basement, on the floor, sticking out from under a bookcase, I found this sign. "How much?" I asked the guy at the counter. He looked me in the eye and said, "Just get that thing out of my sight."

It so happens that I knew the thing to be at least approximately local—the text is the first line of "Shine on Me," by Ernest Phipps and his Holiness Singers, ca. 1928, collected in *The Music of Kentucky*, volume one, on the Yazoo label. I recognized that by conventional standards the sign exudes a deep and rebarbative ugliness—its fifth-grade draftsmanship, its clubfooted asymmetry, its witless line breaks and lack of question mark, its ink mixed with glitter, its ancient clots of tape and the places where the tape was torn off—and that as a printed sign it doesn't even carry the aura of a singular work of folk art. I also recognized the world of guilt and fear it represents, curdling something inside even me, and I haven't been a Christian since I started wearing long pants.

I could understand how some combination of those three factors—familiarity breeding contempt, aesthetic revulsion, the clammy hand of holy writ—could have led the Kentucky shopkeeper to want the thing erased from his consciousness. He might have been a snob, but he might also have been driven out of his evangelical family on account of being gay, for example. In any case, whether or not I was influenced by his reaction, I found that at first the sign made my flesh crawl. I took it home and stowed it away in an envelope. Then I found it again a few years later, thought it was more interesting than I'd allowed, and propped it in an empty recess in a bookcase in my office. Then I thought others should see it, so I hung it in the outhouse. Admittedly it made a striking addition to the rough-hewn interior.

Now that I no longer possess an outhouse, it has migrated to the indoor bathroom. I'm set to move again, though, and I'm beginning to think the sign belongs in the kitchen. I've grown to love the sign. Although the whole subject is just lousy with ironies of various sizes, I don't think my appreciation is a matter of mere contemptible irony. But I do love it, in large part, for its very awkwardness and ungainliness. Does that mean I value it for its authenticity? But while it is easy enough to appreciate anything unprofessional, amateurish, and even slipshod these days—in reaction to a time in which clever design always means a direct threat to your wallet—not everything made by artists whose enthusiasm outran their skill and patience manages any panache. Most homespun framed homilies are just dull. This sign, by contrast, looks combustible. It is so crazy that it looks as if it will eventually consume the wall it hangs upon. Everything that is seemingly wrong about it adds up to a massive—if small-scale—imposition of will. I love the sign because it insists on squaring off with me every time I look at it. It probably wishes me ill.

SUB-CULTURE

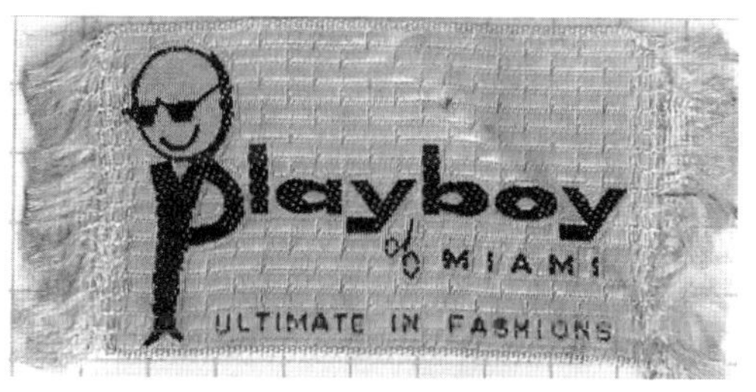

It took me until today to understand what the word "hipster" has come to mean. When I heard people complaining about neighborhoods infested with hipsters, bars ruined by hipsters, I didn't really give it much thought beyond remembering Yogi Berra's lament: "The place is too crowded—nobody goes there anymore." The red herring was the word "hipster," which to my mind couldn't possibly be synonymous with "yuppie" or any of the other terms for people who have more money than you do but no souls, and who spend their free time subjecting all you hold dear to unfriendly takeover.

In my mind the hipster stood for fingerpops, harlequin-pattern banlon shirts, cuban heels, toothpick and cigarette both at the same time, mohair suits, shirt-jacs, chesterfield overcoats, comb in the breast pocket, use of brylcreem years after the British Invasion, Jimmy Smith records, Mongo Santamaria records, Arthur Prysock records, unfiltered Kools, the novels of Richard Stark, the pornographic novels of Alexander Trocchi, the glory days of *Gent* and *Cavalier*, never raising the voice above a throaty whisper, clipped hand gestures, wakefulness despite half-shut eyelids, communicating volumes entirely with the eyebrows, walking with a rolling shuffle, having a substantial number of friends whose race is different from yours.

You get the picture, I think. Yes, it was largely a male phenomenon—there were hipster women in black leotards, but they didn't look all that different from beatnik women in black leotards. It was a style that may have peaked between 1957 and 1963, but it remained, persistent and underground, for decades afterward, ignoring all movements and trends, implacable in its deep and nearly unreadable coolness. I myself didn't really get it until it was way beyond my grasp, a school of elegance I could no longer even aspire to. By that time you'd get at most fugitive glimpses—in jazz clubs, at the race track, in a few fringe neighborhoods, occasionally among old-school bikers. By now the true hipsters are mostly in their 70s, and less visible than ever. They'll take their secrets to the grave.

So it's especially disheartening that their name has been reassigned, and not to any foolish but vigorous crop of tyros, but to parasites. Eric Fredericksen defines the hipster as "a consumer of (sub)culture, a person who substitutes taste for creative drive." That sort has probably been around forever, but didn't really become an identifiable genus until maybe the 1980s, when the vastly increased size of the market made it possible to pursue consumerism as a full-time activity. Hunting esoteric cultural kicks turned into connoisseurship; possession of items distinguished chiefly by their obscurity at once inflated the desirability of those items to others and became tantamount to having produced those items oneself. Now hipsters have gone way beyond Scandinavian psychedelia and Japanese bondage photography. They collect neighborhoods. Soon those will run out, too. You are advised to protect your neck.

DEATH LETTER

At one time the news arrived this way. The fact was on the outside, the particular name was within. It got to the point immediately. As fixed and universal as the skull and crossbones on a bottle of poison, the black frame precluded any mush-mouthed circumlocution. Nobody had "passed away," or "departed," or 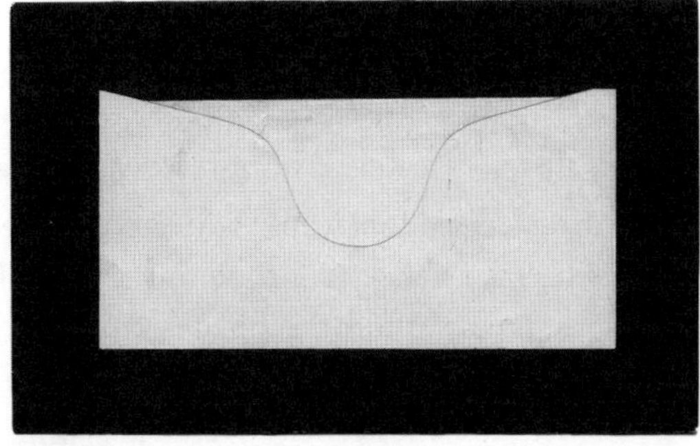 been "called home." They were dead, Jack. The bell tolled, the coffin was carried from house to church to pit, often by human strength alone. A few sentences read aloud out of a book, and the cadaver was food for worms. Happened every day, more often in winter.

When people stuck relatively close to the village, the death letter wouldn't come as a surprise, since you'd been hearing that someone had been doing poorly, was on their last legs, that the doctor had shaken his head and the priest had been hovering around. It got harsher when you moved away for work and didn't always hear what was happening back home. When you were far from your people, finding that letter in your mailbox could knock you for six. (I refer you to Son House on the subject.) Eventually the telephone took over the job, and by then death was always a shock, like it wasn't supposed to happen. People no longer remembered waves of epidemics, no longer saw farm animals die.

But then the black moved from the fringe to the center, and death happened to other people, and you *consumed* it, for fun. Yes yes, I do know—murder stories have been around since our ancestors first figured out how to use tools, and murder stories were always prurient. The shift had mainly to do with black. It was the color of rectitude, of clerical sobriety, of mourning. Then, when widows stopped wearing weeds, it became the color of the hard case. Black stopped commemorating death and began spitting at it instead.

As far as I'm aware, Maurice Heine was the first to use the term *roman noir*, in the 1930s, to describe the common ground between the works of D.A.F.

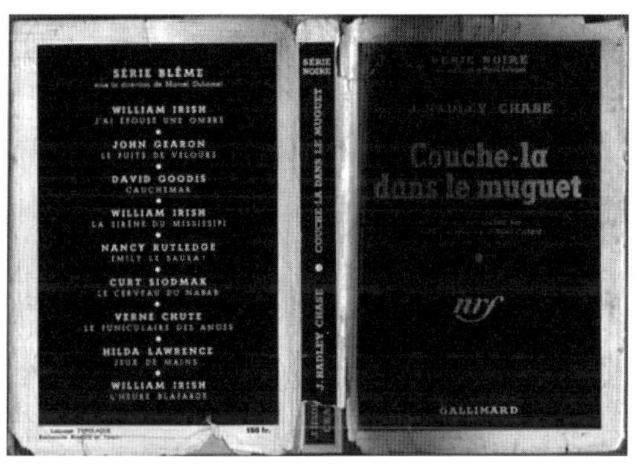

de Sade and the English Gothic novelists. In 1945 Gallimard initiated its *noire* series in distinction to its high-lit *blanche*. Nino Frank coined the term *film noir* in 1946. Black was still harsh then, still reminded people of crepe and worms and finality, and the shock value was enhanced by the recent memory of wholesale death. For decades there was a near-taboo on black in many areas of life. When punks began wearing black in the mid-'70s, in part as a reaction to complacent hippie optimism, they often had to resort to dye.

Nowadays black is shorthand for a generalized and indefinite willingness to kick ass. It is sported and consumed by some people who lack the capacity for sympathetic identification with others, but also by a great many who earnestly hope their bluff won't be called. Black stands for a kind of armor, but by now it's usually made of paper. Black has lost its connection with mourning; the color of death nowadays is probably beige, or powder blue. Maybe soon it will be generally recognized that the most sinister images are the smile, the hug, the smock printed with a pattern of cartoon animals. It will be interesting to see how thugs will adapt to this change. ❧

DEATH TO THE WORLD

An interview with Will Oldham

by Justin Taylor

ILLUSTRATION BY SCOTT MEYERS

In August 2006, Will Oldham and his brothers played four shows over two days at Joe's Pub in New York City. The Oldhams shared the bill with country legend Hazel Dickens to mark the closing of an exhibition of material from the Alan Lomax archives. They played a mixture of traditional and folk tunes, as well as a Shel Silverstein poem set to music and two different songs titled "John the Baptist," conjoined in a medley. (Unfortunately, there were no R. Kelly covers.) After the show, Oldham agreed to an e-mail interview, though what follows actually took place over the phone (thankfully) some time later.

JUSTIN TAYLOR: *Are you in Kentucky?*
WILL OLDHAM: I'm in Chicago; I just DJ'ed with John Langford for a radio show he's got on Tuesday nights.
I picked up the John Martyn album Stormbringer *and really liked it. But I realized when I listened to his song "John the Baptist" that it was only half of what you guys covered the other night—you did* two *John the Baptist songs. And I couldn't find the other one.*
The other one is on a record by a guy named E.C. Ball and his wife, Orna. I'm pretty sure it's in print, maybe on Rounder[1]. It's a great record. As far as I know they didn't release a lot; they weren't recording artists as much as performing artists. They'd perform where they lived, in far western Virginia—deep western

---

[1] "John the Baptist," on *E.C. Ball with Orna Ball* (Rounder)

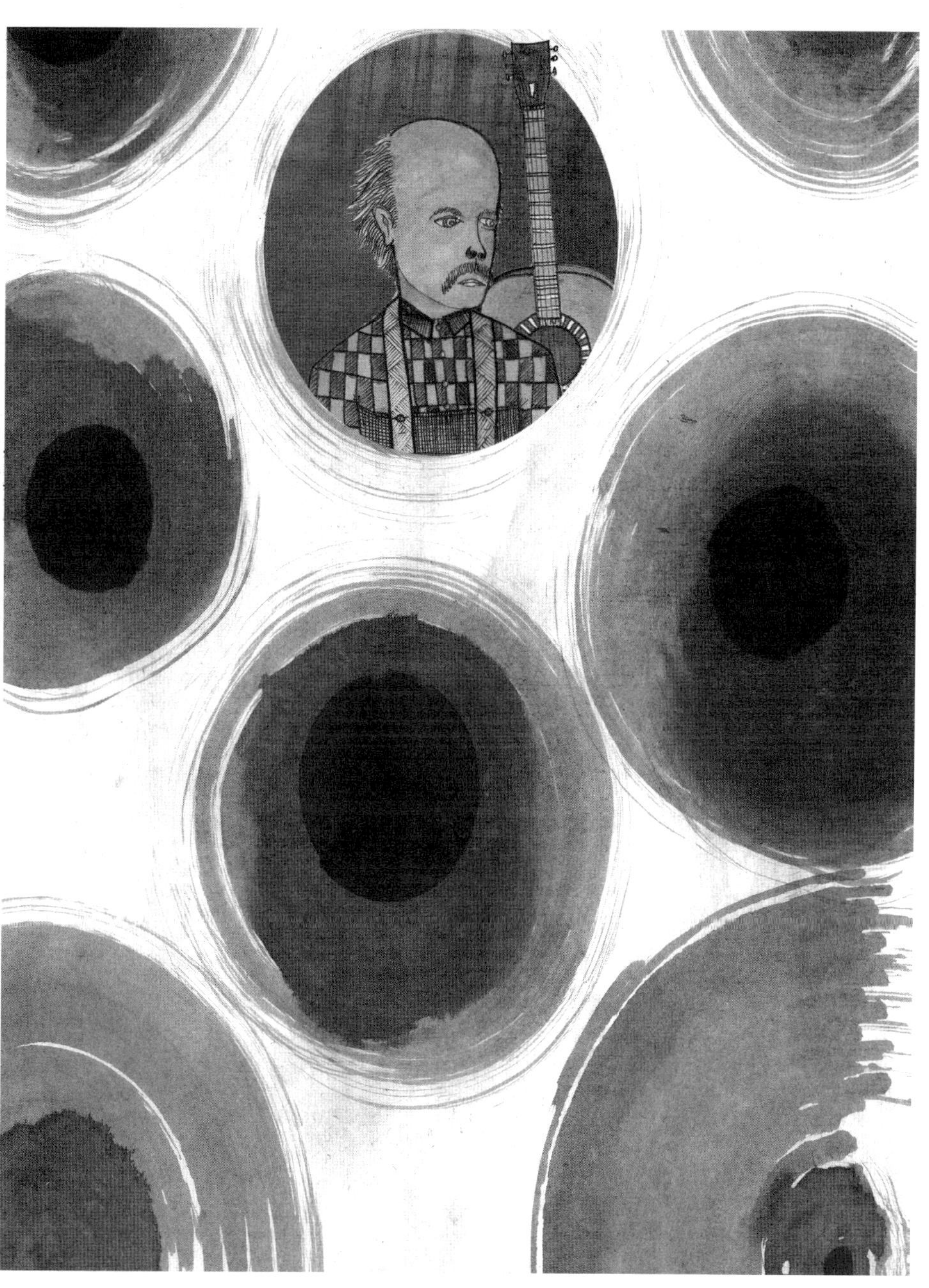

Virginia, not West Virginia—and there were maybe just a few recordings made of them. I think Lomax recorded them at some point, but I don't know if he made that recording that's available on Rounder. A good friend of mine in Louisville, Oscar Parsons, is from that area—from Sugar Grove, Virginia. He has a guitar made by this guy named Wayne Henderson, who's becoming a world-famous luthier. And when he was little, Wayne Henderson learned some of his picking stuff from E.C. Ball.

A lot of this stuff seems pretty hard to come by. I spend a lot of time trying to track down field recordings and, you know, the—uh, I don't want to say "authentic" but I guess it's what I mean. It can be really tough. There's just so much of it. Is this a big interest for you? Do you spend a lot of time looking for this sort of stuff?

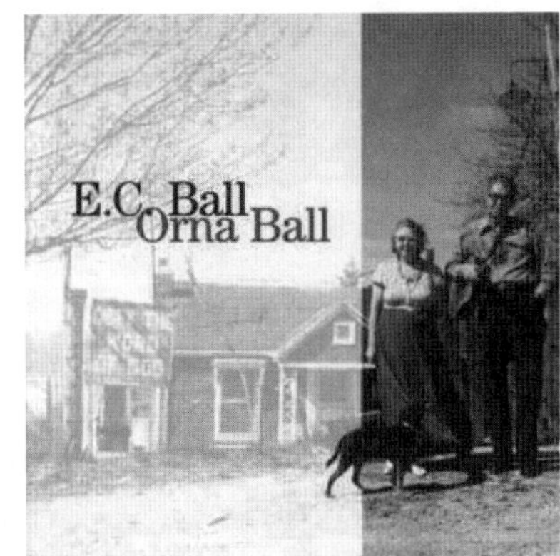

I guess so. It's not an overwhelming task. If you want to find music that you really like you have to put a little work into it.

Any other finds?

Are you asking where to look?

Maybe. Or maybe it's just another way of asking what you're listening to. I've been listening to these recordings of rural children's songs from the '20s and '30s, The Story That the Crow Told Me. *Each performer is like an arrow potentially pointing in another direction.*

That's the nice thing. Once you start to accumulate different things you know you want to track down, you don't have to track it all down at once, you know. You spread it out over the rest of your life, and you know you're never going to be without something. If you find everything right away, you won't have anything to do the rest of your life.

That's fair. Well let me ask you another of the questions I e-mailed you, about how you came into this kind of music, the folk tradition—if that's something you grew up with or more discovered, and where it's gone for you.

Yeah. I think that those shows in New York were, in some ways, a little bit of a red herring. You used the word "obvious" in one of your questions, that something was "obviously" something . . .

[In reference to folk and old-timey music, I had written, "Obviously, you draw heavily from those traditions…"]

. . . and that's interesting, because it's super overt in that a guy said "You want to play these shows? I'm looking for these old kind of songs," and I said, "Okay, I can do that."

But it isn't necessarily the dominant musical influence for me. I figure you just come up with it like everybody else. It's impossible to avoid folk and country music, and whether you turn on to it is another thing. I think whenever you hear somebody sing a song that turns you on, you've got to make some kind of note of it, create some kind of link to it, because you're not necessarily ever going to run into that song again. Sometimes you hear folk records, or whatever other kind, and there'll be great songs. It's the chain that's worth following. My folks had all different kind of records and some of them might have been folk and country. But you get turned on by listening to anything and everything that's played, in your folks' house, or in an elevator, or on the radio.

I think the music you grow up with is a big influence. I was never exposed to folk or country music; if I'd never left Miami I might have gone my whole life without ever finding it. My folks were playing Queen, or Chicago, or something.

Well I heard Queen and Chicago on my folks' stereo too. But they also had other things playing. And probably there would be more of an American folk tradition in Louisville, Kentucky than in Miami—I don't know. I don't know what you hear more, or on the street, randomly, in Miami. Did you have any of that?

If it was anywhere, it wasn't in the suburbs.

When I think of the suburbs I think of the *E.T./Poltergeist* type suburbs. They fill me with dread, because I know how poorly I would have fared in that kind of environment. The isolation and lack of random stimuli would frighten me to no end, make me a recluse. If the only world that stimulates you is a world of your own creation, reclusive tendencies get a real steroid boost.

So how would you describe Louisville?

There was variety. My folks' house that I grew up in was built in the 1950s. Within 100 yards of it was a house built in the 1860s or '70s. And because of a weird school system, starting in fourth grade, I started being bused downtown. Just on the trip from our house to downtown—first the school bus changes and then the city bus changes that required—the neighborhoods we went through were so varied. Just having that kind of trip through universes and cultures on my way to and from the learning institution every day made the world seem a lot bigger than if I had gone to school in my own neighborhood, or if my neighborhood had been uniform. From early on, I was forced to be aware that there was no single reality.

When did you leave Louisville?

I left when I was eighteen, when I graduated high school, and then lived more or less all over the place. Maybe about four years ago I was passing back through and decided to sort of resettle my belongings there.

I don't know why, but I thought you lived in Nashville.

I've made a couple records there, and I go see shows there fairly often. It's only a three hour drive from Louisville, so I can go and come back in a single day. One of my best friends lives there.

Is that David Berman, by any chance?

Yeah.

Can we talk about him?

Sure.

When I interviewed him, he told me he played on Joya, *but I never got out of him what instruments or songs he played on.*

He said that he played on it?

I think that's what he said—

Because he didn't play on it.[2] There's a song on there called "Apocalypse, No!" One summer I moved to the Charlottesville, Virginia area, in part to be near him because we were going to make the Silver Palace record. We would meet to try to figure out how we were going to do this,

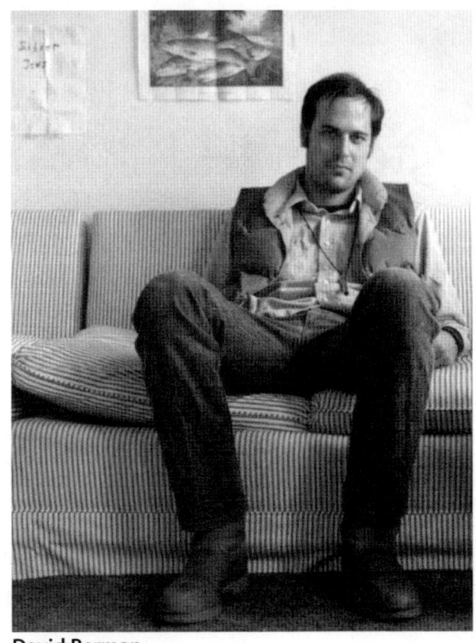

David Berman

exchange ideas for it, and one day he put a huge roll of paper up on the wall and wrote the first two lines of "Apocalypse, No!" on there and was like, "Okay, now you write a song from this." And so I did, and that was one of the only concrete fruits of that summer of supposed collaboration. His song "Like Like The The The Death" also came from that summer, and there was another one as well, but I can't remember what it is right now.

Why didn't the Silver Palace record ultimately come together?

One, it's really hard for two writer-people in writer mode to write together. But also, he had just finished a record—I don't remember which one it was— so he was feeling like a huge weight was off his shoulders. And I was more preparing—in the year of writing and preparation for a record—so we were totally going in different directions, energy-wise. At that moment, because he was done and alleviated, he had a more carefree attitude towards writing. And since I was tense about this impending record, I was more thinking, "Okay, how is this going to work? It has to be like this." We ended up having lots of good exchanges, and we also didn't stress either that we didn't come up with a Silver Palace record at the end of the summer. It was fine.

Meanwhile both your fan bases have been shitting themselves for ten years, hoping this record appears one day. What do you think?

Did you hear that seven-inch? It takes steps toward solving the mystery of the Silver Palace expedition.

---

[2] After I got off the phone with Oldham, I checked the transcript of my e-mail interview with Berman. I had asked him several questions about Oldham, one of which was whether he played on *Joya*. I don't know what made me think he had played on it, but in any case he never answered the question.

I'll track it down, then. But will the answers be on that seven-inch?
Oh yeah.
Can I ask you if the possibility exists of anything forthcoming?
I get a lot out of contact with David. I would hope that we will continue to—as an excuse even for hanging out—find jobs for each other at least.
Like your playing on Tanglewood Numbers?
Yeah, I played some guitar on *Tanglewood Numbers.*
It's funny. On his record I was listening for you—your voice, really—and couldn't find it. When I interviewed Berman he said you were just playing guitar, and that to assume you would sing because you are best known as a singer wasn't very imaginative.
Yeah that's the thing. Of all the everyday things that I'm involved with, he asked me to do the one that I feel like I'm the worst at on his record. I think he might even say the same about when I asked him to sing on my record, at least at the time. I think he's gotten a lot more confidence, both since making *Tanglewood Numbers* and since playing live. But at the time we were doing that *Greatest Palace Music* record, I think he was still thinking "I'm a writer that sings."
Do you write, other than as a lyricist?
Lots of letters and stuff, but no other words.
Can we talk about lyric writing?
Sure, what was the question [*referring to my earlier e-mail*]?
It was specifically about the song "Death to Everyone" and the word "hosing." It sticks out in my mind every time I hear the song. I was much more comfortable e-mailing this question than asking in person—it's so strange to confront the writer and just blurt out "why did you use this word?" But there it is.
I thought it was both more polite and funnier than "fucking."

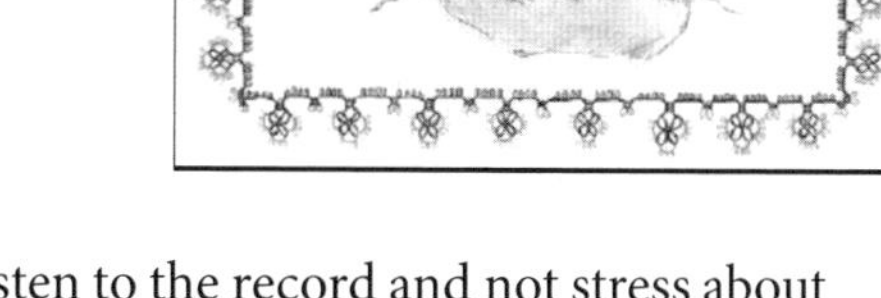

Well it's definitely funnier.
You don't think it's more polite?
Uhhhh…
It's more polite because old women can listen to the record and not stress about hearing the French language on what they're listening to.
What made that a concern with this record, or that song? You certainly use "the French language" when it suits you.
Different songs play different roles. One thing that I've thought about since reading that question is this idea that making music is, in some ways—for me, as the singer of these songs—like being the architect for my own world of signs and symbols and melodies and rhythms that to some extent or another I may

live in, increasingly, for the rest of my life. And, therefore, if I'm building this house or this universe, it has to be as expansive as possible. And it has to include silliness and humor and things that are comforting and things that are offensive and things that are supportive, and so there it is in that song. It's one or more of those things because I have to live there. Know what I mean?

But there's another interesting thing about that, in relation to another question you asked in the e-mail, about titling the Apocalypse collection.[3] Sometime when I lived in Virginia—I've lived in Virginia different times, but I think this was during the Silver Palace summer—down on the mall in Charlottesville, there was this young group of teenage or early-twenties boys with beards who dressed in severe, Russian Orthodox-looking black robes. They were this sort of strange cult/gang/sect thing. And they had a fanzine, totally like a punk-rock zine, called *Death to the World*. It was a great fanzine, but it was a religious fanzine. I was just so excited about the content and the existence of this zine and this group of people that I started writing that song. That summer was long before I had any day-to-day access to what we now know of as the Internet. But after you sent that e-mail I looked them up to see if they're still around. I searched for "death to the world" and it came right up. So I was thinking that you might look to that for possible titles for the collection. I know I bought

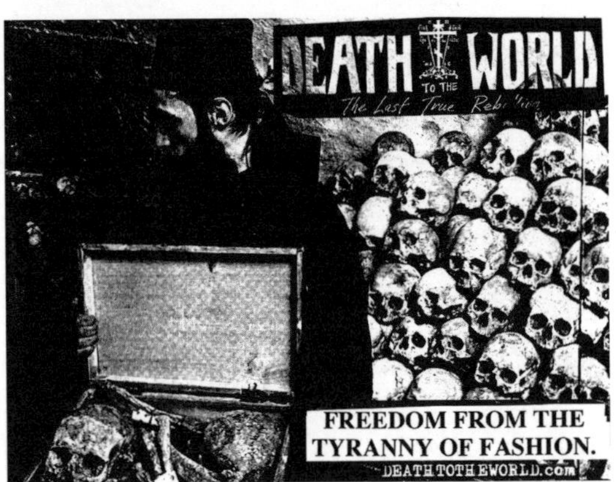

a paperback from them called *Children of the Apocalypse*, sort of a summation of their ideas and theories. The fanzine and the book and the website are all full of quotes from letters of followers and quotes from biblical text, all personal-apocalypse-oriented. You might find something cool.

What are you reading right now?

Two books. One by a guy, pretty sure his last name is Lopez, he's a naturalist and it's called *Of Wolves and Men*. It's a survey of the history and evolution and current state, although the book is twenty or thirty years old, of the wolf. It was a gift from Dawn and Nils of Faun Fables. And then I'm also reading *The Tao of Willie*, the book that Willie Nelson wrote with a ghostwriter which sums up the weird things that he's learned over the years into one succinct, easy read.

I think I'm more curious about the wolf book. Coming back to what you were

---

[3] At the time of this interview, I was editing an as-yet-untitled anthology of short stories about the end of the world, which was subsequently published as *The Apocalypse Reader* by Thunder's Mouth Press in June 2007.

saying about the way you write and the music you make as building a house, the wolf seems to play a longtime, and maybe increasingly prominent, role in your music—recording under the name Super Wolf and then the song "The Signifying Wolf," on the recent Cursed Sleep *EP, seems to maybe embody it best. You want to tell me about the wolf?*

Ah, I could try. I mean, it's probably better done just through the songs that exist at this point. That song is a paraphrasing of someone else's work, in a way that I hadn't done in a long time. It's from a short story called "Sealskin Trousers," about a man who comes up out of the sea—I will try to remember how the story goes versus how the song goes—I used the song to make the story go how I wanted it to go, which was that the man came up and wooed the woman on the shore and then took her back down with him to live as a sea creature. And the man was such a badass in the story, and, being a man, I like to think of myself as a badass in that way.

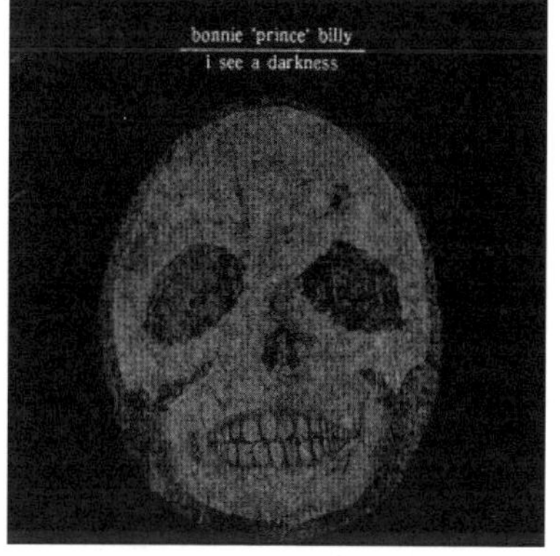

I've always liked the idea of this blues song—or maybe it's just a blues term—"The Signifying Monkey" (it might come from the Willie Dixon canon). I always thought that was a really great term for what being human is. But then I thought that as the signifying monkey, it's my prerogative to use language and what we like to think of as complex concepts, and transform it a step further into a walking talking ethereal snarling singing wolf that can leap up out of the ocean, grab a woman, pull her down, and the whole time simultaneously be making an MGM musical out of it.

That's pretty badass.

So that's that wolf. I remember I took an Italian class a long time ago and we had to make t-shirts, and mine said "come un lupo solitario sono willaccio" which means "like a lone wolf I am bad Will." So I know that at least as far back as when I studied the Italian language I've had a love for the lupine.

I'm interested in the idea of paraphrasing that you mentioned. How about the Get On Jolly *stuff?*

That was a sort of combo paraphrasing/covering venture. The English words of [early 20th-century Bengali poet Rabindranath] Tagore were pretty closely adhered to, but then every once in a while it got to a phrase where I might change a word to one I'd want to sing. But then there's the song called "Come In," that was, musically, an attempt to paraphrase this Johnny Cash song called "Come In Stranger" and the Leonard Cohen song "Sisters of Mercy" at the same time. Rather than use whatever storylines they have going for them, to use a new storyline which had to do with this archetypal gypsy character named Johnny

Faa, who's a hero of old ballads, he's the king of the gypsies. At the time those ballads were propagated, the idea was that the gypsy race came from Egypt—that's why they're called gypsies, I think—instead of coming from Northern India or any other places along the way. I was trying to make a song about somebody trying to rationalize or understand her relationship with this Johnny Faa character. So that's another sort of paraphrasing of multiple sources.

What record is that song on?

It was on a seven-inch, then it was on *Lost Blues and Other Songs*.

How did Johnny Cash's cover of "I See A Darkness" come about? Did you know him well?

I'm not precisely sure how it came about. Matt Sweeney had heard from someone he knew that Rick Rubin had some of my records, and he saw him at a show and went over to talk to him. And Rubin said, "Oh yeah, in fact we just recorded 'I See A Darkness.'" Matt called me right away and said "they just recorded 'I See A Darkness,'" and that was the first I'd heard of it. We had a show a week or two later and invited Rick Rubin to come to the show and he came, then afterwards he asked if I would want to play on the song, so I went out there.

I don't exactly know for sure what made Rick Rubin hear any of my records or what made him choose that one. They'd already recorded, but he said he wanted me to play piano on it. And I didn't tell him that I don't know how to play piano, because I thought it meant I wouldn't be allowed in the studio. I went there, and my impression is that if I hadn't gone there that maybe they wouldn't have even ended up using the song. There were a lot of songs they recorded and didn't use, but Johnny Cash is so gracious that when we met and Rick Rubin said, "Yeah, this is Will Oldham, he wrote that song 'I See A Darkness' that we did," Johnny Cash said "Oh, that's a great song, why don't we work on that right now?" So we went into the studio and pulled it up, and Johnny Cash said "I'm not happy with the way that I sung this," so we spent the next few hours going over his singing of it and redoing it. And in the course of that, there was one point where my voice was recorded. We pulled them both up and the timbre of the two voices sounded nice together, so we decided that I would then record a proper vocal to go with his.

When I sat down with June Carter Cash in the studio, she told me that the first time they heard the song, she turned to Johnny and said "Johnny, you have got to record that song." It's a moment I'll always remember.

What kind of acting were you doing before you appeared in Matewan?

Mostly stage stuff, theater. Occasional local TV spots or industrials, and I'd been in one movie, directed by the great country singer and guitar player, Jerry Reed.

What movie was that?

A terrible, terrible, terrible movie. It was unbelievably bad. Called *What Comes*

Around. I played a young Bo Hopkins. Bo Hopkins and Jerry Reed played brothers, and the first ten minutes or so of the movie had younger versions of them and this guy named Daniel Jenkins from Louisville was the young Jerry Reed. His dad was a member of the repertory company of Louisville at the time, and was an idol of mine. I think Daniel went on to play Huck Finn in the original Broadway production of Roger Miller's *Big River*, which is pretty cool.

I know you still appear in films from time to time, but what made you move away from, say, a career in acting?

It took me a while to realize that acting was not as well-rounded a profession as I imagined it could be. I finally learned that after moving to Los Angeles when I was 19, and signing with an agency that I stayed with for maybe two years, living in Los Angeles, then in New York, going on different kinds of auditions, getting a couple of jobs…

Is that when you did the Baby Jessica movie[4]?

That's when I did the Baby Jessica movie, yeah, and another movie called *Thousand Pieces of Gold*. I began to realize that it wasn't going to provide for me the things that I needed out of life.

How do you pick your film roles now?

Mostly I let them pick me. Anyone who's willing to work with me, that's fine with me, because I don't have an agent. I'm not going to audition for anybody. I don't think there's any justification for me getting a part over a professional actor unless some director or writer-director specifically feels like there's a reason for me being there. That's

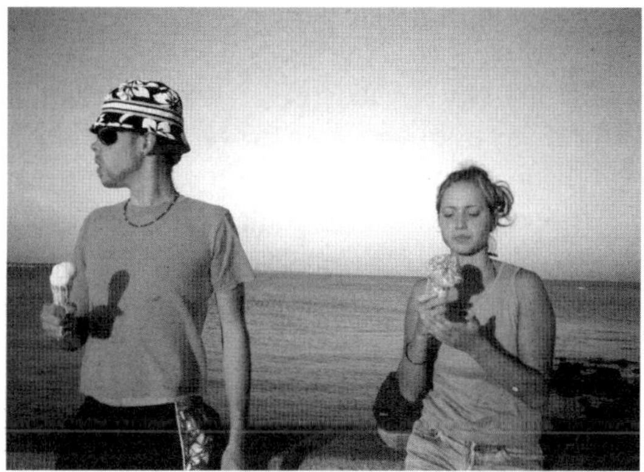

Still from Dianne Bellino's short film, Slitch: Will Oldham as the Surfer, Dina Cataldi as Slitch.

pretty much it. I've spent so much time thinking about it and doing it. And it's very important to me still, but I know other people should have priority over me, because I've already got a job. ❧

---

[4] *Everybody's Baby: The Rescue of Jessica McClure* (1989)

SAUL CHERNICK

Recent Drawings

INTRODUCTION BY CHRISTOPHER MARTIN

Seeing is not easy. Beset by an overwrought commercial landscape and subject to the inescapable retouching of our neurology, seeing is a very difficult mode for us to consciously embody. Certain artists, however, seem to provide direct access to the better halves of our seeing selves. From the vantage points their works convey us to, we begin to see what would otherwise be the most obvious things: being, existence, spirit. And while this may sound exceedingly grandiose, the work of these artists is quite the opposite; it is characterized by its humility. I want to call these artists seers of the veer. What sets them apart is the diligence, precision, and generosity with which they attend the world, seeking past it into the real. Their eyes are always trained on the moment of the real as it veers relentlessly off course. And through their looking, we are allowed to share the keyhole, to join in at the crucial moment when existence flinches, improvises, and barrels oblique. Franz Kline is such an artist. So is Janet Cardiff. And Saul Chernick is most definitely a seer of the veer.

In Kline's work, the veer is enlarged to an almost architectural scale. The best of his paintings resemble black-and-white poster illustrations of nuclear movement. Cardiff works on a much more human scale, redirecting the viewer/listener/walker toward the real through a phantom-based phenomenology. The world, through her intervention, is questioned at the most fundamental level of possibility: what might have been dramatically throws what is into stark, dynamic relief.

From about three feet away, Chernick's drawings share Cardiff's unapologetic enticement, but as the viewer nears, the brazenness of their imagery dissolves into the simple power of the line. A simple, humble power underlies these images. And at the same time it weaves, welds, joins, and entrains them. The varying proximity of the lines to one another seems to describe a magnetic field, each constituent string held between the oppositional forces of attraction and repul-

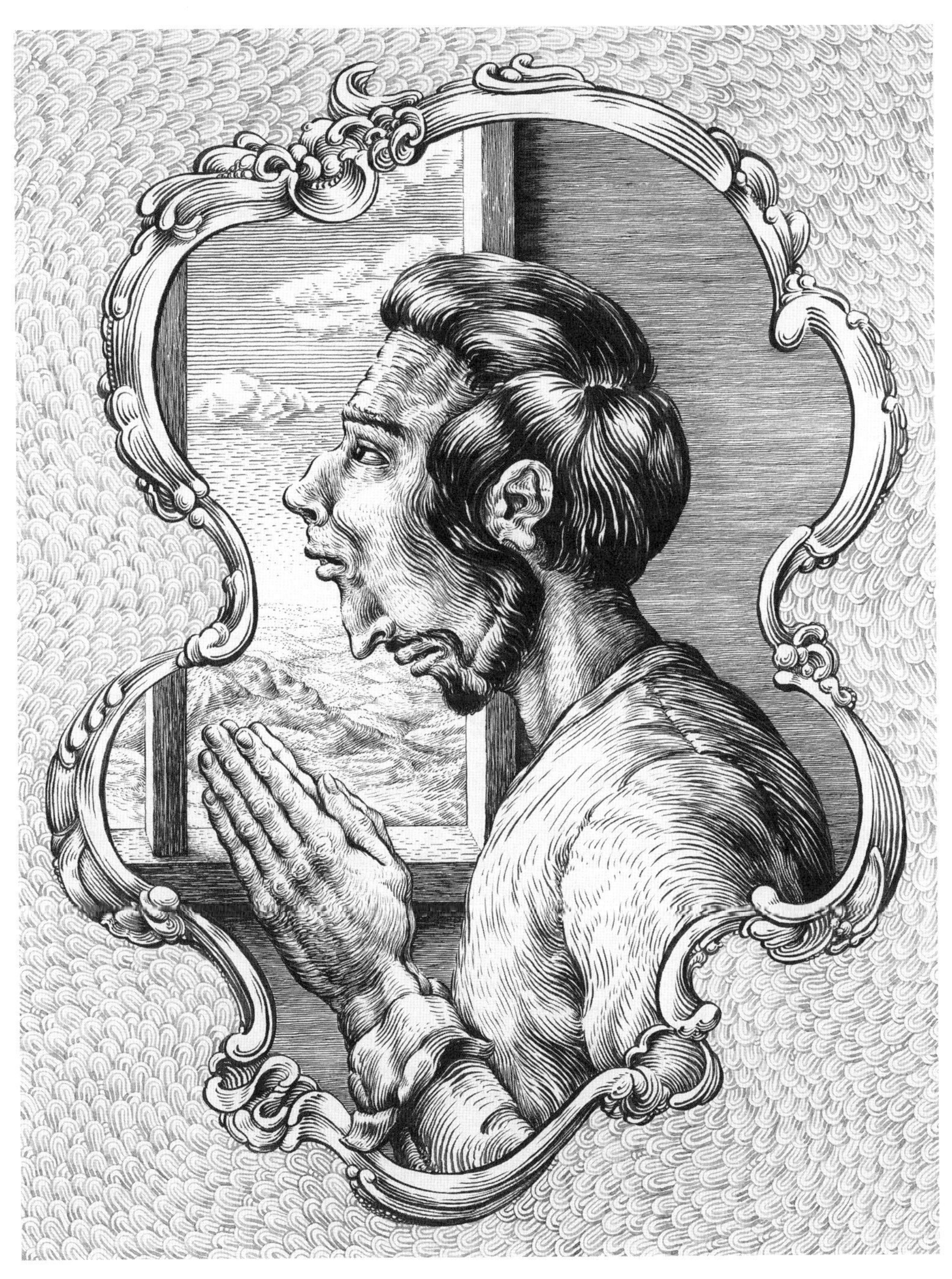

sion. In this way, Chernick's drawings literalize the latent choreography at the heart of any scene. His seemingly static portraits are composed entirely of movement, great figures adrift on a sea of oscillating wires.

So if I liken his drawings to string theory, you will have to forgive the lameness of the analogy. And at least it serves to introduce one of Chernick's most prevalent themes: the collision of past and future. Though a thrust toward antiquity is evident from one's first glance at these drawings, there is something futuristic and utopian about them as well. The playful references to religious iconography seem shot through with a contemporary sense of fashion, as if the gods are preening for their appearance on the red carpet of white clouds. In fact, there are endless numbers of intersections here: the technical and the expressive, restraint and excess, serenity and menace. For my money, the greatest of these intersections is at the nexus of the spiritual and the real.

According to Chernick, "One of the unique purposes of art has been to pictorialize the metaphysical." The pictorial content of a Chernick drawing may be a dog attacking a child, but what are the lines doing? They waver, bend, push, swell, swirl, wrench, verge, and most importantly, veer. And as your eyes draw closer to the beginning and ending of these individual marks, their collective effect becomes more astounding. This line, this one, turns exactly at the point where it may have turned otherwise. In this way it evokes Janet Cardiff's work. These lines, so abstract in close-up, form a small dance, a moment of energy on the shoulder of the dog, evoking the work of Franz Kline. The spiritual resonance of the line builds and pervades the more commonplace religiosity of the images. The real, which has been transferred to the page through the personality of the wrist, sutures the metaphysical back to earth.

Or, if not to earth exactly, perhaps to Protosapia—Chernick's experimental world of human forms, a place where traditional concepts of humanness are rethought and subverted. For this is what a seer of the veer is here to do: having crouched over the moment where existence improvises its zag, the seer sees how things are, and how they might be otherwise.

DRAWINGS BY SAUL CHERNICK: page 37, *The Supplicant*, 2007, ink on paper, 23¾" x 18¼", courtesy of the artist and Max Protetch Gallery; page 39, *Triumph of Death*, 2007, ink on paper, 21" x 14¾", private collection; page 40, *The Abandoned*, 2006-2007, ink on paper, 23¾" x 19¾", Collection of Mark Pollack; page 41, *The Abandoned*, detail; page 42, *Furious Cherub*, 2007, ink on paper, 14" x 12", courtesy of the artist and Max Protetch Gallery; page 43, *A Perilous Way*, 2007, ink on paper, 15" x 18½", CB Collection, Tokyo; page 44, *Misfortune in the Woods*, 2007, ink on paper, 14¾" x 18½", CB Collection, Tokyo; page 45, *Laws of Attraction*, 2008, ink on paper, 17" x 14", courtesy of the artist and Max Protetch Gallery; page 46, *Bouquet*, 2007, ink on paper, 40" x 28", Collection of Beth Rudin DeWoody; page 47, *Bouquet*, detail.

All works reproduced courtesy of the artist (saulchernick.com) and Max Protetch Gallery, New York. To learn about available work by Saul Chernick contact the Max Protetch Gallery at maxprotetch.com, 212.633.6999.

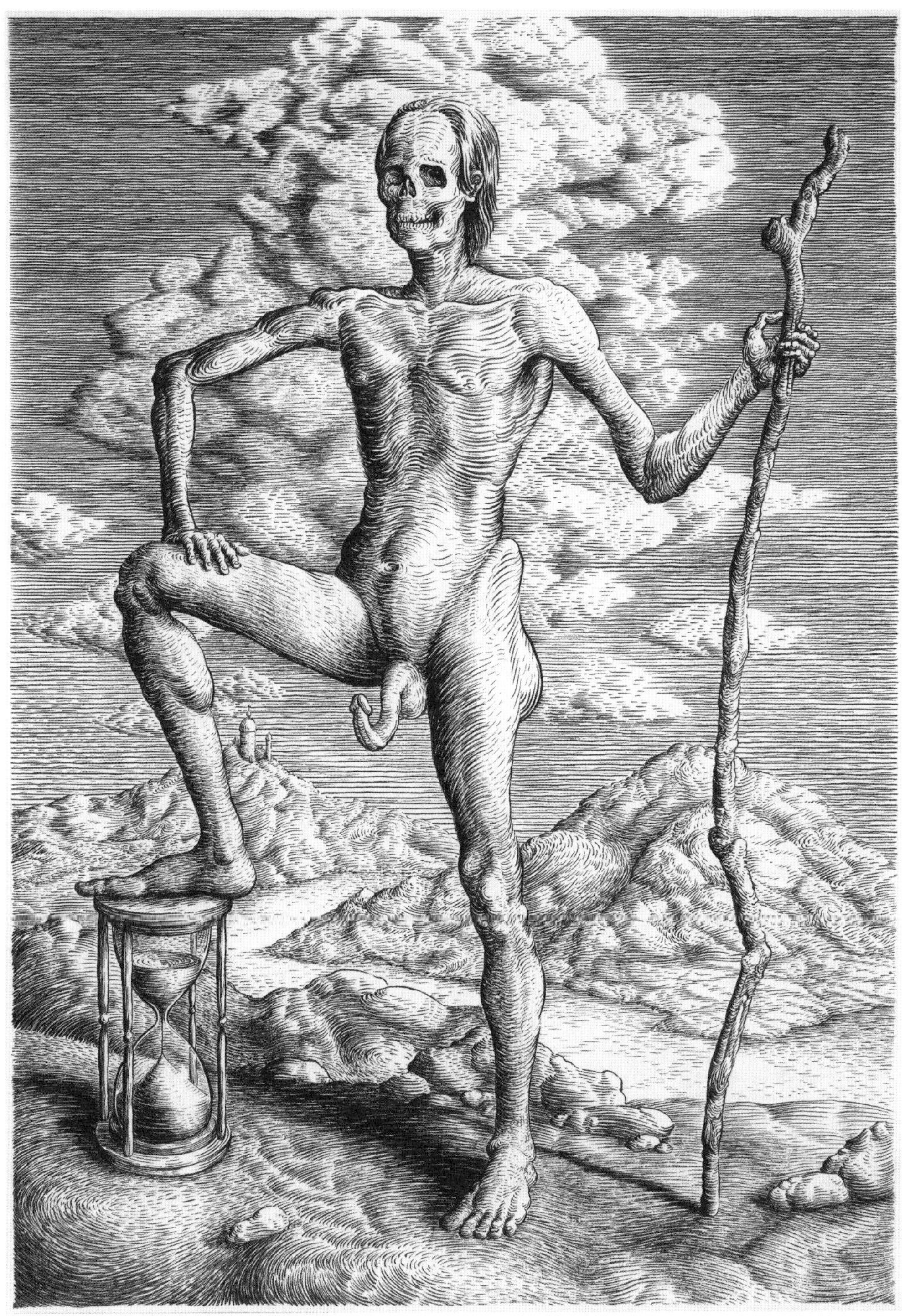

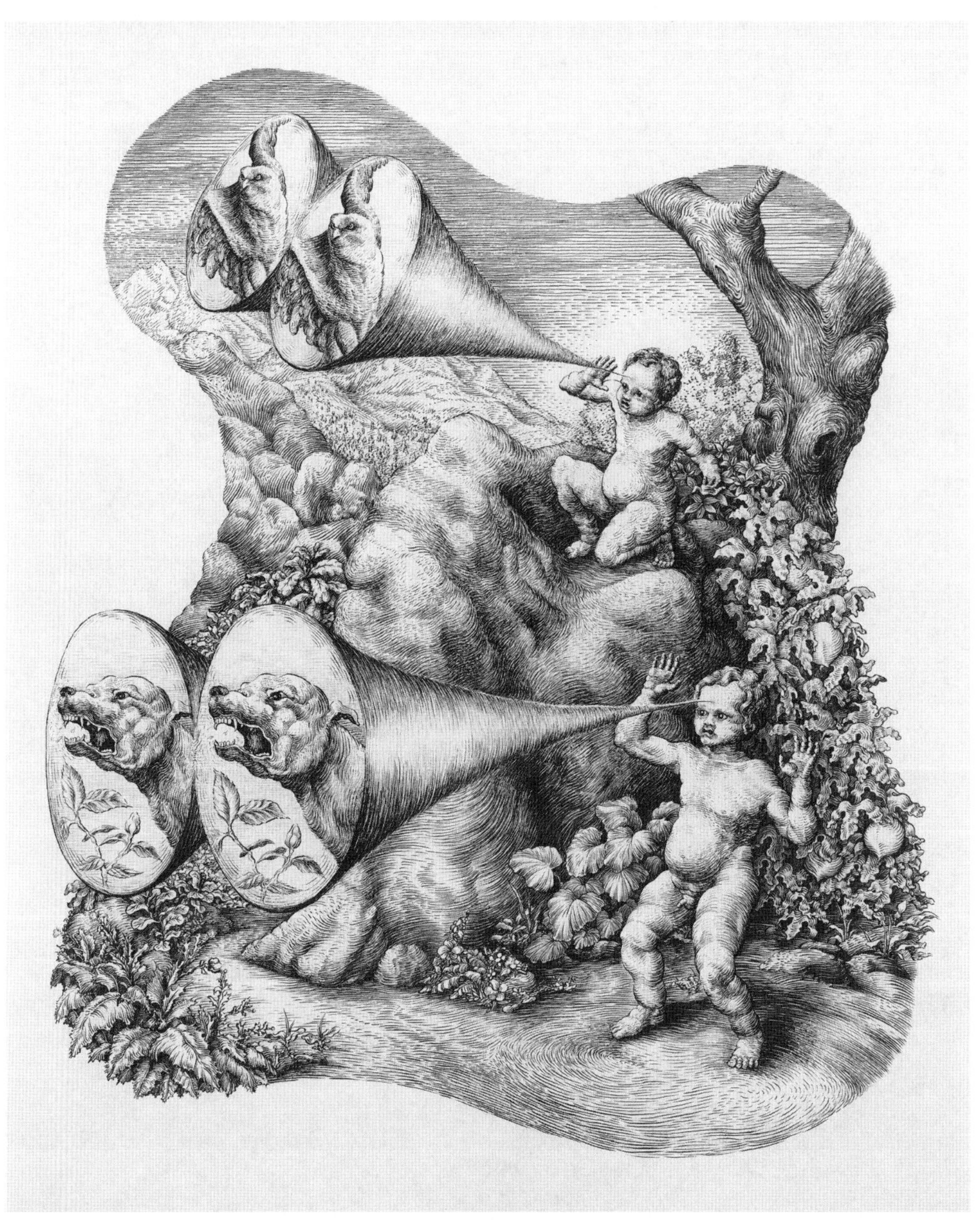

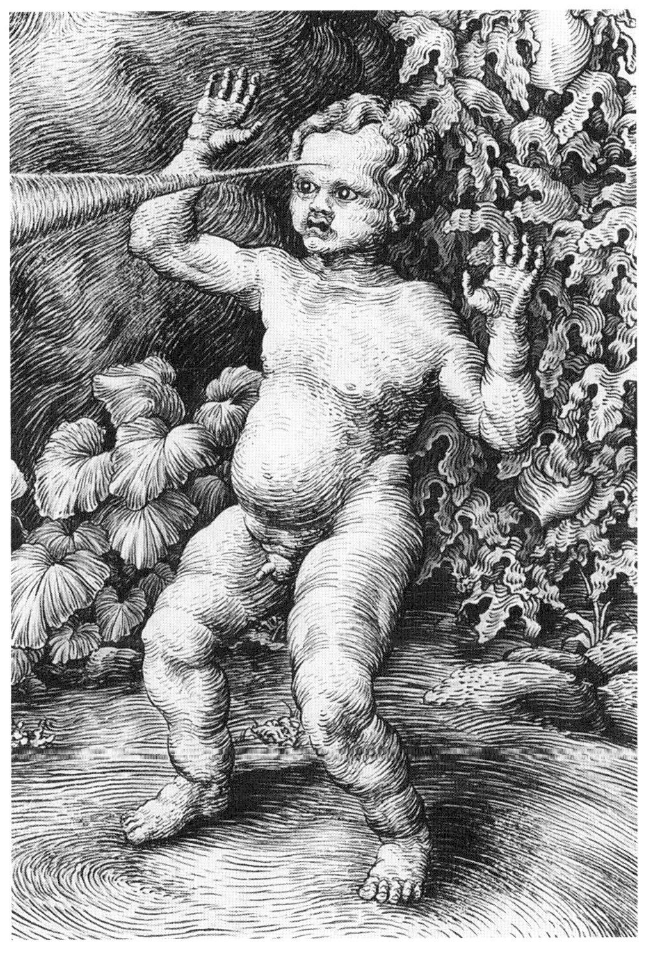

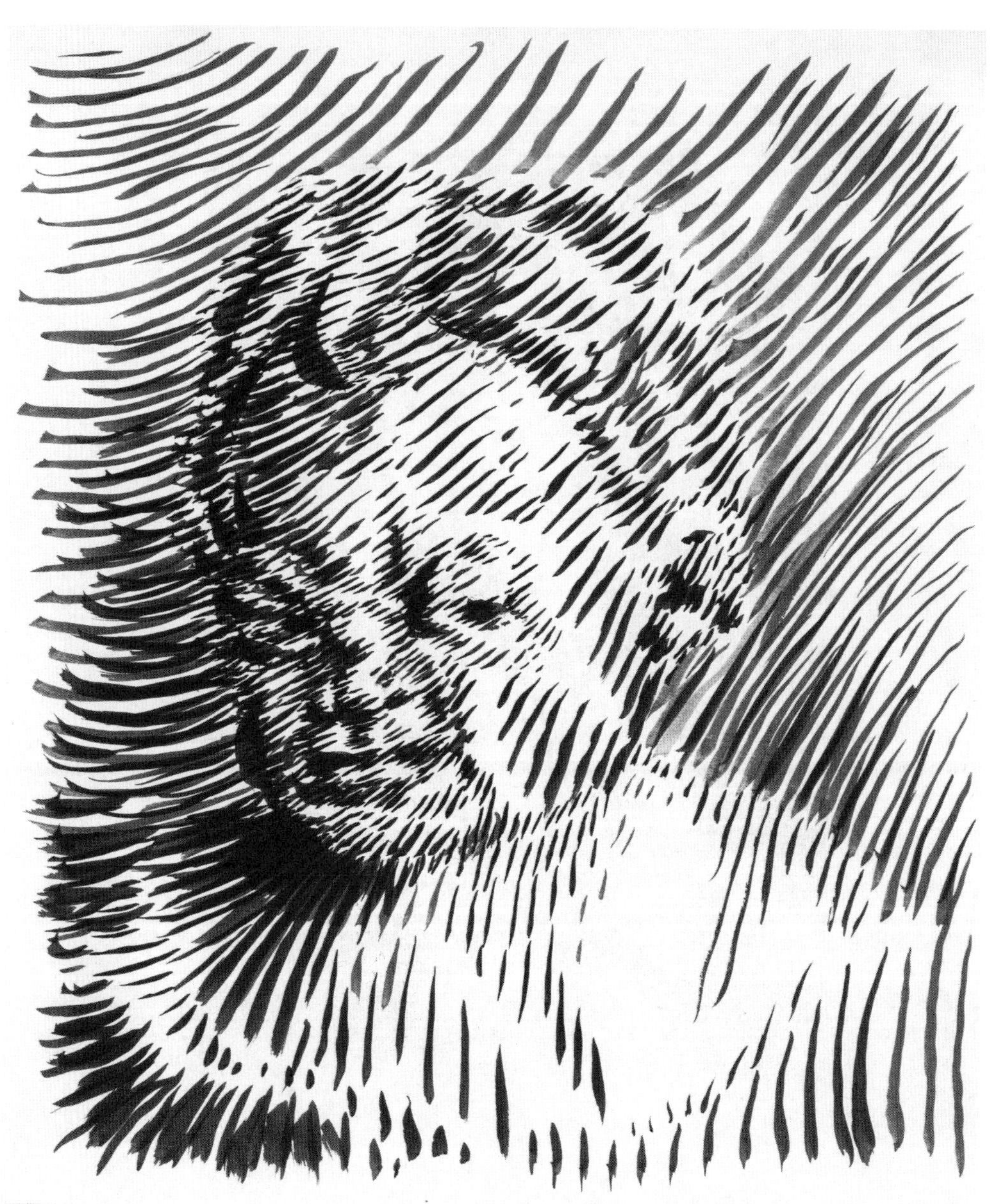

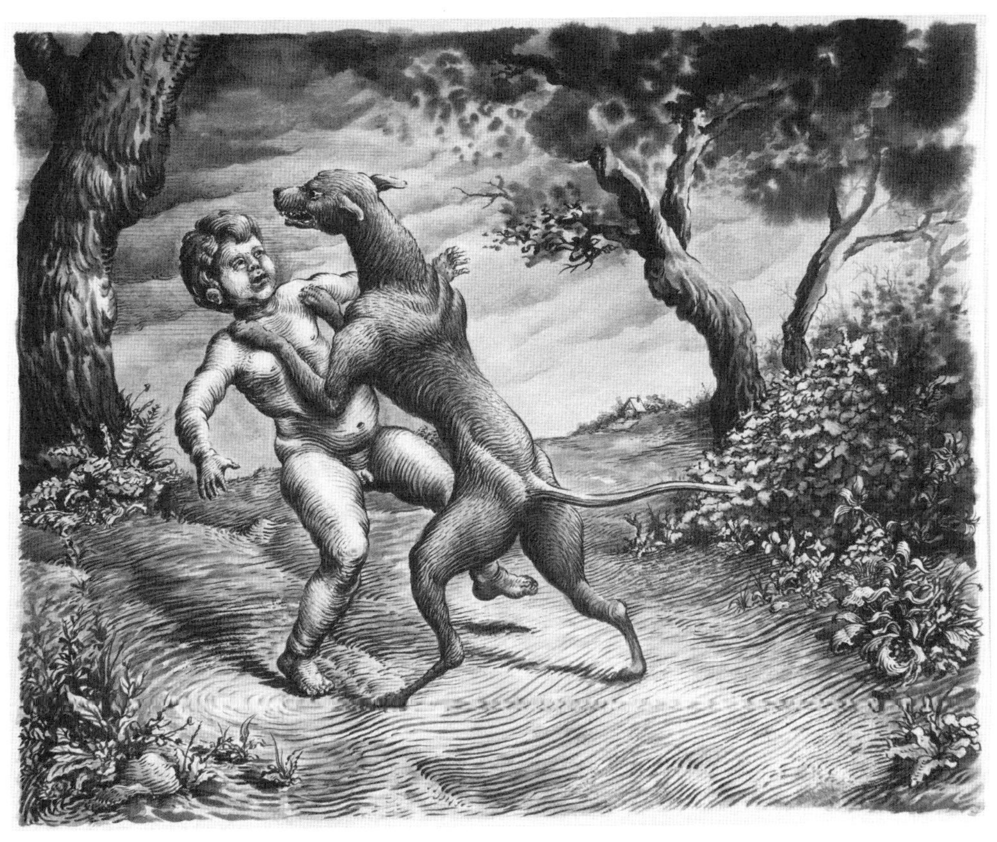

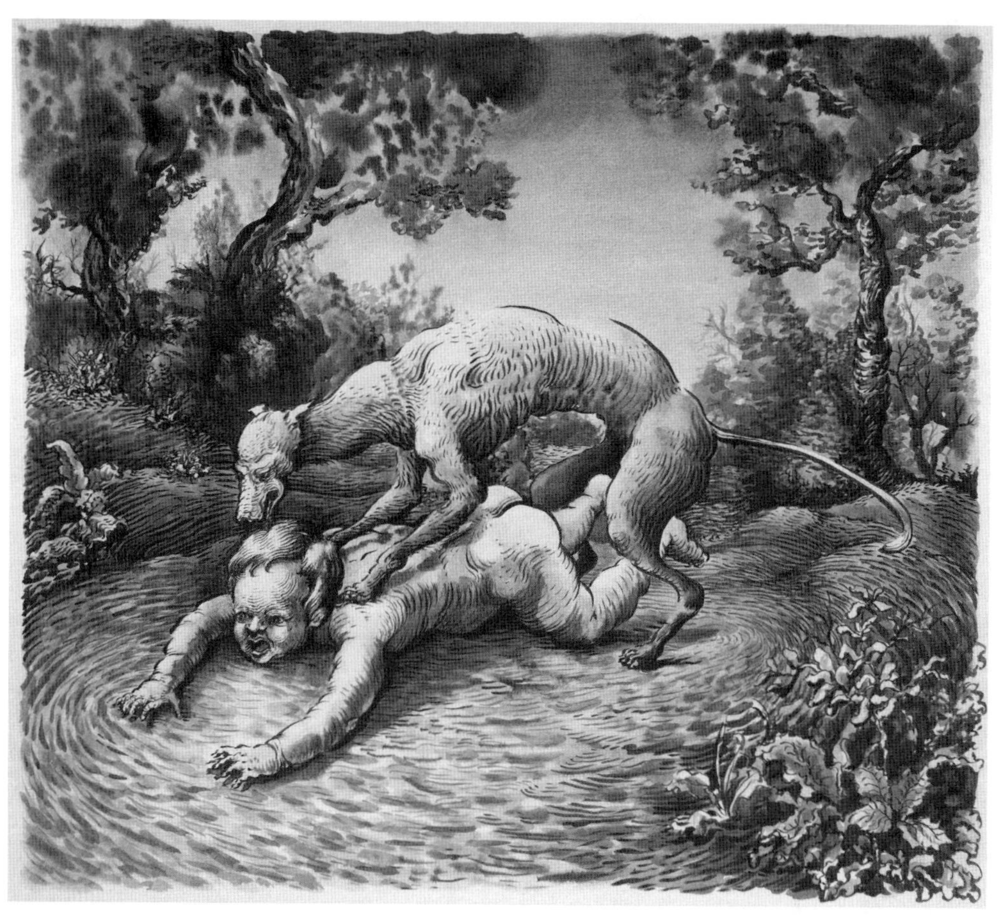

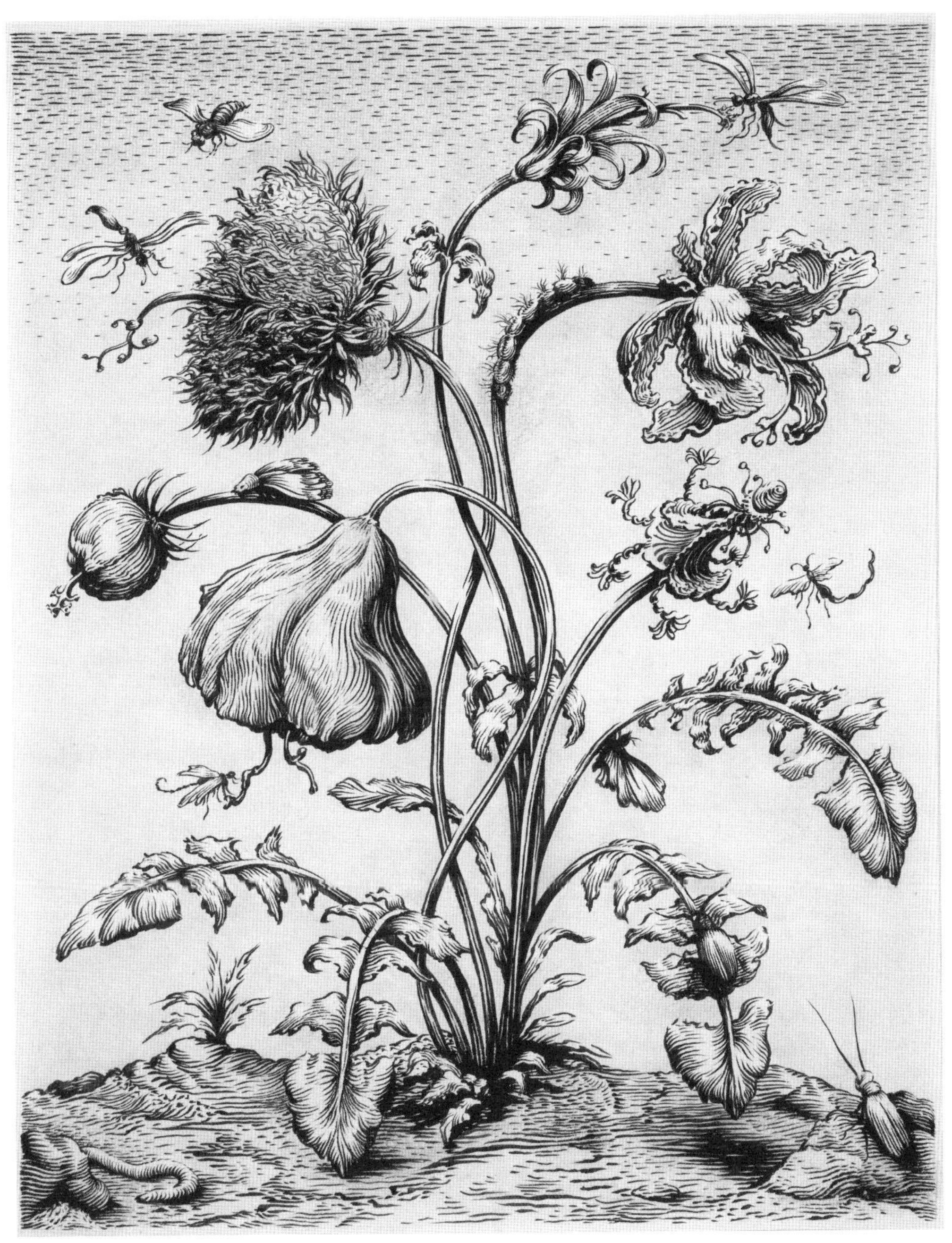

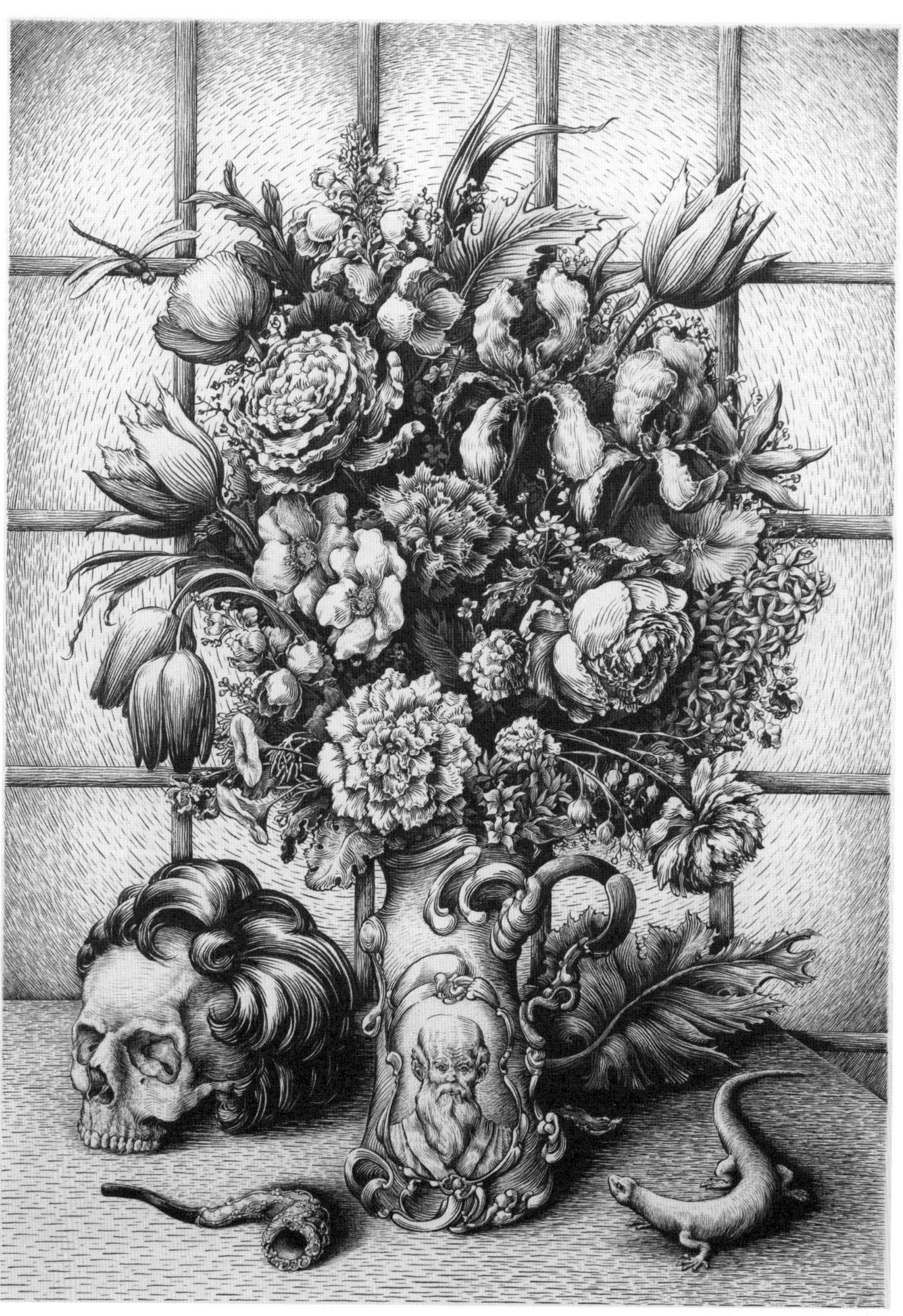

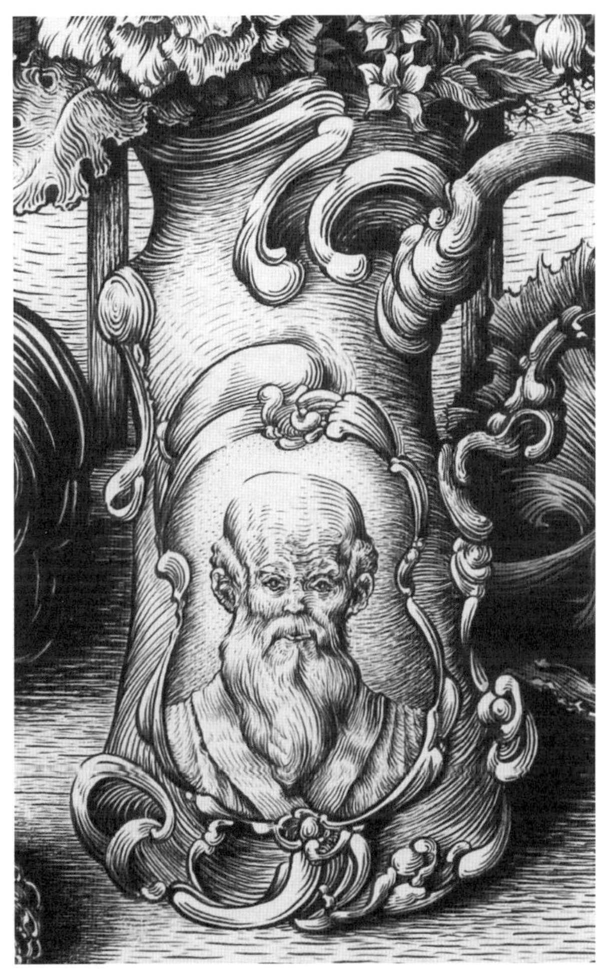

VOYAGER SONG

Blind Willie Johnson's "Dark Was the Night, Cold Was the Ground"

by Mike McGonigal

ILLUSTRATION BY DIMITRI SIMAKIS

Nine notes are played in rapid succession on the fourth string, then repeated in a slurred style using all the strings in an open tuning with a slide capable of producing a steely rattle (most likely a knife). The singer moans and then plays a similar simple-but-affecting line, stringing those notes out, wringing a tremendous silence from between the mostly wordless song's verses.

The 78 "Dark Was the Night, Cold Was the Ground" appears on (backed with "If I Had My Way I'd Tear This Building Down") was a bestseller in its day, moving more than ten thousand units (according to OG blues historian Sam Charters) before later going through multiple pressings on Columbia and subsidiary labels. The only contemporary review I've found is from a New England magazine published in the '20s called *The Bookman*. The notice speaks of the record's "violent, tortured and abysmal shouts and groans" and Johnson's "inspired guitar playing in a primitive and frightening Negro religious song."

Blind Willie Johnson recorded for Columbia until April 1930, when the Depression hit and ruined the market for what were called "race" records. "Dark was the Night" was his third release. He was thirty years old at the time. Some of his 78s outsold even Bessie Smith's, at least for a brief while. This record was the last to be released from his initial Dallas, Texas recording session on Saturday, December 3rd, 1927. And it's the only song from that session to have been completed in a single take.

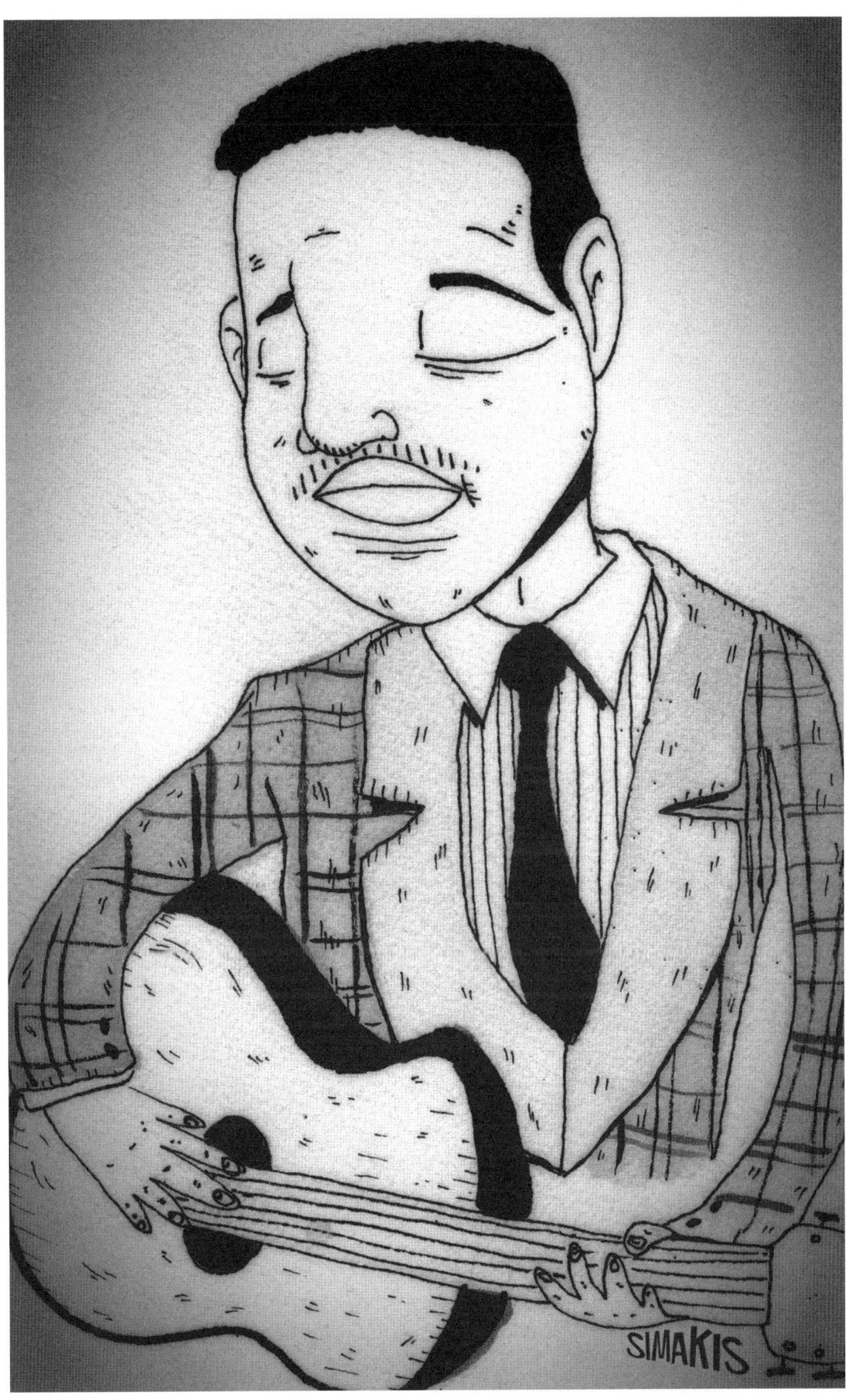
SIMAKIS

I would like very much to avoid the sort of traps that so many well-meaning white people get into when confronted with awe-inspiring works created by African-American artists some eighty years ago. My aim is to briefly contextualize this song (the most haunting piece of music I've heard)—in particular to discuss it in relation to the street corner evangelists and bluesy gospel musicians of the time, noting that gospel as we know it today, rooted so heavily in the arrangements of Thomas Dorsey and (later) James Cleveland, did not yet exist, and that modern gospel as a musical form is in fact younger than jazz.

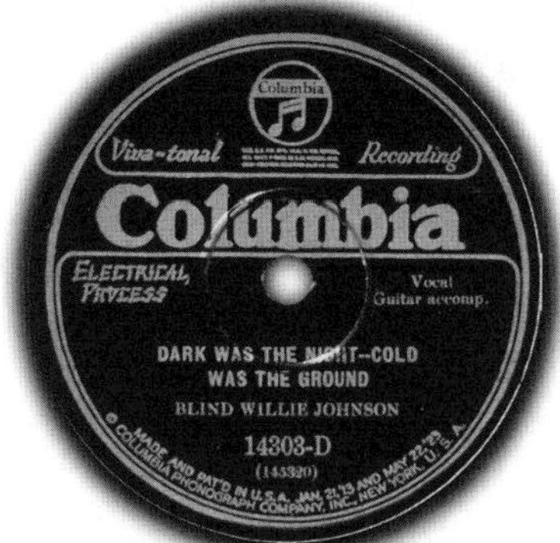

The song seems like it's always been there, like I've always heard it, always known it, though I've only become obsessed by it in the last few years. I've heard it so many times by now I can simply think of it and hear the entire thing in my head, start to finish. This one song has greatly influenced some of the music I like, or liked when I was younger, most notably the work of guitarist John Fahey, who would seem to owe much of his career to it (along with a smattering of Elizabeth Cotten and the work of Willie McTell, of course). In fact, Fahey became physically ill when he first heard Blind Willie and admit he was unable to get the sound out of his head. So it *was* there, I just didn't know it yet. Johnson's influence was also apparent in covers of his songs by Led Zeppelin, the Grateful Dead, Dylan, and Ry Cooder. With his gruff vocal style, intense lyrics, and nimble slide guitar technique, it's easy to see why rockers were and remain so attracted to Johnson's work, which has been covered more recently by White Stripes and Jack Rose.

Many people's first introduction to Blind Willie Johnson is the song "John the Revelator," thanks to Harry Smith's inclusion of it in the "Social Music" section of the famed and venerated *Anthology of American Folk Music* set (Folkways, 1952). It's a fairly typical Blind Willie song: a man's voice growls "Who's that a-writing?," and is answered by a sweet female soprano (believed almost certainly to be Willie B. Richardson, later Willie B. Harris, Blind Willie Johnson's first wife), who sings "John the Revelator" three times in a row, until they both croon in unison, "A book of the Seven Seals." I cannot think of any other song that makes the act of writing (which here sounds to me like "riding," but then again I also misheard the subsequent line as "book of the seventh seal," which shows how many times I ditched Bible study) sound so intense, so active. It makes sense when you consider the song is about the Apostle John penning the onslaught of apocalyptic imagery that is the Book of Revelation.

Love in Vain director and screenwriter Alan Greenberg has written that "in the history of recorded blues and spirituals, there is no greater singer and songwriter than Blind Willie Johnson," perhaps unaware that most of Johnson's songs are rewritings of older hymns and spirituals, but no matter. Greenberg goes on to praise Johnson's vocal range and talking guitar. After singling out "Dark Was the Night" and three other numbers, he asks the reader to "try to find equally visceral conviction any other place or time."

Johnson sings in two clearly distinct styles—at times he sings an octave lower and with different intonation. On "City of Refuge" it can be argued that the two styles denote separate people, though the song is told in a third-person narrative. In her book *Who Set You Flowing*, Farah Jasmine Griffin describes how Johnson begins the song narrating a scene in the style of a "blues singer," but by the end has adopted a preacher's tone—deeper, raspier, almost a shout. "Dark Was the Night" is also a dialogue of call and response, in its own way. Francis Davis writes in *History of the Blues* that "to an even greater extent than Son House's, Johnson's music was charred with purgatorial fire. He was a man of God, perhaps even a religious fanatic, but he ranted like a man possessed by demons." Johnson could just as easily be seen as channeling the intensity of a rural black preacher from a Pentecostal, Holiness, or Baptist church. (Many blues writers and scholars, with the notable exception of the great Paul Oliver, seem compelled to issue caveats when discussing gospel blues, essentially saying that such and such bluesy musician is authentic *even though* she or he sings spiritual songs.)

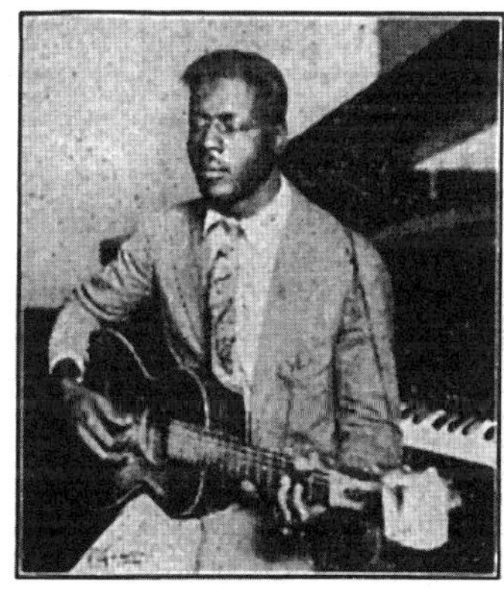

There's one known picture of Blind Willie Johnson. To me, he doesn't look like much of a religious fanatic in it, though it can be hard to tell these things. Johnson is seated in front of a piano and a tin cup hangs from the tuning pegs of his guitar, evidence of the way he made his living, singing on street corners and in churches across his hometown of Beaumont, Texas, and beyond. Johnson was born near Waco, Texas, in 1892. He was not blind at birth. There are several stories about how he lost his sight; the most credible has his stepmother throwing lye into the child's face at the age of seven to get back at his father. From an early age, Johnson was drawn to music; his father made him a guitar out of a discarded cigar box until he could afford a real one in his teens. Willie was a popular performer at dances as soon as he began to play them, but the call to glorify God prevailed. So he infused his blues with a gospel message—a new and radical thing back then.

It was not called gospel blues at the time, but this music was a pretty popular form in the 1920s and '30s. These sanctified singers can be grouped in several categories. There are the so-called guitar evangelists, the first of whom to record was Blind Joe Taggart and the second the Reverend Edward Clayborn, whose label credited his early recordings as simply "The Guitar Evangelist." He's often derided because his jaunty yet vaguely halting little songs all sound basically the same, but as I've said before (see my notes to the song by him on the *YETI* 4 CD), I rather like that about him. Then there are the street-corner singers—with whom we'd surely group Johnson—who often affected booming or otherwise ear-catching vocal styles so as to be heard from blocks away. There are also the recordings that shout-singing preachers made with their congregations. Many early bestselling records were preacher recordings (this was in the period before radio became a mass phenomenon). A further sizeable element of sanctified blues is composed of the spiritual and gospel songs recorded by blues singers and blues-affiliated songsters—many pre-war country blues singers cut gospel songs, including Charlie Patton and Bukka White, both of whom recorded sanctified numbers under aliases for a variety of reasons.

If we are to place "Dark was the Night" into any sort of tradition simply based on the way it sounds, it would most likely be under the small but exciting heading of sanctified blues numbers recorded with idiosyncratic accompaniment. This also includes, for example, the work of Luther Magby. His "Blessed Are The Poor In Spirit," (from his only 78, on the OKeh label, of which supposedly only one copy still exists!) is just mumbly, gruff vocals set to organ and tambourine. I love Magby's voice and think of him fondly as the Biz Markie of this kind of music. The instrumental coda sounds like somebody tap-dancing along to a carousel pump organ. The tune's title refers to a bit of scripture from Matthew: "Blessed are the poor in spirit, for theirs is the kingdom of heaven." Writing about Magby in the *All Music Guide,* Prof. Eugene Chadbourne makes the rather unbelievable claim that "in 2002, he was still maintaining a busy performing schedule, including gospel shows at a variety of state fairs." How this could be true and yet Magby remain unrecorded beyond two songs from 1927 is tough to fathom.

Then there's the Texas-based Washington Phillips, whose recordings usually consist of a short sermon followed by vocals accompanied by an unknown instrument which has best been described as a "celestial ice cream truck" (I forget who said that). The instrument has long been presumed to be either an autoharp or a dolceola. It might actually be something else, a homemade instrument made from either an old banjo or piano innards. The experts (including musician/producer Jim Dickinson) lean towards the dolceola, a sort of miniature piano that was sold door to door in the '20s and never took off in popularity. If you want to know more about Phillips, the best source is the chapter on him in Michael Corcoran's 2005 *All Over the Map: True Heroes of Texas Music*; Phillips's music is readily available on compilations and via online mp3 stores, and we included a track on *YETI* 3..

The final song in this category I want to address was recorded in Memphis ten months before "Dark Was the Night." It's Blind Mamie Forehand with her husband, AC (or Asey). "Honey in the Rock" seems to me the perfect companion song to "Dark," from the similar way the slide guitar is used to "answer" certain lines (though of course that is a common conceit of country blues). Mostly it's just the tune's ethereal, ghostly nature. Gospel historian Horace Clarence Boyer wrote about Forehand's recording in a songbook for the group Sweet Honey in the Rock, relating how "the song became widely popular among Pentecostal, Baptist and Methodist congregations but, as often happens, it underwent a slight textual change on its way to popularity." So while Forehand titled it "Honey in the Rock," as various congregants sang the tune later, they added "Sweet" to the title and it became known as such. In the early '70s, Bernice Reagon formed an all-female a capella gospel act which took their name and part of their inspiration from Mamie's tune. That's understandable; it's unbelievably beautiful. A friend who'd never heard it before enthused, "holy moly—that's ambient blues!" One bell, which is either a triangle or (most likely) an untuned service bell, is struck repeatedly throughout. And then there's Mamie's strong yet quavery voice, which never moves above a moan, though you want it to. It's that restraint, and the absolute strangeness of the arrangement, that forces me to listen to the song over and over. (Listen yourself—it's track 23 on the CD accompanying this issue.)

The 1920s and '30s, when all this music was made, was a time of great religious fervor and upheaval throughout the United States. Entire new denominations and sects sprang up, many of them newly energized by the torrents of the Azusa Street Revival, held in Los Angeles from 1906 to 1909. Among other things, the Azusa Revival begat the Church of God in Christ (COGIC). In the excellent study by C. Eric Lincoln and Lawrence Mamiya, *The Black Church in the African American Experience*, the COGIC is shown to have given unprecedented roles to women; it had uncharacteristically interracial origins as well. Today it is by far the largest African-American and Pentecostal church, with almost six million members.

In the liner notes to a recent compilation on Dust to Digital culled from his extensive collection of 78s, Joe Boussard writes of "Dark was the Night": "I think it's a moaning song that was probably sung in the slavery or Civil War days while they were picking cotton. I think it was handed down. It is incredible that they would make a record of a song like that. But they did it. It shows you the kind of feelings people had in those days." I personally don't think emotions themselves have changed too dramatically in eighty years, but I have come to realize in my research that the song *is* sort of a moaning song, one that's part of the kindred tradition of lined-out hymnody.

"Lining out" is the practice of rapidly singing or stating the upcoming lines of a hymn for the congregation by a song leader or preacher. Leadbelly is quoted in Harris's book as saying that "sisters in the Amen corner" just as often performed the role. Today it's the principal form of singing—purely a capella lined-out hymns—in the Southern Old Regular Baptist church; there are several excellent recordings of this material on Folkways. What "Dark Was the Night, Cold Was the Ground" is above all else—and this would have been instantly familiar to his audience at the time—is an example of a capella hymnody that just happens to be largely wordless. Those first nine notes picked out on the fourth string mimic the song leader, and the moaning melody is then repeated back using the slide.

The original hymn "Dark was the Night" was written by Thomas Haweis, an English physician and clergyman who wrote hundreds like it. First published in 1792 and originally titled "Gethsemane," it was one of the many hymns taught to American slaves in the 1800s by British missionaries. Gethsemane was the garden where Christ prayed and suffered for the sins of the world, the night before he was crucified. According to Luke 22, Jesus's anguish in Gethsemane was so deep that "his sweat was as it were great drops of blood falling down to the ground." It was also on that night in Gethsemane that Christ was betrayed by the disciple Judas Iscariot, an event that was dramatized in Pasolini's 1964 film *Gospel According to St. Matthew* using Blind Willie's song as the soundtrack.

Also included on the accompanying CD is a version of the hymn sung by a woman named Mary Price, recorded in the mid-1950s by Frederic Ramsey Jr. The fieldwork that led to Ramsey's recording came about when he "sought to explore sources that would lead listeners back to the decades between the emancipation of the slaves in 1863 and 1900." This version is a solo a capella performance, but in the space between verses you can hear Price speak-sing the "lead" line rapidly before repeating it back, as the congregation would.

Johnson is justly revered today (*All Music Guide* calls him "perhaps the finest singing evangelist of all time"), but he never recorded after 1930, though he continued to sing on the street, attend revivals, and eke out a living playing music. Michael Corcoran writes of further sightings of Willie, most notably his appearance on the radio in the Second World War when he sang about God moving on the water, updating his tremendous song about the Titanic to reflect current fears of German submarines and warships. Johnson died an awful,

pauper's death in 1945. After a fire destroyed his home in Beaumont, Texas —
and after being denied treatment at a local hospital because he was blind, or
black, or both—he returned to his house to sleep in his rain-soaked bed, where
he died of pneumonia days later.

I wanted to save some of the accolades for last; they've all come since Blind
Willie passed away, in any case. Ry Cooder has described "Dark Was the Ground"
as "the most soulful, transcendent piece of American music recorded in the 20th
century," while Joe Boussard says, "There's more feeling and meaning in that
record than anything I have ever heard." Samuel Charters weighs in with this:
"What Willie did in the studio was to create this mood, this haunted response
to Christ's crucifixion. It was the only piece he played like this, and nothing else
similar to it was ever recorded. It remains one of the unique masterpieces of
American music."

Perhaps the greatest honor is this, however: the song is currently hurtling
into the farthest reaches of our solar system, included on the Voyager Golden
Record, copies of which are attached to two separate space probes launched by
NASA in 1977. The probes themselves were conceived not only as a means of
collecting information about Jupiter, Saturn, and the outer reaches of our galaxy,
but also as a friendly "What's up" to any alien intelligence out there.

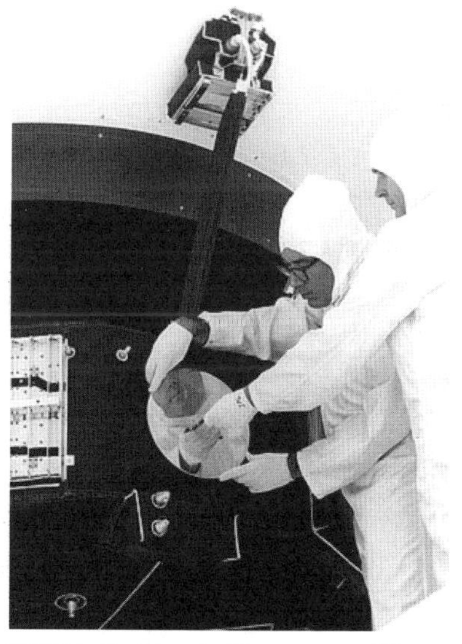

NASA technicians bolting a copy of the Voyager Golden Record to one of the Voyager space probes.

The Voyager Golden Record comes with its
own self-playing stylus and contains 90 minutes
of music from the history of recorded sound.
The anonymous blogger who calls himself
Celestial Monochord argues that Voyager
record compiler Carl Sagan, who got his PhD
around 1960, at the height of the folk revival,
was clearly influenced by the humanistic, global
aesthetic of the Folkways label in deciding
what to include on his golden record, adding
that Alan Lomax served as an advisor. Lomax
made specific recommendations that are known
to have wound up on the record, such as John
Cohen's 1964 recording of a young Peruvian
woman's wedding song; Beethoven and Chuck
Berry also are included on the record. I just love
the idea that this song with the word "ground"
in its title, this work that's simultaneously so visceral and ethereal, is hurtling
farther out into the cosmos every day, as if to say, "Hello there; please don't hunt
us down and kill us. I mean we can't be too bad—look, we recorded Blind Willie
Johnson!" to alien species who might encounter the thing and play it on their
intergalactic hi-fi. ❧

MARJORINE

(I Drove for Chang & Ma)

by Meredith Brosnan

ILLUSTRATION BY JASON TRAEGER

At Heathrow, the old man was escorted off the plane in handcuffs by airport security. He was a sorry sight, still shouting about the papal nuncio and the Virgin Mary as he was being led down the aisle. Because of the disturbance, the passengers on board flight BA0189 had to sit on the tarmac for nearly forty minutes. Colm passed the time reading The Big Book and writing e-mails. Once he exited the plane, things moved quickly: his suitcase appeared almost immediately; the Paddington Express got him into the city in no time. He arrived at his hotel at twenty to ten.

The hotel was at the north end of the Tottenham Court Road. On previous trips to London, he had stayed at some quite ritzy places; this hotel was not even two-star. The lobby was small and needed a paint job. A thin boy with a dark complexion stood behind the reception desk. He looked Spanish, or possibly Turkish. He took his time getting a porter for Colm's suitcase and was slow giving him his room key. His manner, Colm thought, bordered on cheeky. Colm waited for the lift with the porter, a middle-aged guy with a long sad face. He had a sticking plaster on his lower jaw and looked half-asleep. The lift door's shiny metal surface reflected the reception desk. Colm saw the boy was watching them. He was relieved when the lift finally came. It was slow-moving and cramped; there was barely enough room for two people.

The elevator stopped and they got off. The porter started down the hallway with the suitcase. Colm followed with his overstuffed briefcase. It was a long hallway, paneled in dark wood, with doors on both sides. The lighting was

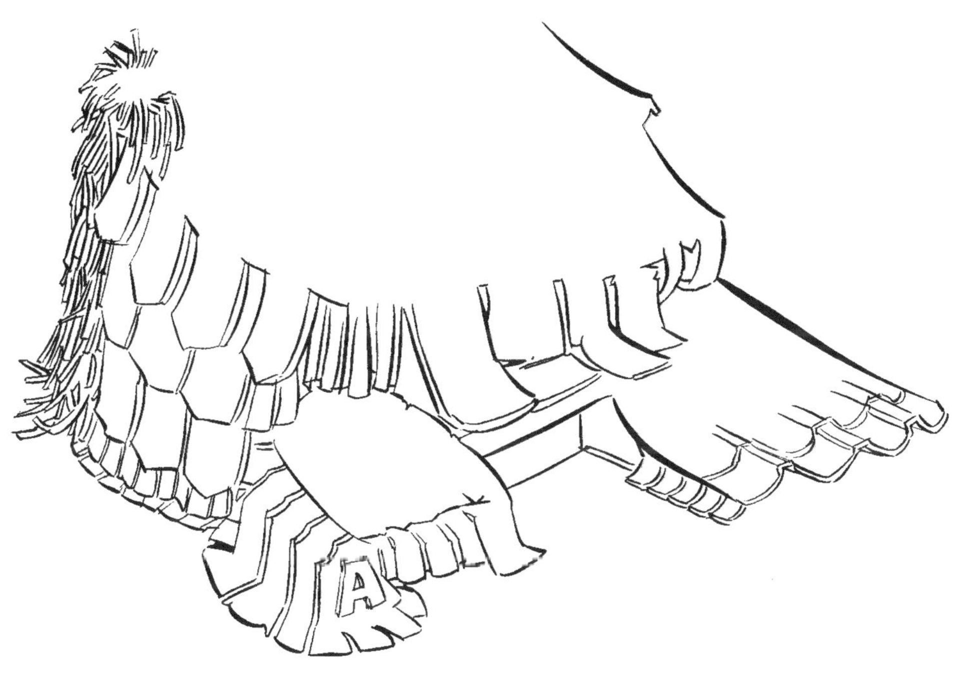
A

very subdued: every three or four feet, a thin column of pale blue light struck the floor. He had a feeling he had walked down this hallway before. But that was impossible. Colm looked up. Those illuminated star-shaped holes in the ceiling looked very familiar. Perhaps the hotel was part of a chain: on a previous trip to London he might have stayed at a different hotel owned by the same company—upscale in relation to this one, but with the same general interior design. He was about to ask the porter if the hotel was independently owned, but at that moment the man stopped abruptly, setting Colm's suitcase down on the carpet. He took out a pass card and used it to open a door on the right.

The room was surprisingly large and bright. As promised, it was equipped with a wall jack for Colm's laptop. He gave the porter a tip; the man touched a nicotine-stained finger to his temple and withdrew. Colm unpacked his clothes and his computer, hung up his suit, and took a shower. Before getting dressed, he went on-line and found the UK AA web site. There were a lot of meetings in London and it took a while to scroll through the list. Ideally, he was looking for a noon meeting in central London, not in some far-flung suburb like Croydon or Finchley. He wanted one he could get to easily; a meeting he could slot in between the two appointments he'd scheduled for the earlier part of the day. His first appointment, at eleven, was with Mr. Chang, the Chinese kitchenware importers' representative, at his office near Piccadilly Circus. They were going to meet for forty-five minutes to look at some new product lines and review sales figures. At half one, he had his second business meeting of the day, with Marko Malevich and his assistant, Renata, in a coffee shop near Marble Arch. Malevich represented a group of Croatian potters and batik-makers whose work Colm wanted to feature in the shop.

According to the web site, there was an AA meeting on Fowl Street at noon. Apparently Fowl Street was just off Piccadilly Circus and quite near the offices of Chang & Ma Importers (UK) Ltd. It seemed his best bet. It was an open meeting—a meeting open to the general public, not just to alcoholics—and would go for an hour. This would take him up to one o'clock—which was perfect, because he could get a quick bite to eat before his meeting with the Slavs. He remembered that Peter, his sponsor, had warned him that finding a meeting in a foreign city could be tricky. Sometimes addresses and start times weren't current. Colm called the AA London hotline. A helpful young man confirmed that, yes, there *was* a meeting today at noon at 39 Fowl Street.

Mr. Chang, the meeting, Marko at half one: his first day in London was shaping up nicely. It gave Colm a good feeling. These days, he liked to have all his ducks in a row.

While buttoning his shirt, he looked around the room. Opposite the bed there was a red upholstered chair with a fake antique finish. Next to it stood the small writing desk where he'd set up his laptop. To the right of the desk was a tall mahogany dresser. The top of the dresser was empty except for one small object, dead centre. He hadn't noticed it until now. Colm put on his pants and walked over to the dresser for a closer look. It was a thimble: a bright silver thimble standing on its narrow end. Thimbles were familiar objects from childhood; he remembered his mother using one as she sat sewing in the kitchen of their old house in Blackrock. You didn't see many nowadays. What was it doing there? He went to pick it up but stopped, surprised. Floating inside the silver rim was a reflection of the room's ceiling light; the thimble was full to the brim with liquid.

He leaned down and sniffed. There was no smell. He picked up the thimble and carried it into the bathroom, walking slowly so as not to spill a drop. He poured the liquid into one of the disposable plastic glasses standing on the sink and held the glass up to the light. Colourless. He carefully poured the water—obviously, water—back into the thimble, which he'd placed on the rim of the sink. As he was straightening up, he caught his eye in the bathroom mirror. He had definitely aged since the beating. You could see it in his eyes, in his sunken cheeks. He'd lost a lot of hair in the past year. "You suffered a very severe beating, Colm." Dr. Shine's words came back to him. "The insomnia you've told me about, the panic attacks—these are symptomatic of something called post–traumatic stress disorder…" He remembered her quiet, educated voice; her gray eyes, full of intelligence and sympathy. Colm picked up the thimble and drank. He knocked it back in one, like doing a shot of whiskey. Colourless, odorless; he'd honestly expected it to taste like water, but instead it had a hot, sweet taste—basically citrus-y but more complex. A hint of ginger, was that it? With a feeling of dread, he put the thimble down on the sink.

He didn't feel drunk, he didn't feel even slightly tipsy. From an AA point of view, that didn't matter. If he *had* drunk alcohol, even if it was only a thimbleful, he was back counting days. He knew he should call his sponsor and ask his advice. It was a strange situation. He could see himself recounting this incident at future meetings. He'd probably talk about it later today at the Fowl Street meeting. It occurred to him that he should bring the thimble back to Dublin and show it to Peter L.—his sponsor, with his medical background, would know where to get it analyzed for traces of alcohol. But the thimble was either the property of the hotel or of some previous occupant of the room; to take it would be stealing. After a few moments of indecision, he wrapped it in a piece of toilet paper and hid it in an outer pocket of his suitcase.

Colm looked at his watch. He'd better get a move on, or he'd be late for his meeting with Mr. Chang. He could call his sponsor on the way. Colm put on his tie and jacket and shoes. He grabbed his coat and scarf and briefcase and took the lift down to the lobby. He pushed through the glass doors and walked up the street towards Warren Street tube station. It was a cold January morning; the wind was strong and from the north. The sky above London was slate-gray and seemed filled with the promise of snow. Colm paused at the top of the stairs leading to the underground and left a brief message on Peter's voice-mail (a message that his sponsor would later describe as "incoherent"). Colm walked down the stairs, bought a ticket and passed through the barrier. He had only a short wait before the Victoria Line train arrived. He changed at Oxford Circus for the Bakerloo Line and took it one stop to Piccadilly Circus.

Mr. Chang's office was on Blefaro Street, which turned out to be a narrow side street off Piccadilly. Following directions copied down from his business associate's e-mail, Colm found number 23. It was next door to an Asian-owned hairdresser's. He rang the top bell and was buzzed in immediately. He took a slow-moving, rickety elevator to the fifth floor.

He got off and followed a sign on the wall that pointed the way to CHANG & MA IMPORTS (UK) LTD. He walked around a corner, then to the end of a short corridor, and took another left. At the end of the hall was a green door. Chang & Ma. He rang the bell. After a few moments he heard the door unlock with an electronic buzzing noise. Pushing it open, Colm found himself in a tiny waiting area, facing a white door. Beside the door, at head height, was a frosted glass window with a lime green tint.

After a few moments, the white door opened and a man came out. Smiling, he held out his hand:

"Mr. Shields! How nice to see you. Please, come in!"

"Thanks. Sorry I'm a bit late."

The man was tall for an Asian—over six foot. He released Colm's hand and made a small bow.

"Mr. Chang has been called away on urgent business. Unfortunately, he will not be able to meet you today. He sends his regrets and best wishes."

"You must be Mr. Ma, then."

"No, no, Mr. Ma is in Aberdeen today. I am Mr. Han."

Half-turning, the tall man indicated with a slow sweep of his hand that Colm was to precede him into the other room. Colm made an awkward bow and stepped through the doorway. On the left, just inside the door, a young black woman sat at a desk in front of a bulky, old-fashioned computer monitor. She had short, copper-coloured hair. As the two men passed her work station, she gave Colm a quick, searching look. He noticed her eyes were large and beautiful; he noticed, too, the big gold-coloured hoop earrings she wore and the extraordinary length and metallic sheen of her dark red nails. Surely they had to be fake, glue-ons? The woman wore a frilly powder-blue top with a plunging neckline; she had shapely breasts. Beside her mouse pad stood a carton of sesame noodles and a pair of chopsticks. At her feet he glimpsed, in passing, the glowing orange bars of an electric heater.

Mr. Han stopped, turned and bowed again. Colm was ushered through another doorway into an inner office. The tall man shut the door behind him. He took Colm's coat and scarf and hung them on a wooden coat stand. Colm took a seat in front of a big wooden desk. On the desk, next to a black phone, was a framed photograph of a man Colm immediately recognized as Mr. Chang, the co-owner of Chang & Ma. He had met Chang only once—in Dublin three months ago. They had dined one evening in a restaurant called the Magic Wok on D'Olier Street. In the photo, the Hong Kong–born businessman stood smiling in front of a flowering bush. Beside him stood a smiling middle-aged woman, presumably Mrs. Chang, and a tall, round-faced boy with glasses, presumably their son. As Colm stared at the photograph, the tall man slipped into his chair on the other side of the desk. He smiled: "Yes, that is Mr. Chang and his family. This is Mr. Chang's office."

Mr. Han's smile abruptly vanished as he cleared his throat: "Mr. Shields, if you will permit me, I should like to begin this morning with some preliminary observations."

Colm didn't like the sound of that but he thought he'd better play along.

"Sure, go ahead."

"First of all, I cannot help noticing that you are much thinner than the last time we met. And you seem to have lost a lot of hair. You face is gaunt, very careworn. I cannot help wondering, *is business really so bad?*"

Colm stared at him. He didn't know what to say. For a start, he had no recollection of ever meeting this man before.

With an effort, he rallied: "I wouldn't say that. I wouldn't say business was bad. It's good, actually. I'm growing. Sure, I've had a couple of setbacks but I'm on track now. I can show you recent sales figures—"

He reached for his briefcase but Mr. Han held up his hand, a peremptory gesture: "Thank you. That won't be necessary."

Colm took a deep breath. *Stay calm. Let him take the lead.*

Mr. Han continued: "Mr. Shields, Chang and Ma is more than kitchenware. We are a long-established firm with an international reputation for all-around excellence. We have high operational standards. We have always made it a point to know as much as possible about our business partners, both here in the United Kingdom and overseas. As a routine precaution, we employ impeccable investigative resources."

He paused. Looking Colm dead in the eye, he continued: "Sad to say, we have it on very good authority that you will most likely fail to meet your projected sales targets for 2007 and 2008. In fact, we predict that by early 2009 at the latest you will be forced to seek bankruptcy protection.

"But my point here is not to criticize you. My point is to give you hope. The fact is, Chang and Ma may be able to help you out of your present difficulties."

Colm nodded slowly. *Were they going to make him an offer for the business?*

"Thank you, Mr. Han. But I don't quite see—"

"One moment, please."

Mr. Han reached in his trouser pocket and produced a set of keys. He bent down and unlocked one of the desk's drawers. He took out a large three-ring binder with a white plastic cover. He set the binder down on the desktop, turned it to face Colm and pushed it across the table.

"Please look at these."

On the cover of the binder was a photograph of a young Asian woman. Standing in profile with her face turned towards the camera, she wore a very short black and white polka-dot dress and black stilettos. She was smiling and pointing at a large pink and yellow star-like object that shone in the picture's top left-hand corner. She wore very pale makeup; her lips were painted bright red. Her eyes, big and brown and full of mischief, regarded Colm from under arched black brows. Chinese characters swirled around the woman's legs and torso and formed a sort of halo above her head. Behind her, he saw skyscrapers, tall black rectangles dotted with row upon row of tiny golden lights; the nighttime skyline of some unknown city. Printed underneath the photograph in a scrolly red font and bracketed by stylized hearts were the words *For Your Lasting Pleasure.*

Colm opened the binder. It was full of colour head shots of young Asian women. There were several black girls and one or two white girls as well. Each head shot hung in a transparent plastic sleeve. On the back of the photos he saw the girls' names–a first name only–their vital statistics, their favourite film, favourite flower, favourite song. There must have been more than a hundred photographs.

As Colm leafed through the photos he was uncomfortably aware that the other man was watching him. After half a minute, he thought it safe to close the binder. "Very nice. Nice photos."

"Yes, they are all very nice girls."

"Well, Mr. Han—"

"Well, Mr. Shields, here is the situation. Chang and Ma have recently embarked on a new and exciting business venture. You might say we have expanded into the entertainment sector. Last year, our public-affairs division identified an emerging market among visiting businessmen and foreign dignitaries for . . ."—he paused and smiled—"charming and youthful companions."

Colm pointed to the binder. "These, you mean?"

"Precisely."

"That's great . . . but what's it got to do with me?"

Mr. Han nodded, very serious now: "The girls must remain fresh. They tire easily. They cannot drive themselves to their rendezvous."

"I don't see—"

"We know you like to drive. And you miss being behind the wheel."

Colm stared at the man. He felt himself going red. "Let me get this straight. I don't want to misunderstand you. You're offering me a job?"

"Yes, we are."

"And the job would be driving call girls—hookers—to meet clients? Here in London?"

"They are not call girls, Mr. Shields. They are artistically gifted models from very good families. Each one has undergone a lengthy training to make her fit to serve as an exclusive female companion for the successful businessman."

"Mr. Han, I don't know what to say— "

"Say yes! We will pay for your relocation and find you a nice flat in a good part of London. We will help you find a buyer for your failing business. We will give you a new driver's license. You would have a very smart uniform with a peaked cap, a grey serge tunic and comfortable leather boots. It would never be your responsibility to clean or otherwise maintain the Bentley Mark 6. Under certain circumstances and with prior notification you would be permitted to use the car at the weekends, to take your best girl for a spin in the country. You could take her to see Stonehenge or the Cheddar Gorge, for example."

Before Colm could reply, the phone on Mr. Chang's desk started ringing. Mr. Han apologized and picked up the receiver. He listened for a few moments and then spoke rapidly. To Colm it sounded like Italian.

Mr. Han replaced the receiver and stood up. He addressed Colm with a smile: "Please excuse me. A matter of some urgency has arisen in our production department. I must give it my immediate attention. I will return very soon so we can continue our discussion. Regarding our offer of employment, please think it over carefully. It is a respectable and well-paid position with opportunities for advancement for the right man. We think you are the right man. If you decide you want the job, you could start today. In the meantime, if you would like some tea, all you have to do is ring the bell." He indicated a little silver bell that stood beside the phone. "Charmaine will bring you a pot of tea and a plate of assorted biscuits."

Mr. Han bowed and walked out, shutting the door behind him. Colm sat there for several minutes, staring at the photo of Mr. Chang and his family. What was going on? The job offer was … absolutely outrageous. Were they fucking with him? It seemed like it. But why? What did they have to gain? Colm stared at the little bell. He thought about ringing it to summon Charmaine—presumably she was the black girl in the outer office. A cup of tea and a chocolate biscuit: that would hit the spot, all right. But instead of picking up the bell, he sat there, deep in thought. The things Han had said, those "preliminary observations," had cut him to the quick. His loss of hair, his thinness—his physical deterioration since the beating must really be apparent. He saw it now: he was going to have a hard job convincing business partners and potential investors that he was back on his feet and that the new shop would make money. Han was predicting he'd be out of business by '09. He'd like to know what that forecast was based on, but maybe they were right, maybe he couldn't make it work. Should he take Han's job offer seriously, then? The Bentley Mark 6. That was a beautiful car. About the license, he assumed it would be no questions asked; he wouldn't have to take the UK test.

Fifteen minutes went by. Mr. Han did not return. Colm got up and went into the outer office to ask Charmaine if she knew how long he would have to wait. He was surprised to find her chair empty and her computer turned off. The electric heater was switched off too. He returned to the inner office and sat back down on the chair. He sat there, brooding, his thoughts ranging far and wide. (He came to a decision about the thimble: As soon as he got back to the hotel room he would flush it down the toilet.) At some point he must have drifted off to sleep; he saw Suzanne and Thelma and the Airport Girl sitting around a big black table, playing strip poker. A noise woke him. He thought he heard movement in the outer office, but when he went out to investigate the room was empty.

He looked at his watch. It was ten to twelve. Time to go. If he didn't go now he'd miss the start of the Fowl Street meeting. Colm took out his pen and a business card and wrote a note to Mr. Han on the back, explaining that he had another appointment. He wrote: *I will consider your job offer carefully and let you know tomorrow.* He placed the card beside the phone, facing Mr. Chang's chair. He put on his coat and scarf, picked up his briefcase and opened the door to the outer office.

When the lift didn't come immediately, he took the stairs. He hurried down the five flights and out into the street. It was eight minutes to twelve. Walking quickly past 21 Blefaro Street, he glanced in the window of the hairdressers'. A teenage girl with bright orange hair knelt on the floor of the salon. She was sweeping the broken pieces of a glass vase into a dustpan. A heavy-breasted woman with a towering black bouffant stood over her, scowling, a fat freckled fist on her hip.

A cold north wind was blowing down the street. Colm pulled his scarf up over his face. He stopped a bearded man in a bowler hat and asked for directions. The man barely glanced at him but pointed down the street with his rolled umbrella. Colm thanked him and set off. Coming up on his right was a newsstand. As he passed it, the cover of a popular laddie magazine caught his eye. The cover girl was naked, kneeling on a white rug, with her back to the camera. She was lit so that the lower half of her buttocks vanished discreetly in shadow. Her left arm was raised to give an unobstructed view of her left breast – the shot was carefully angled (or air-brushed?) so the nipple was invisible. The girl had short dark hair and the kind of facial features that are often described as "exotic" and "sultry." She stared back at Colm with a sulkily provocative expression, her narrow chin almost touching one smooth brown shoulder. Above her head was a small rectangular caption box that read:

**JAMI: HER BODY
MAKES GROWN MEN
WEEP WITH JOY!**

It struck Colm as an extravagant claim. He knew that stopping would probably make him late for the start of the meeting but he felt a strong compulsion to buy this issue of *Bloke*–just to see if the caption writer's boast was justified. He took a handful of shiny pound coins from his wallet and handed them to the newsagent, a bald middle-aged man with a fat mottled face. The man handed the magazine over with a friendly wink:

"Syphilis, guv."

Colm thought he must have misheard: "I'm sorry?"

The newsagent smiled: "Oh, you will be. Mark my words, guv, you bloody *will* be!" He pointed a nicotine-stained finger at Colm's copy of *Bloke*. "Pox-ridden 'ores, guv, poxy doxies! Diddiko dollymops, keenetseeno rollers! In cahoots with cash carriers, duffers 'n' snoozers! 'Dem as 'ud roll a cove fast as blinkin' and not stop at kinchen-lay, neever! Take it from me, guv, Jackie Papadakis! They ruined me 'ealth, they sucked me brines out me arsehole wif their liffle teeth, they emptied me bank account, and I STILL kept comin' back for more! Ha! Ha! Ha!"

The newsagent's laughter boomed. His face had turned brick-red. His eyes were screwed tightly shut, his shoulders were shaking. As Colm watched, the man reached for a copy of *Jugs*, rolled the magazine into a tube and began whipping himself on the backside with it, laughing all the while. In his confusion, Colm dropped his copy of *Bloke* on the pavement. He was backing away from the newsstand, then he was running. Lewd taunts and jeers pursued him down the street:

"Oy! You! Come back! Wot are ya, a fucking FAIRY?"

Excerpted from the forthcoming novella, *Marjorine (I Drove for Chang and Ma)*

UNICA ZÜRN

Graphic Work from the 1960s

INTRODUCTION BY MIKE McGONIGAL
ILLUSTRATION BY SCOTT MEYERS

Born in 1916 in Berlin, Unica Zürn grew up surrounded by "exotic, ephemeral objects collected by her father, a cavalry officer stationed in Africa," to quote her American gallerists, Ubu. "Inspired perhaps in part by her father's gifts from afar and a longing for greater contact with him, Zürn developed a rich fantasy life and a vivid imagination. This is evidenced in her dense, otherworldly drawings of fantastical creatures meticulously constructed out of finely rendered, obsessively repetitive shapes and lines." A rich inner world is certainly evident in the first art that Zürn created for public consumption—a series of stories and radio plays she began while in her early twenties.

Zürn's writings brought her to the attention of the Surrealists, and in 1953, she moved to Paris in order to live with the Surrealist-affiliated Hans Bellmer; she soon began to collaborate with him, and they also became lovers. Together they worked on a series of "notorious" photographs that showed her nude torso bound with string. In addition to tying her up, Bellmer encouraged her to try automatic artwork, and she embarked on a series of anagrams for which she remains well-known in German-speaking literary circles. Both the anagrams and automatic drawings were natural extensions of her established interest in hidden meanings and coincidences. The anagrams also allowed Zürn "to dissect the language of everyday, to personalize it, and to make it reveal hidden at its core astonishing messages, threats and evocations [and] formed the basis of her interpretation of the split between her inner & outer lives," according to the great translator and author Malcolm Green.

Bellmer introduced Zürn to many of his Surrealist pals, including writer

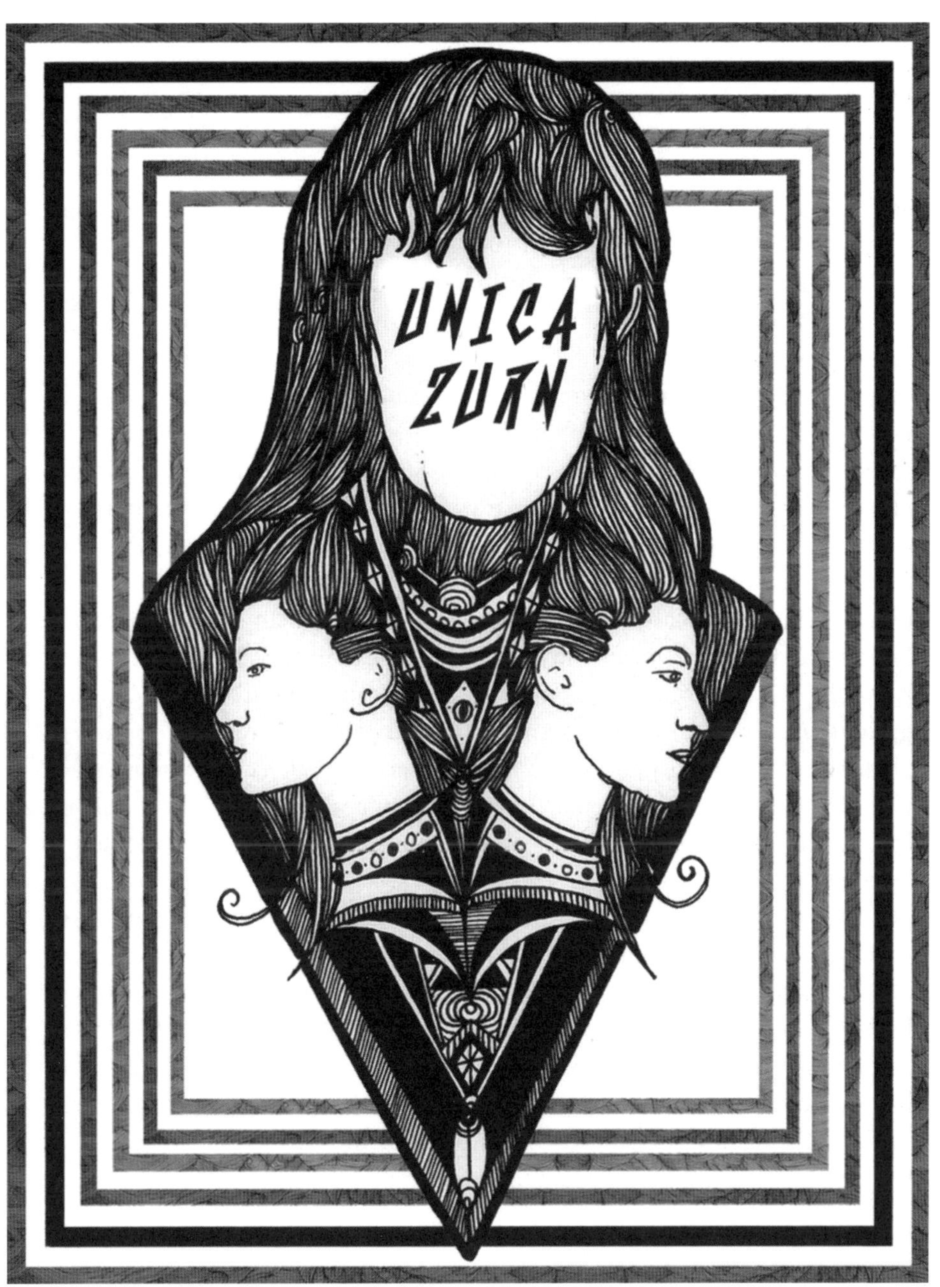
UNICA
ZÜRN

and visual artist Henri Michaux. Meeting Michaux in 1957 had a profound effect on Unica; in fact, it would be fair to say that she never recovered from it. She felt that Michaux was the physical embodiment of her childhood fantasy figure, "the man of jasmine." Meeting him plunged her into a world of hallucination in which visions of her desires and anxieties, and events from her unresolved past overwhelmed her present life. Her return to "reality" was constantly interrupted by alternate visionary and depressive periods. She was treated at various clinics in France; one of her doctors was Gaston Ferdière, who was also Antonin Artaud's psychiatrist. Her illness inspired much of her writing, above all *Man of Jasmine* (*Der Mann im Jasmin*)—subtitled "Impressions from a Mental Illness"—written between 1963 and 1965. It remains one of the most haunting and lucid descriptions of mental illness ever written.

Zürn's graphic works have much to communicate—they are beautiful grotesques, heavily imbued with psychic energy. The drawings look very modern, of course, especially in their resonances to fantasy and sci-fi illustration. To me, there are also reverberations with the watercolors of the German Tachiste painter and photographer Wols; with the sublime strangeness of the work of the anonymous artist known as P.M. Wentworth; and with the intricate, animistic drawings of Scottish artist Scottie Wilson. I also see affinities with the weirdness-from-another-planet aspects of the art produced by Milwaukee-based multi-disciplinarian Eugene Von Bruenchenhein and the mediumistic imagery and *horror vacuii* of British spiritualist Madge Gill. And something about the way she draws faces looks very Moroccan to me. It's all so subtle and graceful. And kind of druggy/sixties-y. Yet she played no role in the nascent "counterculture" of the period. It is clear that her work often comes from a place of torment, but there's a great playfulness to her flotational combinations of text and image, human and animal, representational form and whatever the hell that is.

Most of the works printed here were made during the 1960s, a productive time for her but a tough one. The '60s were marred by the unraveling of her relationship with Bellmer and further slippage into depression and hallucinations. In late 1970, Zürn leapt to her death from the balcony of the Paris apartment she had shared with Hans Bellmer. This act was allegedly foretold in her last completed work. On his own death in 1975, Bellmer was buried next to Zürn, their grave marked with the words Bellmer wrote for Zürn's funeral wreath: "My love will follow you into Eternity."

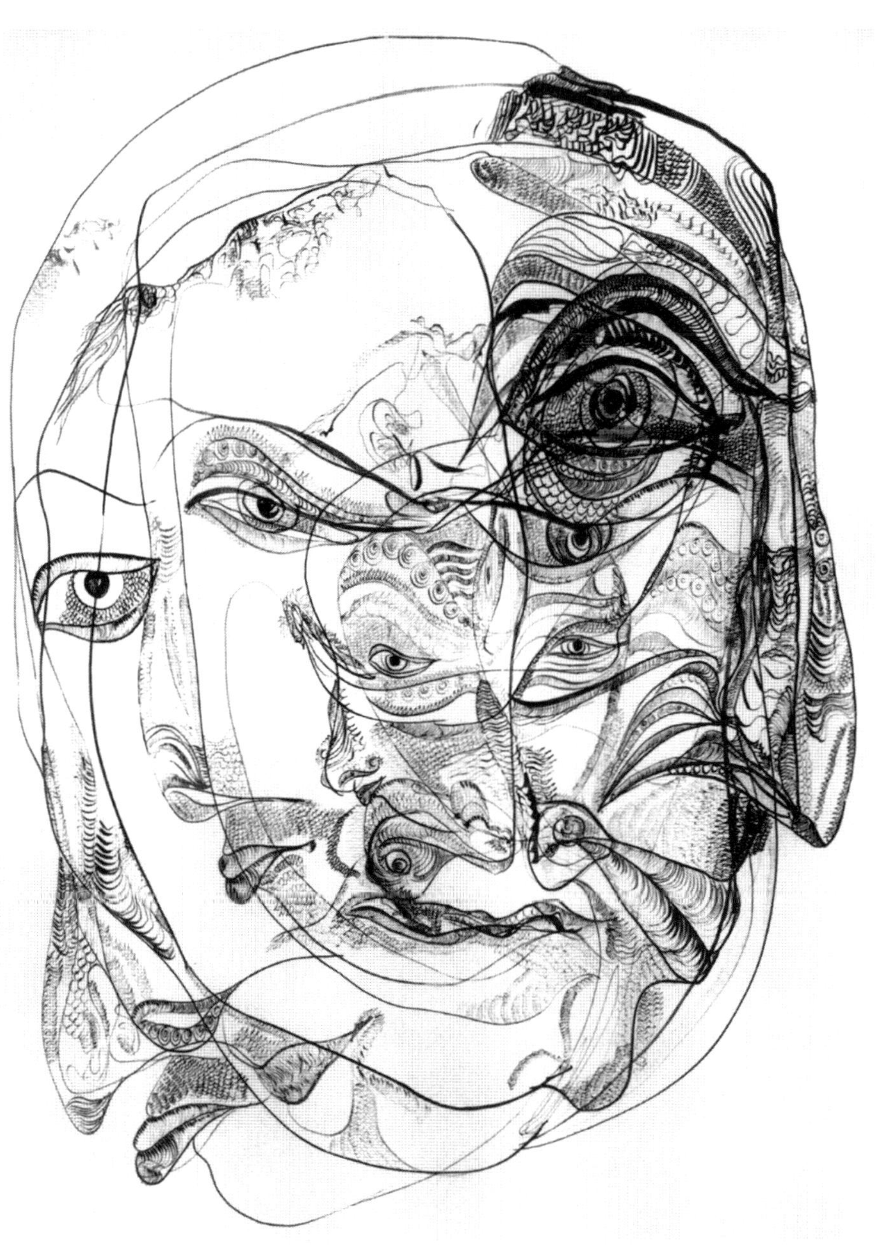

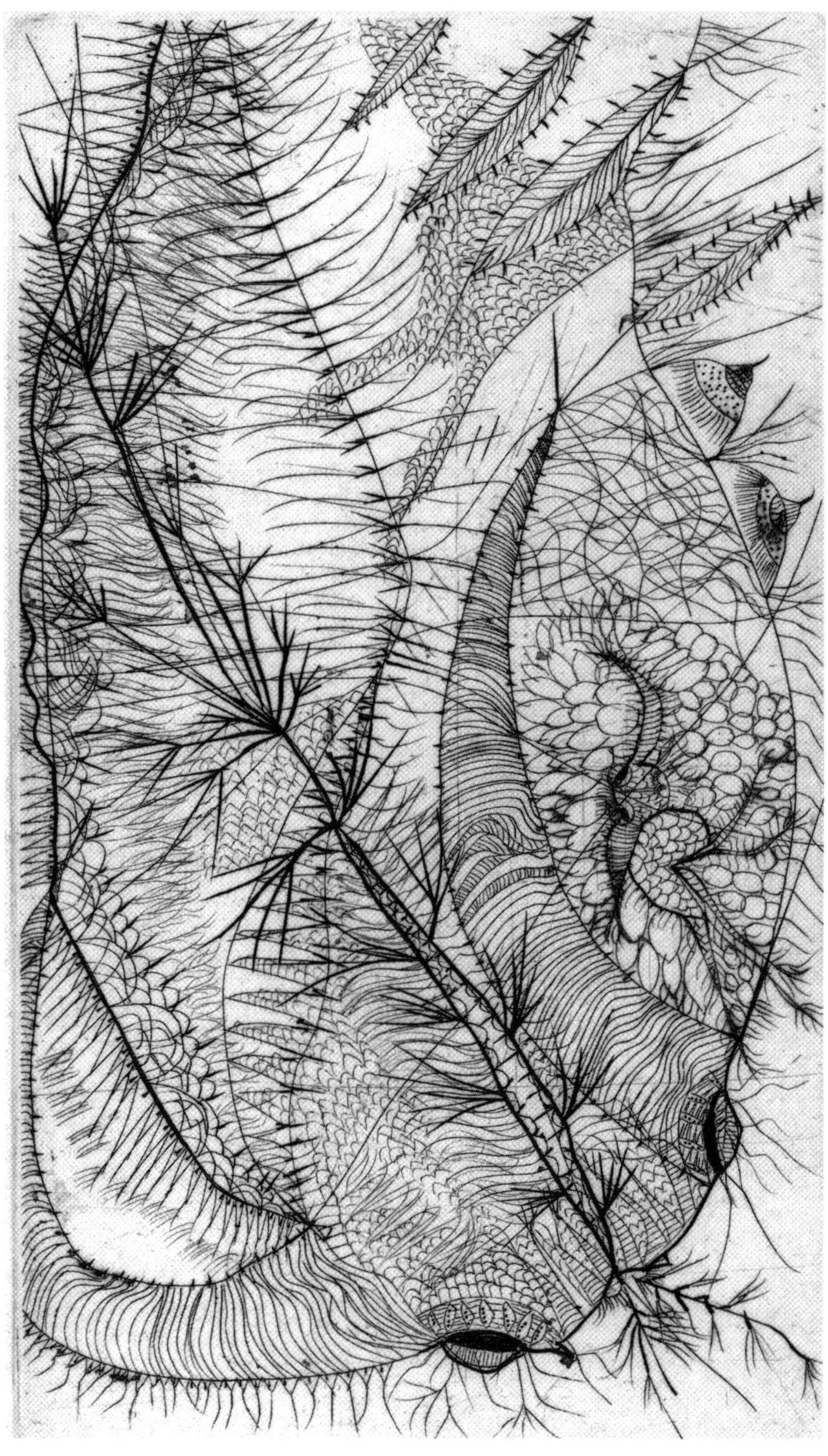

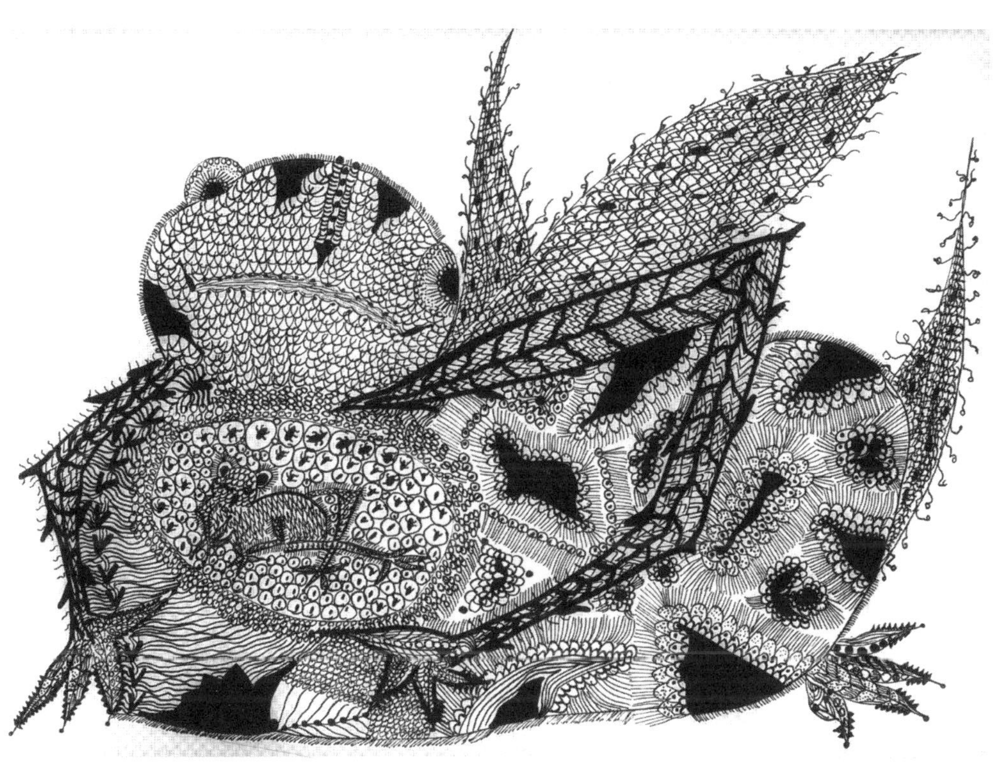

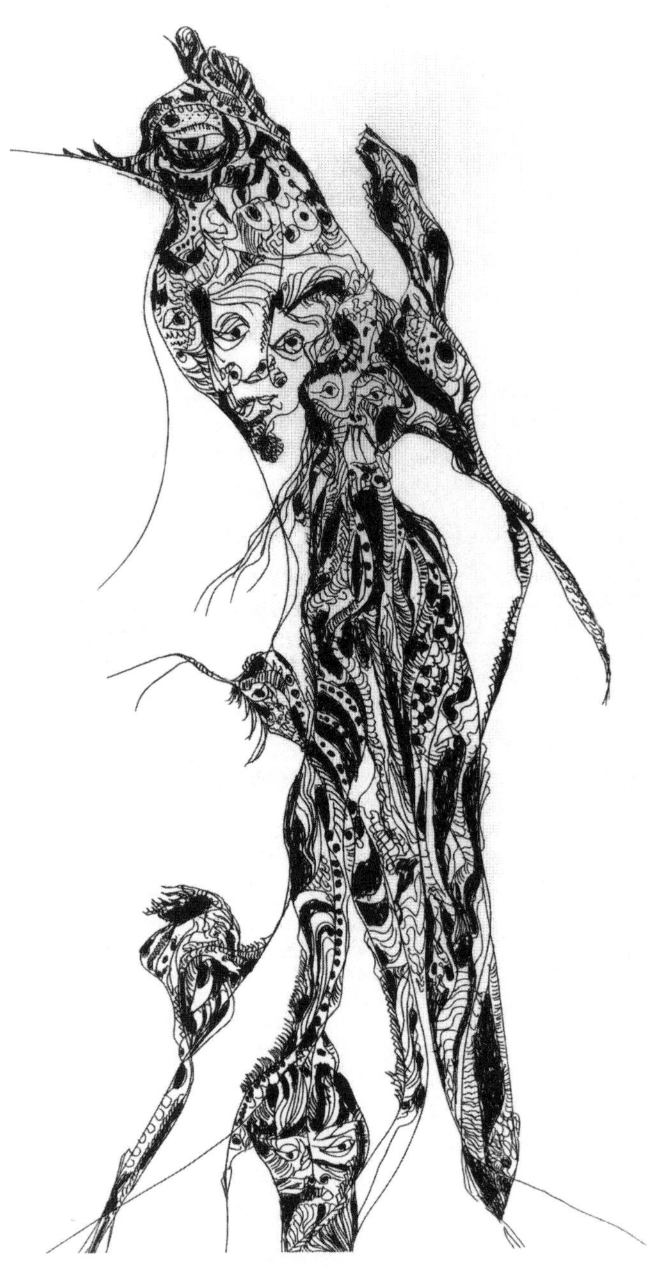

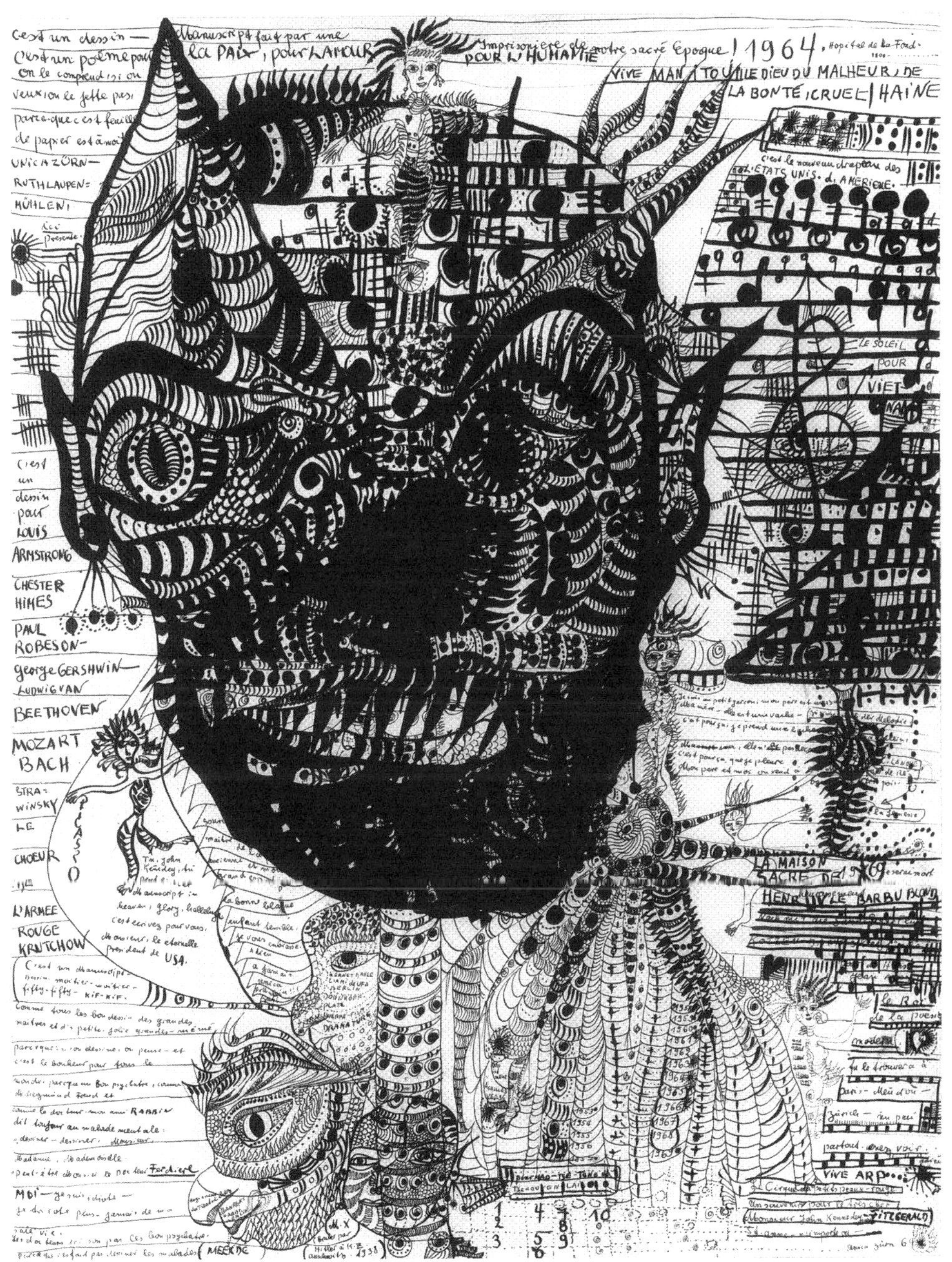

C'est un dessin
C'est un poème pour
on le comprend ou on
veux ou le jette pas
parce-que c'est feuille
de papier est à moi
UNICA ZÜRN
RUTHLAUFEN
MÜHLEN!

la PAIX, pour L'AMOUR

Manuscript fait par une
Imprimerie de notre sacré époque 1964, Hopital de la Ford.
POUR L'HUMANITÉ

VIVE MAN TOUTE DIEU DU MALHEUR DE
LA BONTÉ ICRUEI HAINE

C'est le nouveau drapeau des
ETATS UNIS d. AMÉRIQUE.

LE SOLEIL
POUR
VIET
NAM

C'est
un
dessin
pour
LOUIS
ARMSTRONG

CHESTER
HIMES

PAUL
ROBESON

george GERSHWIN
LUDWIG VAN

BEETHOVEN

MOZART
BACH

STRA=
WINSKY

LE

CHOEUR

L'ARMÉE
ROUGE
KRUTCHOW

H. M.

LA MAISON
SACRÉ DE

HENRI IV LE BARBU BLOND

VIVE ARP

FITZGERALD

MEERIE

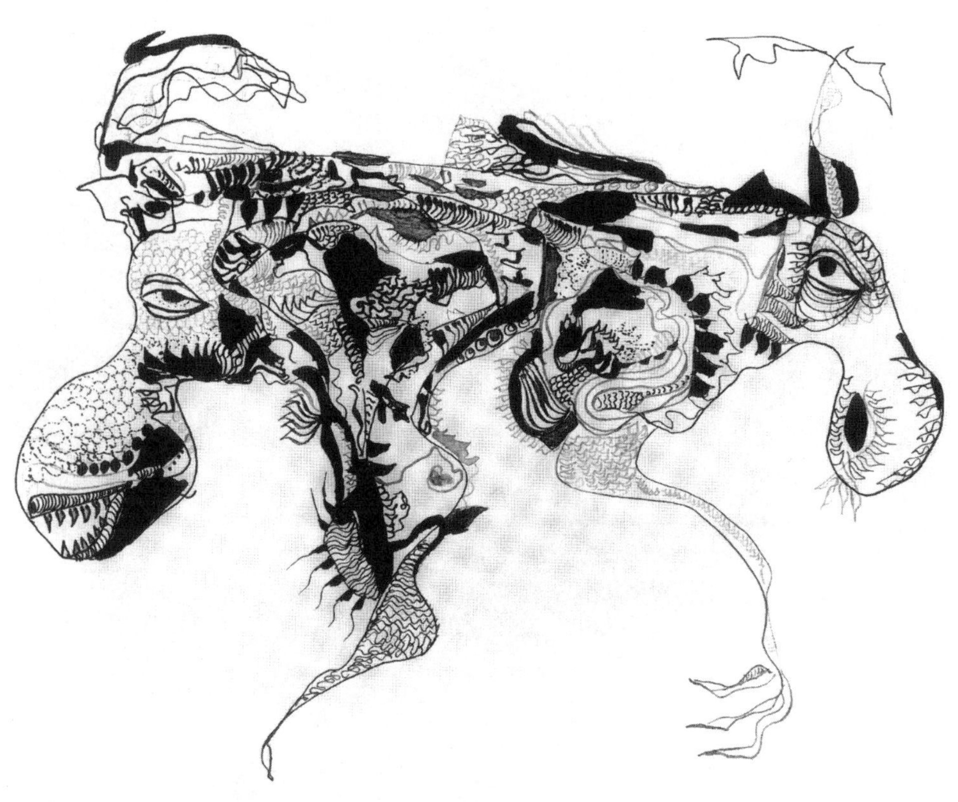

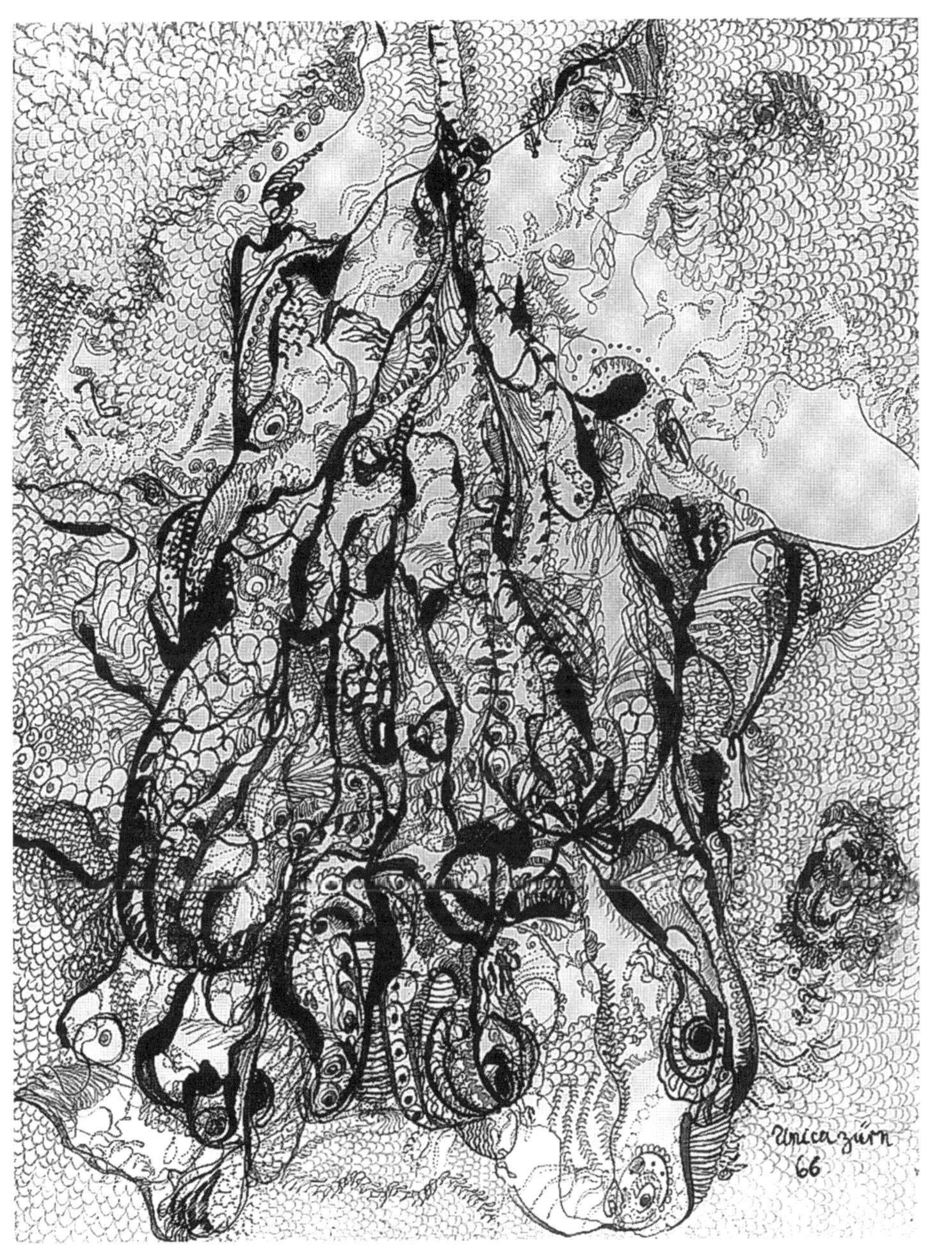
Unica Zürn
66

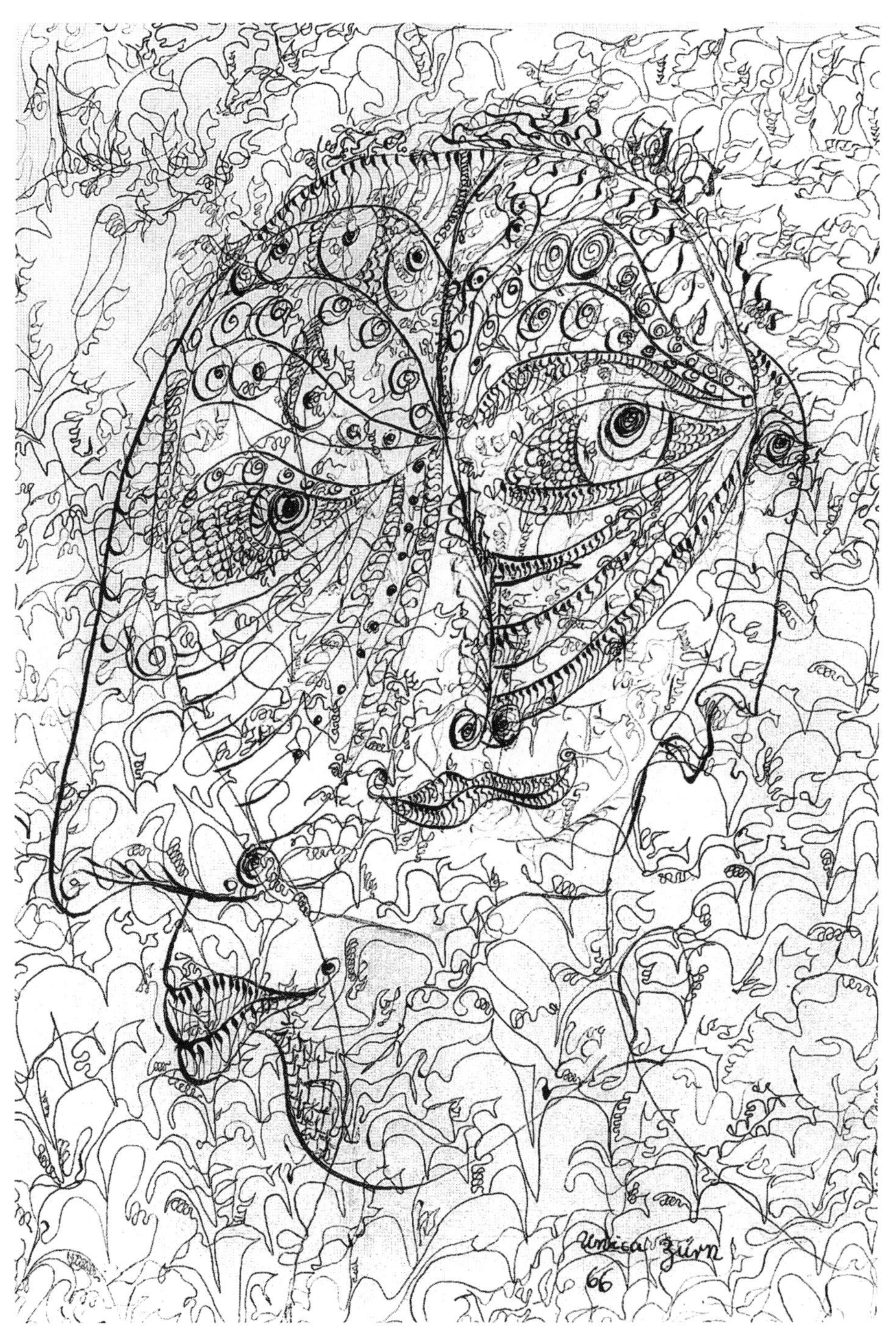

Unica Zürn
66

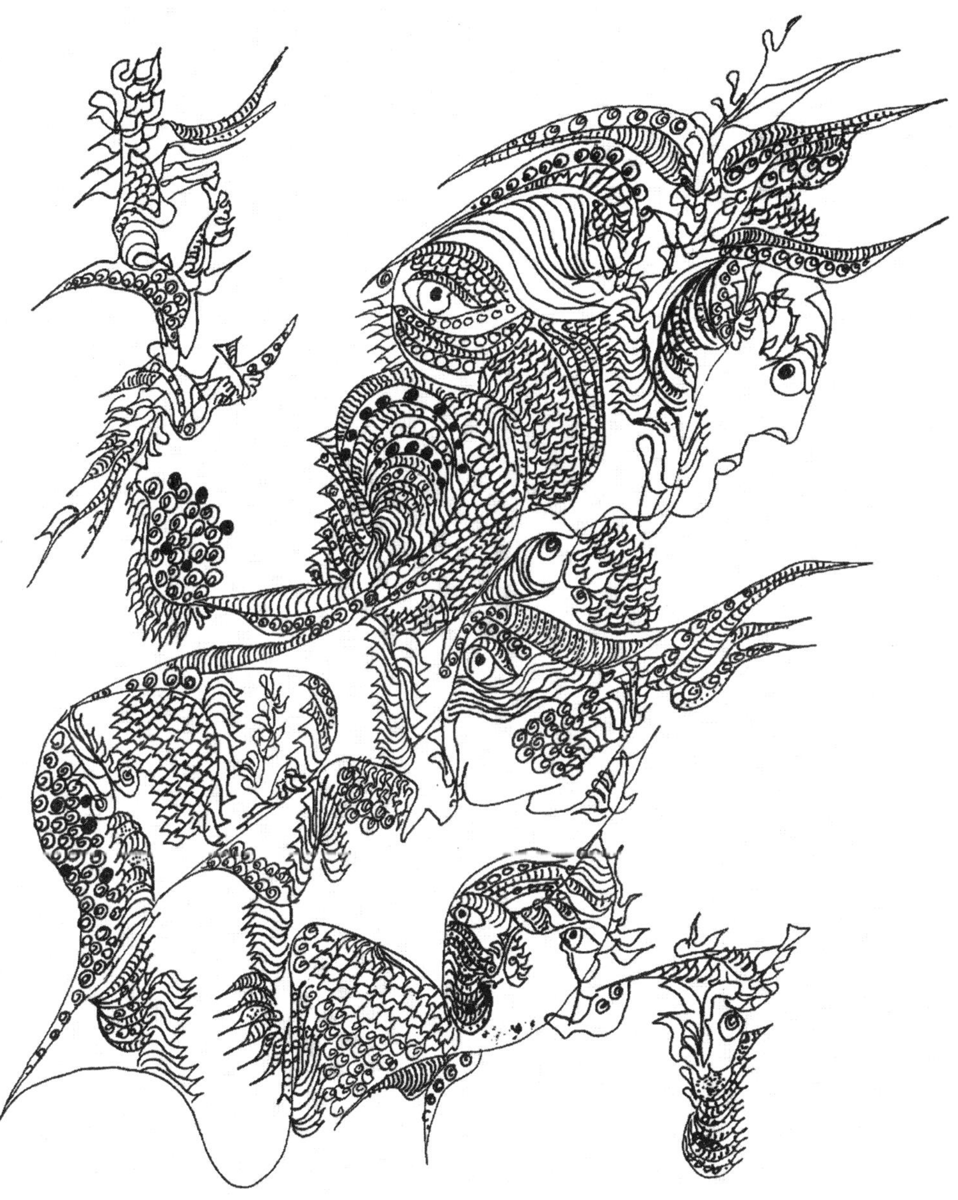

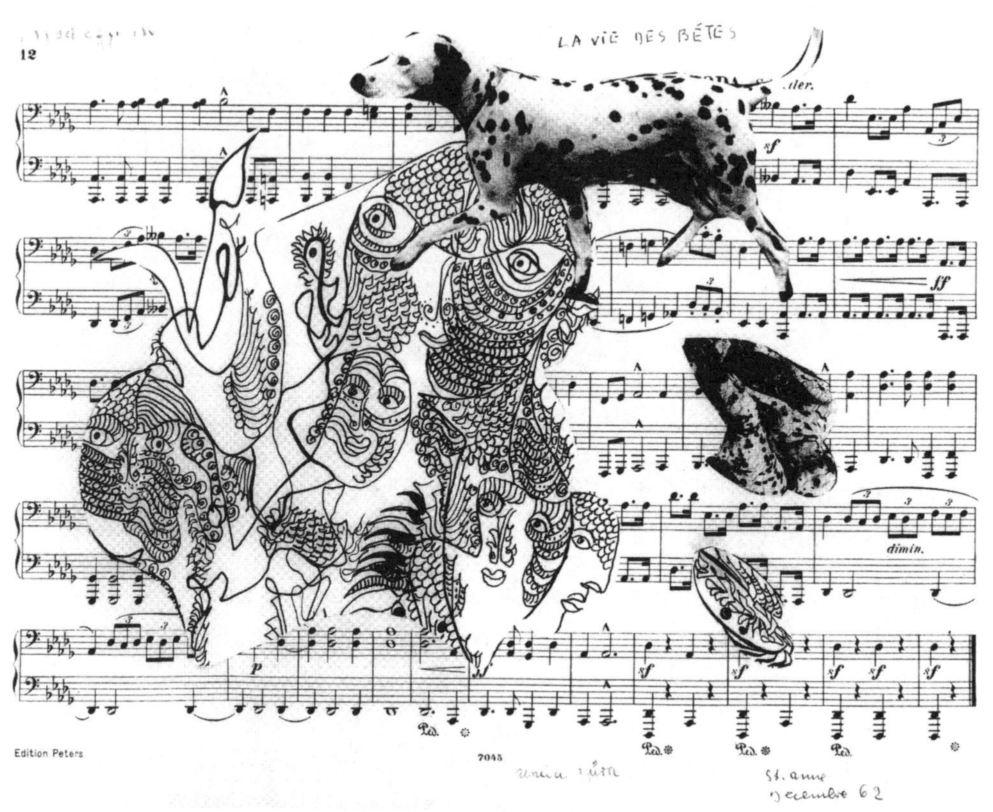

12
LA VIE DES BÊTES
Edition Peters
7045
St. anne
Decembre 62

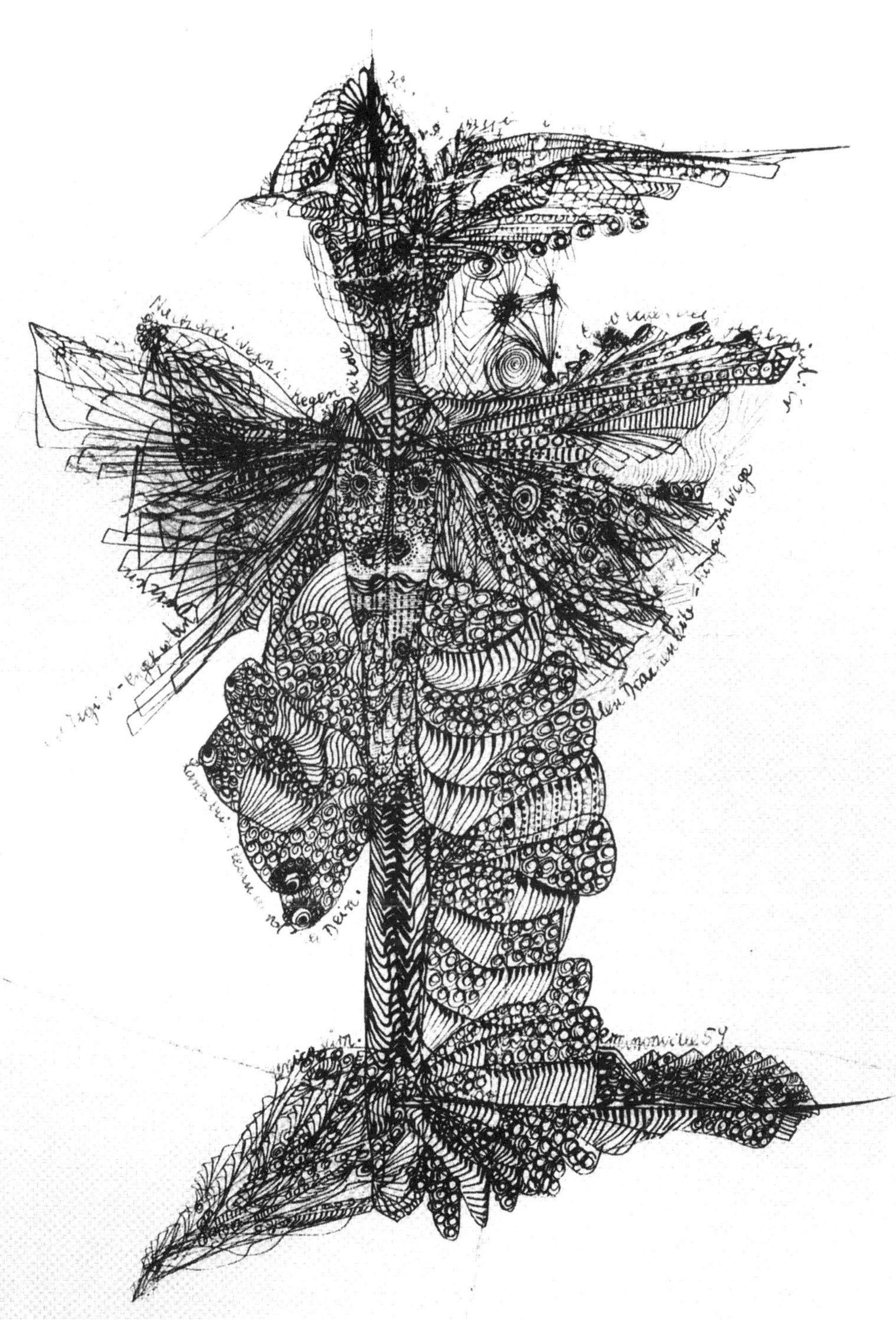

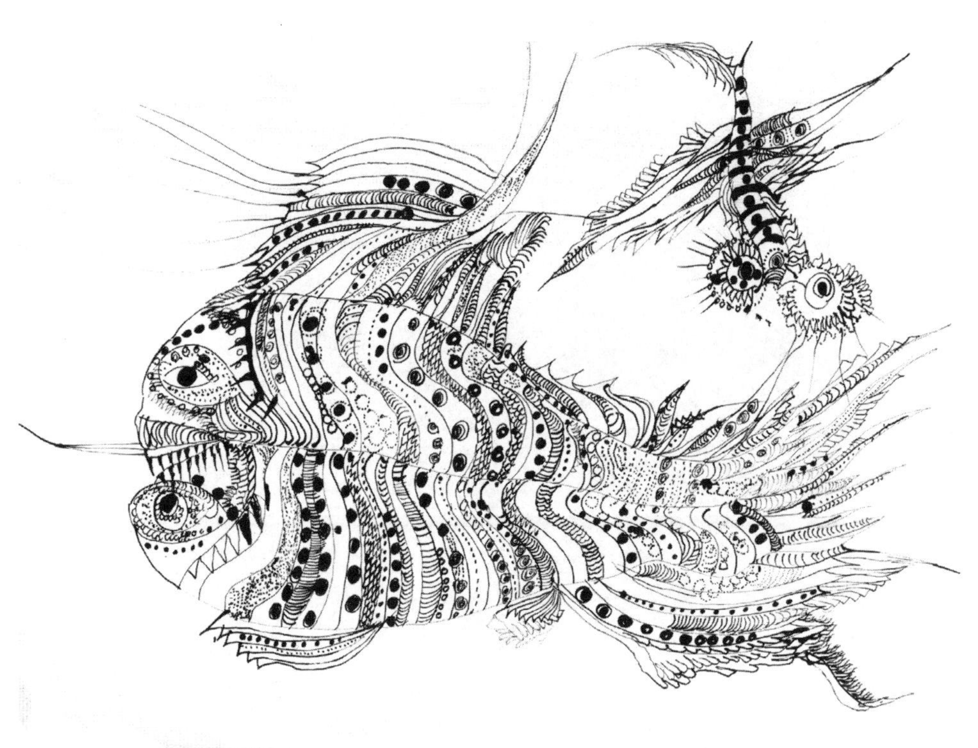

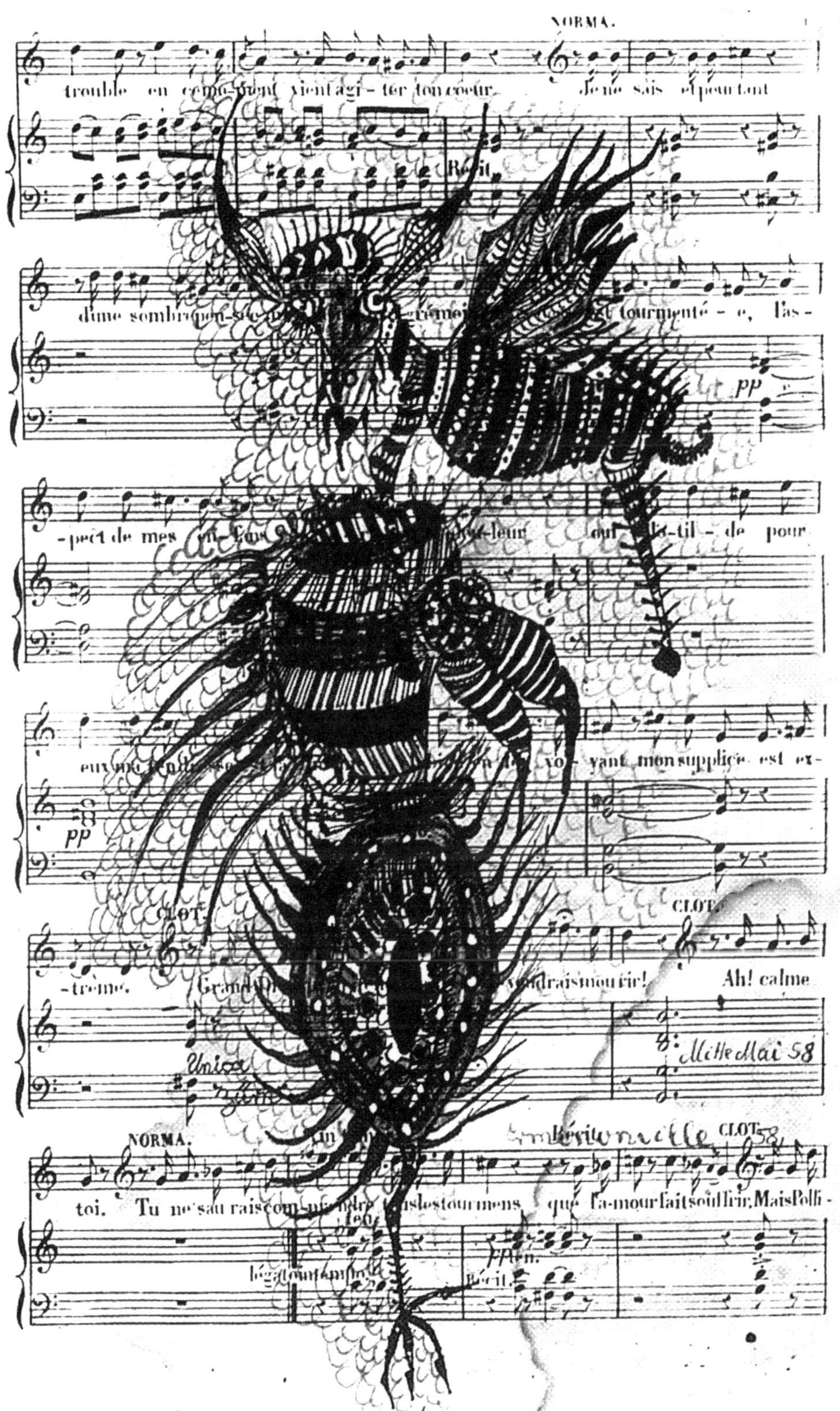
NORMA.
trouble en cemo-ment vient agi-ter ton cœur. Je ne sais cependant
d'une sombre pensée tremblé et tourmenté - e, l'as-
-pect de mes en-fans leur malheur tout fa-til - de pour
eux me fait frémir vo-yant mon supplice est ex-
-trême. Grand Dieu voudrais mourir! Ah! calme
PP
CLOT.
CLOT.
toi. Tu ne sau rais compren-dre tous les tourmens que l'a-mour fait souffrir, Mais Polli-
NORMA.
PP
Récit.
Récit.
Mlle de Mai 58
CLOT. 58

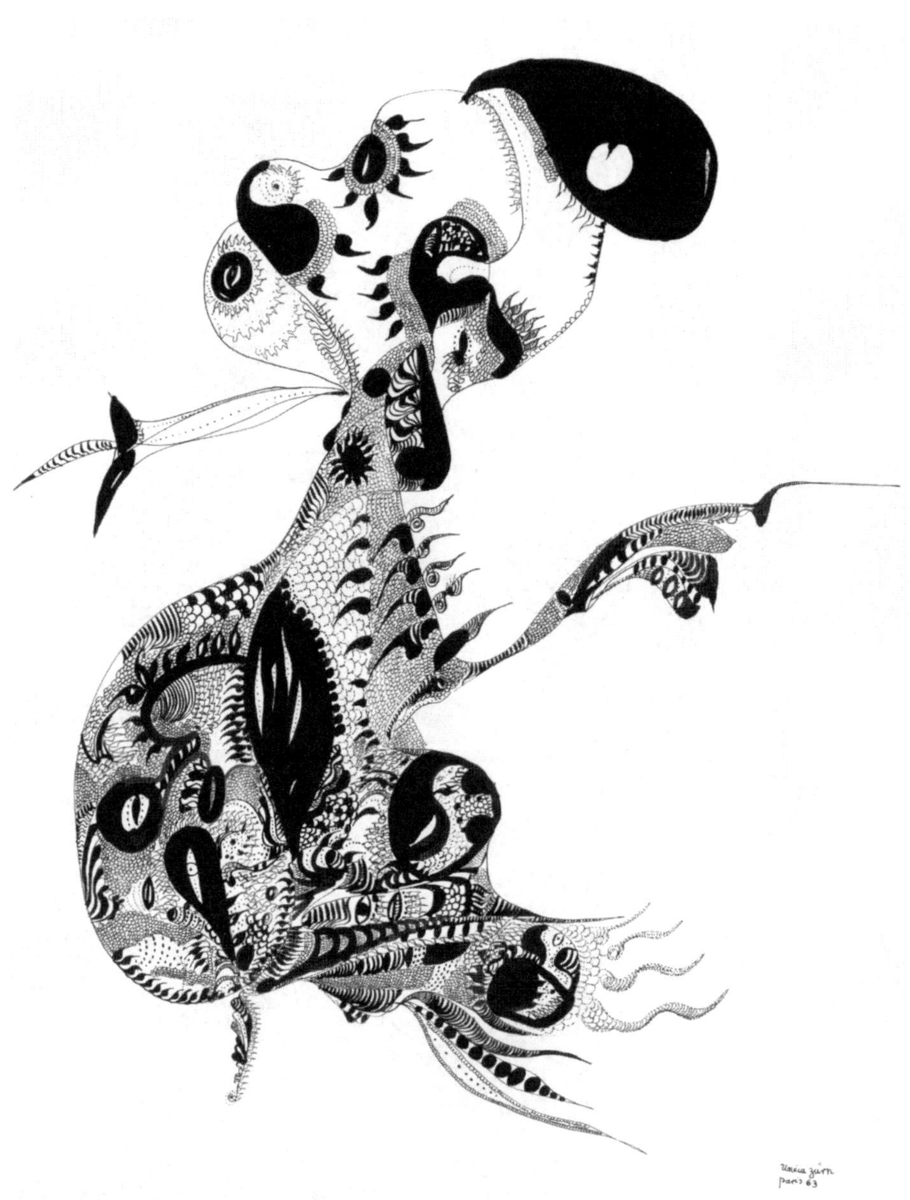
Unica Zürn
Paris 63

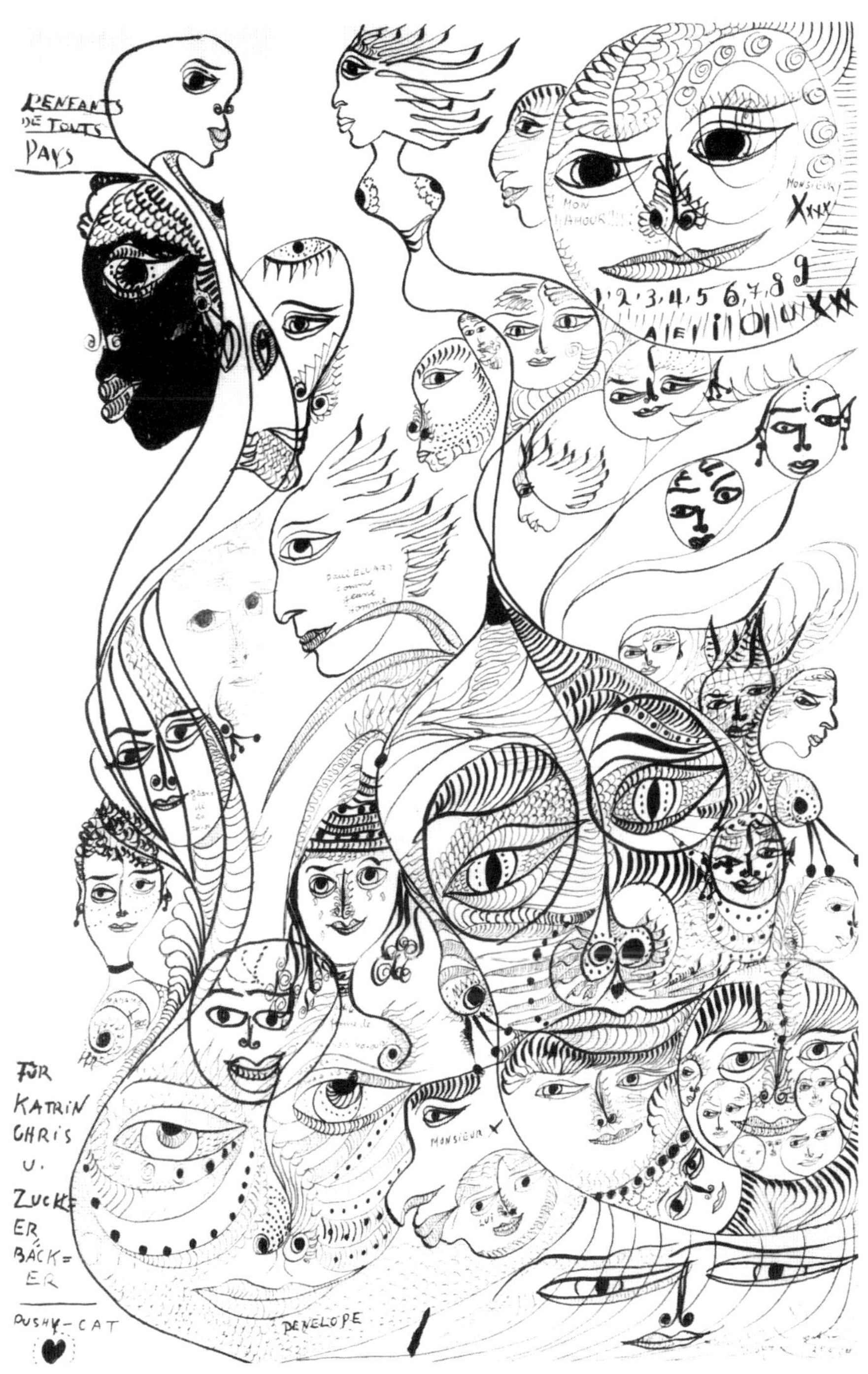

L'ENFANTS DE TOUTS PAYS
MON AMOUR!!!
MONSIEUR XXXX
1. 2. 3. 4. 5 6. 7. 8 9
A E I O U X W
FÜR KATRIN CHRIS U. ZUCKER ER BÄCK= ER
PUSSY-CAT
PENELOPE
MONSIEUR X
LUI

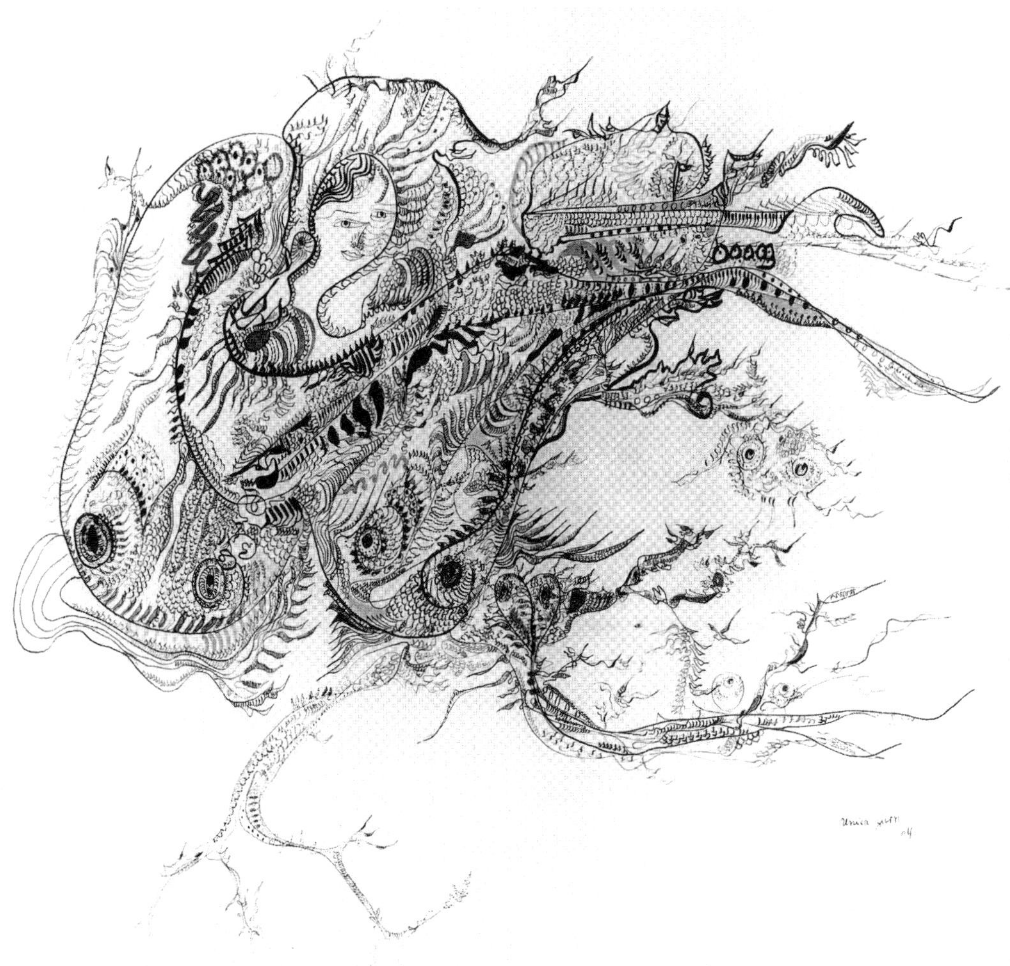

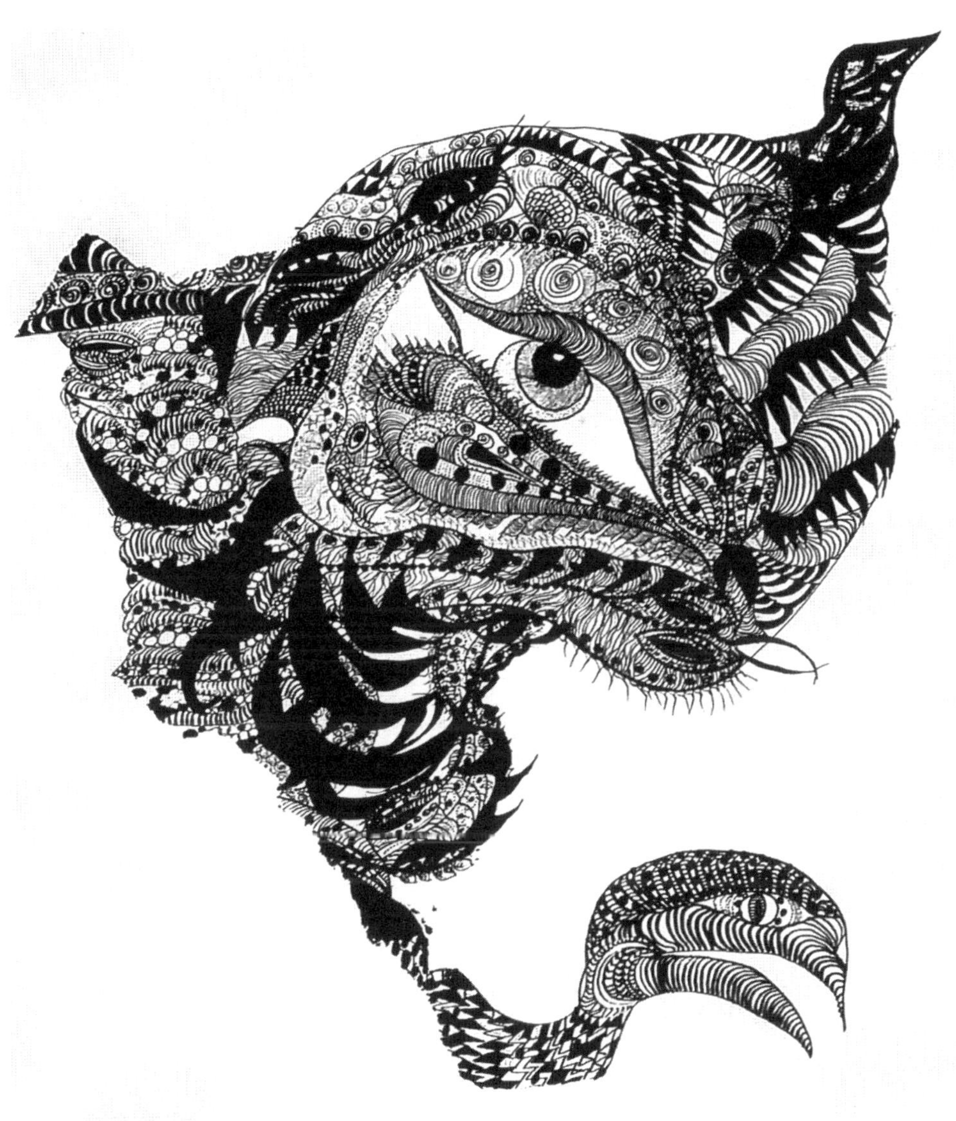

ALL MUSIC IS SIMPLE

Akron/Family

by Martin Beeler

ILLUSTRATION BY E*ROCK

Akron/Family, a quartet from Brooklyn, is creating some of the most compelling, profound, uncannily lovely rock music today. They released a self-titled debut on Michael Gira's Young God Records in early 2005. Since then they have toured incessantly, both as Akron/Family and as the backing band for Gira in his Angels of Light project, and recorded and released 3 more records for Young God: *Angels of Light Sing "Other People"* by the Angels of Light, an untitled Akron/Family/Angels of Light split EP, and *Meek Warrior*, an Akron/Family mini-album. At the time the following interview took place, in fall 2006, the band was about to record a new LP with producer Andrew Weiss, and had recently recorded the basic tracks for a new Angels of Light record. The band—Dana Janssen (drums, percussion, instruments), Seth Olinsky (guitar, voice, instruments), Miles Seaton (bass, voice, instruments), and Ryan Vanderhoof (guitar, voice, instruments)—has built a devoted following based largely on powerfully charged live performances. Their music, which is at once familiar and strange, draws on myriad sources: space rock, folk rock, hillbilly breakdowns, post-everything experimentalism, and jake-legged free jazz, to name only a few. This eclectic mix is unified by Akron/Family's unmistakable, yet elusive, sonic identity.

Note—1/27/08: Since this interview took place, the Akron/Family has, understandably, moved on. In September 2007 they released a new full-length (double vinyl) album—Love is Simple—which the band describes as the "completion of one cycle" of their work together. Ryan Vanderhoof quietly left the band soon after the album was completed to live at a "Buddhist Dharma" center in the Midwest. The Family continues, though. The core group of Olinsky, Seaton, and Janssen draws on fellow travel-

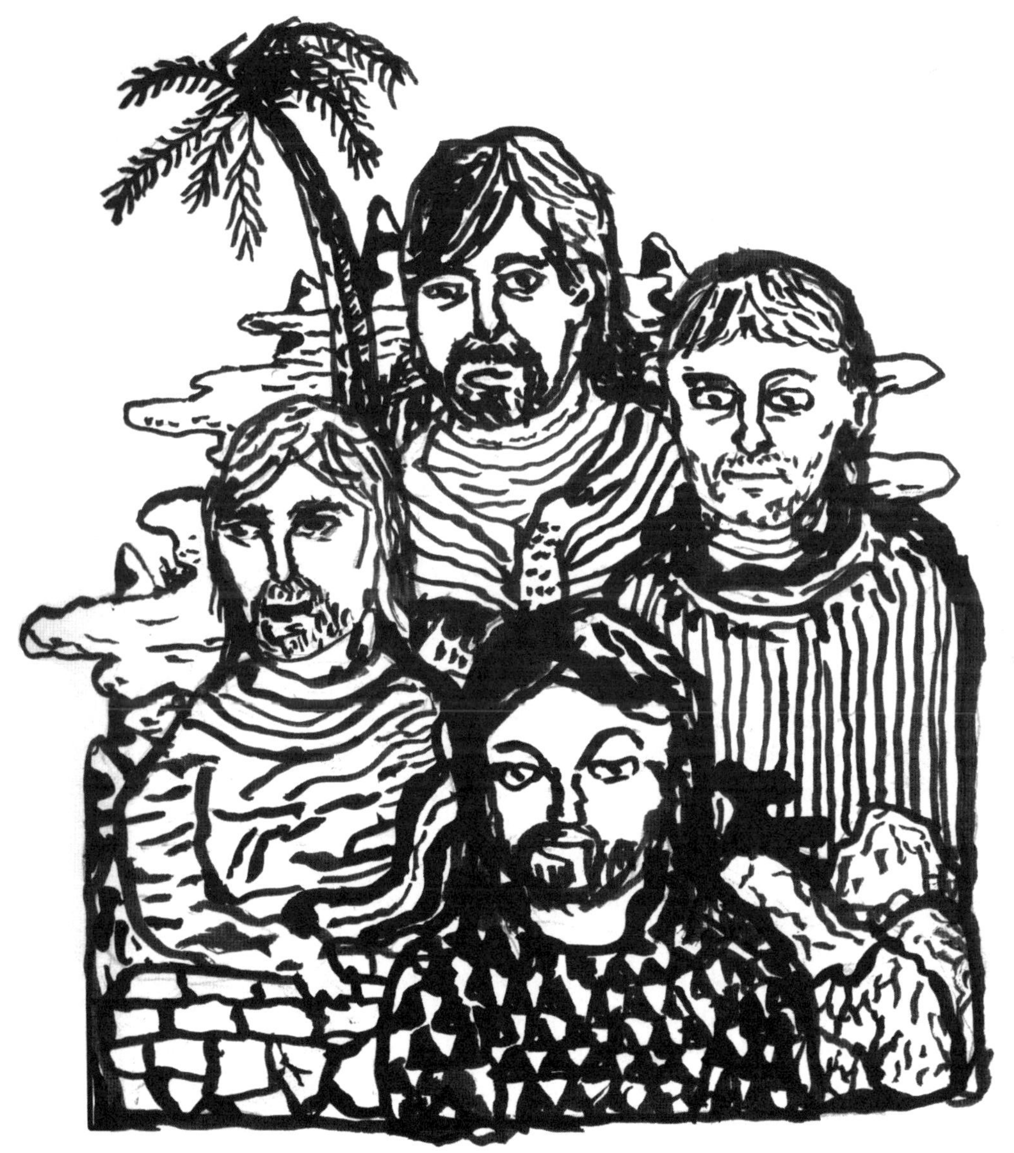

ers—like Vermont-based guitarist and sound artist Greg Davis, as well as various members of Megafaun—to augment their live sound. Live tracks available on the internet show the band to be as fearsome, confounding, and joyous as ever.

INTRODUCTION TO "AK-AK"

The first Akron album grew on me, but I wasn't immediately a fan. What put me off? It may have been something about the production—a coldness or flatness to the sound—that prevented me from falling fully under the spell of the music. Or I may simply have listened too quickly, judged it to be a competent and somewhat interesting instance of something (what?—post-rock, avant-folk experimentalism?), and filed it away. But something in the sound intrigued me, and I returned to the CD from time to time. I also heard Seth and Ryan discuss their music on David Garland's excellent *Spinning on Air* radio show on WNYC, and, more importantly, saw the band perform live.

What really hooked me, though, was the ineffable atmosphere of the music, which slowly worked its way into my consciousness. The great strength and charm of the first album lies, I think, in its evocation of inwardness and reverie, of the liminal state between waking and dreaming. The atmosphere is intimate and chamber-like without being fragile or precious, and the songs have a lapidary quality, as if it they had been worked repeatedly until they gleamed just so. Like dreams or reveries, the music draws life in part from the dark and violent side of things: this is a world of shade and shadow, as well as sunshine and flowers. Above all, for me the album is suffused with a melancholy hopefulness, a feeling that the profound sadness of things can be transformed, momentarily at least, by art.

Lyrically, the themes are, I guess, typical of certain albums made by sensitive young men: love, loss, longing, philosophical musings on identity and knowledge, vague, lingering memories of better times. All of which is conveyed in language that suggests rather than making plain. No matter. The real focus of the album is on the creation of a unique soundworld, and the lyrics, while not throwaway, are not carriers of meaning so much as occasions to create additional sounds—more grist for the musical mill.

Sonically, the album is anchored by the solo voice accompanied by guitar. From such simple beginnings, however, extravagant and myriad forms grow. The basic guitar/voice duo is fleshed out in some songs by the full quartet— second guitar, drums, and bass—but more often (and more interestingly) the instrumentation often includes less familiar forms, including: banjo, glockenspiel, bells, chimes, melodica, hand claps, finger snaps, air forced from pounded chests, field recordings of: birds, crickets, night sounds, rain, thunderstorms, fireworks, grass crunching underfoot, and the voices of children at play, off-station TV or radio fuzz, penny whistles, the click and capstan whir of a cassette recorder, syrupy low-grade synthesizer strings, wheezy trumpet, electronically manipulated organic sounds, computerized gimcrackery, furniture creak, white noise, group singing (about which more later), and God-knows-what-all-else. This profusion of material could create a mess. But the song is the sonic Sun at the center of Akron/Family's solar system, and its strong gravitational force aligns all this junk and jumble into orderly, if complex, orbits.

"Before and Again", the first song on the album, gives a good view into the Akron soundworld. The song begins with a melodic guitar line and hummed, wordless, vocals by Ryan Vanderhoof. The voice is warm, grainy, and intimate; the singer could be sitting next to you, singing to your ear alone; or, even more intimately, it could be an inner voice, a tentative wakening of consciousness, ruminative yet indistinct. High-pitched staticky electronic noises and background voices soon join, puncturing the dreamy bubble created by the first few bars of the song, Vanderhoof's voice reenters and strains toward the upper limits of its register, creating a tension that is only somewhat relieved as it descends to a more comfortable place and is joined by bowed cello in the chorus. This pattern continues until the scene changes radically. After the final chorus, static bursts, the space surrounding the sound takes on a different, more open quality, and a different voice counts "1-2-3, 1-2-3". The full quartet then enters, plays a loping instrumental, is joined by intermittent, breathy trumpet until the piece ends, unceremoniously and abruptly, with the sound of unvoiced air blown through the trumpet in quick motion, replicating the sound of backwards-running tape.

Melodicism, songcraft, and an open, resourceful, and experimental attitude toward sound and form are the threads woven through "Before and Again" and, indeed, through all of Akron/Family's music. Other examples of this uniquely Akron combination of elements abound on the album. Just to cite one more, the song "Part of Corey" begins with a long, loud blast of white noise that tapers eventually to a lingering wave-like lapping, at which point Vanderhoof's voice and guitar enter with a brief elegiac verse and trail off to an unresolved nothingness. It's instructive to compare this song with the full version of "Corey," which appears on an A/F tour CD. In its original form, Corey is a longish, folky number that is fine as far as it goes, but doesn't go nearly far enough. The Akrons solve the problem of this song with verve and brilliance—the solution: lop off 7/8ths of the song and replace it with a seemingly random burst of noise. Magically, inexplicably, it works; the song is saved.

The combination of disparate and unexpected elements in a tense but unified whole may be what Michael Gira calls the band's "playful but hermetic quasi-religious/sonic world view/creed, known as 'AK' or sometimes 'AK-AK'." As Gira explains, "As we worked, a song would sometimes be described as too 'red' or not 'aluminum' enough or some other arcane (to me) reference, but inevitably, corrections made with the aid of a screwdriver or maybe the sanded metal rails of a staircase resulted in an unpredictable but 'correct' result."

In any event, whether attributable to the faithful application of the doctrines of AK-AK, or to something else entirely, *Akron/Family* does manage to create and convey a unique and appealing sonic world view, one that is firmly rooted in the song, attuned to sound in the widest possible sense and submitted to a rigorous, yet intuitive and eclectic, understanding of musical form.

BECOMING WHAT ONE IS

In retrospect, though, the debut album may appear to be something of a hothouse flower. It certainly reflects the conditions under which it was made. As Seth explains, "the early recordings were made up of a lot of songs that were started at home, recorded in an apartment, and usually worked on by one person at a time." According to Miles, the home recording software that the band used was more like a sequencer than a multitrack system, which created definite limitations on what the band was able to do with the recordings. This may be what gives the first record that sculpted, lapidary feel; in fact, many of the songs were laboriously crafted piece by piece. The limitations of the technology provided, it seems, a fruitful constraint, which the band was able to embrace and turn to its advantage. The consequence is that however beautiful the music on the first album may be (and I unequivocally endorse it as such), it sometimes feels a bit inert and static, when compared with the music that would follow.

Although the first album does include some songs or passages that derive from and suggest the band's live sound (e.g., I think, the end of "Italy" and "Lumen"), it only hints at the organic and dynamic sound that Akron would develop. Between the release of the first album, at the beginning of 2005, and August 2006, when they came skidding to a halt, Miles estimates that the Akrons played between 200 and 300 shows, as the Akron/Family and/or the Angels of Light. That's a lot of touring. The result of which, according to Seth, is that "Akron/Family really congealed as the four [people] as one unit, with the split really showing that, and so we have really focused on that up to now."

You can hear the difference in sound on the first two Akron/Family tracks on the split EP. "Awake" is a gentle, reflective number that would not be out of place on the first album. (In fact most of the songs on the split were written at the same time as the songs on the debut. As Miles explains, Akron has been able to draw on their voluminous initial "trove" of songs—Seth, in particular, is a prodigiously productive songwriter—to provide material for the split and for "Meek Warrior.") Again, the song is built around the solo guitar and voice, with a melodic bass line and harmony vocals filling out the structure. Superficially, this is similar to the sound of the debut, but the way the sounds come together is different. It's difficult to pinpoint, but the various component parts seem to interrelate more, to cohere into a single organic unit, rather than feeling like elaboration or filigree of the basic design. The vocal part is also more assured and up-front, I think, reflecting the Family's increasing mastery of their collective voice. "Moment," the second song on the Akron side of the split, is a different beast entirely. It's an example of a distinctive musical form that the Family has perfected through live playing: the stylistically heterophonous mini-epic. The piece begins with a blast of free improv skronk—recalling a (slightly) more melodic version of Masayuki "Jojo" Takayanagi's New Direction Unit—then segues to a stomping, swaying, shouting, declamatory bit, recalling nothing in particular, then on to more skronk that resolves into extended minimalist vocal droning, which is undone by a forward racing bit of ensemble riffing that finally comes to rest in a delicate verse or two of finger-picked, tambourine shaking, sweet, sweet, song, buoyed by Beatles-ish harmonies. The cumulative impact is that of being sweetly bludgeoned by your beloved into a harmonious and resonant catatonia.

COMING TOGETHER OR FALLING APART

During that year of incessant touring, Akron/Family became a great live band. I saw them 6 or 7 times during this period. Each concert had an individual and distinctive shape and feeling; and each was also one of the best live shows I've seen in a long time. One remarkable thing about Akron live, I think, is the way that open-ended passages of blissed-out, Popol Vuh-ish jamming and more or less straight renditions of songs exist within a coherent overall structure, so that the entire concert comes off as a single unified musical event—although it may contain many chaotic moments and appear to be on the verge of collapse at any time. Does the band plot out the structure of live sets meticulously, or was this something that developed organically and intuitively?

"The Grateful Dead had a wonderful system that went: concise songs first set, jam out second set." Seth explained. "We've tried to do this multiple set thing a few times, but people get confused, and think they're only allowed to be around for one or the other. Consumers. So we've had to try in different ways to combine the two into one set. I think over the past year of touring we have done this to a varying degree of success. Mainly, because something that works one night often fails the next. We find patterns generally of songs that work next to each other, or spaces in the show that are conducive to being open, but generally something works for a time and then doesn't, so the live show is always vacillating between coming together or falling apart. Each show is like this, openings fall apart and then come together in a song or whatever, and then over the course of a tour, things get tightened up, work better and better, and then for whatever reason stop working, and must fall apart again to make room for something new to start."

This phenomenon of the live set always being in the process of coming together or falling apart creates a tidal pull that gives the band's shows great energy and creative tension. Akron is fundamentally concerned with keeping the experience of the music fresh and real, for themselves and the audience. As Miles experiences it, when the music isn't working right, isn't flowing or firing on all cylinders, it creates a certain "taste." "It's a bitter, metallic sensation," he explains, "it just tastes wrong." The solution, as with any recipe, is to adjust the spices until the taste is right again. For Akron/Family, this adjustment usually takes the form of one or more of the members veering away from whatever course the music is taking at the moment—"jumping off," as Miles describes it—in an attempt to create a new perspective, or timbre, or feeling. This can take many forms: a sudden burst of kazoo bleating or tape noise in the midst of a melancholy lament, or one instrument repeating a part or phrase beyond the normal time allotted, creating a pivot around which the other members describe arcs and spirals of sound until the piece resolves into a new shape, and takes off racing along its new course.

The results of this experimentation are not assured. An Akron concert includes a real sense of risk; the risk that something boring might happen, that the form toward which the band is groping may elude them, that the music might fail. I've never actually seen that happen, but the prospect of failure, and the band's willingness to court failure as a means to uncovering something new and unexpected in their music, gives their concerts a palpable edginess, a feeling that an event is taking place, that something real is happening.

ONLY CONNECT

Akron/Family's relation to the live audience is singular and noteworthy. They manage to create a wild, celebratory environment at their shows that's also somehow trusting and open. This sounds corny, but it's apt. At most shows there's at least one spontaneous sing-along moment—for example, the crowd taking over the long coda of "la-la-lah-lahs" at the end of "Running, Returning"—as well as songs or bits of songs in which audience participation is led from the stage—for example, the sound of surf created by collective sibilation in "I'll Be on the Water." The band also does things that muddy the distinction between audience and performer, like turning up the house lights and playing from within the audience. One senses that these practices arise from a sincere regard for the audience; these aren't mere signifiers of authenticity and spontaneity, but rather a true reaching out, an attempt to connect with the audience in an authentically human way.

"Oftentimes we are scared shitless up there, so we just try and make that the common ground," Seth explains. "'OK guys . . . you are scared, we are scared, it is hard to have a good time, but if we can all slowly agree to not take ourselves so seriously for at least a little bit, and maybe try not to judge the people around us for a little bit of time . . . and remember we can go right back to feeling bad as soon as the show is over.'"

"It is *not* performance art. It is *not* conceptual. We are just trying to get on the subway and convince everyone to talk to each other, if only for a short ride."

ALL MUSIC IS SIMPLE

"Blessing Force", the first song on *Meek Warrior*, features propulsive, polyrhythmic drumming by Hamid Drake. Drake, who is one of the greatest living free-jazz drummers, is probably best known for his work with reedsman Peter Brotzmann and bassist William Parker. That Akron/Family could assimilate a strong "foreign" influence like Drake's drumming while still maintaining their own musical personality proves, I think, how firmly rooted, if somewhat elusive, the Akron sound is. (It also shows, of course, that a great musician like Drake will conform his playing to the music, rather than overrunning it with his own personality.)

Seth: "Hamid is a truly amazing person and musician. We became friends with him about a year ago, and then we just e-mailed him to see if he would be around when were near Chicago to try to do some recording. We just recently did a CD release at Tonic in NYC for *Meek Warrior*, and got the chance to perform live with William Parker. It was a real dream come true. When I first moved to NYC a few years ago, what I really wanted to do was play free jazz with these guys, but realized that it was not the path for me. I have too many interests musically, and what these guys do takes such specific focus and dedication—I feel like these guys and their scene are grossly underappreciated for what they do and how they commit themselves to their art. Anyways, it was truly amazing for me to be able to come full circle and within 2 or 3 years be able to play and record with these guys and try to meet somewhere between what they do and what we do."

"Technical differences aside, I think that there are some very similar intentions of spirit that we share, and these can bridge any minor aesthetic or technical gaps. Before going on stage, I was explaining the songs we were going to play to William, and I told him 'don't worry, our songs are very simple.' He looked at me and replied, 'All music is simple.'"

"All music is simple." I cherish the phrase—and the image of the ferociously talented Parker gently putting the young Akrons at ease. I like to think that Parker was expressing, somewhat elliptically, something fundamental about the "similar intentions of spirit" behind his music and Akron music, to which Seth alludes. Both Akron and the free jazzers are seeking, it seems, something primary, unmixed, absolute and unalloyed—"simple" in the chemical sense—in the experience of music.

IN THE TRADITION

Akron music, for all its experimental and open qualities—its ability to embrace free jazz and free noise—seems to me to be firmly rooted in some sort of rock and pop tradition. The classics of rock, I guess (though not necessarily "classic rock"), are in there, as well as the source material for great rock music, all that Harry Smith *Anthology* stuff. Indeed, sometimes Akron/Family overtly references or uses the Beatles (especially late Beatles), Dylan, or American vernacular styles.

Are there any particularly influential or important models from "the tradition" (whatever that may be) that the Akrons have in mind when playing or writing?

"Isn't there a famous saying about stealing instead of borrowing?" Seth replies. "Yes, indeed, we rip off everyone all the time. I've been wanting to move out of NY for a while now, because there is too much junk around here. Too much fashion. Trees and rocks and water NEVER go out of style. But yes, all the best steal. Dylan stole. Beatles stole. Coltrane stole."

"I think it is a rather absurd idea that with the amount of information available to us all these days, anyone could really digest it and move forward into something truly new by the age of 25. Dylan was working with a much more limited palette, and was able to move on young, but I don't see it anymore. I think more original stuff, at least for me, will come out in my thirties. There is just too much information. . . . [H]opefully we will be able to kill our rock idols with [the next] record and move on. We'll see."

I think Seth may be selling the Family short on the issue of "originality," maybe not looking at the issue from the right perspective. When Pound enjoined poets to "make it new," the "it" in question (at least in Hugh Kenner's reading) was the tradition. Pound meant that the only way forward in art, the only method for discovering something original, was by working through inherited forms to uncover the root poetic impulse. That work itself, from within the tradition, can be original. From this perspective, I think Akron/Family has succeeded in creating something original; their music speaks in its own inimitable voice but also manages, by comparison and contrast, to highlight qualities that may have been latent or dormant in canonic rock music. After hearing Akron/Family, for example, I listen to the Beatles in a different way. (I also listen to Yes in a different way, but I'm wary of mentioning that here, fearing ridicule and censure.)

The timeless qualities of Akron music make me think that they should be able to record a classic studio album. Something like *Led Zeppelin III* or *Harvest*, a record that captures a feeling, creates a distinctive imaginative space for the listener, and has narrative unity. The debut Akron record has some of the qualities, but doesn't quite have that single-minded quality that would make it a classic. I asked Seth if the band thought about this type of classic studio recording, and if there were any particular albums that had a particular feel that they might be striving toward with the new record.

"I think we are all always wanting to make that recording: *Harvest, Sgt. Pepper's, Astral Weeks, Blonde on Blonde, Abbey Road*. I'm hoping that this new record will be our chance to kind of take a real shot at that, making our classic record, and then hopefully we can move beyond that and make some new models of possibility. Everything changes. We all need some new shit. The album is quickly becoming outdated, don't you think?"

Seth may be right. The album is certainly being made unnecessary by technology, it seems, as mp3 shuffling becomes the primary way that music is experienced. But I'm not sure (and I rather doubt) that the album is becoming outmoded as an aesthetic matter. At any rate, the band is currently working on their new record, and a couple of things are different about the process this time. As Miles explained, the band will be working on completely new material—their trove of songs from the early days is now empty. They will also have several weeks of recording time with producer Andrew Weiss, who is known primarily as the producer of Ween, and is the first "outsider" (i.e., not Gira and the Akrons) to produce the band. This is a significant departure from the Akron/Angels split. And *Meek Warrior*, which were both recorded under intense pressure in relatively short amounts of time. The time pressure, according to Miles, was both a result of dire necessity—the band's touring schedule wouldn't allow more recording time—and was a feature of Michael Gira's production style. Gira, he explains, thrives on the pressure and uses it to fuel his creativity. Although that method has worked well, Akron/Family is looking forward to have more breathing room, which may give the recorded music the chance to develop more organically.

YOUNG GODS

Akron/Family have undeniably found a unique voice, and it's likely that they would have found that voice with or without the intervention of Michael Gira. But it's also undeniable that the particular timbre of that voice in its present form owes much to Gira's influence. Young God Records, Gira's label, has released all of the band's albums so far, and will release at least one more studio album by them next year, as well as another Angels of Light record with the Akrons as band/collaborators. Gira himself has given the band a great deal of personal attention, and that attention has been repaid both in terms of the development of the Akron/Family's music, and the development of Gira's own creative projects.

The relationship began with the band sending Gira periodic samples of its home recording sessions. Gira responded to these recordings with detailed and constructive criticism of the material. Eventually, Gira witnessed a live performance of the band at the tiny, but beloved, Pete's Candy Store in Williamsburg, Brooklyn, and decided to sign them. Akron/Family would turn out to be the principal post-Devendra project of Young God, and would further establish the label's reputation for championing highly individual voices with surprisingly broad appeal.

I wondered what exactly Gira's role was in developing the "works in progress" that A/F shared with him, and was curious about what it was in the early recordings that caught Gira's ear, what elements he encouraged them to develop or discard, and what his role as a "producer" of their music has been.

"I tried to point the way toward what I thought was original and irreducible in what they do," Gira replied. "Number one was the great singing, sense of play and experimentation in the music, and just the way their group personality expressed itself in many disparate ways, from nonmusical sounds to quick, elliptical perceptual changes and references. But most of all there's a sincerity (though not of the mawkish variety) to their music that I find compelling. Even when they're 'funny,' which they often are, they're still right in your face, not at all cynical. They can also be incredibly poignant and spiritually moving, too. I get the impression they are always searching for a personal truth in what they do, which is rare and really deserves to be encouraged. So, my role as producer was just to try to help them see the things in them that were unique to them and jettison any obvious references or influences that might have obscured their originality. The multi-layered vocal harmonies were a nascent aspect of their music before we went into the studio for the first time, but when we got in the studio and they started exploring that further, it was obvious to me that they were really lit up and completely effervescent when it came to that, so I pushed them as much as possible in that direction. My goal as producer, aside from the usual sonic concerns, is to help bring out the truth and originality of the artist, to get them to realize what's unique in themselves. If I helped Akron do that, I'm a happy man."

THE GRAIN OF THE VOICE

Group singing is one of the most distinctive features of the Akron sound. It's the aspect of their sound that is most likely to immediately grab your attention, prod your memory and imagination, draw to mind a crowd of comparisons, none of which quite work, and, finally, leave you with a bemused but satisfied feeling of "Wha' fuh?" To my mind, the source of this sound must be beyond reach, it lies too far back in collective memory, or too deep within some animalistic region of the brain. It's a sound that seems at once generic and utterly unique, coming from everywhere and nowhere at once. It's a mysterious and, to quote Gira, "irreducible" element of the Akron/Family music.

Seth confirms that the band owes the development of this polymorphously perverse vocal identity to Gira's influence: "This was something that Michael Gira really pushed us to develop. He really had a great foresight in seeing the potential in it. We all thought we were bad singers, but he got us to focus on it, and it has really provided a lot of possibility for us and our music."

It's an interesting phenomenon. None of the Akrons are "bad" singers. Seth and Ryan, who carry most of the lead vocal parts, have distinctive and emotionally evocative, if technically limited voices; Miles and Dana have pleasant and strong voices. Yet when the group sings together they create a voice beyond good and evil. It's an almost primal, chthonic force that embraces sweet harmony, painful squawk, chaotic, irreverent, nonsensical, Dadaist blather, and a demotic sort of sing-shouting that reminds me of the lock-grooved stuttering of hyperactive children. Some reviews have mentioned the Beach Boys as a reference, but that seems only partially right. There's a wildness and roughness to Akron's singing, even at its sweetest and most polished, that is alien to the Beach Boys aesthetic. It reminds me sometimes of the Beatles in their more ragged moments, or the cracked, farmer harmonies of the Grateful Dead, or the frayed, difficult beauties of shape-note singing, or the faltering, unintentionally Orientalist blendings of the amateur gospel groups I heard growing up in Tennessee and North Carolina.

"We are certainly far more Grateful Dead than Beach Boys," Seth offers. "People compare us to all sorts of things that we do not really sound like." A frequent contemporary comparison is to Animal Collective. The urge to compare the two is understandable, since there are few bands that foreground group singing the way these bands do. But the sounds are at root dissimilar. The Animal Collective sound is bright and bouncy, and sometimes comes across as merely kooky or whimsical (I had to quit listening to them for a while when I suddenly felt I was listening to a children's singalong record. Nothing against children, you know), whereas the Akron sound springs from a more primitive source; it flows from something, well, older and weirder.

The focus on the voice also connects the Akrons to other Young God artists of the moment, most notably Devendra Banhart, Mi and La'u, and Michael Gira himself, all of whom possess strong, distinctive, and idiosyncratic voices. Gira's thoughts on this aspect of the Young God aesthetic are illuminating with respect to the Akrons. "It's something I'm beginning to realize about why I choose certain artists to be on the label. It has to do with the core quality of the voice. I don't care about skill, or even tunefulness, but I look for a quality in the song and the singer, where it doesn't need much (or maybe not any) accompaniment to convey the essential message of feeling contained in the song to really go right into the center of the listener. Devendra is a prime example of course. He is supremely lupine, like some weird hairy dude in a cave summoning the spirits. His guitar playing is great, but he doesn't even need that. Same with Akron too. All they need to do is slap some stones together and howl at the moon, as far as I'm concerned. Everything else is just aesthetics and intellect, which are fine and useful aspects and may be pretty or challenging or interesting sometimes, but maybe also not really crucial to the experience of what the music has to offer, in the end."

I feel certain that at some point the Akrons have gathered in a cave to slap stones together and howl at the moon, but so far as I know there is, alas, no recording of such an event. (Maybe the next tour CD?) The recordings and live shows do, however, confirm the power that Gira discerns in the Akron voices. "Love and Space," for example, is an almost unaccompanied (a lightly strummed guitar keeps time and leads the changes) devotional/invocational number that the band has performed live for a while—often moving into the audience and forming a song-circle for the purpose—and which appears on "Meek Warrior." In the song, the individual members take turns singing the lead part, beginning "Lord, open my heart," while the others intone "Love and Space" in harmony.

It's a simple, sincere and powerfully moving piece, all because of the uncanny penetrating power of the Akron voices. The image it brings to mind is of a circle of frail and fragile humans convened in the wilderness to invoke the oldest magic of the species—the song—to keep the darkness at bay and to summon the light.

ANGELS OF LIGHT

Michael Gira loved the Akrons so much that he invited them to join him in the Angels of Light, with the Akrons taking the part of backing band and full collaborators on the arrangements. The issue of this union, so far, is some of the most compelling material that Gira has recorded in years, in the form of one full-length Angels record, *Sings Other People*, and the split EP with A/F. As Gira describes it, working with the Akrons "contributed greatly to the revivification" of his music. Miles explains that playing in the Angels of Light and learning Gira's songs gave the band the opportunity to see their own music from a different perspective and to apply a different kind of discipline to music making. The 2005 tour in which Akron/Family opened for Angels of Light also gave the Akrons their first extended touring opportunity and exposed them to audiences throughout North America and Europe. After that first tour, Akron/Family has worked like mad, but one gets the impression that it was that tour and collaboration that gave them the push they needed to get where they've gone.

Gira is expansive on the effect of the Akrons on Angels of Light. "After we'd worked on their debut together, I had a new Angels of Light album planned, and I'd been floundering about, wondering what direction the songs I'd written should take. It suddenly dawned on me that Akron should just be the interpreter of the songs, for the most part, since our initial contact in the studio on their own album had been such a great and creative time. So I basically let them walk all over my songs. Ha ha! I'd never relinquished control to such an extent before, but I felt really comfortable in this instance. It was liberating. It was the best time I've ever had recording, just working with these crazy hippy inspired genius monkeys in the studio. I don't recall ever having laughed so much."

This intense form of collaboration may have ended though. "[T]he new Angels album I'm working on now, on which they just played the basic tracks, was a different matter. Much more subdued and considered on their part. Now I'm in the process of orchestrating it much further, to a much greater degree than I did when they worked on *Other People*, using other friends and musicians too, letting the songs take shape that way. Akron did a great job of course, but it was interesting to see their wild enthusiasm tempered through the prism of their now having toured incessantly and achieved the success they have now. They have so much going on I couldn't expect them to bring the same degree of vitality to it as they did on the first recordings. It was kind of awkward actually, but now it's provided me with the opportunity to grow musically, so it's all good."

It is all good, Mr. Gira. Having seen Swans live way back in the day, and lived through the ensuing psychic damage, it's with great delight that I imagine Michael Gira, tickled and giddy, secluded in the studio with these loveable crazy hippy inspired genius monkeys making sincere folkish melodic music. Nature, thank goodness, knows only transformation.

THE LIGHTNING BOLT OF COMPASSION

As Michael Gira points out, one aspect of the Akron appeal is the band's ability to make music that is emotionally compelling and spiritually moving. One of the earliest extended articles on A/F, a piece by Peter Bebergal on the "Killing the Buddha" website, addressed what the author called the "transcendent" aspects of Akron music. Other articles have exhibited a similar concern with what might be called the spiritual dimension of the music. Listeners—particularly at live shows—seem to be strongly affected by the music; it touches them in a profoundly emotional way. This is a most difficult subject, and I have no clear idea how or why Akron/Family affects people this way. I don't think it's necessarily something formal in their music that produces this effect. Unlike much rock music that attempts to evoke a feeling of transcendence—from psychedelia to doom metal— Akron music is neither drone-based nor does it allude to putatively mystical and/ or non-western musical traditions. The "spirituality" of A/F has, I believe, more to do with the openness of the performers, and the emotional intensity that goes into the music. Akron/Family enact, it seems, a very basic human process—the creation of meaning out of the chaotic jumble of experience—infuse the process with a palpable joyousness, and invite us to join in.

"Music has been focused on spirituality far longer than it has been focused on popularity, image, or consumption," Seth explains. "We live in a very strange world filled with many sad things. I think that music is one of the great few things that has a power to be positive and transformative in people's lives. And all this without boundaries. I do not need to be a Christian to be lit up by gospel musics, or Jewish to have my heart opened by devotional Hassidic music. It all seems to me to be a very *human* thing. Unfortunately, we are a somewhat boring band. Our songs are generally not about drugs or sex or mysterioso conceptual blather. I would never try and say that we attempt to do what guys like Hamid Drake or William Parker do, but this is what I mean when I say that I think what we do has a similar intent."

It's a good point. Why shouldn't we expect the experience of music to be a spiritually significant event? That, after all, is one of the oldest functions of music. And for many of us music—or art, or literature—is the only true religion that remains.

As for the similarity of intent with respect to Akron and the free jazz guys: didn't someone say that music is the healing force of the universe? ❧

YOU MUST BE BORN AGAIN

An interview with Nicola Bowery

by Francesca Granata

ILLUSTRATION BY DIMITRI SIMAKIS

I visited Nicola Bowery—the wife of the late fashion/performance artist Leigh Bowery—in her Brighton, England home last summer. I was interviewing her for my PhD thesis, a big chunk of which revolves around Leigh Bowery's extravagant costumes and performances from the 1980s and '90s. My interest in Leigh Bowery had been spurred by Hilton Als' profile in the *New Yorker* (March 30, 1998). That piece discussed Bowery's varied career from fledging fashion designer to notorious club figure to performance artist—three strands of his practice which remain firmly intertwined.

Nicola was extremely kind in showing me a number of her husband's elaborate costumes which—having been painstakingly made to accommodate Bowery's considerable girth—appeared eerily empty. (This was particularly evident since a complex system of understructures keeps them in shape, further highlighting Bowery's absent body.) She also discussed her role as the slime-covered baby in the humorous, unsettling "birth scenes" that Bowery staged as part of his band Minty's performances from the early '90s until his untimely death in 1995.

Leigh Bowery's status changed both during his lifetime and posthumously: from a cult figure of the London club scene, he became a performance artist whose work is routinely included in prominent international shows (most recently the Venice Biennale). His image remains consecrated in the art-world pantheon via Lucian Freud's intense nude portraits of Bowery (who sat for Freud over the course of two years, as often as five days a week). Bowery's life as an openly gay man married to a woman and his multifaceted art practice still have the ability to confound; his lively work actively resists and destabilizes classifications and borders of any kind.

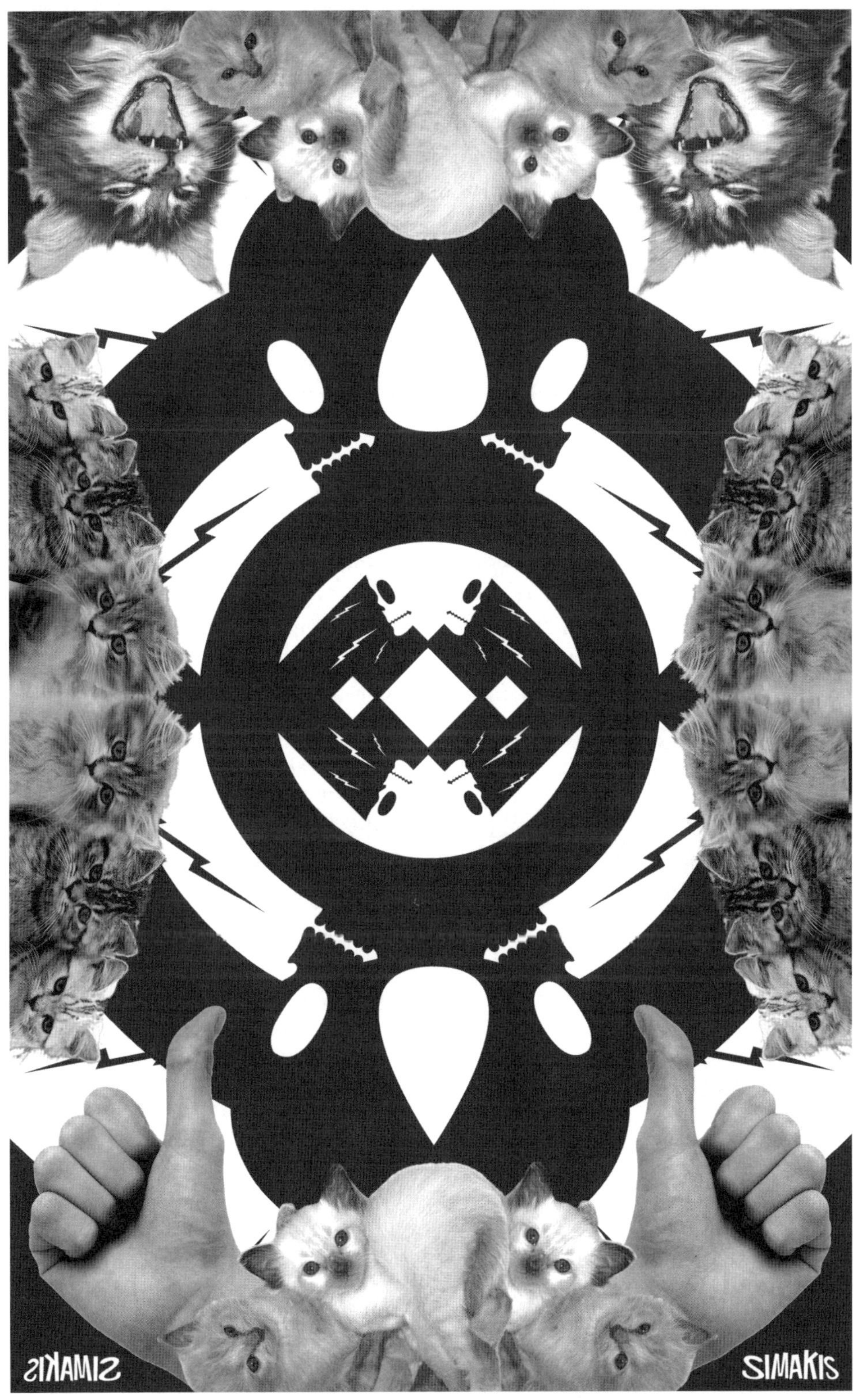

SIMAKIS
SIMAKIS

FRANCESCA GRANATA: Leigh Bowery seemed really interested in manipulating his body through his increasingly complex costumes, and by accentuating parts of the body like the belly, which normally tend to be restricted and de-emphasized. Do you know why he was he so interested in accentuating the belly in his looks?
NICOLA BOWERY: Because he had one! When he first came to London he was quite conscious of his weight and he dieted at some point as well. Then he started to use his body for the fashion he was making at the time. In the early '80s, he started emphasizing his body (particularly his better points) and squeezing himself into corsets that you couldn't really see from the outside. So a lot of his garments were a more restrictive look. It was probably after he started sitting for Lucian Freud. Lucian was so into his body . . . They both loved his body, so Leigh started to use more of it in his costumes.

It started with his bum in the very early 1980s, with a lot of jackets which exposed the bottom with knickers or frilly knickers. Then he got into breasts because he had quite a lot of blubber up there; he could make boobs. He wasn't like every other drag queen. He didn't want to be like a woman, he just liked to emphasize certain parts of his body.

And, of course he emphasized the belly in the infamous birth scenes! You mentioned how the birth performances, in which you played the baby, were inspired by Divine in the movie Female Trouble. *Did Leigh talk to you about playing the role of the baby before planning the piece?*

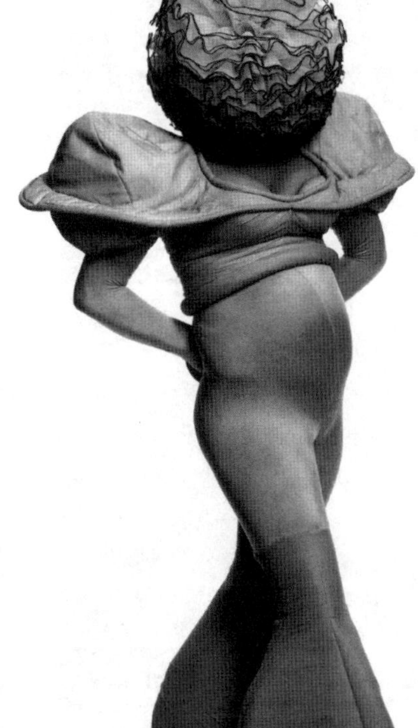

He didn't talk about his ideas so much. He would just get on and do them and then tell me what I'd be doing with it. In *Female Trouble*, Divine is wearing a yellow-and-black striped dress and a head scarf and glasses just before she gives birth to little Taffy. For the very first performance he did of the birth scene, Leigh remade that dress and wore a head scarf and glasses. We did a performance at Kinky Gerlinky and he enacted the bit where Divine is in the telephone booth and she's telling her boyfriend that she's pregnant and he tells her to get the hook. So, he reenacted that bit, and I was rolled in a ball inside it at the time. It was the first birth that we ever did, and nobody knew I was underneath him! Leigh had to go up on the table to give birth to me and I came out. And I can say it did shock a lot of people; nobody was expecting it *at all*.

I'm guessing the audience wasn't made of straight stuffy people?

Not necessarily. Kinky Gerlinky was a major night club event every month and everybody dressed up to the hilt to go there. All the drag queens would look fantastic.

Was it hard to shock that type of audience?

Yes—plus they were used to Leigh wearing some sort of extravagant costume. They obviously didn't realize there was a person underneath, but it wasn't unusual for him to have a sculpted belly.

So the birth performance came about because he was a fan of Divine?

Yes, that's how it initially came about. Leigh absolutely adored Divine.

And then he thought it worked and he continued to build on that?

Yes, and it changed obviously after the first time, when he did the Divine costume. That's the only performance we did with that. Afterwards, he made outfits that were more sculpted around the birth. When we did Wigstock he made a lovely velvet jacket and a velvet skirt. He constructed this massive bosom and I used to have to go inside it. Lee Benjamin, the guy who was helping with this, would cut around it. The bosom was cut to conceal me so nobody would know I was there and it would all look in proportion. He also had a sculpted face for it, a face mask made of Lycra stockings with great big lips and cheekbones so he would look like a caricature of a person. After that, we did a few performances with this outfit and then he would strip down so people could see me actually inside.

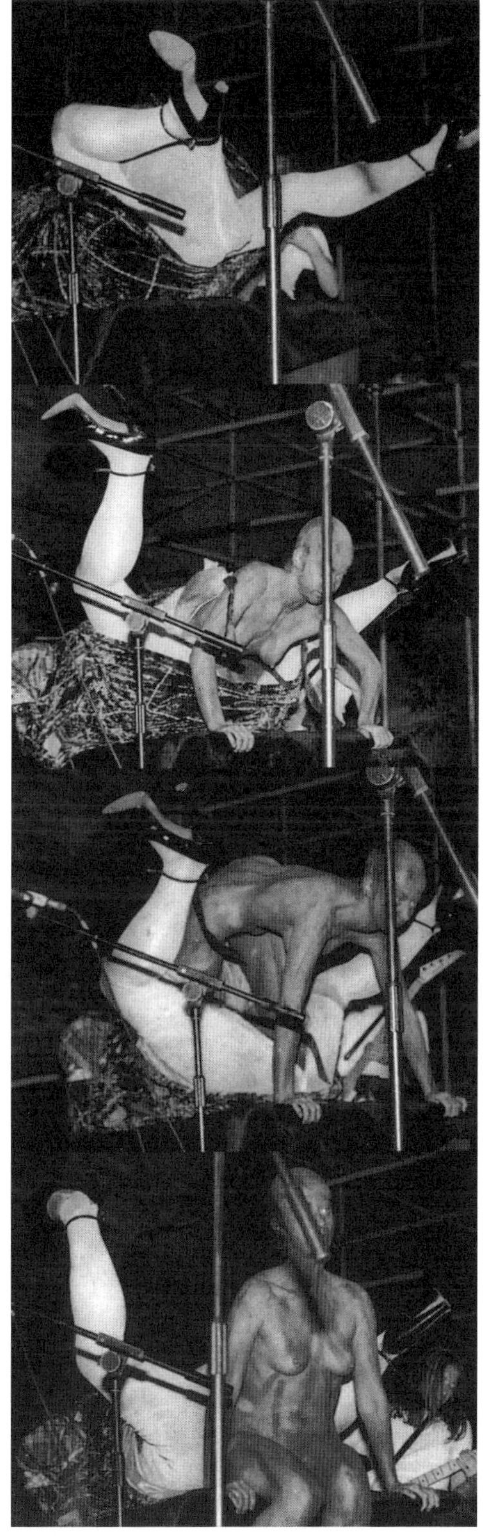

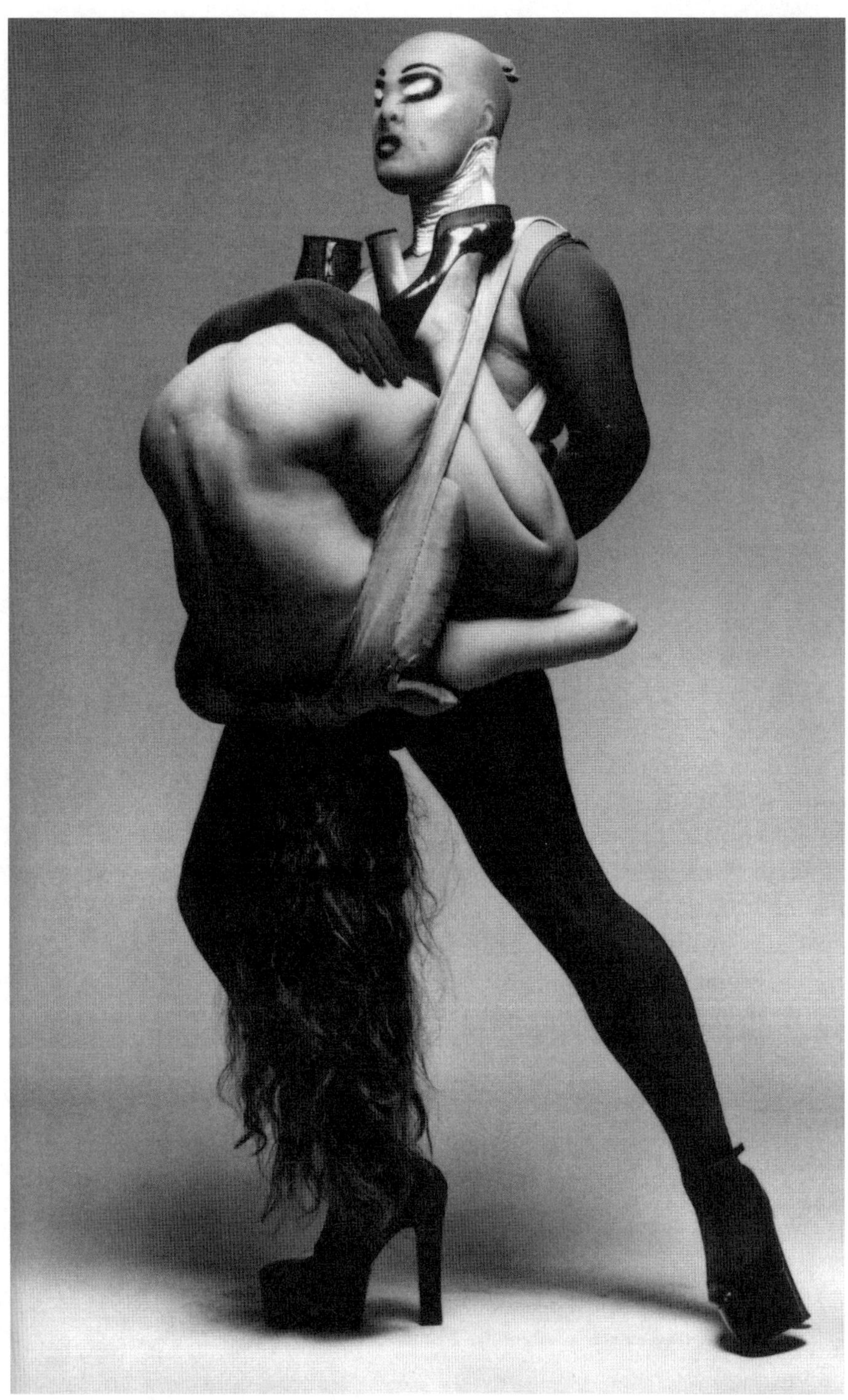

CREDITS. Photographs on pages 102, 104, and 107 by Fergus Greer, from *Leigh Bowery Looks: Photographs by Fergus Greer 1988-1994* (Violette Editions, 2005). Page 103: photograph by David McCairley of Minty perfomance at Joshua Comston's Fête Worse than Death, Hoxton Square, London, 1994, reproduced from *Leigh Bowery* (Violette Editions, 1998)

At some point you were doing a performance of the birth as part of a residency and they told you had to stop because of the Westminster Council.
It was at the Freedom Café. Apparently, you are not allowed to have full frontal male or female nudity in a performance. After Leigh gave birth to me, I was obviously nude, and he stripped off as well to change into something else. Actually you *are* allowed to be nude but if you move you are not, so you could be still and be nude. It had to do with the olden days in Soho, with strip clubs and things of that sort. It's a really old law that's not usually put into effect. Somebody rang up the Westminster Council and warned them that would be the case. They didn't mind about the peeing, the fact that I was drinking his pee—not that I really was, but it looked like it—and they didn't mind Leigh pretending to lick chocolate off of Richard Torry's bottom. But the nudity ...

It was a bit of silliness, a bit of a scandal—ridiculous, really. But that was the last performance Leigh did before he died. We got shut down after that first night and then he started to get headaches and ended up in the hospital with meningitis, and died.

Did you enjoy performing with Leigh? Did you do other performances with him?
We were great mates. I loved him to death and we enjoyed performing together. Why wouldn't I? It was exciting.

The birth performances might have been the only ones, I think. I sang a bit with the band. Oh ... no, there *was* another performance I was involved in. He did a performance in Holland in Fort Asperen, in which he hung upside down. I was dressed as a ballerina of sorts and was spraying the audience with air freshener. So I was in that performance too. I'm sure there is something else but I can't really remember.

In Tokyo, from the photos, it looked like you and Leigh were performing together.
In Tokyo he did a series of performances in the Parco department store. He did a small performance which included him bending over and puking on me. I was dressed quite normally in a black t-shirt and black trousers, and he pretended to puke over me. It was just mainly soap, but it really freaked out the Japanese audience. They actually came up to me asking whether he was sick. Leigh quite liked it. He had a mischievous sense of humor, and definitely liked to confuse people.

What about the Wigstock audience? Were they pretty shocked? I saw the Wigstock tape and the other performers seem more traditional drag types.
I don't know, to be honest. You know how New York drag queens are: sometimes they love you and sometimes they hate you. Leigh always got along with them, because he used to go to New York quite a lot. He went to clubs in New York and that's where he met a lot of drag queens. He had extreme respect for them because he thought they were fantastic, Lady Bunny in particular. They really got on well; they both had a very similar sick sense of humor. Perfidia is

another one he got on really well with. Michael Alig at the time was hosting the Limelight, and he'd bring Leigh over to host on some nights.

There was a lot of press on Leigh because of the Wigstock show in New York. How was the press in Britain? Did they take him seriously right away or did it take a while?

There was a piece about him in *Flash Art*; there was an article in *Lovely Jobly*. A lot of magazines started to take him seriously as an artist after he did the performance at the Anthony d'Offay Gallery in the late '80s. That's when he realized he wanted to be thought of more as a performance artist.

The costumes he did for that gallery performance looked really labor-intensive.

Yes, all of his stuff was.

Did you work on a lot of his clothing?

I did quite a few of his garments. I was always helping with various bits and pieces, but I was mainly known for sewing all the sequins on his garments. I was good at beading.

Did you learn that in college?

No, I studied printed textiles. After I left college I was just working with some friends of his and they basically just gave me a bag of bugle beads. They were doing a fashion show and asked, 'Can you make these bras look nice?' He came around to the studios and saw what I was doing and really liked me and asked me if I could work with him on some of Michel Clark's costumes.

Did you guys make all the costumes yourselves, or did you contract it out?

He pretty much did most of the things himself. He never contracted it out. There were three main people he worked with: Lee Benjamin, Pearl and myself.

Did you do this costume? It's pretty elaborate.

Yes, I stitched all the feathers. It would take six to seven days to sequin something like that because they are tiny bugle beads. It took a long time to do a lot of the costumes. That's all we worked on. We were quite lucky, really, because Leigh had a regular amount of money coming in from sitting for Lucien, and so did I, so we had enough money. Usually sitting for Lucien was at night, so we could work on the costumes during the day. And before we started sitting for Lucien we were on the dole.

Did he want to sell his garments or did he not really care?

Leigh was not very materialistic—as long as he had enough to get by. He wasn't extravagant, you know. The extravagances were in the work, in the art. Then Lucien would take him out for expensive meals, which he liked. He didn't make much money at all. The money he made went toward the costumes. And fortunately, because Leigh became so well known as a performance artist, he was asked to host clubs and exhibitions and the expenses were paid to go out there. So we traveled a lot. What would you really want: money for food, living, your art and also to go traveling.

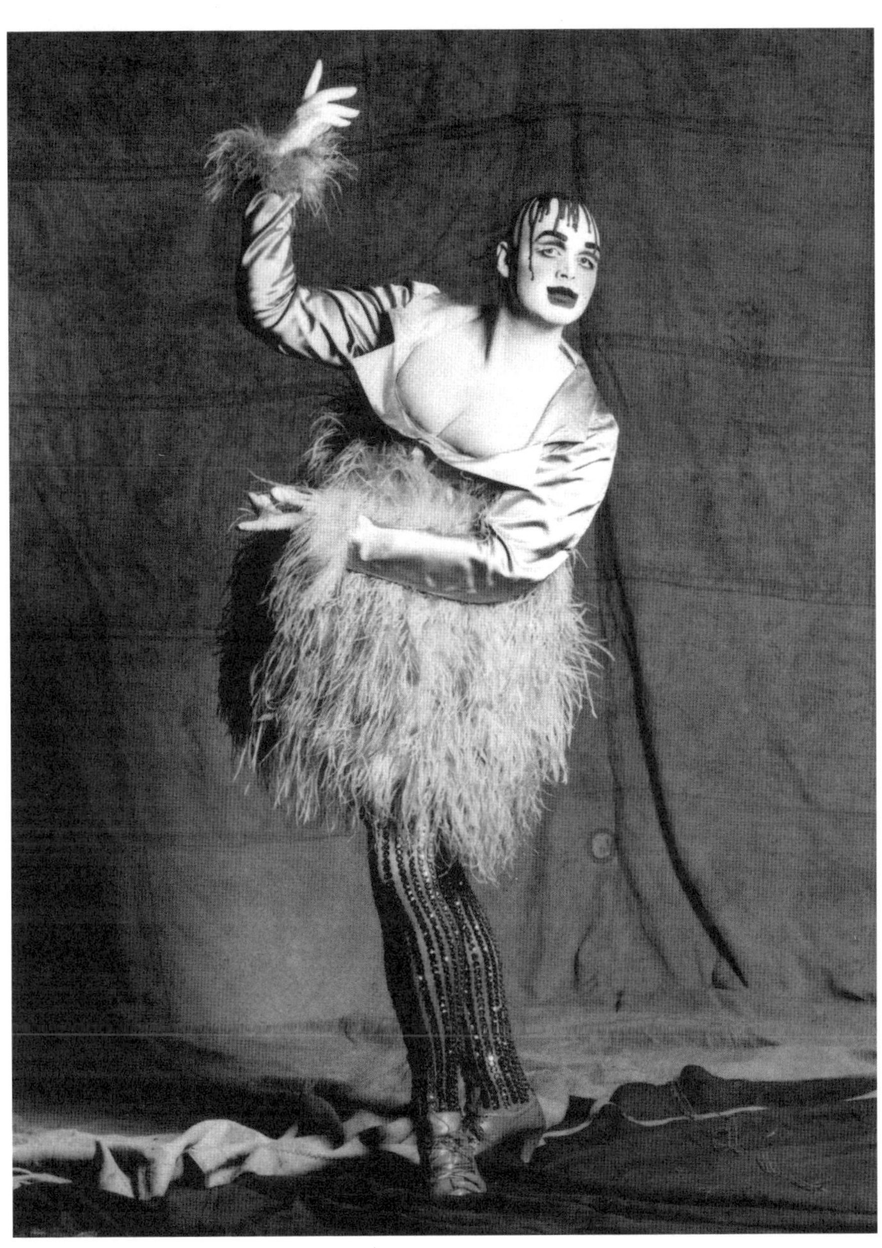

Did you continue working on costumes after Leigh's death?
Because I was very good at sewing on sequins, I made a living at it. Together with Pearl, we worked with Christian Lacroix, Thierry Mugler and Westwood. We were really good mates, so we worked together on more up-market stuff.
It seems a lot of designers were influenced by Leigh. Did he mind that?
At times he was influenced by the same people that were influenced by him. He thought Vivienne Westwood was great. Jean-Paul Gaultier was influenced by Leigh, too. 🐾

107

KYLE FIELD

Some Drawings

Kyle Field makes music under the name Little Wings, and draws a lot under the name Kyle Field. In the last year Kyle has released his first book of drawings, *Put It In A Nutshell*, as well as his eighth Little Wings album, *Soft Pow'r*, on the Rad Records label. His website is at kyledraws.com; it's a phenomenal way to spend a half hour or so.

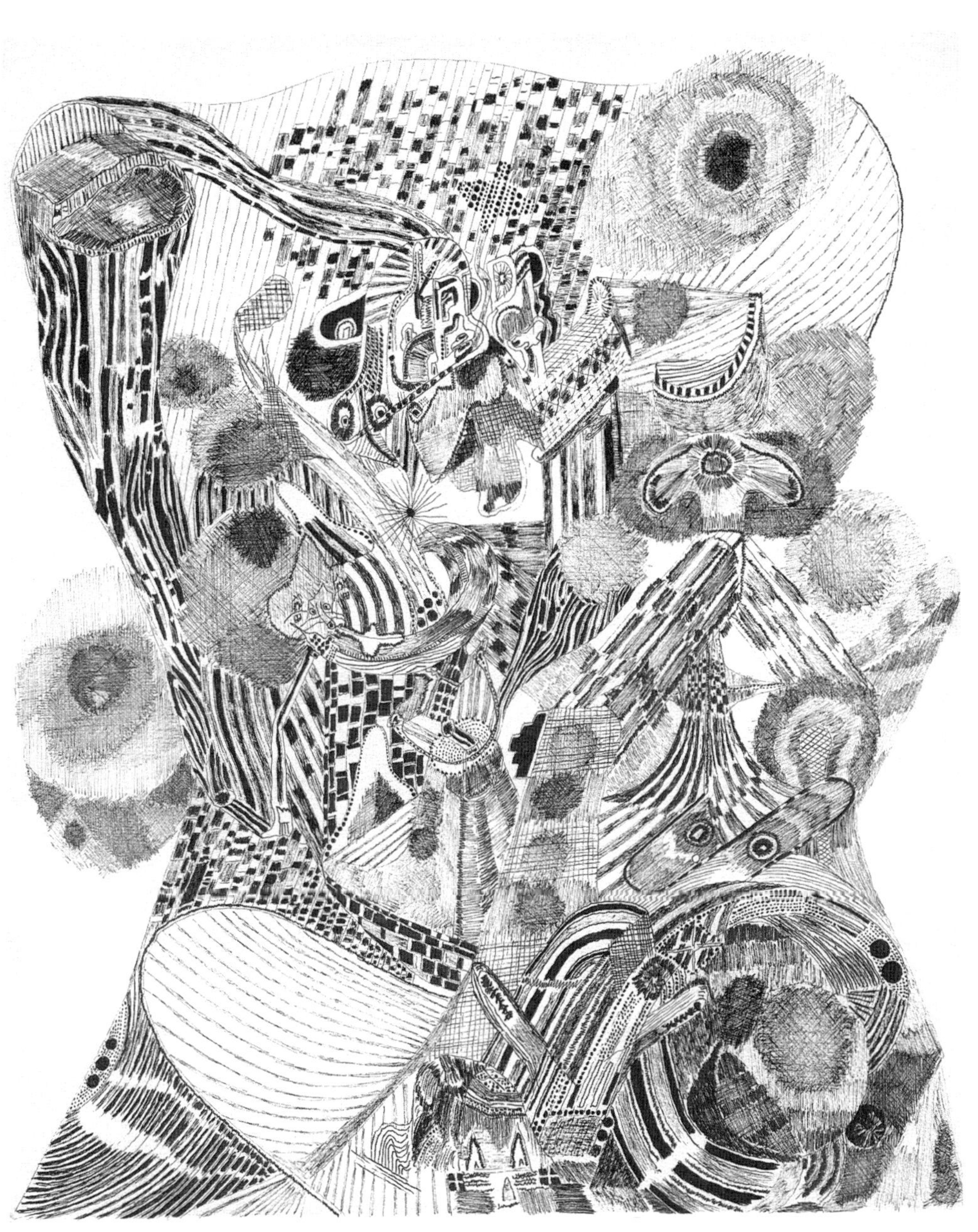

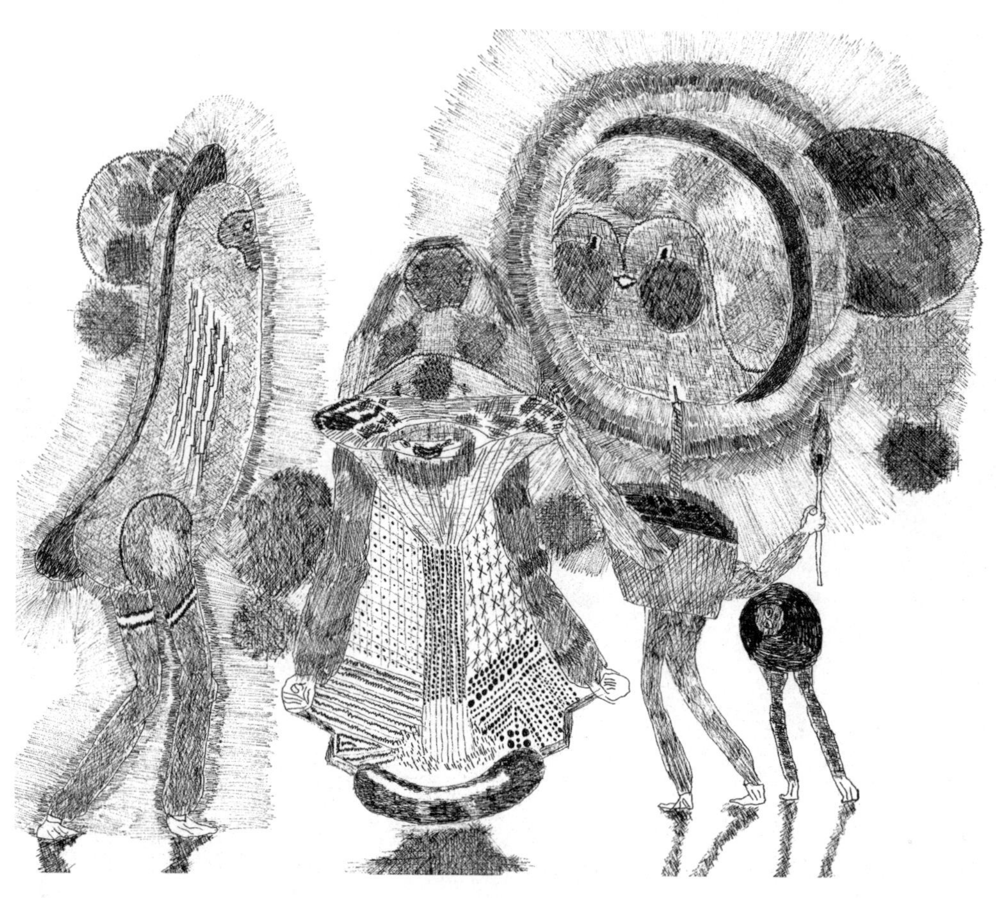

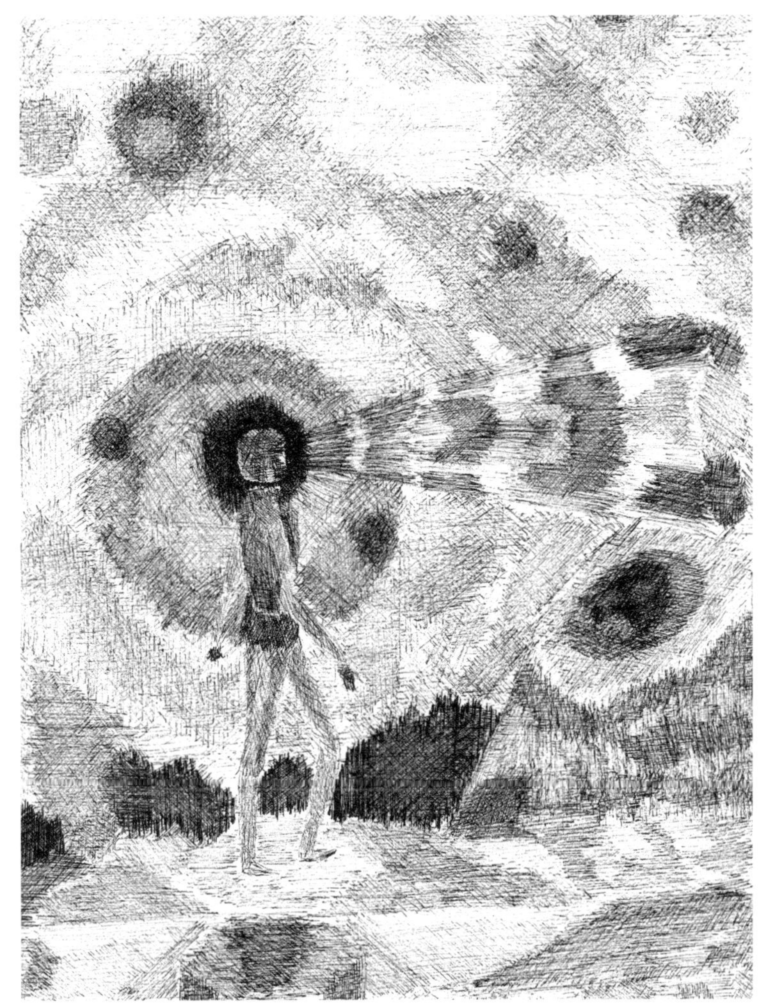

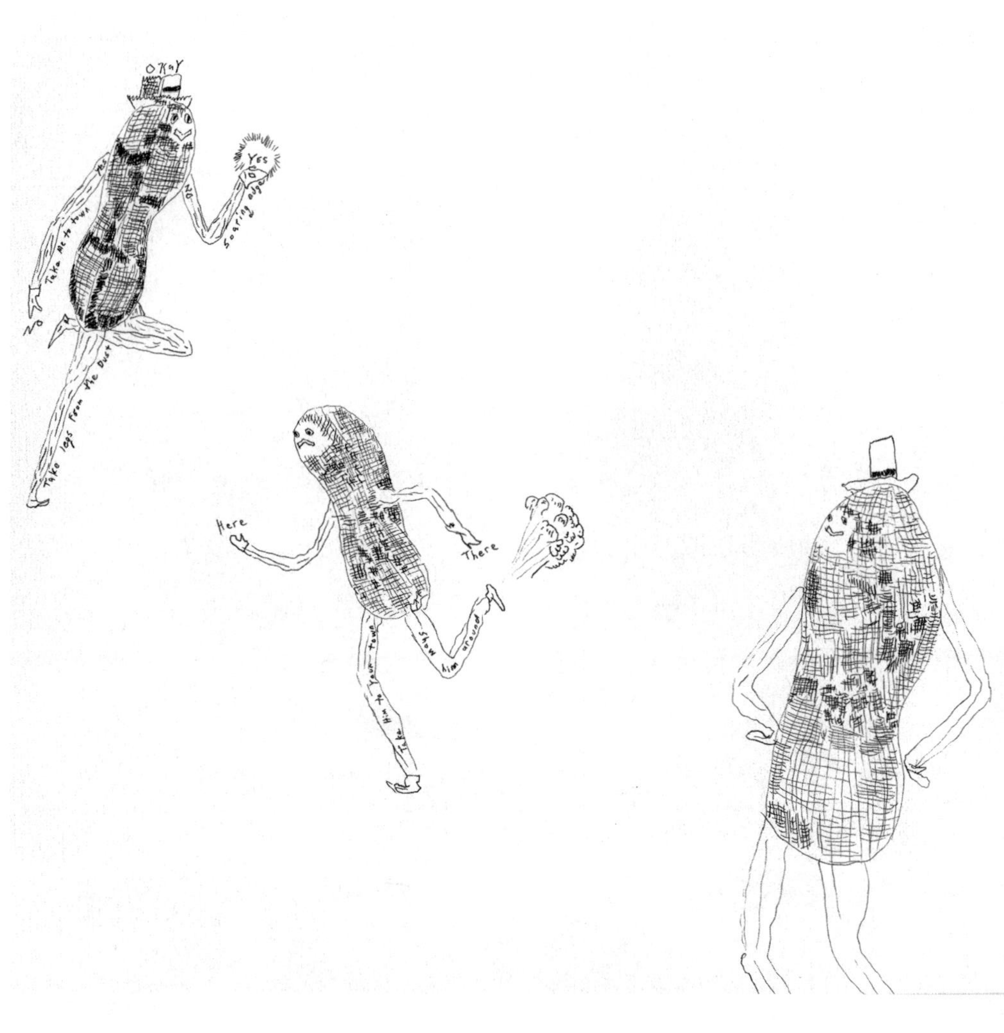

OKaY
YES
NO
Take me to town
No
Take legs from the Dust
soaring edge
Here
There
Take Him to your town
many ways
him around

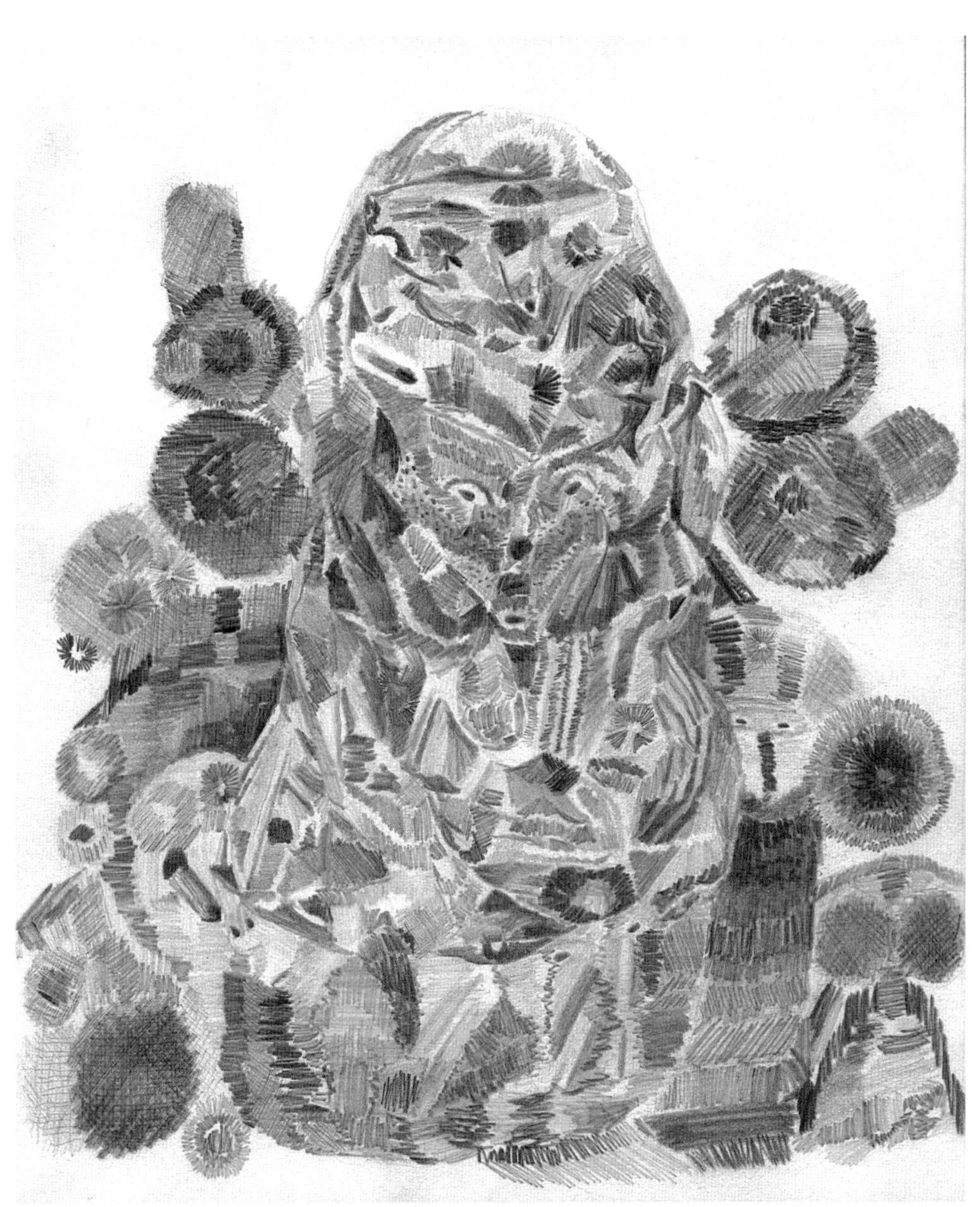

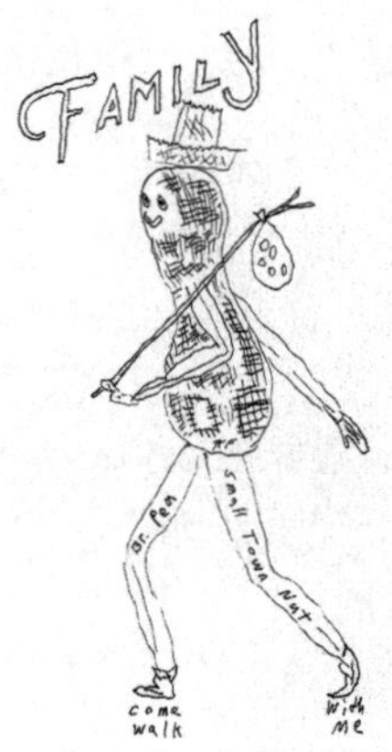
FAMILY
or. Pea
small Town Nut
come
walk
with
me

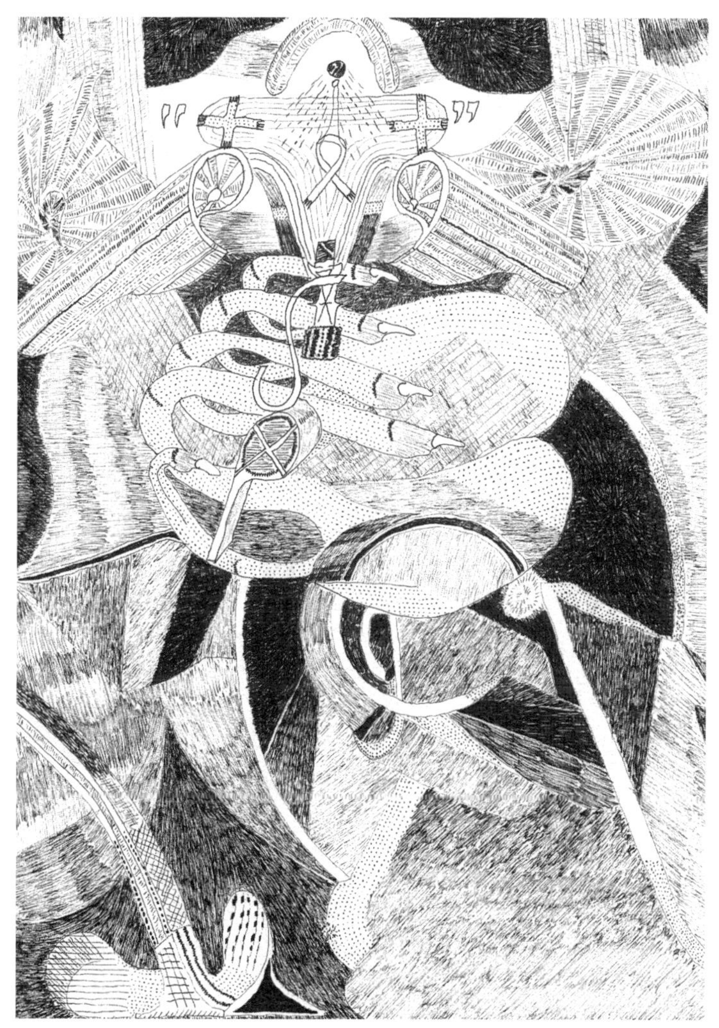

WHERE IT STARTS GETTING SWEEPY

A chat with P.G. Six

by Erik Davis

ILLUSTRATION BY JASON TRAEGER

The first time I heard P.G. Six's solo album *Parlor Tricks and Porch Favorites,* I had that spooky, rare, and altogether priceless sense that the artist behind the music—the singer and multi-instrumentalist Pat Gubler—had somehow tapped directly into my soul. Actually that's not quite right—a lot of the time I'm not sure I have a soul. Maybe it's just a neurochemical fiction, right? So it's more like the music reminded me what having a soul feels like, at least for me, which means a beautiful but tart melancholia, a paradoxical nostalgia for some golden world I've never known, or at least cannot remember.

I do remember listening to *Porch Songs* while suffering through a late night layover in some European airport I have forgotten, hunkered down with an iPod in a crowded but silent cafe, with nothing to do but sit and wait to sit some more. I was drinking beer and staring onto asphalt and rain, and listening to this short stately tune, whose single distorted guitar melody threaded the sad and modestly majestic minor chords on the piano. I heard the almost whispered words as if they were directed to me:

When the shepherd is calling you home
Are you ready to put down the yoke
Or will you punish yourself still?

This is where I started getting sweepy. Staring at the dark haze beyond the raindrops, encased in the posthuman anomie of contemporary travel, I felt the stirrings of some deeper pilgrimage that I could not, as yet, really embark upon.

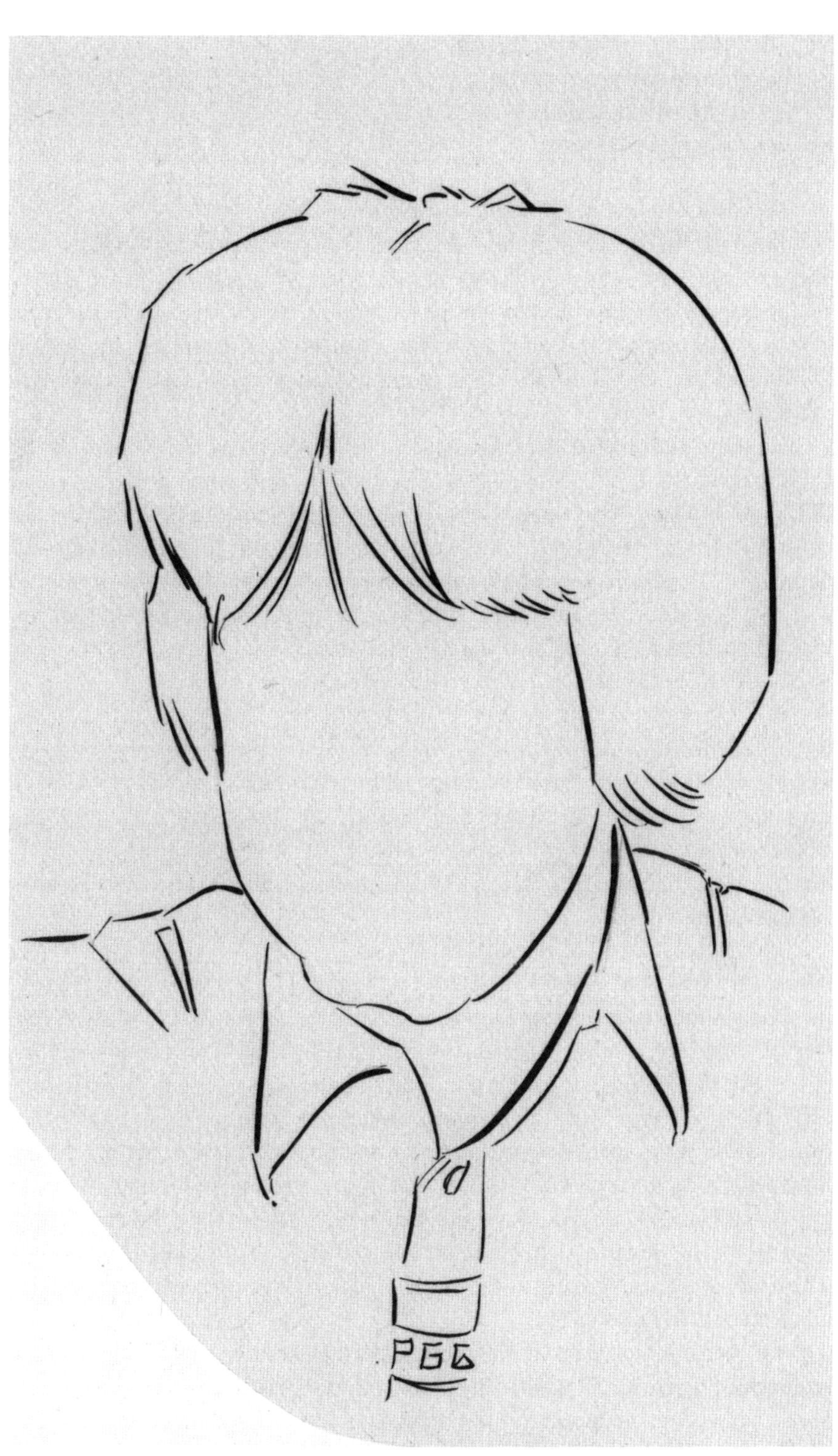

Like its follow-up, the only slightly less marvelous *The Well of Memory*, *Parlor Tricks and Porch Favorites* is a short album of gnostic folk, intimate and haunting and odd. Mr. Six, as the *New York Times* would have to call him, is not a strong singer, but a fragile one, and so you pay attention. He is a spectral finger-picker, whose guitar playing is more indebted to UK elven lords like Bert Jansch, Robin Williamson, and John Renbourn than to the Takoma primitives who loom over so many American hepcat neo-freak pickers.

On these albums, P.G. Six also weaves the songs together with spacey improvised passages conjured on weird old resonating instruments. Because while Gubler can do the coffee house thing, he also played for years in the strange and surprising Tower Recordings with Matt Valentine, Helen Rush, Erika Elder, Tim Barnes, etc. Tower redefined improvisation for the bastard indie children of folk and rock. On discs like *Folkscene* and *Furniture Music For Evening Shuttles*, they tapped into deep currents of collective experiment and psychedelic invocation years before that whole furry freak thing went down.

Gubler's archaic avant-gardism shaped his third record, *Music for the Sherman Box Series and Other Works*, which consists mostly of chiming, ancestral explorations of odd-ball harps. Unfortunately, neither instrumental improv nor acoustica play much of a role on last year's *Slightly Sorry*, his first record on Drag City. A solid rawk rekkid, the album includes an unforgettable Neil Youngish ballad ("The Dance") and a matchless trad cover ("Lily of the West"). But the format still seemed, IMO, to clip his wings.

Before May '07 rolled around, P.G. Six had yet to play on the West Coast. So when he lined up a slot opening for Gary Higgins during San Francisco's Mission Creek Festival, I was psyched. The Swedish American Hall is an atmospheric Ren Faire space, but the sound was too bright and the hall was pretty empty. (Where the fuck was everybody?) Gubler was joined on stage for a couple tunes by MC Taylor, the guitarist in the local alt-cow act Court and Spark, who had just gotten back from a wedding and was kinda drunk. Gubler played some of his best songs, and one unfamiliar one, a cover of a weird hippie tune called "Not I the Seed" he got from a Raccoon record by a guy named Jeffrey Cain. Gubler plucked and fluttered with quiet intensity, wincing at the occasional flub. I'm a moody picker too, and I just watched his fingers.

We met the next day. Gubler work a black jacket over his t shirt and thick, rectangular glasses. He was friendly and comfortable with the awkwardness of it all. He sometimes seemed tongue-tied but persevered with my queries, and his laughter was full-throated and geeky. I wish him well.

ERIK DAVIS: I didn't read about you beforehand on the internet, so my first questions are pretty basic. How did you first hook up with Tower Recordings?

P.G. SIX: I knew Marc Wolf, aka the Spanish Wolfman. We were at SUNY Purchase. He studied classical guitar but played a lot of rock music and experimental music. He had a few different bands with Matt Valentine, and I wound up being in this band called Memphis Luxure. That was kinda like a scrappy rock band, with a little bit Beefheart influence, a little bit Pussy Galore. You know, obnoxious. I was playing keyboards – Wurlitzer organ, and we had a Farfisa organ that we would use for a lot of the bass parts. That deep fuzzy sound.

We were living in the suburbs, Portchester, right on the New York-Connecticut border. The drummer moved to the West Coast, we were looking for another drummer and then it sorta fizzled out. At the same time we were starting to do more acoustic jams. I moved in with Matt Valentine and his girlfriend Helen Rush, and we would have Walkmans around, just recording these mostly acoustic jams on whatever was lying around. It was really loose and liberating.

What was liberating about it?

With Memphis Luxure, we rehearsed really diligently, three times a week, workshopping all this stuff. That's really fun too, but it gets depressing when the stuff gets cast aside because all this work went into it and now where is it? With the Tower stuff, it was really like, anything can happen. Turn on the tape, go.

The thing is, Tower doesn't really sound like freeform jamming.

Sometimes we would improvise in a way as if pretending there were a through-composed song. Guided by Voices' *Bee Thousand* was high on the listening list, and some of the Sebadoh stuff—you know, capturing these home recordings of a really embryonic version of a song.

Did songs sometimes emerge later?

One of my approaches in working on that music was going back and listening to little sections and going, "This is really a strangely beautiful moment that I'd like to make peek out more. What if another instrument doubled those sets of pitches?" I found that fascinating, going in and learning a little section of something and bringing that to the fore in the overdubs. It makes it more mysterious: "Is this composed? How improvised is this?"

Were the vocals ever improvised?

Absolutely. A lot of on-the-spot vocals. Not everything, though. There were some songs that were in progress and then we would record them. Record it before it gets too old! There was definitely an opinion that the first impulse was the correct one.

Did that resonate with you?

It did, especially after being in school for music. I wasn't a hugely academic person as a musician, but I was trying my hand at theory and composition. So I might have been a little intimidated in school by people who were in the tradition of highly academic and really technical avant-garde jazz and classical music that incorporates improvisation. These people had a vast knowledge and extended techniques. I was coming at it with less time invested. It wound up being freeing for me to be able to play and to express and to not feel like, "This isn't valid 'cause I don't have the chops."

Did a lot of that encouragement come form Matt?

Partially. Being around that can free you up. Just actively doing it.

It's a weird kind of trust, improvising without a net. What was it like, building that kind of trust?

I think at its most successful, we were being free enough to let the band sound like itself. Whenever you get people together, its always going to be something different, something other than your intentions. I think we were respecting that impulse at times. At times we were trying to put a square peg in a round hole.

One thing that also comes through Tower Recordings and especially your stuff is a strong sense of folk tradition, which is a quality that just fascinates me. You'll play old songs, or things that sound like old songs. That sense of drawing from tradition is part of the pleasure. Even if it's made up, like with the Incredible String Band. But with you and Matt Valentine, and with some fellow travelers as well, there is also this commitment to improvisation, which is almost like the opposite impulse. Because then it's not about tradition, but about what's in the moment. Like on Pelt's Ayahuasca, they play a twenty-minute tripped-out improv drone piece, and then you get "Coo Coo Bird."

One way to be respectful of a folk tradition is to incorporate elements of it into your own music and make a point of trying to make it different and your own. Like those first wave '60s and '70s bands, amping up traditional songs—some traditional musicians probably thought it was bullshit, crass, stupid. But in some ways it's respectful, especially in hindsight. Look at Fairport Convention. They start off playing American blues songs, and then they are like, "We're not really born into this." So then they're mining English dance music like jigs and reels. They are seeing, "It's appropriate that we investigate this music."

That's such an amazing moment, when UK musicians turn from the American folk model of the early "60s and start doing British songs. I loved that you cover the Anne Briggs song "Go Your Way" on The Well of Memory. *You could have done one of the traditional songs that she was known for. But you covered one of those numbers that she wrote herself, but that sound all of a piece with the traditional material. It's like covering this tune was a way for you to acknowledge an ancestor who also straddled tradition and her own music, who's not just keeping it under glass.*

If she had been born earlier, if she had been a singer and written some songs, those songs would have become "anonymous" or traditional songs. They would have made their way into the repertoire.

The more people study modern folk traditions, the more clear that that's what's happening a lot of the time anyway.

It's really interesting when people who are really hardcore traditional players do actually write a tune. People from the '40s or something, they may only be known for a couple of tunes, but they make their way into the repertoire. It sounds like the original version of the tune could have started in the 1700s. But somebody tracks the history and finds out its composed by this fireman in Chicago in 1950. And somehow it makes its way.

The blues are a great example. When white people heard country blues in the early "60s, they heard it as traditional anonymous music. There's this desire to have access to some sort of culture that's uncontaminated by modernity and the idea that there are individuals who create cultural objects, sell them on the marketplace, deserve royalties. When Robert Plant rips those guys off, he's not going, "Oh I'm gonna rip those guys off." He was thinking he was drawing from a well of collective memory.

Yeah, they get a bad rap for that. I don't think they were necessarily being rip-off artists or insincere. They were just short-sighted.

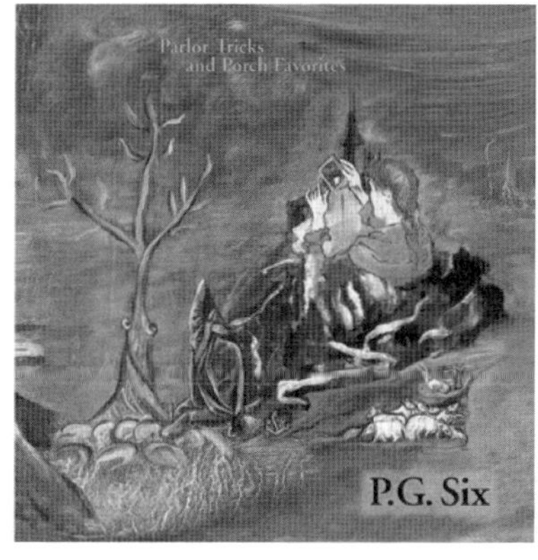

When you wrote some of the folky songs on your first two records, were there particular tunes you were spinning off of?

Well, I really liked that traditional song called "The Deserter," which Fairport does, and Robin Williamson does. I wanted to play that song, but I was feeling like I couldn't really pull it off. Some of the language is archaic, and I felt a little funny playing it. I wanted to write a song that was still in that vein, so I wrote that very short song "When I Was a Young Man." Sometimes now I use my verses and then sing the rest of "The Deserter," so it winds up being a fusion of my song and this traditional song. That kinda shit is interesting, to me anyway.

What about "Old Man on the Mountain"?

That's another one where I based the melody directly on a traditional tune, this "Cherry Tree Carol" song I learned from that Shirley Collins record *Folk Roots, New Roots.* I just assumed it was a traditional melody. But she actually recomposed the melody for that recording. So I was like, "Great!" [*laughs*] But it's an awesome melody, really beautiful.

Anyway, I wound up using that melody and I wrote this weird "Old Man" song that's about a folkloric devil. I like the song, but it also falls short. I'll be singing it and I'll be like, "This doesn't have a rhyme scheme to it. It's like fake." If it was a traditional song, it would rhyme but you wouldn't notice it rhyme.

What's the original song about?

"Cherry Tree Carol" is this weird creepy Christmas song, a Christian song. It's this apocryphal story that doesn't make it into the standard scriptures.

What's the story?

Joseph and Mary are walking along and they come to an orchard of cherry trees. And she's like, "Pick me some cherries, I'm pregnant." He freaks out. Then Jesus,

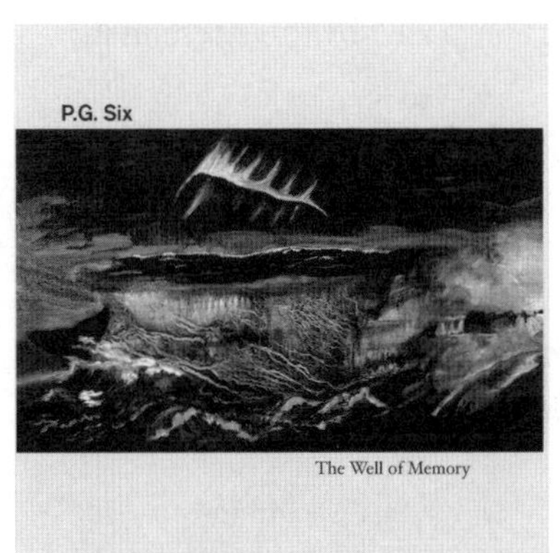

The Well of Memory

who's in her womb, commands the cherry trees to bow down so that she can pick the cherries. And there's this wonderful line: "And Mary gathered cherries while Joseph stood around." Wow. This poor guy. It's like when you fuck up and you feel totally impotent. And then Joseph asks Jesus when's his birthday. And it's not even the 25th! He says it's the fifth day of January. It's such an odd song.

There's a lot of apocryphal stuff in Tower and P.G. Six, whether it's allusions to Philip K. Dick or esoteric religious images. Your tag, P.G. Six, comes from a Brion Gyson book, The Last Museum. In the book P.G. Six is trying to make his way through the bardo. That's pretty esoteric.

The name came from Matt Valentine. He was always coming up with names. At first I was like, "What?" Then he gave me the book and I read it. I was like, "That's fine, that'll be my alias." I though it was only going to be my alias for a certain kind of music. But I was just lazy so there it is.

Are you conscious of creating that apocryphal sentiment or does it just come out of your interests and sensibility?

Sometimes I'm trying to do it. The more interesting stuff just kinda happens and then you look back it. Like I find myself having a lot of pseudo-Christian references in my songs. Later I'll just realize how all those years of going to church snuck in there.

A couple of your songs are about redeemer figures, or the idea of redemption. But it doesn't sound like you're very convinced it's going to happen. A lot of Christian songs that have that image in it are sort of triumphant.

Yeah, like, "We're down with God!"

But in yours I feel more like the yearning you express in the song is the redemption. Those moments don't seem feigned or like you are just using an image from the Bible because it's cool. They're really emotional.

When you reference religion you are walking a tightrope. It can sound awfully fake, especially when you are doing a kind of quasi-roots music thing.

But for you personally, what is it that attracts you to those figures of redemption?
Gosh. [*laughs*] It's a really good question.

This is a funny situation. For me there is an extraordinary poignancy to your music, a haunting quality to your guitar playing, but also to the way you sing, to what you sing about. There's a spookiness there I find very powerful, that really speaks to me. So I have that weird, potentially false sense that I actually know you in some way. And yet all my understanding about how music works suggests that sometimes there is a clear marriage of the personality and the expression, and sometimes not. I mean, I'm hanging out with you and you're not this mystic.
I'm just this guy.

Yeah you're just this dude. It's funny. Those feelings are legitimate on my part—what I feel, and also what I hear. It's deep stuff. But the way you get from you to that stuff, it can follow so many different directions.
Yeah. I've been in the same boat. Like when I've met artists that I'm a fan of, I used to get disappointed by that fact. You want to pick their brain because there's something really special in their music. You are like, "Can I get a little bit of that?" Sometimes they can be nice and polite, and sometimes they can be assholes. I have learned not to expect that anymore, because it's already there, it's already in the music, that thing that you want, they've already put that out there. Then if you meet them and you like them, that's a bonus, and you might actually learn something from them.

I'm thinking particularly about Robin Williamson. I learned some things from him but they weren't what I expected to learn. I took some lessons from him on the harp. It was kind of great, but it was also high pressure, 'cause you only have this half hour to learn something. I wanted someone to hand me the Holy Grail. "Ok, this is how you do it, this is how you make all this interesting music." He was more realistic. He was interested in teaching you something really specific that you could use. So you are not going to get the holy grail of inspiration from someone. You're gonna get someone telling you that you should learn what the good keys are for your voice and write songs in those. Something really mundane, but that actually winds up being really fucking practical advice that actually helps rather than being some esoteric thing.

Music is so capable of inducing that sense of idealism or devotion. Its this place where we allow ourselves to have these powerful emotions, and yet it's circumscribed.
Like I'm playing three shows with Bert Jansch next month. If I was a little younger, I would be—and I still will be—starstruck. I've met him before, he's really quiet, burned out, I mean really nice, but he's just doing what he has to do. Certainly not a very flamboyant person. But everything is already in his music for you to learn about. It will be a pleasure to chat with him a bit, but also to give him his space, because he also probably needs to not be "Bert Jansch."

Speaking of great guitarists, did you take lessons?
I never had lessons on guitar. I've done a lot of watching people. I picked up a lot of things from watching Robin Williamson. Like that open tuning I was using last night.
Do you use a lot of different open tunings?
Not so much. I used to use more. Then I got kinda burned out on the idea of having a whole bag of tricks of different tunings, and having to retune. Every once in a while I'll put the guitar in a tuning I am not familiar with and improvise. I think that can be interesting and really great. There were a few years when I don't think I was playing in standard tuning at all. I mean, I found myself in guitar shops, picking up a guitar and going…
I can't play it any more.
Feeling like an idiot.
How about the harp?
A lot of my musical influences come from my older brother Steve, who is also a musician. When I was 12 he got the idea he wanted to buy a harpsichord kit. It took him like a year to put it together, and my dad and his friend Bill worked on it in the basement. It was the cheapest kit you could possibly get, so they had to solve a lot of problems. It was funny, a fun project.

That sparked Steve's interest in esoteric instruments. He got a harp when I was in high school, so I wound up improvising on it and getting interested. Now I have two harps, a wire strung harp, and a bray harp, which is a medieval harp, with that buzzing sound. That's a real interesting instrument. It has 19 strings. It's tiny. You can get a lot of music out of it for such a small thing.
Where did you first encounter it?
I saw this guy William Taylor play. He's an early-music expert. I'd never heard a bray harp before. When I heard it I was just floored.
By what?
It's the European equivalent to the sitar sound. From what I understand, it was probably the predominant sound of the harp, because you see harps in paintings by Hieronymus Bosch and stuff, and ninety percent of them have these little pins by the sound board. You turn them and they lightly touch the strings. It makes sense – you play that in a room and it's audible. They liked those reedy sounds, they liked bagpipes and shawms. Things that cut through a crowd, that you could hear.
What's your next project?
It's still in an embryonic stage, but I kinda wanna do an instrumental, more guitar- based record. It might wind up being half guitar and half harp stuff, 'cause you know there's an awful lot of guitar records out there, a lot of great ones. I'm just gonna record some pieces and see where it falls. I thought I was gonna be getting started on it by now. When the time is right…

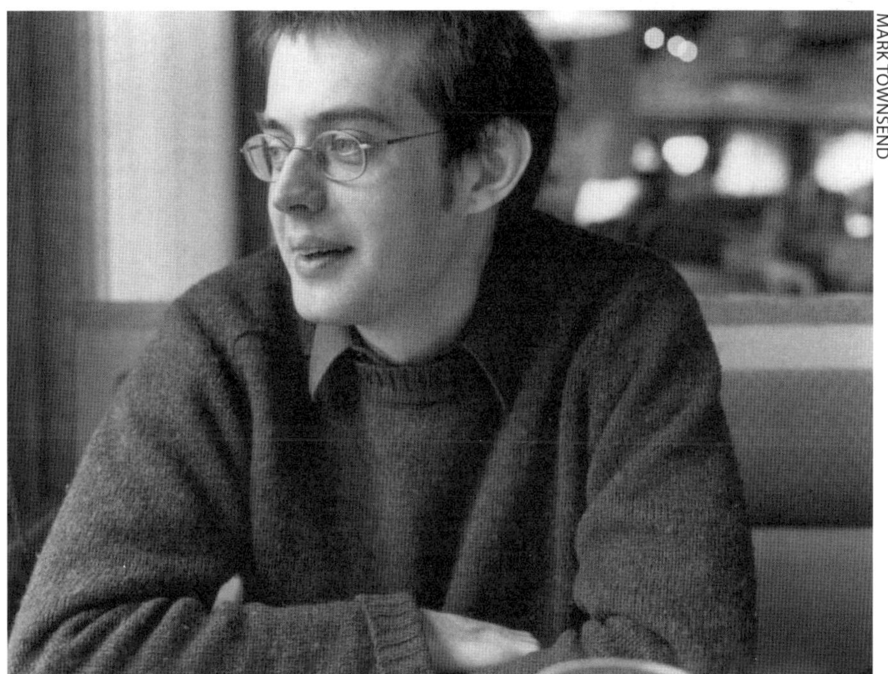

Do you find it harder to get to stuff, what with work, and life, and getting older?
Yeah. Usually the hardest thing is just getting out of the gate, just taking the first step.

When you haven't been playing, do you feel more like, Fuck man, I'm blowing it, or is it more like you're not feeding yourself something you need?
A little bit both. Emotionally, it is the thing I need to do. Some people need to go to the gym or else they will feel frustrated and unhappy. I need to play. If I go away on vacation and don't play for a few days or don't bring an instrument, I'll start to get tense and itchy.

It can be a healing release.
I think it's therapeutic in every way. Even if you play for ten minutes, and you're still angry about what that asshole did at work, there's some benefit, because at least you didn't just sit on the couch going, Fucking asshole! You were at least playing some music.

It's not just that playing helps you get unstuck emotionally. It's also that there are certain feelings or ways or being that you can only access when you are playing.
Often when I have felt like total shit, playing music has been what has gotten me through it. There's not enough booze in the world to fill the voids you encounter in life. But sometimes you just need a little glimmer of hope, a little spiritual food or something, and you'll probably find it by engaging your mind in something like music. ❧

I REST BETWEEN THEM

by Kevin Sampsell

ILLUSTRATIONS BY ALAN GRISWOLD

IT STARTED AT THE MERRY-GO-ROUND. I'm not sure what drew me there. I had no kids and I wasn't a babysitter. I guess it was the novelty of having this big carnival relic inside a fast food restaurant.

I'll go ahead and say it: I was at a Burger King.

Maureen had been running the merry-go-round a long time. It was passed down to her from her father. I didn't ask how it ended up here, at the home of the Whopper. But she charged the company for her services, her machine, and that's how she made her living. It was an attraction. People came from all

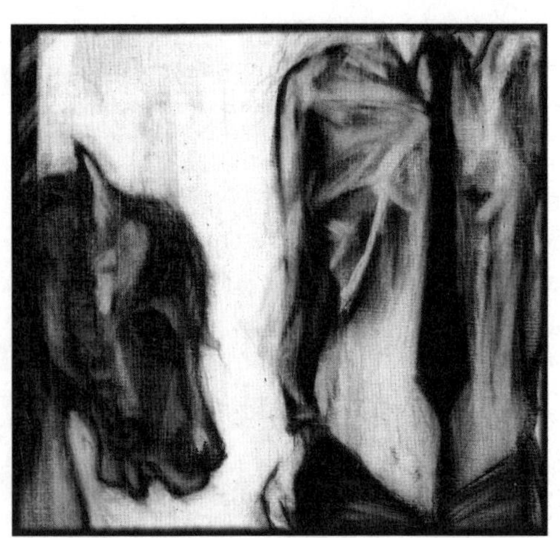

over the county to see it. There were days when the engine would start to overheat and she'd have to shut it down for a couple hours.

I'd go there on the slower days, sit with Maureen and talk about life. She had been engaged before I met her but she broke it off so she could live with her mom and take care of her. She wore a dress shirt and a tie when she worked the merry-go-round. I figured she was trying to cultivate a formal air, of nostalgia and family fun. She was thin and had a nervous energy like she couldn't wait to get on with something else. She had brown, medium-length hair and eyes that always looked a little stoned. She was fourteen years older than me.

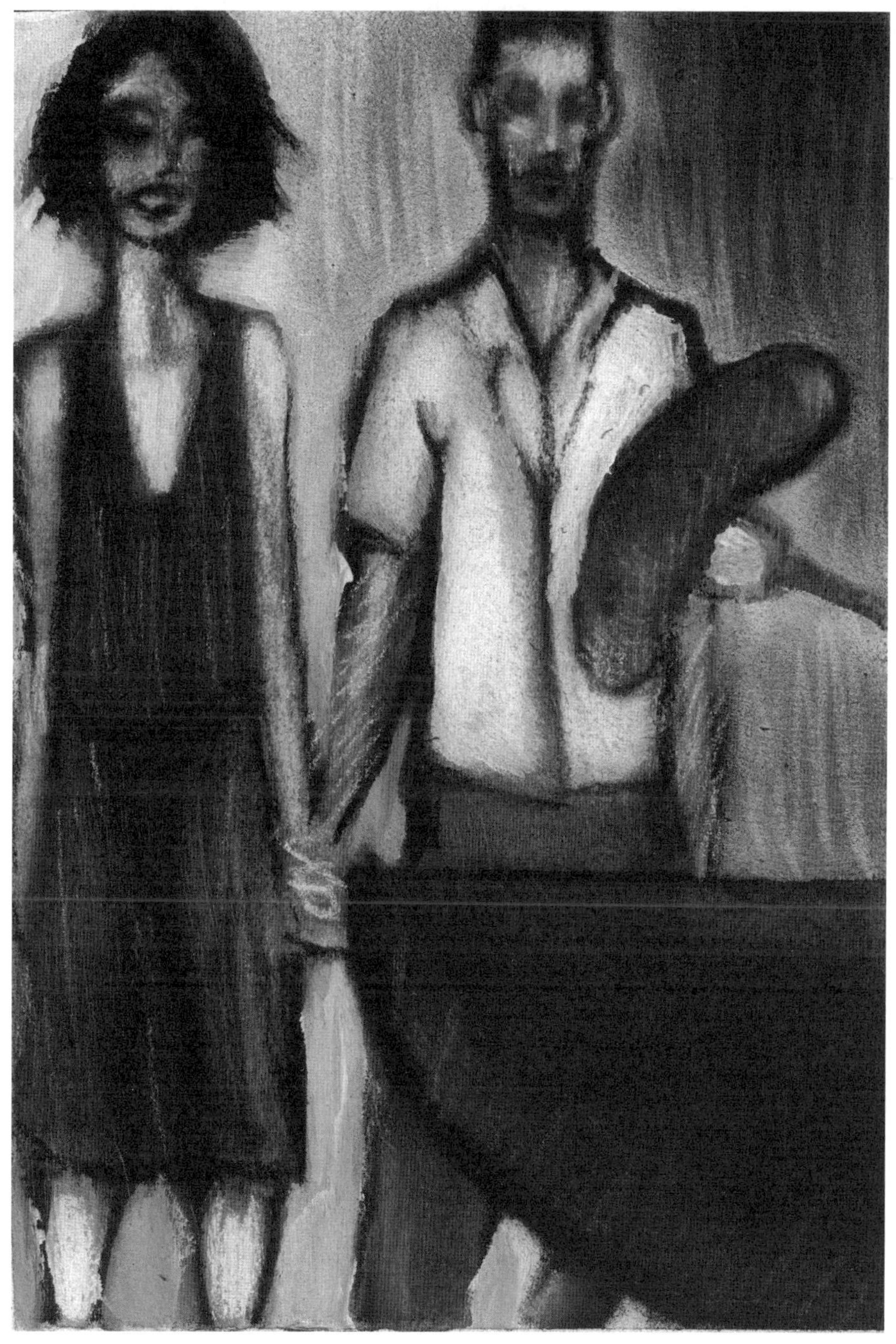

I was on a break from a relationship, meaning I would probably get back into it after I saw how other people felt about me.

Kristi was the girl I was on a break from. We worked at the newspaper together. Not as reporters or anything like that. We worked graveyard shift on the production line, slipping color ad inserts between section B and C before someone else bundled them all up for the vans to deliver to the paperboys. We

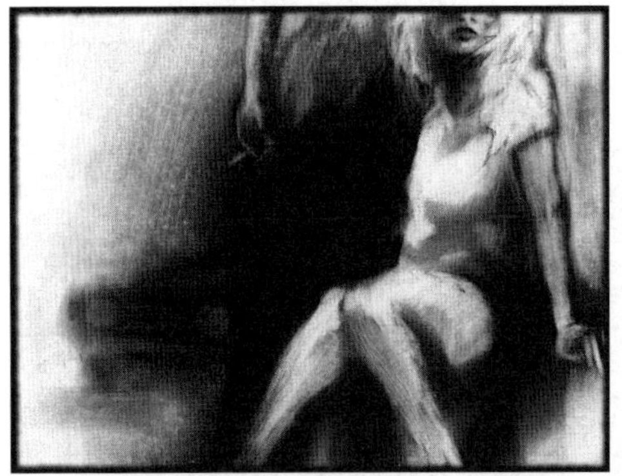

were one step above the paperboys. Maybe even one step below.

Kristi was the only reason I worked there. I met her on a smoke break three nights in and she kept touching my legs as we sat on the back dock. She started calling me her boyfriend after that and we went out for nine months before she freaked out for good.

"WANNA HAVE LUNCH WITH ME?" Maureen asked as she started up her ride for a dozen kids.

"Oh, uh, sure. You want a double cheeseburger meal?"

"No. I meant lunch somewhere else. Like O'Connors or something." She gave me a little jab, to seem casual.

I said it sounded like a good idea. We watched the kids going around in front of us, all smiles except for one. There always seemed to be one who wouldn't smile, as if she'd been forced onto the white horse when she wanted the black horse or the ostrich. I kept watching this one unhappy girl hoping she would grin or do something indicating fun. She kept looking at her parents with that look on her face: *Get me off this thing.*

It was strange to see Maureen outside of the Burger King. She looked better in these surroundings. Neon beer lights brightened her cheeks and gave her figure some shadowy angles. Her tie was off and I could see her bra through her shirt. Our conversation seemed to toggle back and forth, her talking about something in the seventies, me talking about something in the eighties. We seemed a little off, our chemistry tethered to poles far away from each other. Still, she ate her onion rings and drank her iced tea as I picked apart some mysterious sandwich. I couldn't remember what it was I had ordered but it was falling apart badly, the bread a little too BBQ soggy, the crispy fried meat (chicken?) too awkward and slick. I got sauce on my cheek and I didn't have a napkin. I used a french fry to squeegee it off. She saw what I was doing and gave me her napkin. I self-consciously put the fry back on my plate. I realized we were eating the same sort of things we would have eaten at Burger King. I felt a sense of futility about this and started to slouch in my seat.

"I think I'm going to take the rest of the day off," she said. "This is fun." I waited for her to elaborate, but she didn't say anything for about three minutes. "I need some new shoes," she finally said. "Let's go to the mall."

I COULDN'T HANDLE KRISTI'S MOOD SWINGS. When we first started going out she'd try to hide them from me. But about four months in, she finally burst. She said it was PMS. All the women in her family had it bad, apparently. Her older sister couldn't keep a job or a boyfriend and her mother had been divorced three times before she even had kids. I said I would try to help her but I wasn't up to the task. I often felt verbally abused and we'd break up almost every month for three days. "We have to talk," she'd say, and my heart would turn to steel. She'd eventually let me know she was better by pinching my butt at work. Or she would walk up to me and simply say, "I suck."

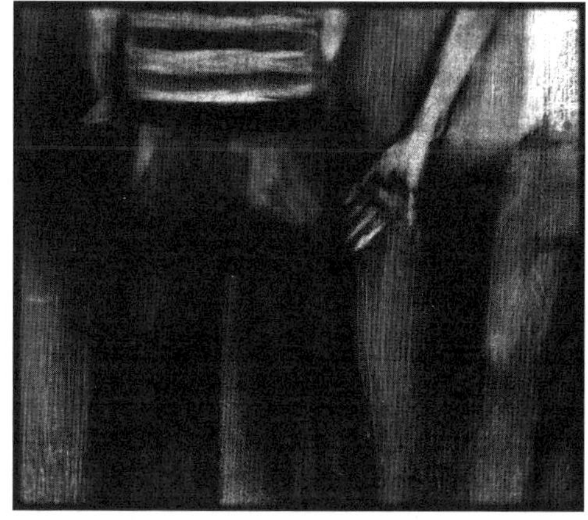

One time at work, we went to my car and made out for twenty minutes. It was about three in the morning; the sky was totally black and draped in humidity. Somehow I was able to bend over enough to put my mouth between her legs. She braced herself against the dash, with her sweats just below her knees, listening for anyone who might walk across the gravel toward us. I tasted her blood and she started to cry. It just made me want her more.

When we went back inside to work I could swear that we stank. But I knew the other people there were not as happy as we were at that moment.

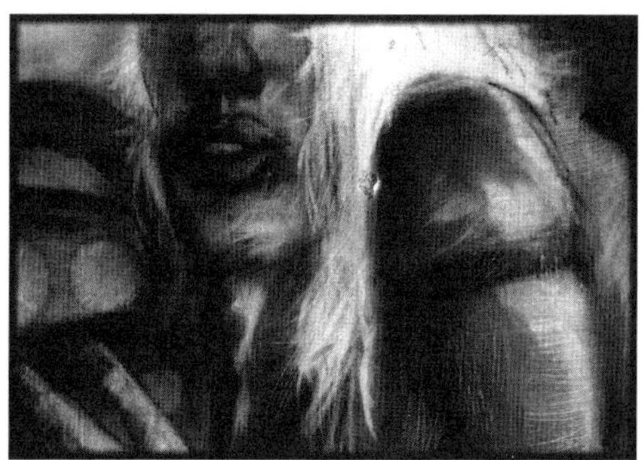

They would look out into the sky as it changed color and they wouldn't see what we saw. They wouldn't feel what we felt. Patty Loveless played on the radio and everything was good and comfortable as we slipped the coupons in, just after the box scores and before the obituaries, our eyes looking up and connecting every few moments until the vans pulled up to the docks.

WALKING IN THE MALL WITH MAUREEN didn't make me feel less self-conscious about being with her. I remembered the days when I actually used to hang out in the mall. Back then, who you walked around with was a sign of your status. If I was seen with one of the popular girls, the other guys would be jealous and maybe give me some respect for a few weeks. But if I was caught shopping with my mom, or some girl from marching band, it was like it went on my permanent shame record.

"I'll make this quick," Maureen said, steering me into a store full of sneakers. She had grabbed my arm for a couple seconds when she said this and it made me think, automatically and uncomfortably, about what it would be like if we were ever a couple. I fell deep and troublingly into this cloudy thought and didn't say a word the whole time we were in the shoe store. It was like I was with a different person all of a sudden. Instead of a person running a merry-go-round, eating French fries, and talking about her favorite Jackie Chan movie, she was just another girl dying for a new pair of shoes. She must have sensed my uneasiness. She settled for a pair of brown suede Converse One Stars. She changed into them once we got out of the store, sitting on a stone bench amid the people passing by. I noticed for the first time that she had nice feet. She flexed her toes and looked at me. "I just wanted some good supportive shoes," she said. "You want me to buy you some shoes?"

"No, it's okay," I said, my voice dry and cracking. She smiled and started to slip the second shoe on. "Wait," I said. I touched the heel of her foot and wondered if she was ticklish. Inside my head, I was still thinking too much, internalizing and overanalyzing, but touching her foot, at least for the moment, made me aware of my hand. "Oh," she said. "That feels good." She closed her eyes. I closed my eyes too. "I'm glad we're friends," she said.

KRISTI SPENT EVERY WEDNESDAY MORNING with her mom, running errands and sometimes drinking Bloody Marys. We had Wednesdays off together and she'd let me sleep until late in the afternoon before she came over and let herself into my apartment.

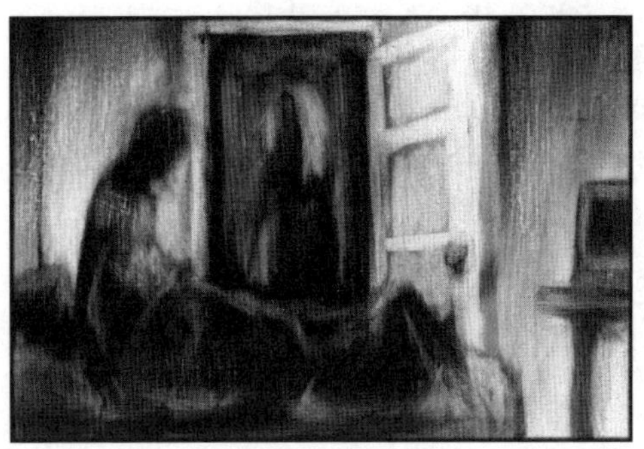

She woke me up on one of these Wednesdays and put her hand in my boxer shorts, trying to arouse me. I turned over and away from her, not ready to wake up. She exhaled loudly and left the room. I fell back asleep but she kicked open the door ten minutes later.

"I know why you don't want to have sex," she said tightly.

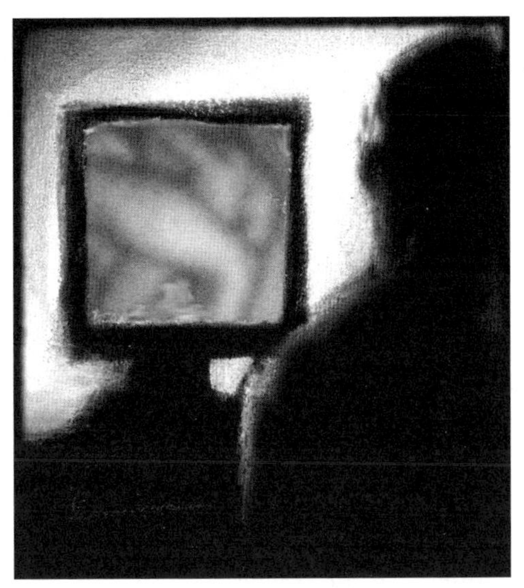

I woke up immediately. I tried to remember what I'd been looking at earlier in the day, when I woke up around noon, when I surfed the internet, image after image, trying to find just the right one. I never knew when I'd find it but I always did, even if I had to look at dozens of women. It was something I did sometimes several times a week, a few private moments of fantasy. Sometimes, after I'd emptied myself of these urges, that hollow space would fill with shame.

She left my place angry and calling friends on her cell phone. I hated to think what she was saying and what they would say back to her.

She called the next day and we talked more. She was still shook up by the whole thing. "I'm taking some more days off," she told me. She was being very stern. I imagined her standing very stiffly somewhere, close to a highway, her eyes rimmed red, staring at a mountain far away.

SOMEHOW, MAUREEN AND I FOUND OURSELVES at a jazz club where one of her friends was playing. Some of her other friends were there, too, and I got this weird feeling that they were treating us like we were a couple.

"At first I thought you were her younger brother or something," her friend Scott said to me. His hair was mostly gray with some red. His mouth seemed involuntarily wrinkled into a frown. I swallowed some beer and tried to tell him we were just friends, but he interrupted me. "My first wife was ten years younger than me. Not to say that's a bad thing. I was in heaven for six months."

I asked him what happened and he looked at me as if I was getting too personal. "The life experience just isn't there yet. I got tired of being her teacher."

"Are you talking about Mandy again?" Maureen asked him. She grabbed my arm and held on. "Stop telling your horror stories. Are you trying to scare my date away?" I experienced a strange mix of feelings then—I felt defensive about my age

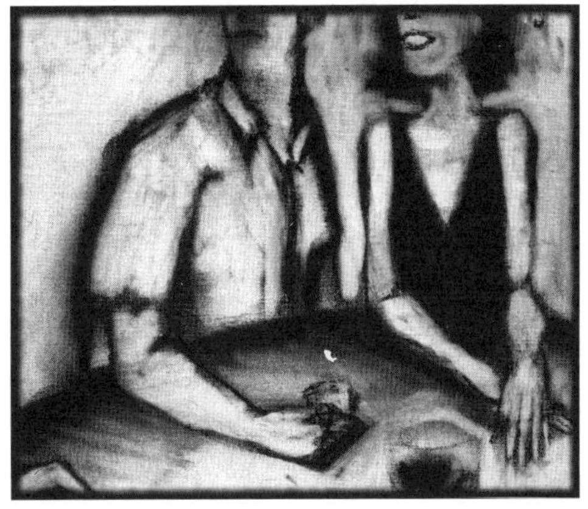

and my "life experience," but I was also unexpectedly thrilled that Maureen had called me her date. It was like I had permission to play a role now. I didn't have to be an individual among strangers. I could scoot closer to Maureen and blend into her. I could let her talk and only offer a comment if she asked me herself. It was easier this way. I kept drinking and felt my nerves unwind. The jazz started to sound good as I held hands with Maureen and tried to play footsie under the table.

I TOLD KRISTI THAT I THOUGHT I WAS A SEX ADDICT, that I felt the need to ejaculate every day. I told her that I had worried about it for a long time—worried about things like becoming sterile or mentally ill—but the habit had become a part of me. Even if I had sex with her every day, I'd still have to masturbate sometimes. Anything could trigger it. Anyone. It wasn't a matter of her not satisfying me, because she did. The images I looked at weren't competition. But everything I said sounded unfeeling and terrible. Words were dumb.

It's a desire to please myself. To be able to do it whenever I wanted. Without ceremony.

She asked if I'd see someone about it and I said I would. Still, she saw it as a betrayal and couldn't stop imagining me, sitting at my computer, looking at other women. It made every part of her burn.

MAUREEN CAME OVER TO MY APARTMENT after the jazz band finished that night. My neighbor, a college dropout named Larry, made small talk with us for a little while outside. He was cooking hot dogs for himself on a little barbecue and he kept looking at Maureen like he was trying to remember where he knew her from. "Oh wait," he said. "You're the one who runs the merry-go-round at BK." We all laughed and Maureen said quietly that yes, that

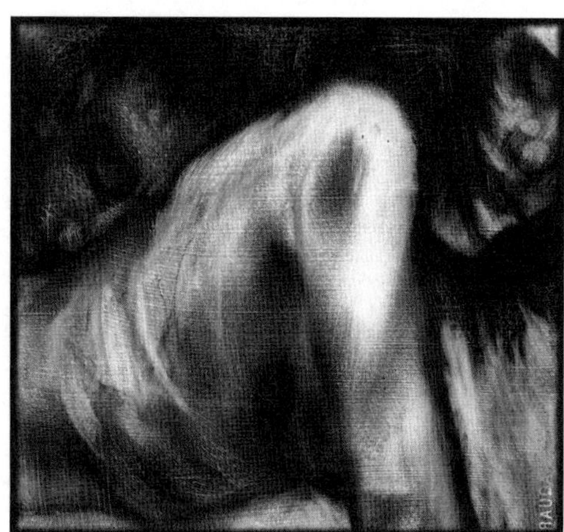

was her. "I did that too for a while," Larry said. "Down at Oaks Park. I was always nervous that people were falling off." He laughed by himself this time. "It's hard to see around the whole damn thing, you know?"

I told Larry good night and he seemed surprised when Maureen and I headed into my place together. I hadn't told him about Kristi yet. "Have a good one," he said.

When Maureen sat on my couch in the front room, I kneeled on the carpet in front of her and held her in an uneven sort of hug. I wasn't sure exactly what I wanted. But I did want to feel her body against me. It was so different from Kristi's. She was smaller but not as soft. Even her head seemed different, and smaller. My mouth felt too big for hers. Her hair was short and dry in my hands. Her neck seemed too thin, and dangerous.

The couch was noisy, even though we were moving slowly. We slid to the floor and she took off her shirt. I kissed her arms, her chest, and her back. I found myself staring at her shoulder blades as if I couldn't tell what they were. They stuck out of her skinny frame almost alarmingly, like wings. I rested my face between them.

Outside we heard Larry putting out his barbecue, the water on the charcoals. We could smell the smoke in the air. Maureen tugged my clothes away. She stood up and took off the rest of her clothes. "I have to go home and check on my mom," she said, then she got back down on the floor with me.

THE NEXT NIGHT I WENT BACK TO WORK and my boss called me into his office. He gave me an envelope and told me that Kristi had switched to another dispatch. He said he couldn't tell me where. Inside the envelope was the extra key to my apartment, a bunch of photos, and a note. *Since you like pictures more than the real thing,* it said.

I found my station and started my shift, slipping in the inserts and advertisements. I felt like I was in a trance and wondered if this was a "life experience." When it was time for my break I didn't really want to stop. But the guy taking my spot just stood there waiting. Finally, he tapped me on the back, hard. I went outside and looked around, almost 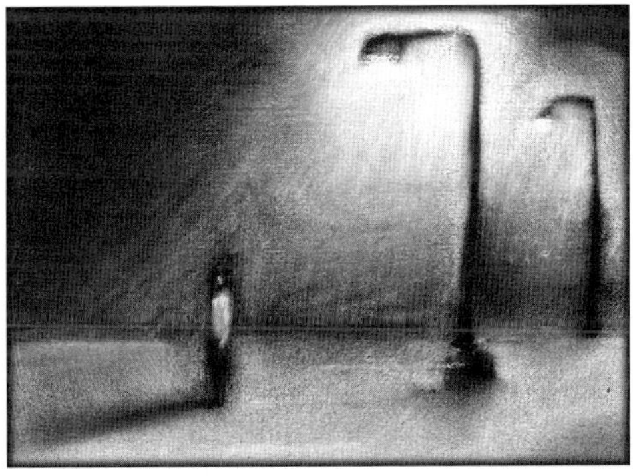 expecting to see Kristi, but also wondering if I could see Maureen in these surroundings. I looked out at the empty parking lot, squinting into the dark, and tried to see the future. ❧

BEEN HEADED UP EVER SINCE

A 1969 Interview with Fred McDowell

by Hoyle Osborne

The following piece originally appeared in the July/August 1969 issue of *Sing Out!*, a magazine that has referred to more than once as the "folk bible." Osborne's interview is one of but a handful ever published with "Mississippi" Fred McDowell. Interestingly, that same issue includes the second part of Peter Cohen's infamous chat with Harry Smith, one of the few interviews ever granted by that cranky artist and architect of the 1952 three-volume Folkways set *The Anthology of American Folk Music*. Among other things, the *Anthology* helped spur the folk and blues revival of the 1950s and '60s, which led to the rediscovery of many original performers, most of whom hadn't recorded since the early 1930s (at the latest). But dozens of newer musicians were also discovered during trips made by archivists, ethnographers, and fanboys.

Fred McDowell was arguably the greatest blues slide guitarist of the postwar era, and the first exponent of North Mississippi/hill-country blues ever to be recorded. Fred was born in 1904 in Rossville, Tennessee, a small town about thirty miles east of Memphis. His folks, both sharecroppers, passed away when Fred was still a boy. McDowell picked up the guitar in his early teens, played at dances around Rossville, and then moved to Memphis proper in 1926 where he was greatly influenced by the thriving music scene. A live performance featuring Sid Hemphill and Charley Patton had a huge impact on McDowell. He stayed in Memphis, working odd jobs, but his own music-making never really took off—largely because he could never afford his own guitar. After getting married to his wife and sometime musical collaborator Annie Mae, Fred settled in Como, Mississippi, about 50 miles south of Memphis, in 1941, just before the U.S. entered the Second World War.

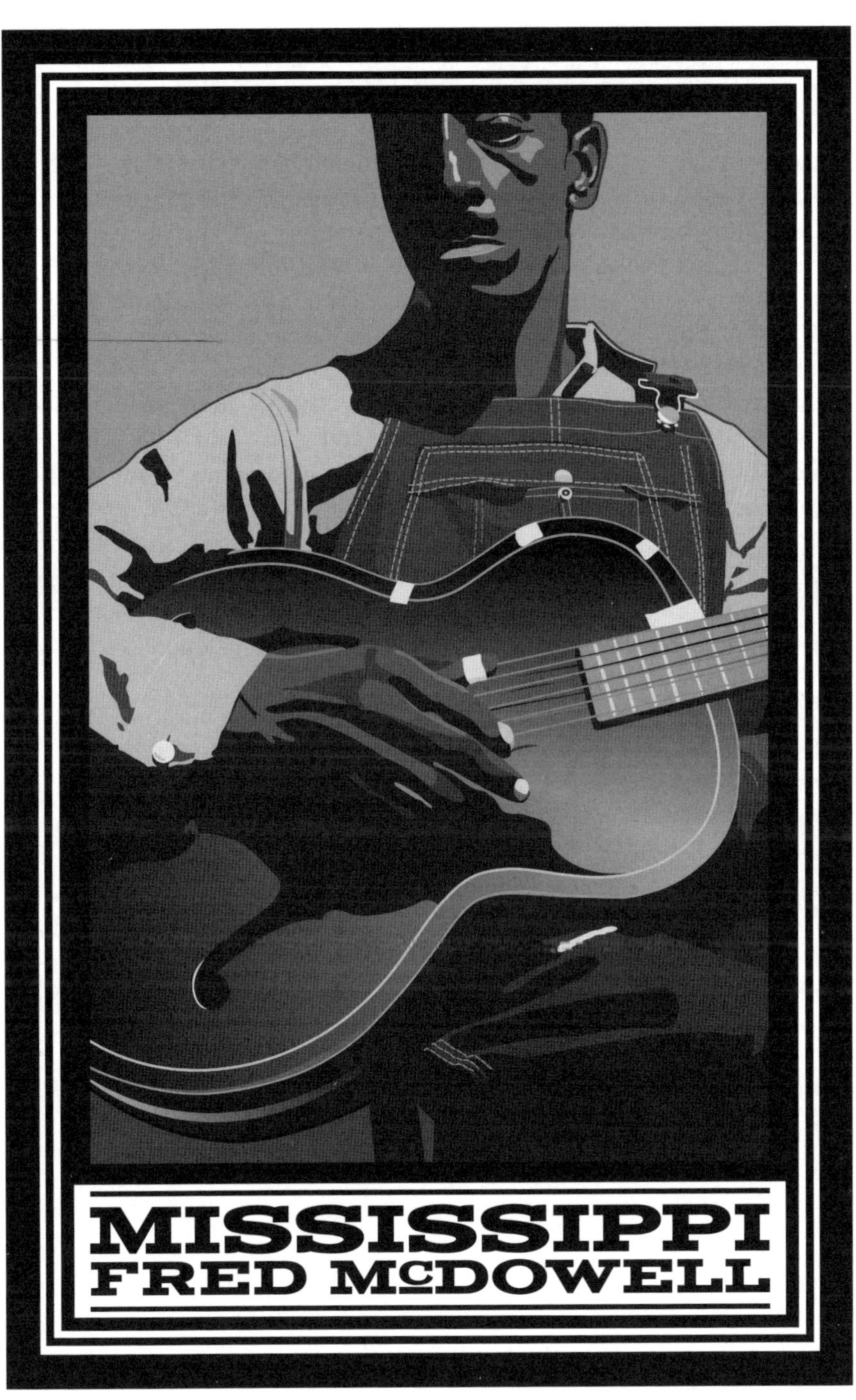

MISSISSIPPI
FRED McDOWELL

McDowell made a living as a farmer, but never stopped playing music at dances, churches, and picnics; he was finally given his own guitar in 1941. In 1959, Alan Lomax "discovered" and recorded McDowell during a trip funded by Atlantic Records. McDowell's music appeared on six of Lomax's brilliant *Southern Journey* album series (the first seven of which appeared on Atlantic, with a few more on Prestige) around 1960. After Arhoolie's Chris Strachwitz heard McDowell, he tracked him down in 1964 in Como and recorded him immediately. Strachwitz released Fred's first proper solo record, *Mississippi Delta Blues*, later that year. McDowell was soon in high demand in the blues revival scene, appearing at the Newport Folk Festival in '64. Before he died in 1972 from a cancer-related illness, he cut over a dozen albums for Testament, Capitol, Sire, Blue Thumb, Milestone and Transatlantic—but mostly he recorded for Arhoolie. McDowell is buried at Hammond Hill M.B. Church, between Como and Senatobia.

We used the internet to find Osborne, who's had a lengthy career as a versatile piano player. He's held down a steady gig at the Diamond Belle Saloon in the Strater Hotel in Durango, Colorado since 1990. For more than twenty years now, Hoyle Osborne has been partner and accompanist to singer and songwriter Jane Voss; they've cut four albums together. When asked how he came to interview McDowell in the first place, Hoyle spoke of coming into contact with Dick Waterman, a controversial Boston-based manager and booker for many prominent old-school blues singers in the early '60s. His Avalon Productions had been the first booking agency formed to represent blues artists.

"Dick made a point of making friends with college-age music fans like me in Philadelphia, because he sometimes had to put one of his old guys up in his apartment," Hoyle explains via e-mail. "In order for Dick to have the time to keep up with his work, he needed someone to keep the old guys company—that would be me. Bonnie, of course, had the presence of mind to have a guitar in her hand while she was keeping company. How I've regretted missing that opportunity. At least I did have private 'lessons' with John Jackson and Elizabeth Cotton." Private guitar lessons with Elizabeth Cotton? Be still our hearts!

The full text of Osborne's original introduction to this interview is as follows:

I met Fred McDowell at Dick Waterman's house in Philadelphia. I wish I could have set down the interview more faithfully. For the impact of Fred's words, you have to feel his fantastic rhythm, wonderfully natural use of repetition. Every sentence becomes a poem. Listen to his recordings, or better still go see him, and you'll know what I mean.

FRED McDOWELL: I'm not like a lot of people. Some of 'em say, "Well, I don't like So-and-So." Well, the next man plays what he plays—it sounds good to him. And I feel like a person ought to go along with that 'cause you can't take the next man's feeling from him you know. Course I know what I play, I don't care if it don't sound good to you, it sounds good to me. That's the way I figure it. And so this other music here, this new style, I likes it. I listen to it. I'll play the new songs in my style. I might change the tune too.

I'm using the electric guitar for the sound. It sounds louder, and then it plays easier too. But my style's the same.

In my home you take just about everybody around there, you know youngsters, when I was a boy coming up, there was mighty few you could find couldn't play a guitar. There was more guitar players around there than any place you'd want to see. All them boys could play guitar. Everybody was playing the same style, 'cause you see that's where I got it.

You see I used to play at those house dances on a Saturday night. I really could sing. I had a good voice then. Well, they'd always get me to sing to the guitar whilst they'd play. And when they'd get tired playing they'd get me the guitar to hold, and that's the way I got started banging on it and singing with it. It didn't make no difference, 'cause it sounded good to them, cause their hearing what they had was bad anyhow. And so I kept on until I learned.

And one little piece, that was at that time a real blues in that part of the country, "Big fat mama with the meat shakin' on your bones." Oh boy, you could play that, you was the best around. So that was the first piece I learned how to play. And they had another one come out, "Milk Cow Blues," that was the next piece I learned how to play. "If I ever learn them two pieces I don't want to learn nothing else." So I learned 'em.

I was a grown man when I went to Mississippi. My home is in Rossville, Tennessee. That's I was born and raised. After my mother died, my sister wanted me and her to stay pretty close together. Well, I wasn't married then, and I went down there where she was. And I married there and I been ever since.

There was mighty few people down in Missississippi where I was, down in Como, where I was, that played guitar, that played blues. You plenty of guitar players, but they playing jubilees.

I went to church. You see I got religion. And I quit playing. My mother she asked me to, before she died, to quit. So I quit about six years. I wouldn't pick up a guitar.

You done heard one of my albums? Well there's two men on there, two brothers, Bob and Miles [Pratcher], one playing the violin and one playing the guitar. Well Alan [Lomax] was over to their house. He'd been there a week and they'd told him about me, and so this guy he came out to me that evening, and I went over there, me and my sister—she are a-blowing a comb on that album with me. And we played ther that night. So he took me out behind the house and asked me, "Can I come to your house Saturday night?" I said, "Yeah." Well you know how a person is if he's not used to a thing, well that's an amazing thing to him, so I was telling all my friends about it, cause we had a lot of gospel singers around there. and they wanted to hear themselves on tape too.

So I told them all, and man my house was full that night. So after he come in I say, "You gonna get them all man?" He said, "Uh-uh. They's somebody else, and I don't want nobody else but you." So after he got set up everything for the recording why he told the boys, "Now I'm going to let you all sing a song. And I'm going to play it back and let you hear it. But I'm not interested in nobody tonight but Fred." So that's what he did. I played from nine o'clock until seven o'clock that Sunday morning. All night. Going back over you know. Until we got it just like he wanted it.

In a way it paid off. When I was playing on a Saturday night, maybe two dollars and a drink of whiskey. And so now they've got me to where I've been all over the world and seen a lot of things that I wouldn't have saw if I hadn't did it. And I been getting a little bread out of it too. Well, that's better than nothing.

I think of it this way: if you've got a gift, you do that, you don't know what may turn up in your favor. That's the way I look at it.

'Course that's what a lot of 'em was telling me at home, "Oh man you going around here playing for these white folks? They ain't done nothing but come in here making money off us." I said, "Well, maybe they are." But now Alan sent me, the first check he sent was to them boys, them two men what I'm telling you all about. Why, he stayed at their house a week. And man they was so crazy about him, till they was buying him whole cases of Coke, feeding him, killing chickens. And he did send 'em a check. They asked me, "Hey may, you heard from that man?" I said, "No, you?" They said, "No, that damn man ain't done nothing but messing us up." I said, "Uh-huh."

The next two weeks they got a check. Fifteen dollars together. They thought, my sister did too, they thought that was big money. She came up to my house one day, she said, "Brother." I said, 'What?" She said, "Brother, they done got their money." I said, "Yeah? How much did they get." "They got fifteen dollars together." I said, "Well no, I ain't heard from him."

So about a month, the first of March that year, I looked in the mailbox, I had an envelope. Mine was a hundred. And boy they got sick. "How come your check's so much more than ours?" I said, "I don't know." Well the next one I got, I got 70 dollars. The next one he sent me I got 75. The next one was 10. Well you see they ain't never got nothing, just this one. They couldn't understand that.

Well, I could. He just like my type of playing better. It sounded better to him. And that was my idea about it. Ever since then I been going, going, going, all over California, New Yorrk, and Washington—been there three time—Newport. And I been overseas, and they're expecting me to go back again. Now ain't none of them been no further than down home. Well you see that's something to look at.

I went to England before. And I played spiritual songs, too. And I had some ladies told me that's the first time they ever had heard anybody play anything like that on a guitar before. They really dug it, man. See I play lots of spiritual songs like Rev. Wilkins. He plays 'em, I play most anything I hear anybody else sing. I learned that when I was learning how to pick guitar.

When I was learning I learned how to sing with it. And also, I don't know whether you pays any attention to me singing and playing, but I can make them strings say just what I say. Anything I say I can make them strings say. And they always told me, they ,"You're complimenting what you're playing."

Ain't but one thing: you have to play with "whamp" when you're playing with a harmonica. But still I'm used to it, cause I've been practicing with it so much. And I likes it. It sounds good to me.

Paul Butterfield's a real nice cat. When I first met him in Chicago—him and Elvin [Bishop] both—was blowing and so on. I asked him one day, I said, "Come on and let me show you something." He say, "Man you can't show me. I can't play with you." I say, "Don't you never doubt yourself. You don't know what you can do until you try. That's all I want you to do. Just make them notes on your harp, while I get my guitar with your harp." So he did it.

I said, "Now you just follow me. As I start it you keep time with me. And he started. And every time I get ready to make a change I say, "Get down!" And he get down on the whinin' part of that harp, just like them little strings goin' over that bottleneck. And I get' ready to get it, I tell him, "Get up! " And he get up. And I say, "Hold it right there man," and he started playing then.

Donna Green—she was a schoolteacher—she asked me to stay over and play at her school. So I did. So that night I had Paul with me. I asked her, I said, "Donna, can Paul play with me tonight?" She said, "No, he ain't good enough." I said, "Yeah, allow him a chance." She said okay. So the guy introduced us and boy, we wore it out. And the next thing I heard from Paul he was making records. And I haven't saw him since. Everywhere I've been he just has left that week before I got down there.

This here bar, this slide part, my uncle, I was a little old boy then, I would sit in the corner. They used to come to our house on a Saturday night. At that time people used to order whiskey from Kentucky and all like that. But my uncle, he ordered it, the whiskey, and the crowd would gather on Saturday night. Well, Elijah Shields and Gene Shields, them was brothers. Well, one would play lead and the other would play second. He had a beef bone, you know a bone cut out of a steak, and he had that bone smooth as I got this ring. And he played it all the time on his little finger. Boy I'm telling you I thought that was the prettiest sound I ever heard in my whole life. I said, if I ever get grown and learn how to play guitar, I'm gonna get me one of them bones.

But I didn't start with no bone. I started with a pocket knife. It's so hard playing with a pocket knife. You gotta play with the guitar laying flat across your lap. Cause I was playing with it in between my fingers like that. Well you see you can't make a chord with the other fingers. And so I studied, I tried a bottle after I learned, and I been headed up ever since. ❧

KEVIN ARROW

Recent Drawings

"I have three main modes of practice: painting, drawing, and archiving 35mm slides and obsolete media. Visual art and music have always been intertwined throughout my work.

"The drawings are me 'marking time' and archiving my experience, or 'Anarchiving' my world. I'm way too lazy and sloppy to actually draw or even copy my subject. Ninety-nine percent of it is traced, but this is not even interesting. In the manner of a collagist, I prefer not to cut up my source, but to preserve it.

"Pop Art is a term that is pretty meaningless for me, unless I'm discussing Andy Warhol or Roy Lichtenstein. I am more a student of everything in the tradition of Harry Everett Smith. I am attempting to illustrate the connections between seemingly disparate experiences through my drawings, paintings, and 35mm slide presentations. I am currently moving forward on a Miami Beach Art in Public Places project, creating a 200-square-foot glass mosaic commemorating the arrival of the Beatles in Miami Beach in 1964.

"The need for me to categorize and archive ideas and objects and my desire to create art work utilizing found, manipulated, obsolete, and recontextualized media stems from my interest in understanding, demonstrating, and experiencing the laws of impermanence, and the intrinsic emptiness of experience.

"Jim Shaw's thrift-store paintings and the Destroy All Monsters collective paintings documenting Detroit have been inspirational. I recently saw them in person; this was a mind expanding experience, seeing Sun Ra, Milky the Clown, and the Stooges in a single painting!

"A work session will often begin with some strong Cuban coffee and a trip to some Miami thrift shops. I'll buy some records and old magazines, and retreat to my studio/garage. Surrounded by stacks of LPs, *Life*, *Playboy*, and *Wee Wisdom* magazines, I place a record on the turntable and begin the act of free association. Like Rashied Ali, I further the composition, with my pens like drumsticks."

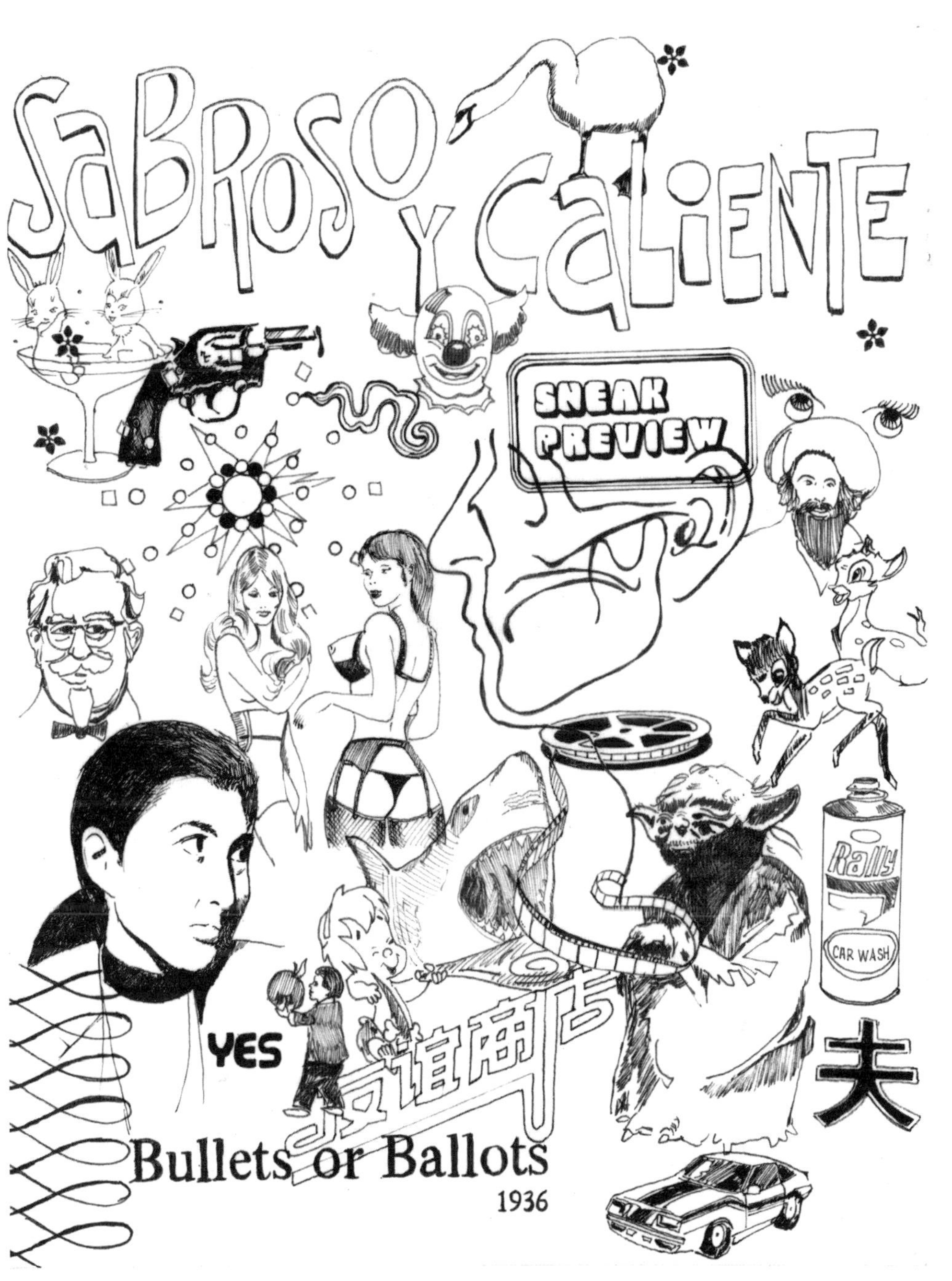

SaBRoSO y CALiENTE
SNEAK PREVIEW
Rally
CAR WASH
YES
夫
Bullets or Ballots
1936

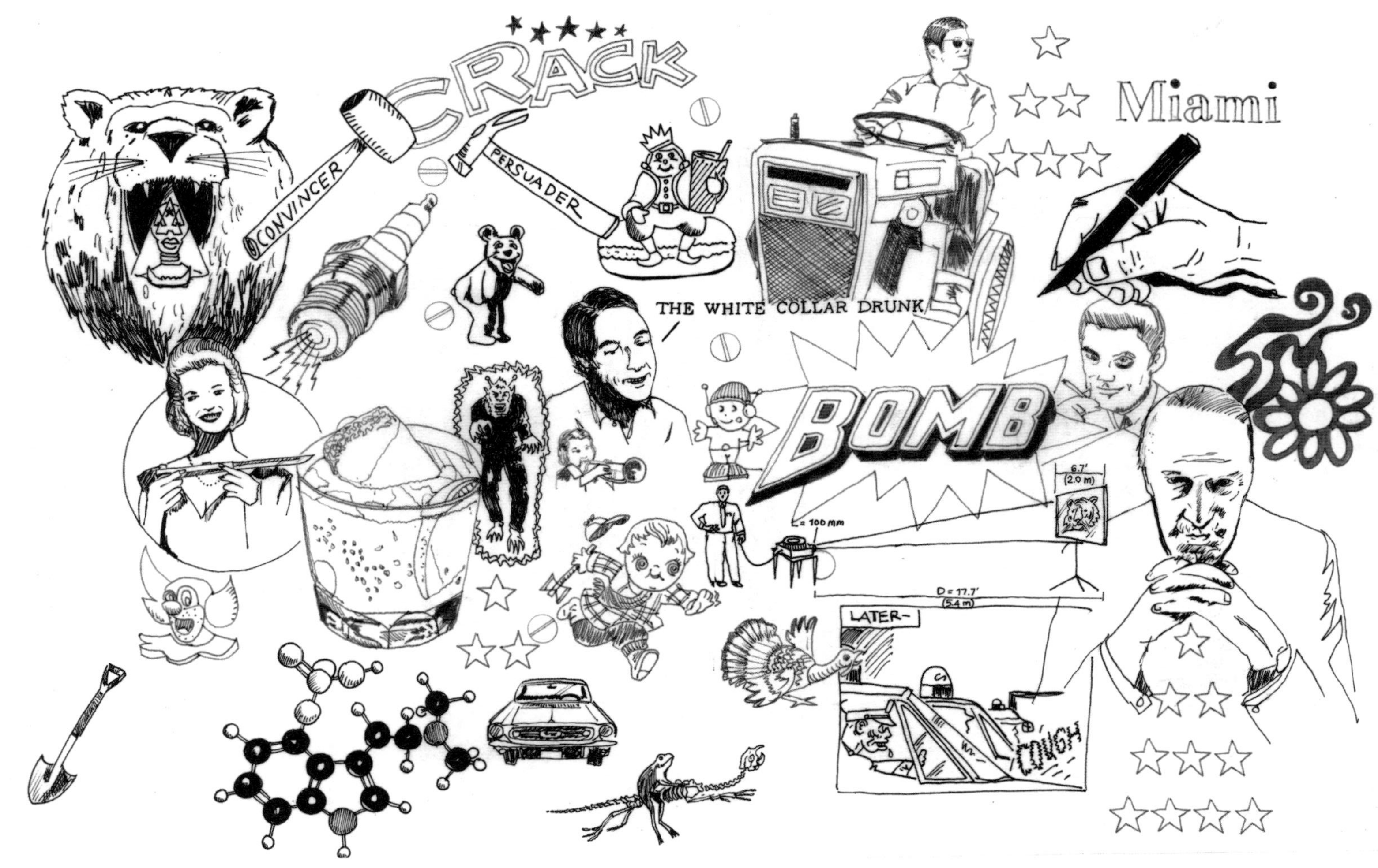

CRACK
CONVINCER
PERSUADER
THE WHITE COLLAR DRUNK
BOMB
Miami
L = 100 mm
6.7"
(2.0 m)
D = 17.7'
(5.4 m)
LATER-
COUGH

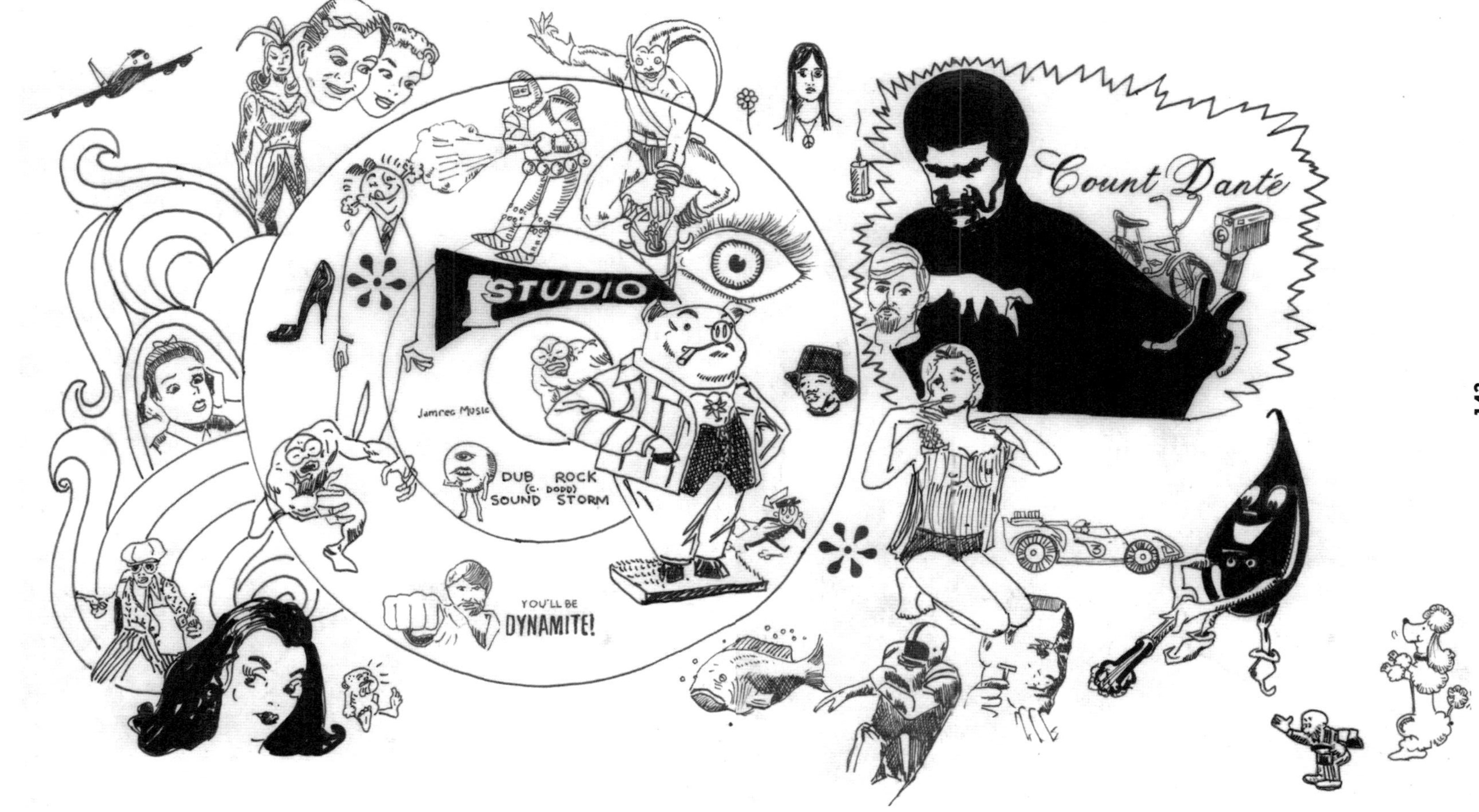
STUDIO
Count Danté
Jamrec Music
DUB ROCK
(C. DODD)
SOUND STORM
YOU'LL BE
DYNAMITE!

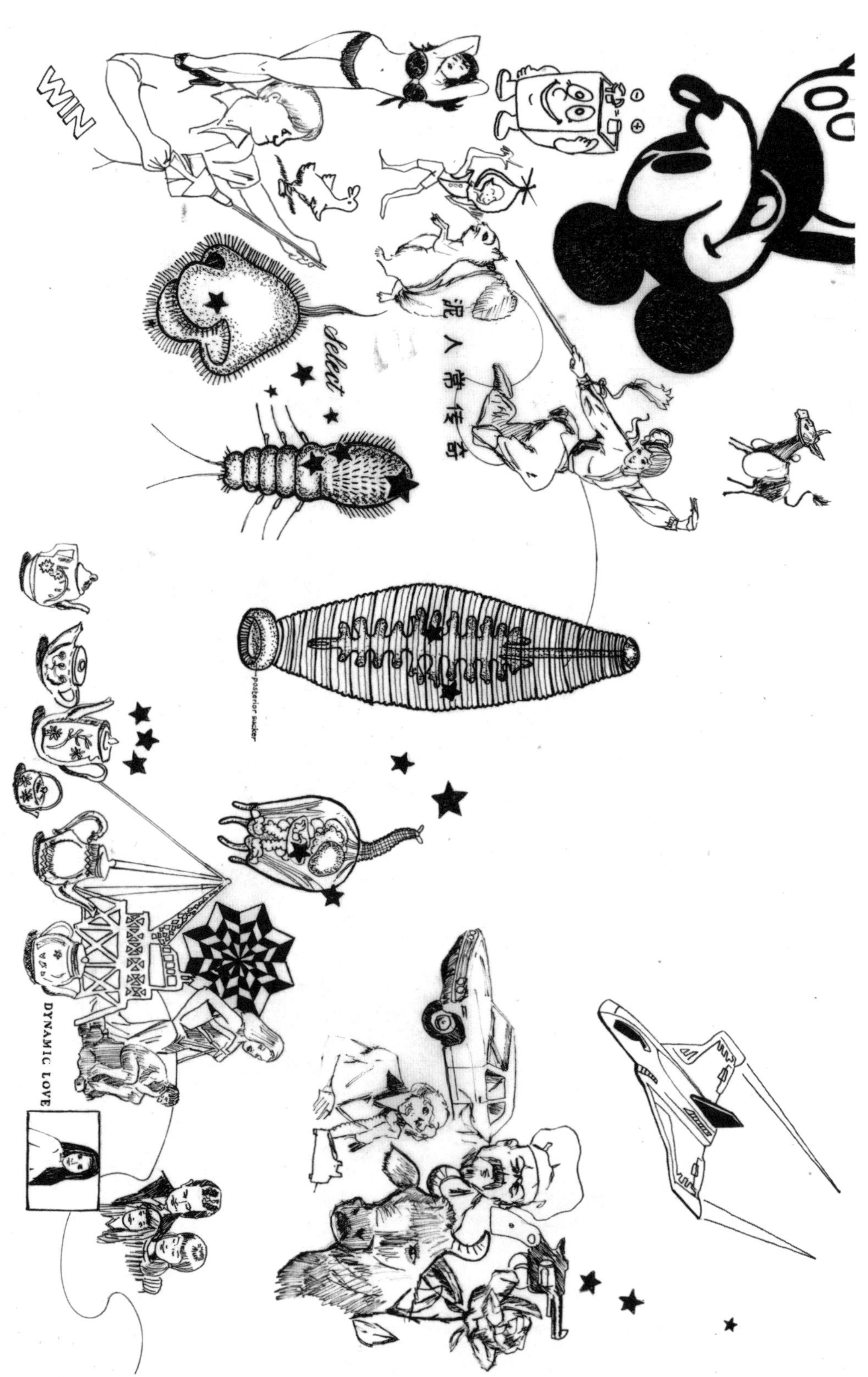
WIN
select
泥人常传奇
posterior sucker
DYNAMIC LOVE
YOO

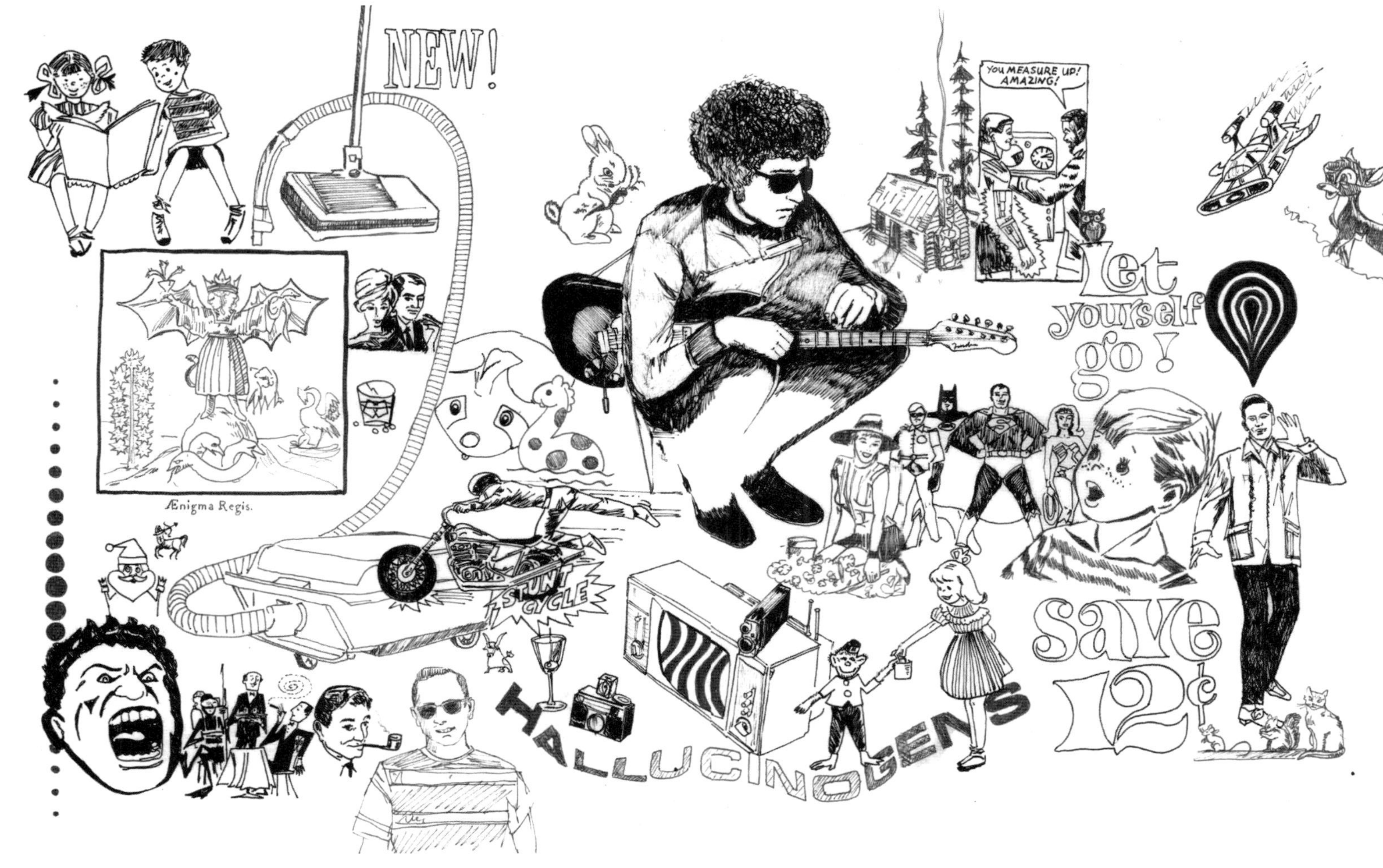

NEW!
YOU MEASURE UP! AMAZING!
Ænigma Regis.
let yourself go!
STUNT CYCLE
HALLUCINOGENS
SAVE 12¢

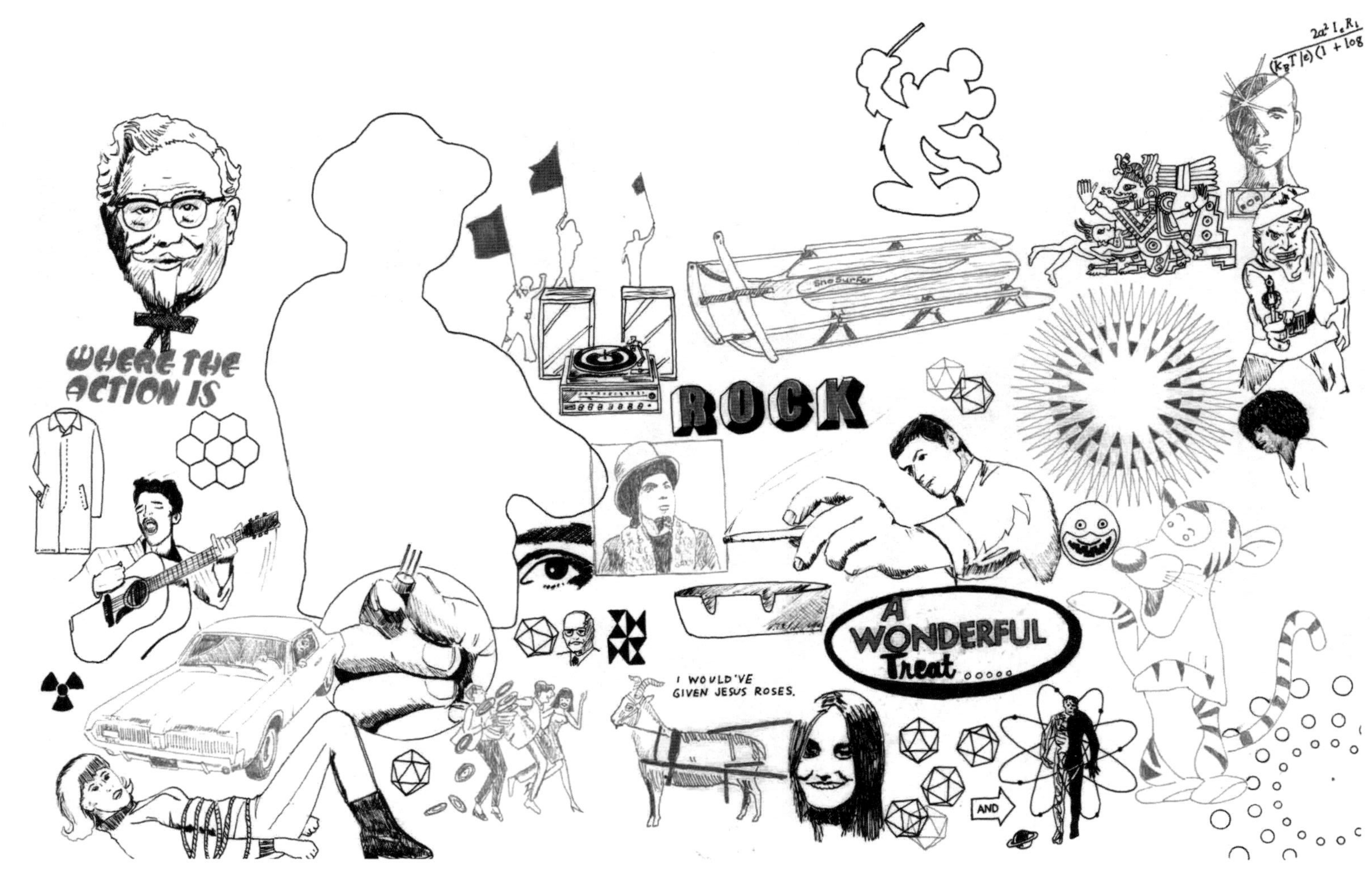

WHERE THE ACTION IS
Sno Surfer
ROCK
I WOULD'VE GIVEN JESUS ROSES.
A WONDERFUL Treat
AND
$\dfrac{2a^2 I_e R_1}{(k_B T|e)(1 + \log}$

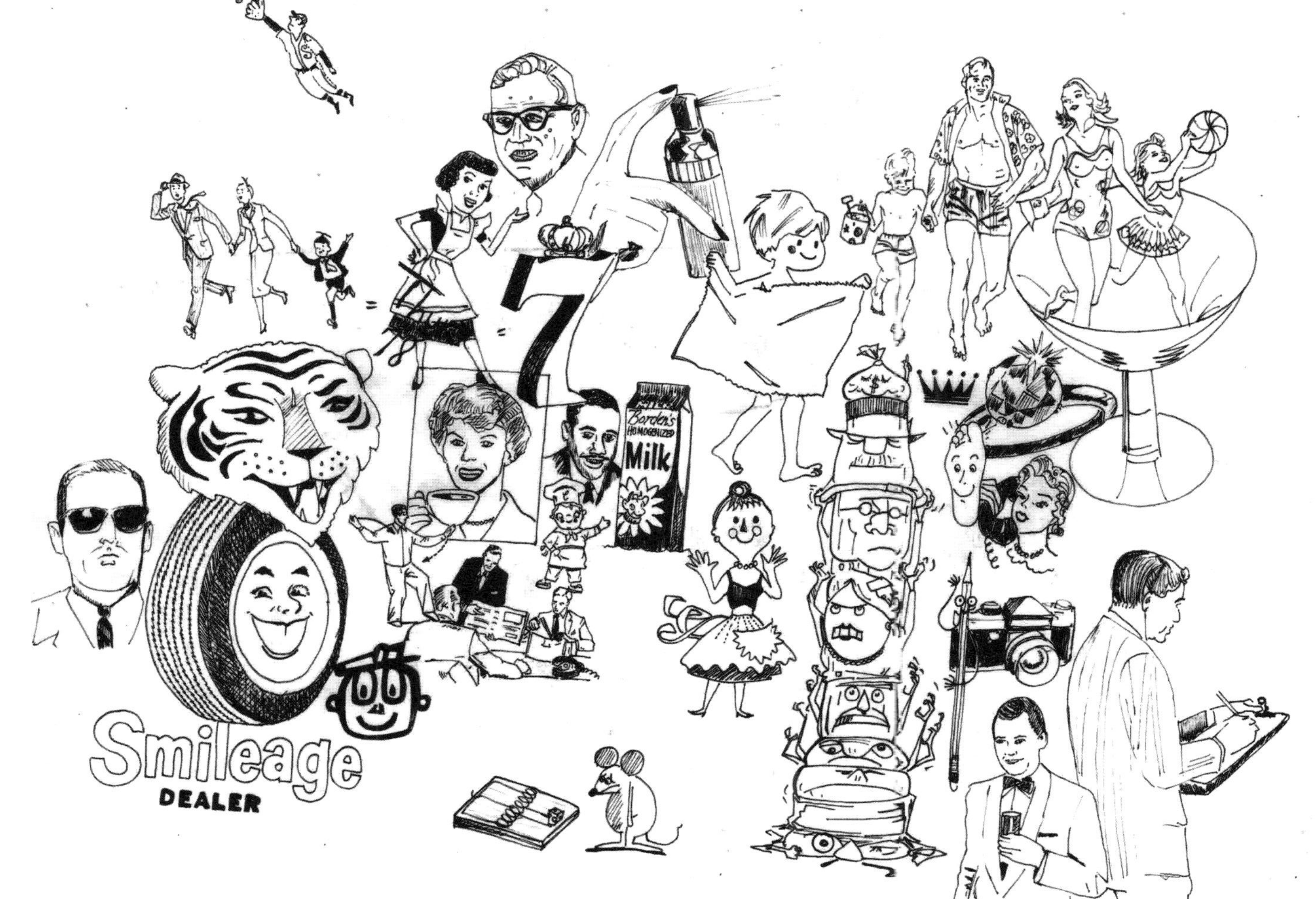

Smileage
DEALER
Borden's
HOMOGENIZED
Milk

DID YOU EVER PLAY WITH SUPERSOAKERS?

by BloodNinja

ILLUSTRATION BY ATHIER MOUSAWI

I. F. : You ready yet? Im bearing to go!

SexyKarla17 : Yhea im slipping out of my clothes right now, what do you look like?

I. F. : a Kodiac bear

SexyKarla17 : ?

I. F. : Im soft naked, fuzzy and waiting for you to come mount me

SexyKarla17 : Oh I love cute fuzzy bears, I walk up and get on top of you stroking your soft hair, kissing you gently as my move my :way down your stomach

I. F. : I growl to warm you my cubs are near

SexyKarla17 : huh?

I. F. : Bears get fuckin pumped when anyone is near their cubs

Sexykarla17: yhea hehe dont be silly. .

SexyKarla17 : I love how you growl as I continue to kiss you, while taking off your pants.

I. F. : Bears dont wear pants and you should cover yourself in Honey now

SexyKarla17 : hehe you would love to lick that off me huh. I pour honey all over my warm wet body waiting for you to start licking :it off me slowly

I. F. : I sniff the air to see where the sweet scent of the honey is

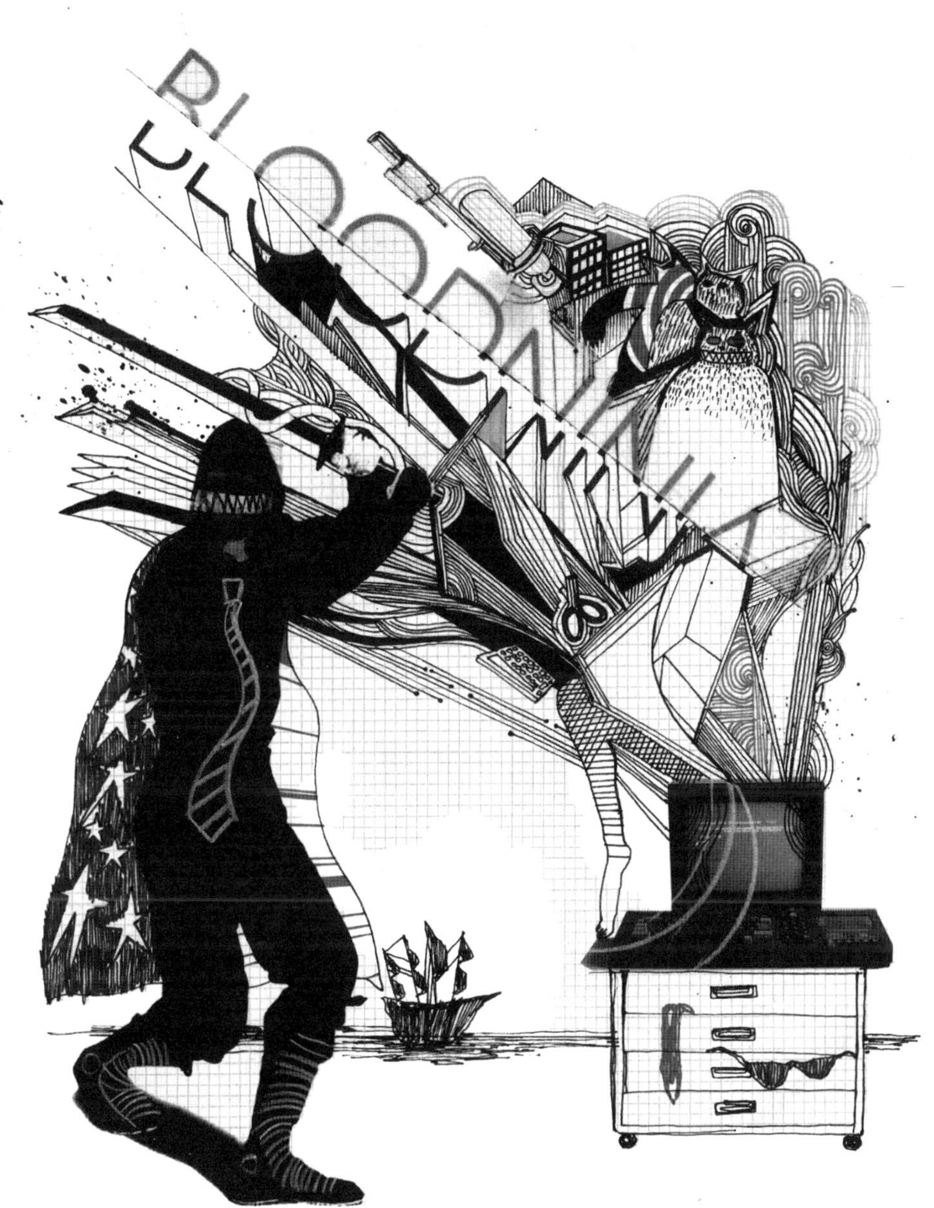

coming from, while slowly snorting and walking towards you
I. F. : I Growl again, and start to bite you
SexyKarla17 : Yhea that feels good. . ooooo. . . not too hard now
I. F. : I bite harder peeling flesh from your stomach, and look
up into your eyes to show you my mouth dripping with your
warm blood :mixed with honey, I then I let my cubs rip apart
your limbs and play with you like a ragdoll.
SexyKarla17 : what the fuck?
I. F. :uuuuuuuuuuuuuhhhhhhhhh and im spent.

▲▲▲▲▲▲▲▲

Wellhung : Hello, Sweetheart . What do you look like?
Sweetheart : I am wearing a red silk blouse, a miniskirt and
high heels. I work out every day, I'm toned and perfect. My
measurements are 36-24-36. What do you look like?
Wellhung : I'm 6'3" and about 280 pounds. I wear glasses and I
have on a pair of blue sweat pants I just bought from Walmart.
I'm also :wearing a T-shirt with a few spots of barbecue sauce
on it from dinner. . . it smells funny.
Sweetheart : I want you. Would you like to screw me?
Wellhung : OK
Sweetheart : We're in my bedroom. There's soft music playing
on the stereo and candles on my dresser and night table. I'm
looking up :into your eyes, smiling. My hand works its way
down to your crotch and begins to fondle your huge, swelling
bulge.
Wellhung : I'm gulping, I'm beginning to sweat.
Sweetheart : I'm pulling up your shirt and kissing your chest.
Wellhung : Now I'm unbuttoning your blouse. My hands are
trembling.
Sweetheart : I'm moaning softly.
Wellhung : I'm taking hold of your blouse and sliding it off
slowly.
Sweetheart : I'm throwing my head back in pleasure. The cool
silk slides off my warm skin. I'm rubbing your bulge faster,
pulling and :rubbing.
Wellhung : My hand suddenly jerks spastically and accidentally
rips a hole in your blouse. I'm sorry.
Sweetheart : That's OK, it wasn't really too expensive.
Wellhung : I'll pay for it.

Sweetheart : Don't worry about it. I'm wearing a lacy black bra. My soft breasts are rising and falling, as I breath harder and : harder.

Wellhung : I'm fumbling with the clasp on your bra. I think it's stuck. Do you have any scissors?

Sweetheart : I take your hand and kiss it softly. I'm reaching back undoing the clasp. The bra slides off my body. The air caresses :my breasts. My nipples are erect for you.

Wellhung : How did you do that? I'm picking up the bra and inspecting the clasp.

Sweetheart : I'm arching my back. Oh baby. I just want to feel your tongue all over me.

Wellhung : I'm dropping the bra. Now I'm licking your, you know, breasts. They're neat!

Sweetheart : I'm running my fingers through your hair. Now I'm nibbling your ear.

Wellhung : I suddenly sneeze. Your breasts are covered with spit and phlegm.

Sweetheart : What?

Wellhung : I'm so sorry. Really.

Sweetheart : I'm wiping your phlegm off my breasts with the remains of my blouse.

Wellhung : I'm taking the sopping wet blouse from you. I drop it with a plop.

Sweetheart : OK. I'm pulling your sweat pants down and rubbing your hard tool.

Wellhung : I'm screaming like a woman. Your hands are cold! Yeeee!

Sweetheart : I'm pulling up my miniskirt. Take off my panties.

Wellhung : I'm pulling off your panties. My tongue is going all over, in and out nibbling on you... umm... wait a minute.

Sweetheart : What's the matter?

Wellhung : I've got a pubic hair caught in my throat. I'm choking.

Sweetheart : Are you OK?

Wellhung : I'm having a coughing fit. I'm turning all red.

Sweetheart : Can I help?

Wellhung : I'm running to the kitchen, choking wildly. I'm fumbling through the cabinets, looking for a cup. Where do you keep your :cups?

Sweetheart : In the cabinet to the right of the sink.

Wellhung : I'm drinking a cup of water. There, that's better.

Sweetheart : Come back to me, lover.

Wellhung : I'm washing the cup now.

Sweetheart : I'm on the bed arching for you.

Wellhung : I'm drying the cup. Now I'm putting it back in the cabinet. And now I'm walking back to the bedroom. Wait, it's dark, I'm :lost. Where's the bedroom?

Sweetheart : Last door on the left at the end of the hall.

Wellhung : I found it.

Sweetheart : I'm tuggin' off your pants. I'm moaning. I want you so badly.

Wellhung : Me too.

Sweetheart : Your pants are off. I kiss you passionately-our naked bodies pressing each other.

Wellhung : Your face is pushing my glasses into my face. It hurts.

Sweetheart Why don't you take off your glasses?

Wellhung : OK, but I can't see very well without them. I place the glasses on the night table.

Sweetheart : I'm bending over the bed. Give it to me, baby!

Wellhung : I have to pee. I'm fumbling my way blindly across the room and toward the bathroom.

Sweetheart : Hurry back, lover.

Wellhung : I find the bathroom and it's dark. I'm feeling around for the toilet. I lift the lid.

Sweetheart : I'm waiting eagerly for your return.

Wellhung : I'm done going. I'm feeling around for the flush handle, but I can't find it. Uh-oh!

Sweetheart : What's the matter now?

Wellhung : I've realized that I've peed into your laundry hamper. Sorry again. I'm walking back to the bedroom now, blindly feeling :my way.

Sweetheart : Mmm, yes. Come on.

Wellhung : OK, now I'm going to put my. . . you know . . . thing. . . in your. . . you know. . . woman's thing.

Sweetheart : Yes! Do it, baby! Do it!

Wellhung : I'm touching your smooth butt. It feels so nice. I kiss your neck. Umm, I'm having a little trouble here.

Sweetheart : I'm moving my ass back and forth, moaning. I can't stand it another second! Slide in! Screw me now!

Wellhung : I'm flaccid.

Sweetheart : What?

Wellhung : I'm limp. I can't sustain an erection.

Sweetheart : I'm standing up and turning around; an incredulous look on my face.

Wellhung : I'm shrugging with a sad look on my face, my weiner all floppy. I'm going to get my glasses and see what's wrong.

Sweetheart : No, never mind. I'm getting dressed. I'm putting on my underwear. Now I'm putting on my wet nasty blouse.

Wellhung : No wait! Now I'm squinting, trying to find the night table. I'm feeling along the dresser, knocking over cans of hair : spray, picture frames and your candles.

Sweetheart : I'm buttoning my blouse. Now I'm putting on my shoes.

Wellhung : I've found my glasses. I'm putting them on. My God! One of our candles fell on the curtain. The curtain is on fire! I'm :pointing at it, a shocked look on my face.

Sweetheart : Go to hell. I'm logging off, you loser!

▲▲▲▲▲▲▲▲

wI. F. : My shit is hard you ready to jump aboard?

1hOttYeVe : oh yhea im so wet right now

I. F. : Why you just shower?

1hOttYeVe : no im wet for you

I. F. : Did you ever play with supersoakers when you were a kid? or that gator shit you would dive and slide down, there was that :badass pool at the end of it.

1hOttYeVe : What the fuck are you talking about? You wanna cyber or not?

I. F. : I do! Sorry. . . I just didnt know why you were wet. . . then you say your wet for me, and im thinking I didnt even throw water on :you. . .

I. F. : Im sorry lets continue!

1hOttYeVe : alright then. . . I walk over to you and start kissing your neck and chest

I. F. : I pop like 16 boners

1hOttYeVe : what the fuck!

I. F. : what?

SOUTHPAW IN A MUSLIM WORLD

Travels through Mauritania and Western Sahara

by Hisham Mayet

INTRODUCTION BY MIKE McGONIGAL
ILLUSTRATION BY PEDRO LORENCO
PHOTOGRAPHS BY HISHAM MAYET
WRITTEN WITH ASSISTANCE FROM CHARLES GOCHER

The street performers all push their instruments—traditional or otherwise—into satisfying distortion for maximum crowd enjoyment. People clap, sing, and dance, and it's hard to differentiate between the audience and the performers. A DJ spins incredibly beat-up singles on the street, tweaking the pitch as it plays to make the notes more bent. It looks like a ton of work getting the grime out of records in the desert.

This is Marrakech's massive central square and Hisham Mayet is there with his camera—working on what would eventually become the Sublime Frequencies DVD release *Jemaa El Fna: Morocco's Rendezvous of the Dead*. The shooting style's what you might call "nontraditional"; he's editing as he's filming, right in his digital video camera. Sometimes Hisham focuses on strikingly beautiful people in the audience and then veers back to the performers, themselves concentrating instead on a group of young kids playing on the fringes of the scene.

"DIY ethnography, punk rock ethnomusicology, subjective anthropology, ecstatic diplomacy." That's how Seattle-based co-founder Mayet describes the music and film label Sublime Frequencies, whose motto is "music thought not to exist is *everywhere.*" It's apt: Mayet—a handsome, whip-smart, 38-year-old racon-

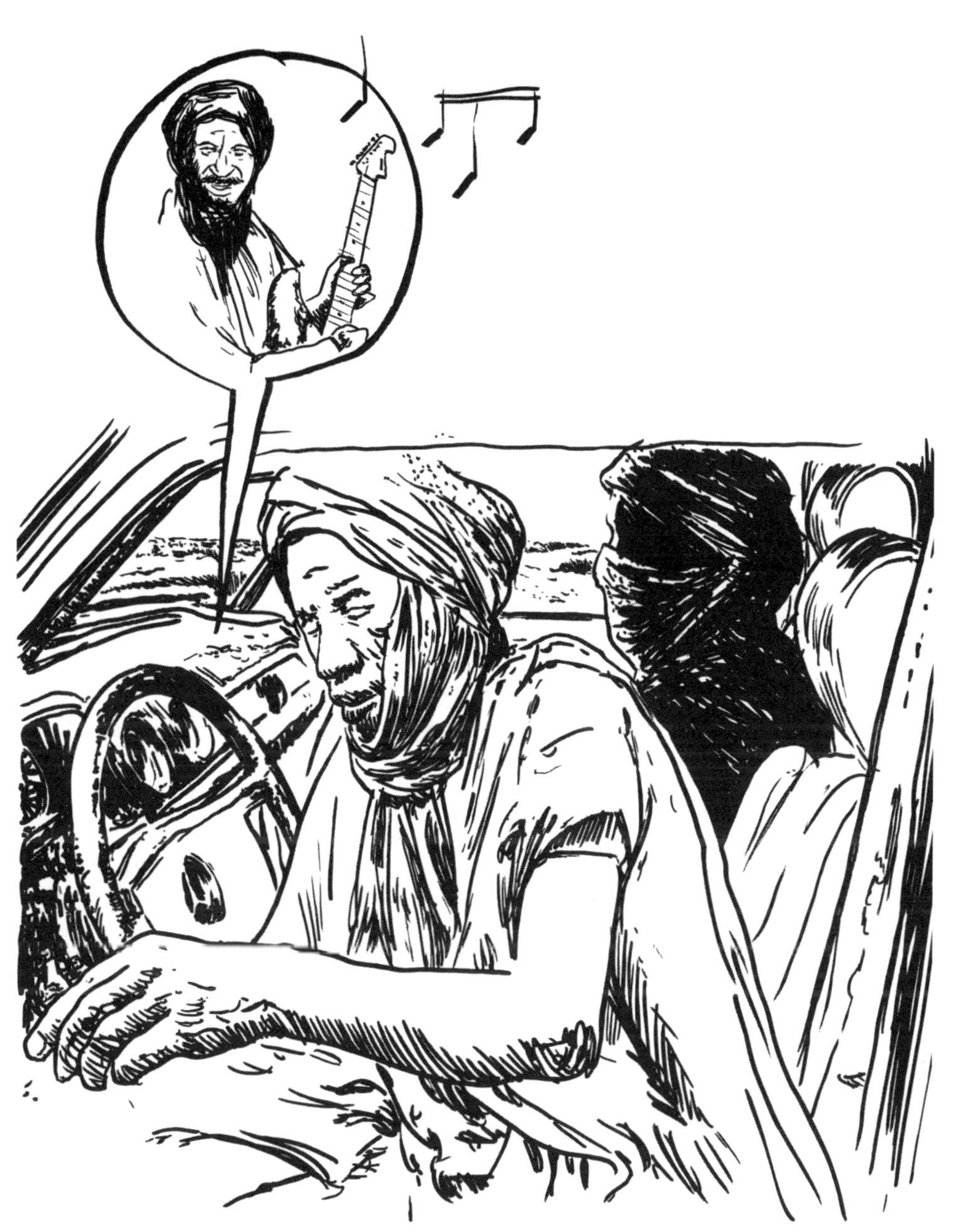

teur—has traveled extensively throughout the Middle East and North Africa, collecting sound and video along the way. He's just spent a month in "Niger to continue my documentation of West African trance possession ceremonies," he says. He recorded "some amazing shit while there. "I wish I could have stayed another month; it really just takes so much time to get rolling there." He also plans to continue his exploration of the Tuareg, a nomadic, matriarchal North African desert people whose music and dance is a strange hybrid of Arab and African styles.

Sublime Frequencies' impressive catalog of the last four years—six DVDs, two LPs, and 33 compact discs—is radically time/space-defying. These releases seem to come from a land where Sun Ra and the *Ethiopiques* series of psychedelic '70s funk are purely for the cocktail hour. "We are covering areas where most ethnomusicologists don't go—many of them are not interested in pop or folk hybrid music," Alan Bishop—the label's other cofounder and bassist for the recently disbanded Sun City Girls—explains, surrounded by his cavernous rehearsal space.

Mayet and Bishop used to get together with Richard Bishop and Charles Gocher of the Sun City Girls to watch and listen to recordings they'd made on world travels. When showings of the material at a Seattle dive bar called the Rendezvous met with great enthusiasm, they decided to start the label. "The label is owned and run by myself and Alan Bishop—we are the day to day operations," Mayet says via e-mail. He quickly adds that, "Mark Gergis, Robert Millis, Richard Bishop, Tucker Martine, Laurent Jeanneau, FM3 from Beijing, Carlos Casas in Spain, and Albano Costillares in Argentina have all contributed releases on the label," not wanting to imply that he and Bishop do everything.

These releases—consisting of (among other things) field recordings from Bali, North Vietnam, and Southern Laos; forbidden "gang funk" from Brazilian slums; radio collages made in Jerusalem and Algeria; interviews with people on the street in Syria; Javanese and Moroccan pop music; and Marrakech street performers—have a gloriously in-your-face approach to what's typically been the realm of academics. Bishop refers to phenomenologist Charles Fort's coinage "extrageography" to describe the Sublime Frequencies modus operandi. "[It's] a term Fort used to describe phenomenon outside of the accepted dimensions and perceptions of science and the common man," he says.

"I use it as a generic place name to describe cultural areas—which have vibrant folklore and music—that are beyond the will of most to entertain as `valid' points of reference to study or merely want to learn about. For example, Niger, Benin, Oman, and Nagaland are extrageography because most people don't know anything about them, yet I could argue that people in those four areas of the world are as valid and perhaps superior to others when it comes to creating music of expressive beauty."

The CDs often have only the tiniest bits of information; the *Radio Series*—literally collages of recordings made from radio broadcasts—do not list the performers or tracks. (You can hear outtakes from their *Radio Sumatra* disc on the CD that accompanies this issue.) The DVDs contain no narration at all, and often include but a smattering of background information. The label leaves it to the consumer to figure stuff out.

"A narrator is a distraction," Bishop says. "There is always an agenda, which `guides' the viewer. The best parts of all ethnographic film—*Herdsmen of the Sun* by Werner Herzog and *Divine Horsemen* by Maya Deren being two of the best— are the moments without narration. I'm not an idiot. I can figure out what's going on most of the time. Many other people are not idiots. They can make up their own mind about how to interpret non-narrated film. Why not completely superimpose yourself into [another] world without some schmuck—even if it's some well-intentioned schmuck—telling you what's going on?"

"This music and its players exist outside the marketability machine, so it's being played [and] presented unadulterated," Mayet says. "It's not necessarily technique that we're after, but rather honesty, passion, and unblinkingly raw interpretations of traditional forms. These performances or celebrations do not exist for the camera. A lot of the footage recorded transpired in a completely serendipitous manner."

Before he passed away early last year, Gocher told me that he felt "the whole Sublime Frequencies thing is allowing people to travel to where the music is without having to physically locate there." "Now, when we travel, we know that we're on the job, trying to get the best and most unusual footage we can in order to release more DVD projects," Richard Bishop adds. "We will most likely continue to use the `no-narration' approach, which is in direct line with our film philosophy—no spin, no agenda, just pure sound and vision—to be interpreted and further researched by those who choose to."

There are those—from wonky message boards I Hate Music and I Love Music to the *International Herald Tribune*—who question Sublime Frequencies' method of unadorned/often unexplained presentation, arguing that it amounts to further marginalization and exoticization of other cultures rather than a true attempt at understanding. Then there's the question of how well the original performers should be compensated or whether it's possible even to *find* half the musicians on these labels. The Drag City-backed and Baltimore-based Yalla Yalla label has also been called to question on these fronts ("Who Is the World?" Best of Baltimore, Sept. 19), what Jess Harvell termed "claims of chauvinistic bootlegging" on Gawker Media's music blog *Idolator*. Such critics should "fight a much larger and nobler battle," Mayet says. "Their time would be much better spent focusing on issues that are affecting all of us in much more sinister ways."

The political import in releases of contemporary music from the Middle East is clear. Brian Turner, WFMU-FM program director, praises SF titles such as *I Remember Syria, Radio Palestine* and *Choubi! Folk and Pop Songs from Iraq* as "timely in their importance" in an e-mail. "It's disappointing to see how the general music world is so immersed in its own problems—complaining about who's getting paid—rather than addressing the mortifying state of world affairs and releasing music to address it. The Sublime Frequencies series casts an amazing light on the cultures of other nations, including those that Bush considers `evil.' This stuff is just so important."

Mayet's films are consistently the best in the SF canon. "I really wouldn't know what else to do if I wasn't doing this right now," he says. "It nourishes me on a daily basis—I love a challenge and doing this is the ultimate test of will and execution." We're super pleased to present Mr. Mayet's 2006 travel diary.

I HAD JUST FINISHED A TEN-DAY RECORDING SESSION IN DAKHLA, Western Sahara—a fishing town of some 60,000 people on the west coast of Africa, more than a thousand miles south of Casablanca—a location as remote as any I have ever visited. I had been on an expedition looking for a musician called Doueh. My only clue was a cassette of music recorded off of shortwave radio which I'd brought along from a previous excursion north of here, in southern Morocco. I'd found Doueh and recorded his group, as I explain more fully in the liner notes to the Sublime Frequencies release, *Group Doueh: Guitar Music From The Western Sahara.* Group Doueh plays raw and unfiltered Sahrawi music from the former colonial Spanish outpost of the Western Sahara. Doueh (pronounced "Doo-way") is a terrific electric guitarist, and the group's sound is loud, distorted, and unhinged. Sahrawi songs derive from the sung poetry of the Hassaniya language. The music is based on the same modal structure as Mauritanian music, though Doueh's style is a looser appropriation, infused with Western guitar scope—it relies, he says, as much on Hendrix as on traditional Sahrawi music.

My next mission was to get to Mauritania: south along the Atlantic coast. Doueh had called an old mentor of his in the Mauritanian capital, Nouakchott, Sadoum Ouled Aida. I wanted to record more examples of Sahrawi music and Sadoum was one of the legendary musicians of the area.

There are no trains or buses along this route, so it took me three days to set up a ride from Dakhla to the border town of Nouadhibou. It's about 300 miles along a single-lane paved road, and can only be done by hitching a ride or getting one of the locals to take you there (for a large sum). From there, I was told, there is no road across the 250-mile wide expanse of desert that lies between Nouadhibou and Nouakchott. I'd either have to fly down to the capital, or do a 30-hour drive along the coast, driving along the beach. I figured I would deal with that once I got to Nouadhibou. By the third day, a ride had been secured. I was to travel with Mohammed, a friend of Doueh's who traveled this route often, because his family lived across the border.

I was told we'd be leaving at 10 a.m., so around 9:30 I gather my bags and wait at Doueh's house for my ride to show up. Eleven hours later, there's still no sign of my ride; I'm getting bleary-eyed watching the African Cup when Mohammed and Doueh come in and tell me it's time to get going. It's a small cargo truck, with a two man cabin. It's loaded to the gills with mattresses, blankets, cloth, plastic buckets, shoes, radios, and a clutch of mystery items buried amidst the cargo. On top of all that merchandise are open cases of eggs

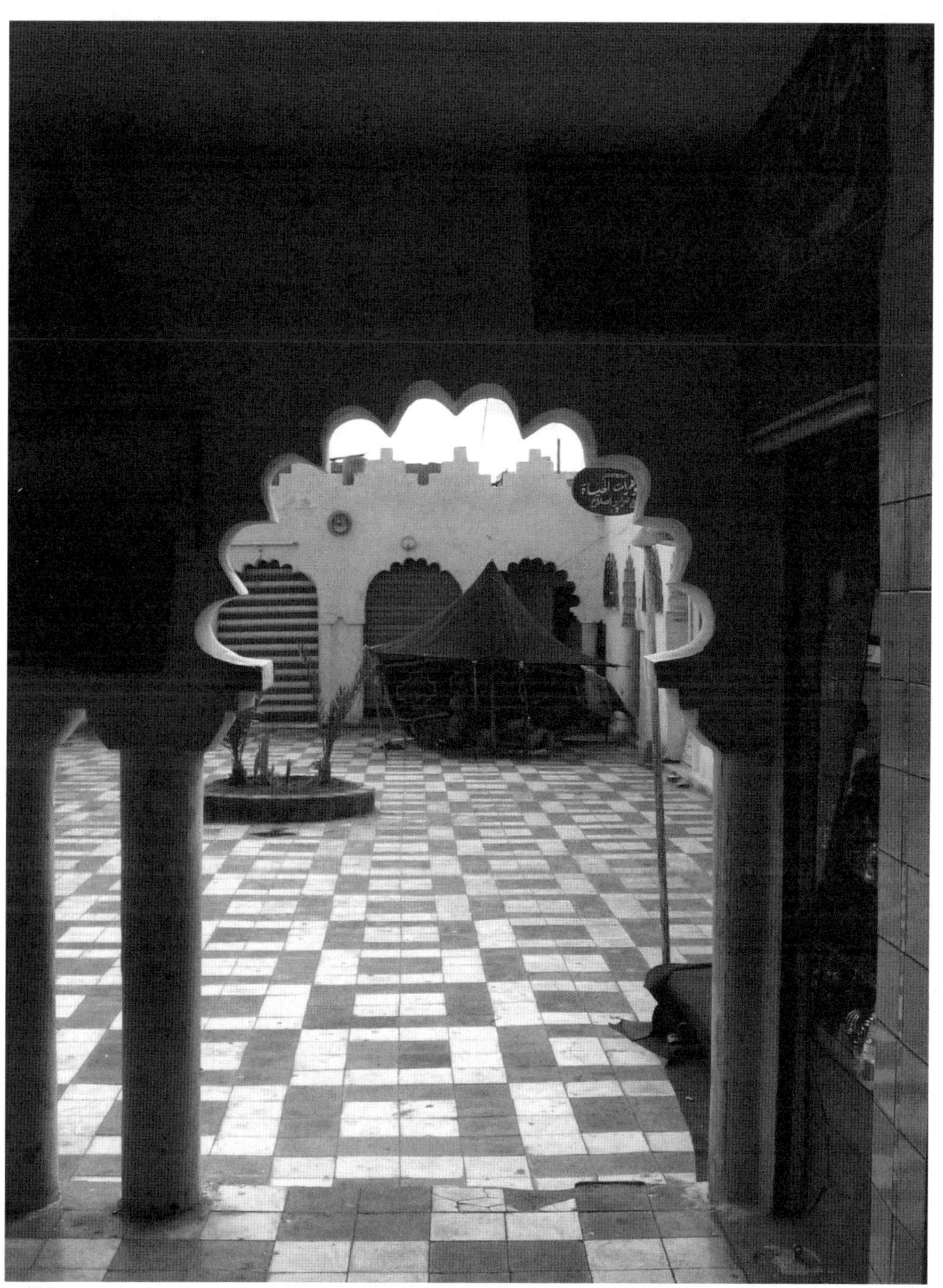

Dakhla

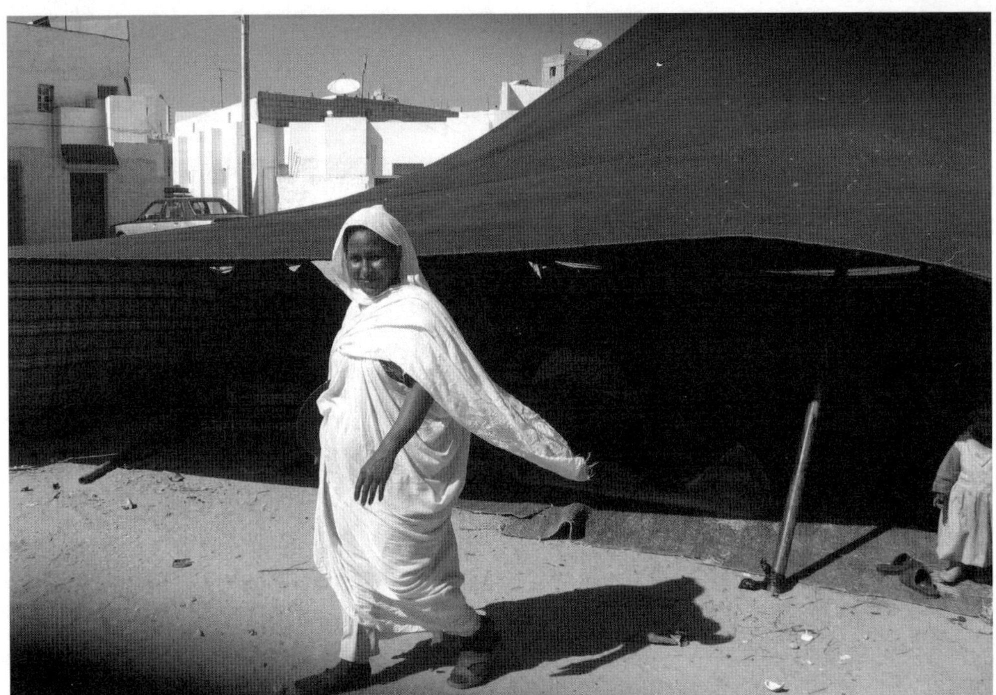

Dakhla

covering everything! The roof is also loaded with everyone's gear: an extra five feet of cargo expertly stacked and roped, making the truck a vertical tower on wheels. Three of us get into the cabin and the rest get in the back with all the goods, pushing the cases of eggs to one side, then off we go. This is the exciting part of any trip, the thrill of the complete unknown—a place you've never been, with people you've never met, and miles of nothing in between you and a destination as remote as any you could ever imagine.

WE DRIVE UNDER A FULL MOON THOUGH A BLEAK LANDSCAPE with traditional Hassaniya music blaring from the shredded speakers right behind my ears. It's a cool, 45-degree, dry desert night. Ten minutes into the drive, we stop by the side of the road. An old man wearing the traditional Sahrawi blue dra'as walks up, literally appearing out of thin air. Mohammed gets out of the cabin and the old man now sits between me and the driver. His face is an ancient face, one that has seen many desert days and nights— jagged and pockmarked with a big cyst the size of golf ball protruding from his cheek. With three stowaways in the back piled on top of all the goods, we're off again— the old Sahrawi man sitting almost on top of me with the raspiest cough, hacking his brains out every few minutes. Glorious!

It's surreal, crossing this pocked landscape under a full moon—there is truly nothing around us, as this is the most barren stretch of the trip. The driver is a pro, able to see through this blurred horizon at night on an unpaved road through the desert. After driving for three hours, we come to a stop at a depot called Damcar, 150 miles from the Mauritanian border, to rest for the night. It's one a.m., and the only place to stay is booked up for the night. So the whole crew has to spend the night with another five travelers in some sort of outhouse in the back, on a cold stone floor. As I look up at the lone fluorescent bulb dangling and buzzing overhead, my jaws chattering like a jack hammer, I realize I need something to lessen the chill. I find the owner sweeping outside and he points to a room where I might find something to keep me warm. In a pile of moldy mattresses I find an old blanket. After shaking off whatever detritus was caked on it, I huddle back among the others. The blanket is an absolute savior. I try to sleep but just sort of float in a dream state, listening to the white noise of the bulb humming overhead. We all awaken around dawn to a really breathtaking view. The desert is beautiful at all times, but at dawn—with its pastel pinks and blues and wispy cirrus clouds—it has a poetry unlike anything else.

We have breakfast: two-day-old bread, honey, and coffee. I get four large plastic bottles of water and we are off to the Mauritanian border where a two-hour wait ensues. Droves of olive drab uniforms are processing everyone like a ballet of Keystone cops. As the sun starts to climb high above, we are engulfed by a swarm of flies hellbent on devouring everything in their path.

Once the Moroccan border crossing officials are done with us, we drive slowly into a sort of nether region: not really Morocco, nor Western Sahara, nor Mauritania, just a patch of unpaved desert about two miles long. A herd of wild camels are grazing amongst the dunes, and it's a stunning sight. When I ask if I can get out and photograph, I'm told to be careful because this border area is dotted with land mines! I shoot video instead, from the safety of the truck cabin.

We come to a meeting place in the middle of this borderless zone, a rogue hangout for all these smugglers and desert bandits. An encampment of rusted out cars and makeshift tents, it's a lawless no man's land. We park and make a pit stop to chew on three-day-old bread (dipped in water so it's palatable) and yogurt amid the auto carcasses. After about an hour, I ask what Mohammed and the driver are waiting for; the sun is burning my face, the flies are merciless, and the pack of wild, mangy dogs are starting to annoy me. I am getting restless, but this delay seems not to bother anyone else. I am told we will be here till sundown because after that the customs agents tend not to check all the trucks coming through. And since we seem to be carrying something that the customs agents would not allow, it is apparently best to wait until then.

I would have been able to deal with all of this in a calmer situation. But these flies are a menacing horde. They cover everything. They get into your mouth, your eyes—any part of exposed flesh at all. The smugglers and bandits had adapted gracefully, but it's different story for me! We all sit around under the makeshift tent for another hour, a tense silence in the air. We pass around glasses of tea so sweet the flies drown in them, me and the other men cautiously looking at each other as if a gunfight in a Sergio Leone film is about to take place.

Fuck this, I think. I gotta get out of here.

I notice other cars coming through and ask our driver if I can get my bags out of the truck. With Mohammed in tow, I find a gentleman who will take us to through the customs on the other side. He's driving a clunky 1980s Mercedes 300E which seems the norm for cars around these parts. He puts in his cassette of lo-fi Hassaniya electric-guitar music, and we're off.

The joy of being in motion again is enough to revitalize everything, though it's a slow drive along the bumpy gravel road. We come to the Mauritanian border; it's nothing more than a clutch of ramshackle huts with brightly colored fabric for doors blowing in the hot, dusty, desert air.

We walk up to customs and I hand over my passport. I look over and see another agent digging into his lunchtime meal. It's a big bowl of couscous with hunks of goat meat that he sucks the marrow from. All the while, a gangly cat jumps into his bowl, more amusing than annoying him. The passport is stamped without incident—unbelievable, probably the easiest part of this trip. I still think I might get to Nouadhibou in time to catch a plane to Nouakchott. The drive down is spectacular: rolling desert dunes that billow like tapestries along the road. We drive by nomadic tents, a sight hundreds maybe thousands of years old, with herds of wild camels motionless in the noonday heat.

WE FINALLY ARRIVE IN NOUADHIBOU, A CITY HARD TO APPROACH from any direction except along the route I was taking. You can get there from the east through a 700-mile-plus stretch of desert via the longest train in the world. It's 26 miles long and carries iron ore—Mauritania's chief natural resource—to the coast. The only other way is to sail into its port from the Atlantic Ocean. It's a town that exists on its own terms, insulated and incredibly poor. The only contact it has with outsiders is via the large fishing fleets that dock outside its harbor, and that contact is limited to the fishermen coming ashore for prostitutes and a warm meal. We arrive late in the afternoon, and I think I am going to the airport.

But we make a pit stop at Mohammed's relatives' house, where we have tea. One has to understand the absolute connection the tea-drinking ceremony has in this part of the world, a continuous ritual that happens throughout the day. It's an integral part of any conversation held between people who are to be together any amount of time. They brew a heady mixture of Chinese green tea with lots of sugar in tiny pots over small fires. They sample it, taste it, smell it, debate its quality. Finally satisfied, they hold the pot two feet above a small shot glass and expertly pour the tea back and forth from pot to glass several times to create a head of foam before they serve the tea — hot, sweet, and strong enough

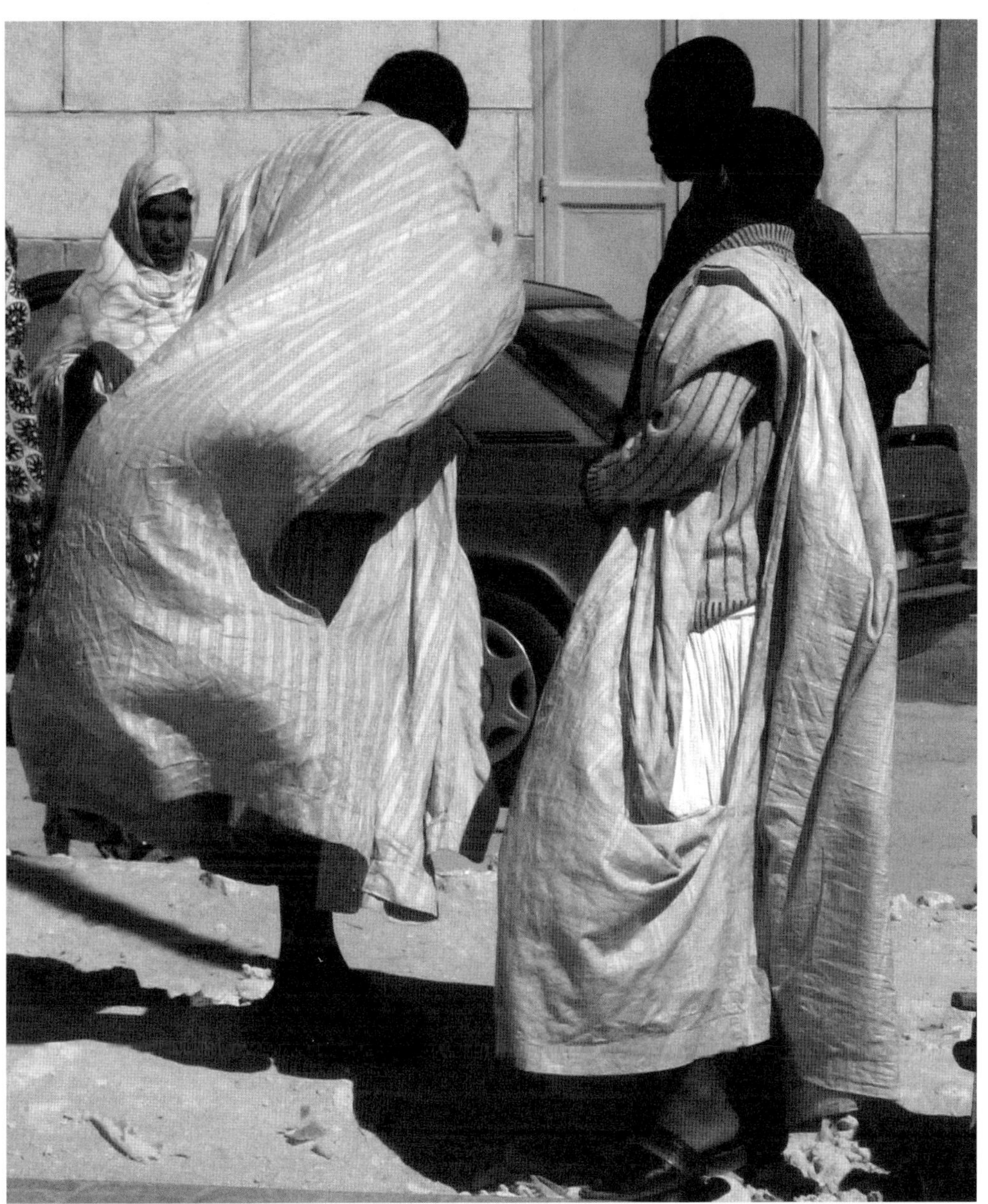

Mohammed in Nouadhibou

to pucker your mouth. When the first pot is drained, the process is repeated using the same tea leaves, adding more sugar. Then it's done a third time. Tea is always brewed thrice. It's a ritual as rigid and formal as a Japanese tea ceremony. It defies any class or social structure; it is omnipresent.

After our meal and some calls around town to decide my fate, I am told there are no flights to Nouakchott until Tuesday. I find out I can hire a taxi and that it's only a five-hour drive and will cost less anyway. My research tells me it's a 30-hour drive along the coast. However, they just finished building a new road a few weeks ago. As I ready to get into a taxi, I realize I've left my travel notes for

Mauritania and small camera bag in the truck cabin back at the border depot. And the bag has a really important tape of incidental footage I cannot afford to lose. FUCK!!!!!!!!!!!

It looks like I'll have to stay in Nouadhibou for the night. Mohammed tells me the truck will show up later this evening. The driver has to drop off the rest of Mohammed's baggage. He will get my notes and tapes, and drop them off at the hotel where I'm staying tonight.

Mauritania is quintessential Sahel country, its very existence is informed by the Sahara desert. A perpetual fog of sand infiltrates everything. And if that subsides, the searing rays of the sun take their toll. This former French colony was carved out for the Sahrawi peoples who have inhabited this area for a thousand years. They are descended from the Yemeni Maqil tribes, part of the first wave of the Islamic conquest throughout the Sahara.

As I settle in, I see Group Doueh—whom I had just stayed with for a ten day stretch in Dakhla—on the state-run TV broadcast. It's a reassuring sight, which confirms my resolve to relax. And the next broadcast is Elvis' *Live in Vegas*, the complete show!

I wake up the next day and the power is out in the city. I need to call Mohammed to set a time to meet. I'm tense, hoping that the notes and tape are coming back to me. I try and make a connection using the lobby manager's cell phone. Fortunately Mohammed knows the hotel I'm at, and arrives shortly—all smiles—with my belongings.

He comes with me to the Nouadhibou taxi depot to make sure I secure a ride to Nouakchott. Once there, it's a snarl of people coming and going in all directions. The hustle is as intense as I have ever seen. Nouadhibou is really intimidating, especially this part of town. The second I set foot out of the car, my bag is grabbed from my hands. It's not being stolen; it's another taxi driver's attempt to get my business. That prompts another taxi driver to declare war. They start to argue about which one is taking me even though I tell both I am not interested. I leave all of this for Mohammed to deal with. As I lurch away, collecting my sanity, the fight escalates into a stabbing.

I have both my bags being dragged through the sandy streets looking for Mohammed who's about 20 yards away, and thinking, "Oh, fuck"! I look back, and a crowd is all over the scene. As I scamper away, Mohammed bellows my name and secures myself and my bags in a storefront. As I try to collect my wits, Mohammed lines up a taxi. All the long-range taxis in this area are late-'80s-to-mid-'90s Mercedes 300Es. We stuff my gear in the trunk. I get the front seat 'cause I'm paying double what everyone else is—everyone else being five Senegalese men and women stuffed into the back seat. Soon we're all finally heading south, down to Nouakchott.

The drive is spectacular, covering some of the most beautiful desert I have ever seen, dunes, camels, and nomads' tents gleaming in the afternoon heat. The ubiquitous electric-guitar-driven Hassaniya cassettes are our soundtrack. After driving for a few hours, we halt in the middle of the desert for a pit-stop. We are being followed by another taxi the whole way. It's best to travel this way when crossing the desert, in case one car breaks down alone out here. We're at a rest area in the middle of nowhere—just a few tents and a shack with supplies. I poke around, filming everything. The lens stumbles on a goat carcass dangling in the sandy wind.

Everyone seems to know which tent they should go to. The Mauritanians (the drivers) are very caste-oriented. They take the better of the tents. After a humble turn at the tent where the Senegalese men and women relax, I am told that my presence is requested with the other men. There we sit with the omnipresent tea and await our meal. It is couscous with squash, potatoes, and goat or camel intestines (I can't tell which). As is customary in the desert, you eat with your hands. As I dig into the communal bowl, little do I realize that this has just come from a boiling cauldron. My fingers are scorched and I bite my

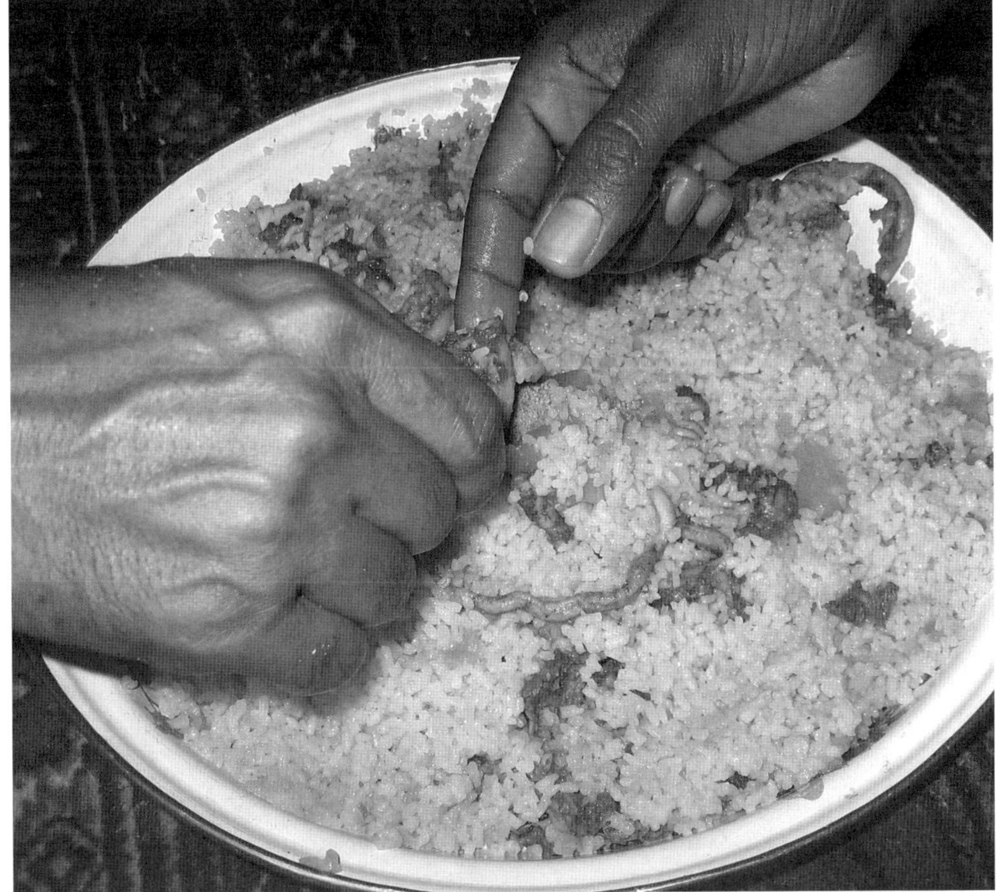

tongue—it's all I can do to keep from screaming. I play with my food a while; that's what everyone else is doing, forming little balls to swallow. The meal is followed by more tea. Some of the men wander off for their afternoon prayers, then we're back on the road again.

As we near the outskirts of Nouakchott, we are greeted by miles of garbage on both sides of the highway. This is where it all ends up, just stretching for miles. Although he agreed earlier to drive me to a hotel, the driver now insists that everyone get out at the taxi depot on the outskirts of the city. It's packed with people and goats and dogs and hustlers waiting for prey. I erupt and call his bluff. I demand he take me into the city center, and finally he relents.

Nouakchott, like many other West African capitals, is extremely expensive. I find something reasonable then settle in for my Mauritanian adventure. I relax and order an $8 beer. I need to contact Sadoum Ouled Aida and make my plans accordingly. He answers and confirms our arrangements. Now I can finally relax.

SADOUM OULED AIDA IS ONE OF MAURITANIA'S MOST FAMOUS and respected musicians (along with Dimi bint Abba and Sadoum's brother Khalife, Dimi's second husband). Simply getting to meet him is really something special. Doueh had called and told him that one of his (Doueh's) close friends— a brother—wants to record some Mauritanian music, so Sadoum has obliged.

I spend the first day getting my bearings. Nouakchott lives up to its Hassaniya name, which means "palace of the winds." A sandy haze is omnipresent; this is where the Sahara meets the Atlantic Ocean—two of the most dominant weather forces on the planet. This is where all hurricanes that come to the Western Hemisphere are born.

When it's time for me to record Sadoum, I'm taken to his house. It is located out in the sprawling shanty towns that make up 95% of Nouakchott. They sprang up after the recent migration here of a large percentage of the nomadic peoples—a consequence of the series of crippling droughts that afflicted the Sahel in the early '70s, and again in the early '80s.

Within the greater Sahara region, as in the entire Arab world, hospitality is religion. Sadoum takes me to his house to meet his family. His wife and newborn child are the pride of his life. His house is a humble compound, three mud-built huts, but he offers a feast of camel meat with couscous plus a medley of vegetables. His court brews us tea in all its ritualistic glory. I am introduced to an older female griot. She is there to accompany Sadoum on some of the music. As I record Sadoum, she calls to me. Even though we've just met, her salutation is to rip part of her gown, to show me that I am completely at home here, and I am welcome to all she owns. A powerful gesture from a woman poorer than the poorest of us.

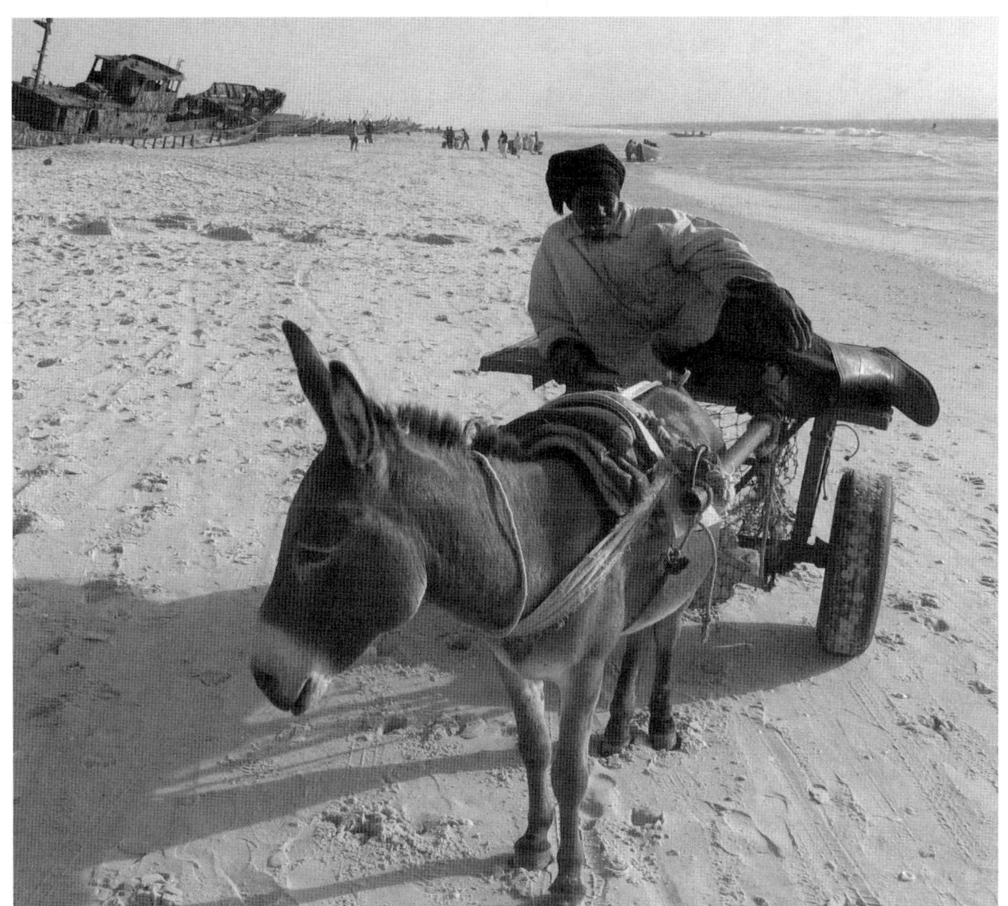

Wolof fisherman, Nouakchott

We are taken to another house in the city, where I am introduced to a local band Sadoum has brought together for me to record. It's a phenomenal session. The band consists of electric guitar, tinidit (a traditional Mauritanian string instrument), tbal (pot bellied clay drum), ardin (a traditional harp played only by the women), plus all the guests hand-clapping and gesturing along. The music is mesmerizing, with sinewy tendrils of string interplay accentuated by grunts and hollers of the sung poetry of the Hassaniya language. Sublime!

I spend a few more days wandering around Nouakchott. One day I decide to go to one of the main attractions, the Plage des Pêcheurs (Fishermen's Beach). The taxi drive out there unveils the huge emptiness of the western edge, vast gravel flats that separate the city center from the water. The beach itself is spectacular: first a solid ridge of dunes, then an impressively straight sweep of fine sand stretching to the horizon. This is the domain of the sub-Saharan Wolof, Pulaar, and Soninke peoples. They are the black Moors who gather the rich coastal bounty in one of the most fertile fishing areas on the planet. Wolof is also the main language group that separates them from the Arab Hassaniya Mauritanians. They are also Muslim and make up the main ethnicity in neighboring Senegal to the south. I'm at the beach at sunset, along with hundreds of other people, waiting for the fishing boats to come in with the day's haul It's an amazing sight. "Sea donkeys" are waiting to haul the catch up to the pier to be weighed and cleaned and taken to market. Old ships that beached along the coast decades ago lean like hulking ghosts, rusted-out monuments to seafaring dreams gone horribly bad. Everyone is courteous and beautiful; the Wolof boats are floating works of art—brightly decorated with reds, greens, yellows, and blues in a striking display of folk craft. I eat fried sweet cornmeal balls and pick through fish bones, enjoying one of the few relaxing moments of my trip.

THE NEXT DAY IS MY LAST IN MAURITANIA. MY FLIGHT TO

Casablanca leaves at three a.m. I'm watching TV in my hotel room; the Muslim world is seething about a political cartoon published by a Danish newspaper that depicts the Prophet Mohammed's turban as a bomb. There are demonstrations in all the major Arab capitals, but not in Nouakchott. This is surprising, as they are quite religious here, and I'm sure everyone is aware of the situation.

Late that afternoon, I decide to head out to the beach and get more footage of the rusted-out galleons and more photos of the Wolof fisherman. I make a pit stop at the Marché Cinquième, one of the more interesting markets around the city. It's an adventurous walk down sandy lanes to gawk at fishmongers' stalls, tubs of peanut butter, rows of mattress sellers, fabric shops with fine-weave muslin in striking prints. As you make your way deeper in, a clutch of medicine and gri-gri sellers— with their displays of monkey and bird feet, and lizard and turtle heads—make for macabre browsing. I wander around and lose myself in labyrinthine corridors.

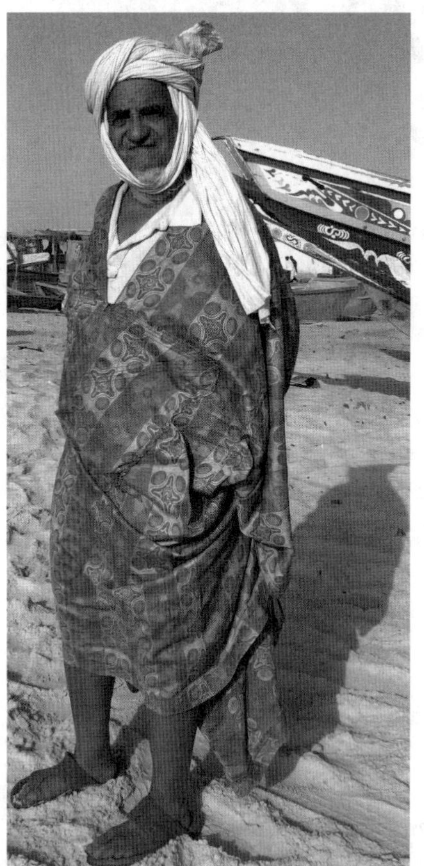

On the beach in Nouakchott

And I find myself at one of the older mosques. It's close to 4 p.m.—time for afternoon prayers. I wander around the grounds and ask if it's all right to use my camera to film. I am told to speak with the Imam. I find the Imam before prayers start, and ask his permission. He is

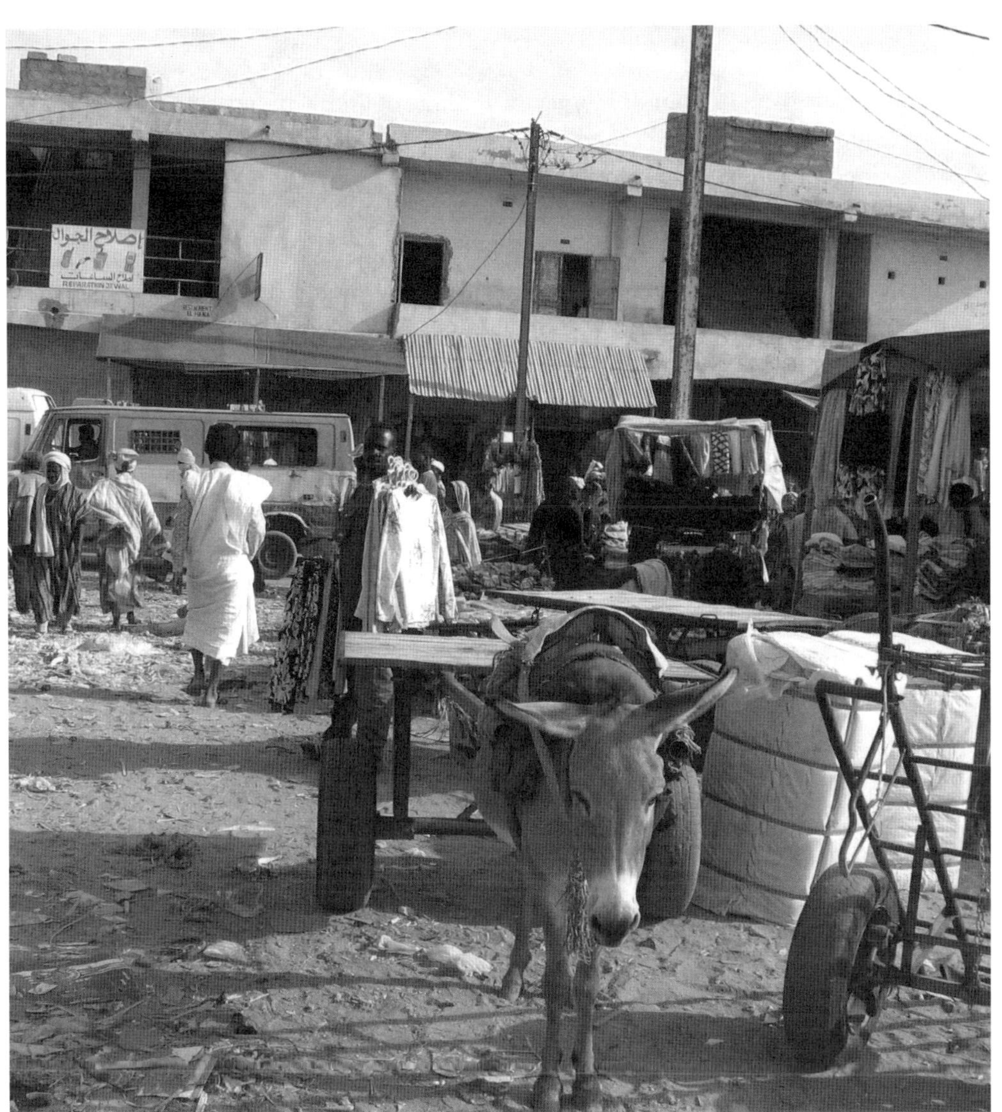

Marché Cinquième, Nouakchott

old and can barely see through his rheumy eyes. He tells me to pray with the others first, and then I have his permission to film.

IT'S A LARGE BUT HUMBLE MOSQUE, AND IS STARTING TO GET crowded; the vast courtyard is filling up with its flock of faithful. The scene is intense. I really look out of place; even if I was in local garb, it would not have made a difference. This is an extremely poor neighborhood, and a bitter analogy to Mauritania as a whole. Mauritanians were completely alienated by the French. While Senegal to the south and its West African neighbors have had some semblance of post-colonial respect, Mauritania was all but ignored and left with minimal resources to eke out some example of modernity. Outside the mosque, I decide to pray alongside two dozen rows of men. I have my camera out of my bag and in front of me, partly as a way of asking permission from all of the men beside me. The mood is claustrophobic. Everyone is looking in my direction. It's a look that any outsider avoids at all costs. Once the prayers are finished, I start to get tracking shots from the outside.

Almost immediately, a crowd surrounds me. This is not an inquisitive crowd; it's a confrontational one. My instincts tell me not to act nervous or afraid. I have to give the impression that I am confident in what I'm doing. It's a tense 10 minutes of shooting. The crowd swells around me. A few people are asking what I'm doing and I explain that I've got the Imam's permission, but no one buys my story. It does not placate anyone. A gentleman comes to my defense and temporarily defuses the situation. He takes me into the mosque. I'm shaking in my boots, but remain steadfast in getting these shots. We enter the mosque while the Imam is giving his sermon. I am in the rear; my camera is poised. I decide to point and shoot, and within thirty seconds an excited fellow rushes towards me, appalled. He starts screaming hysterically at this blasphemous turn of events. Within seconds, half the mosque is running towards me. Echoing murmurs turn to shouts and screams. I am shocked at the velocity of this onslaught, explaining as fast as I can that I am a fellow Muslim. This is not entirely true, but for the sake of argument and survival, I am as devout as anyone else in the mosque.

I deflect all accusations of being a non-believer and almost in mantra fashion, keep repeating, "I am an Arab, a Libyan, a fellow Muslim." This accomplishes nothing. Within minutes, a crowd of approximately sixty men surrounds me. They are getting more excited by the second. I am witnessing the birth of a riot—one I am the cause of. My lone ally is exhausted in trying to deflect the onslaught. It's starting to get physical. People are starting to grab my arms and demanding answers. A few others come to my side and all decide I need to get out of the mosque immediately. I am surrounded. We manage to squirm past all the shouting. I am now in the court yard, being pulled by my guardian angels through the crowds. We are followed by a full-blown mob at this point.

It's strange to witness how a mob comes together; it's the excitement of the moment added to solidarity with the instigator plus general boredom that seems to cause an eruption of this magnitude. I am now really in panic mode, still repeating my mantra. I am being dragged out to the market area, and the whole of the neighborhood is now involved. Children are running and screaming at the excitement. I look back and it seems a hundred people are following us, screaming "ALLAH AKBAR, ALLAH AKBAR." I am thinking of the cartoon riots at this point, which makes the situation psychologically suffocating. I plead with my ally, whose name I don't even know, "Please get me to a taxi." He says it's now too dangerous, we must keep walking. I don't know

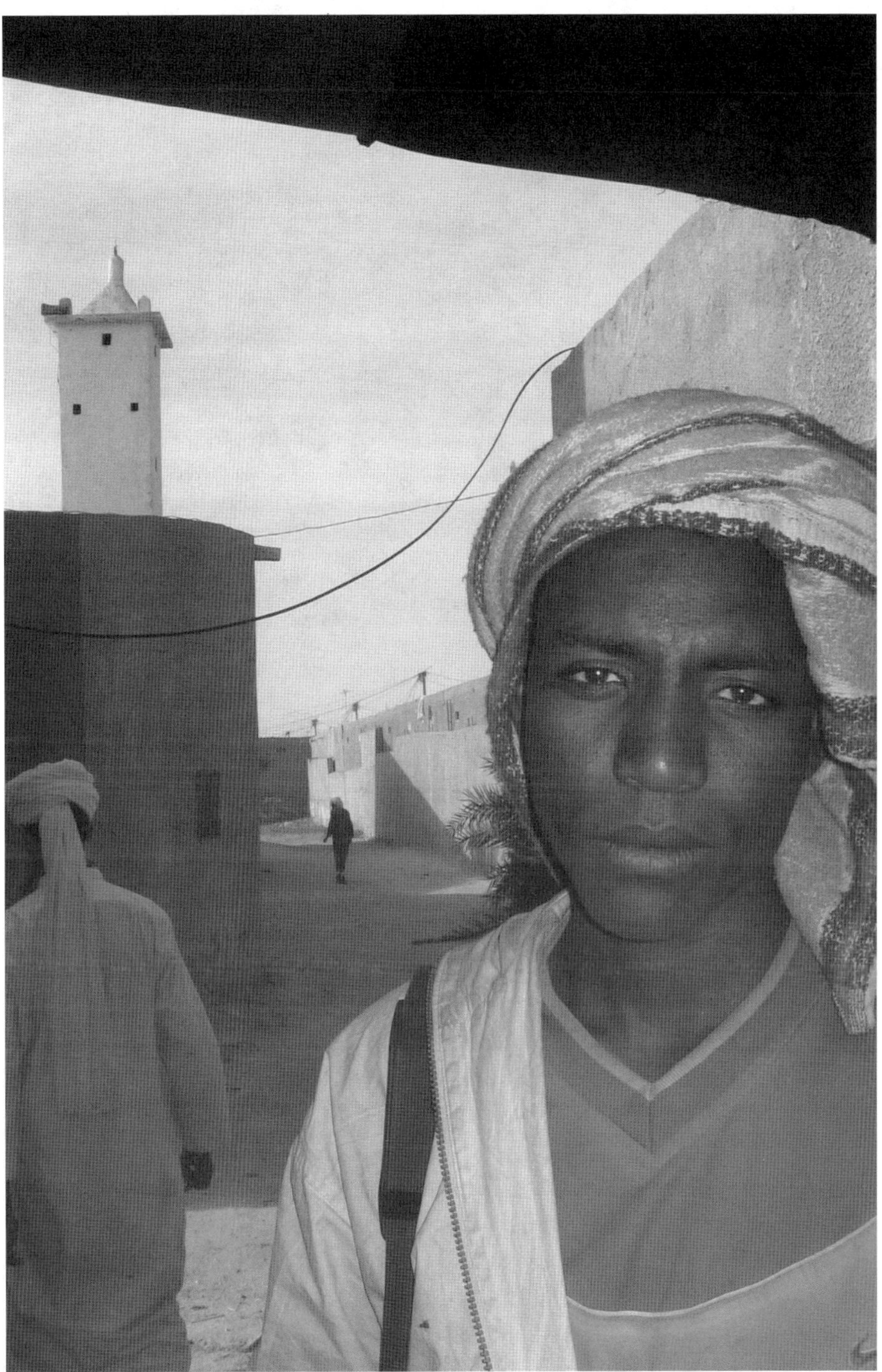

Near the mosque, Nouakchott

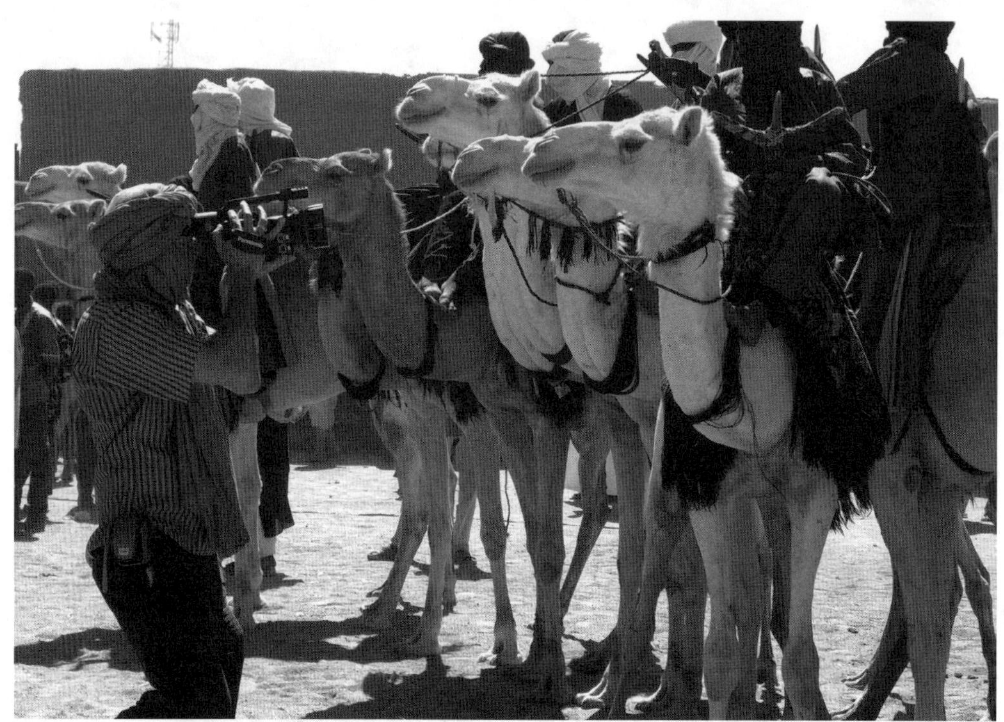

where we are going.

I am being led through the narrow streets; all I hear is the crowd. The mob is getting larger. In a riot, most people don't really know what it is they're rioting about. It's the idea of not being left out of something which seems to create a sense of inclusion, and excitement. I look up and all I see are veiled women looking down from their balconies. I feel like I'm being buried alive. I keep asking my ally what are we doing; he says it's out of control, that he is trying to get me to a policeman. We plod on through the alleyways. The crowd becomes more virulent. I am being pushed and pulled by kids who are just excited that something out of the ordinary is happening. I am truly fearful for my life!

Out of the blue, another gentleman joins us and says he is a policeman; but he's not wearing a uniform. I don't know who to trust. It's complete chaos. We keep running from one dark alley to the next. The policeman is beating the kids away with a stick, and I feel like I'm having a heart attack. We finally reach a green iron gate. It's padlocked, and the man claiming to be a policeman tells me I need to get inside. "Where are we?" I scream. "And what are we doing here?" He tells me it's a police depot and I just need to get inside. I look in and refuse, thinking I am going to be locked up in someone's torture room, or jail. The policeman looks at me and with a serious glare, says, "If you do not get in the room right now, this crowd will kill you."

I grab my ally and run in. And it seems that the fanatic who started all of this in the first place is now in the room with us! He'd been at the forefront of the mob. They lock the door behind us. I can still hear the riot raging outside. We all collect our breath, and the policeman starts asking questions. The instigator, my ally and I are all speaking at once. I explain my story while the others do the same. He asks for my passport and I give it him. It's my American passport. He looks at me and asks me to explain this. I do; I tell him how I am here to record the musician Sadoum. He, like all Mauritanians, knows Sadoum. The fact that I know Sadoum means a lot, and offers a momentary reprieve. As time passes, I can hear the crowd outside thin out a bit. Another policeman shows up and he is briefed. I am told that we are going to the main police station. I wonder how we will get out without me being beaten to death.

One of the policemen goes outside and secures a taxi. We all get ready to exit. Enough time has passed and everyone's side of the story been told. By now the instigator of the whole fiasco and I have found some common ground. Now he too is an ally. Once the taxi is secured, everyone huddles around me and we exit. The crowd has lessened considerably, but it's still dangerous. The taxi is nearby, but in this situation, it feels like we have to walk a hundred miles to get to it. We sprint through the remaining crowd like a herd of zebra escaping a pride of bitter lions. Once we're in the taxi, part of the mob that had dispersed notices, and start to come toward us. The policemen order the driver to move fast. The driver gets us out, and speeds away. I cannot tell you the relief and gratitude I feel just to be alive right now.

We are all taken to the main police station in Nouakchott; I am told it will be a while. There is a line of people ahead of us all giving their stories to the lone judge. One of the men explaining his situation has a hole in his forehead; blood streams down his face. Others are jostling to get their turn at the judge. When my turn comes, I finally get to explain what happened, as does the gentleman who had started the riot. The tape the police had taken from me is now in the judge's possession. It's a tape I cannot lose. At this point I should thankful to be alive, but still I plead and plead to get the tape back. I offer to show the judge what I shot and even to erase any questionable material. He refuses, and tells me I must come back in a few days to pick up the tape. I explain I am leaving the country in a few hours. Unfazed, he moves on to the next case.

FUCK!

I want that tape, but this is clearly a lost cause. I leave the police station with the original policeman; the original instigator whom I now know as Salad; and my first ally, whose name is Miner. They hail a taxi for me, and we chuckle at the madness we've caused. We all hug each other goodbye, and I return to the hotel to pack my bags.

En route to the airport at 1:00 a.m., we drive by the police station. I ask the taxi to stop. I walk inside and make one last effort to get the tape back. But I am told the police chief has it, and he won't return for two days. I trudge back to the taxi, but I'm aware of my good fortune. ❧

MICHELLE BLADE

Recent Paintings

Michelle Blade is a visual artist; she lives in San Francisco. The images on the following pages are paintings she made using acrylic, ink, and/or oils.

"Being in the Bay Area has changed my perception of community a lot, and in turn affected my work monumentally. I'm not sure if I would have been able to make work like this if I was still living in Los Angeles. Most of the time the paintings end up being centered around my own personal disillusionments, desires for communal equality, transcendence, and authentic experience . . . If I had my way, I'd be working in a studio on a mountain top somewhere.

"I've art-directed a couple of music videos, including 'Like a Wolf' for Seawolf and 'Peace and Hate' for the Submarines. The Submarines video was awesome to work on; I had full creative control and made almost every prop by hand. The band was super sweet and the director, Josh Forbes, was really into it. The vibe was exciting. Working on the Seawolf one was fun too, but at times a bit crazy. This project was more of a collaboration between the band's creative desires, the director's, and mine. I'm pleased with how it turned out, but in the moment I remember it getting a little intense.

"I'm starting a new project on February 1 2008, where I wear a uniform for a period of six months. It's just one outfit, but I'll have multiples of it. Built by Wendy has been so kind as to sponsor the project. Two other artists are doing the experiment with me, alongside a sociologist. I'm excited to see what comes about!"

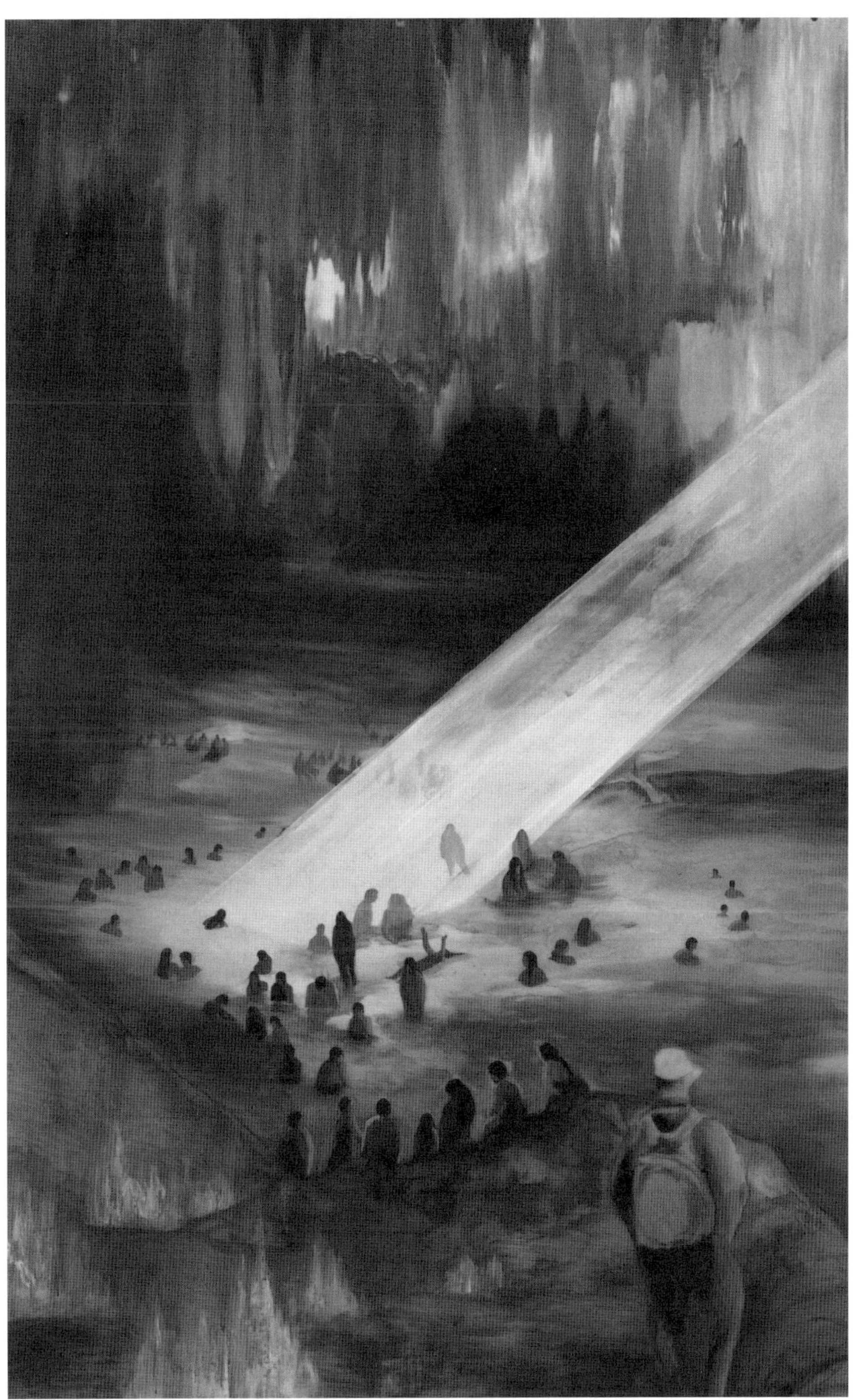

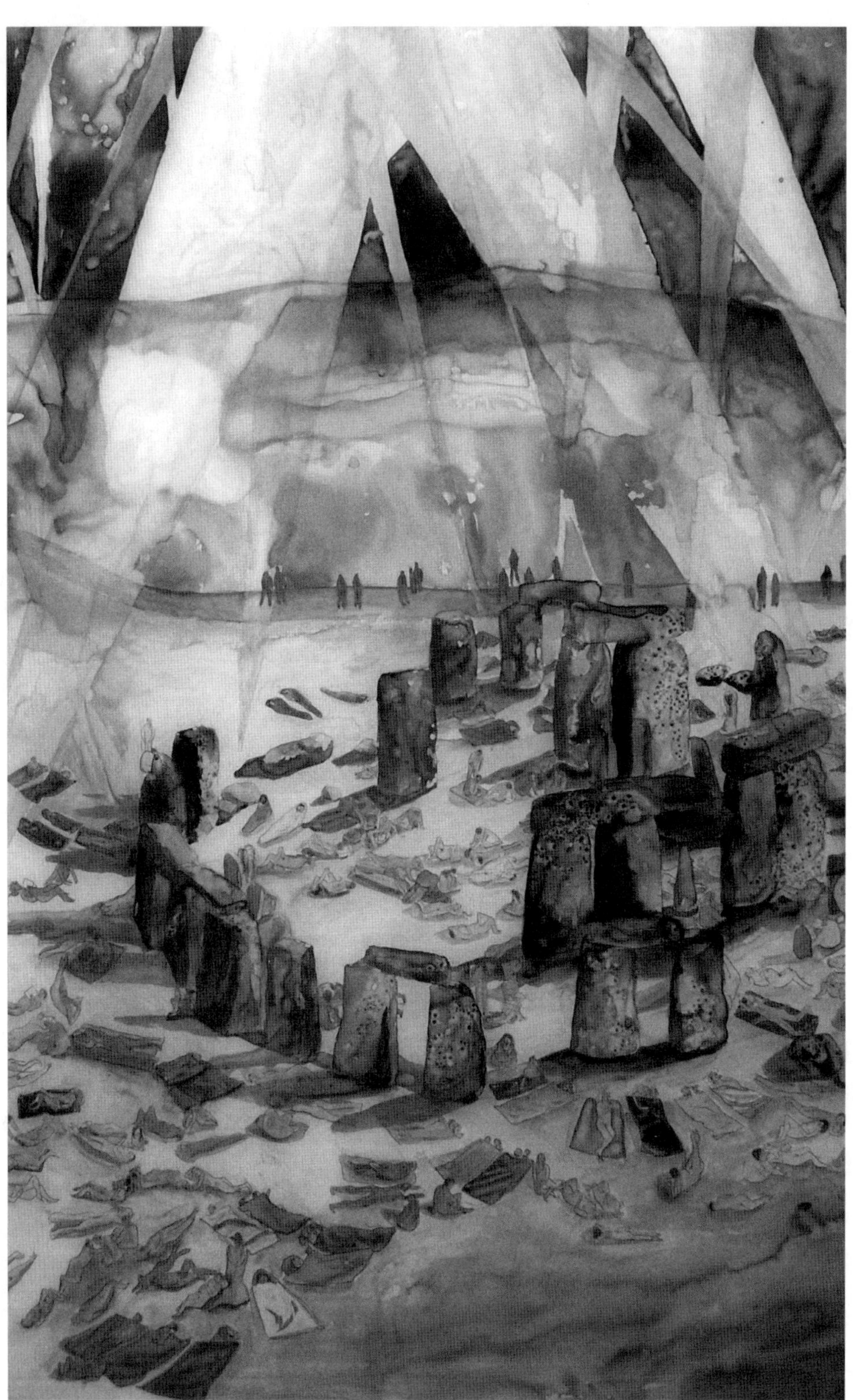

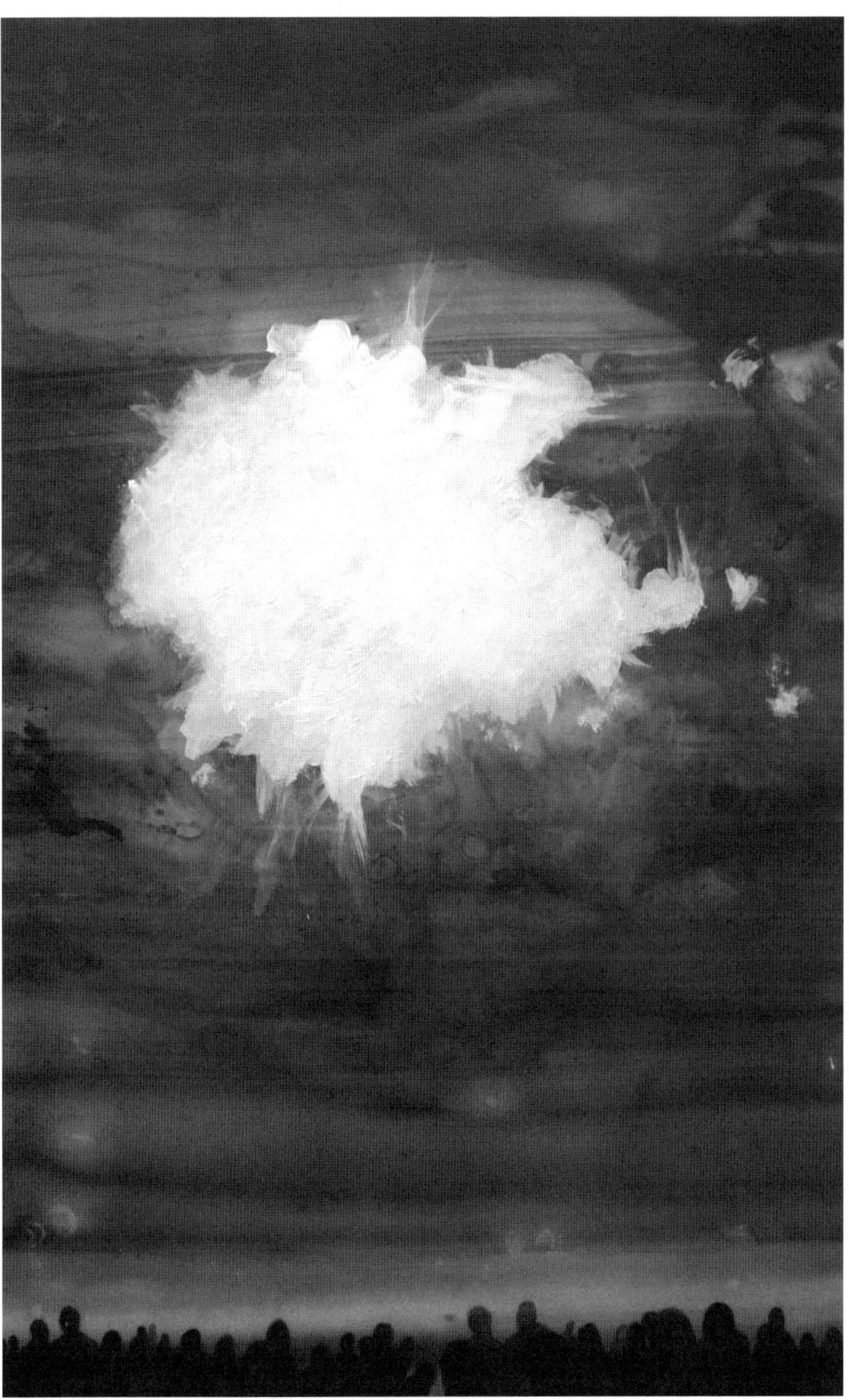

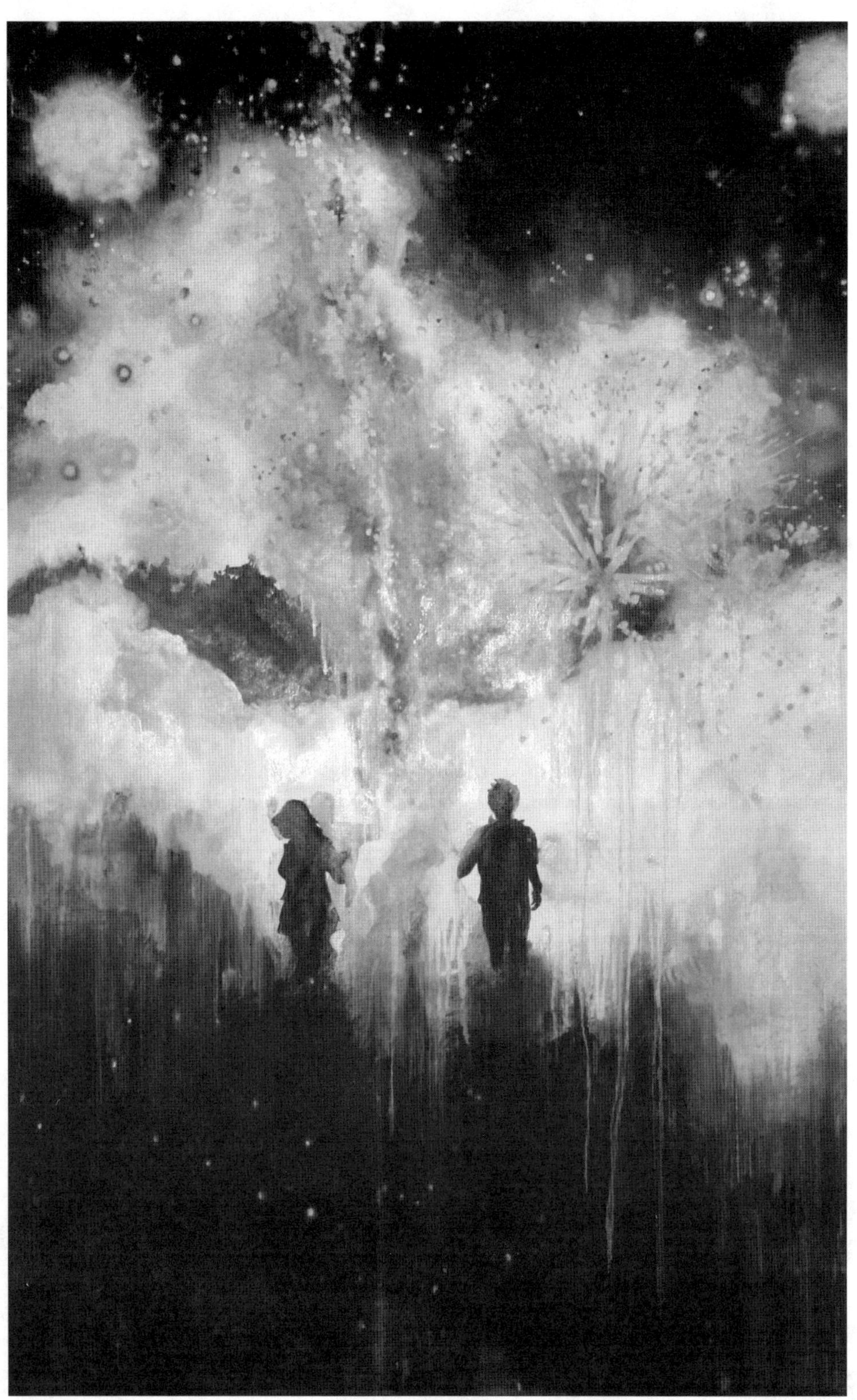

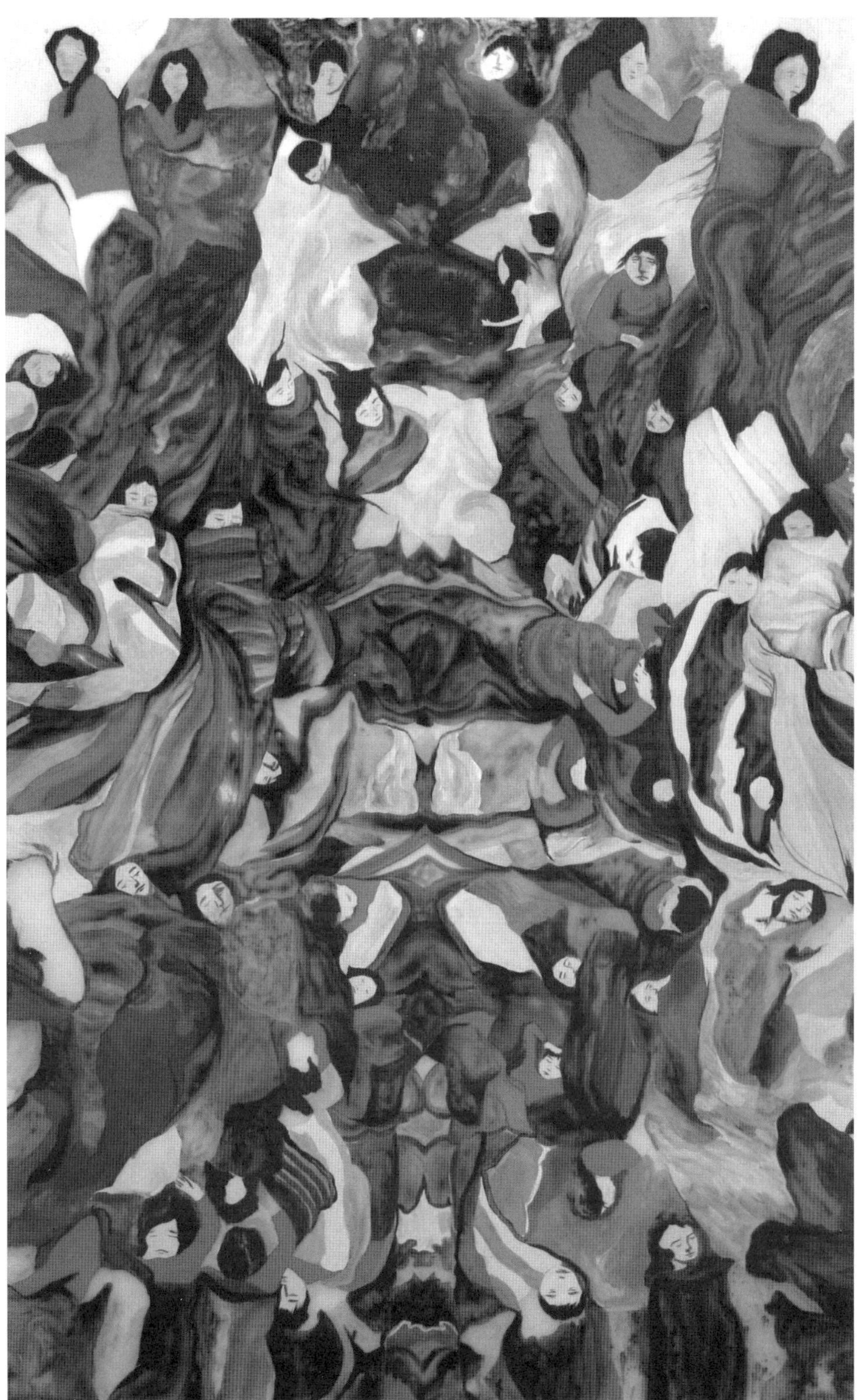

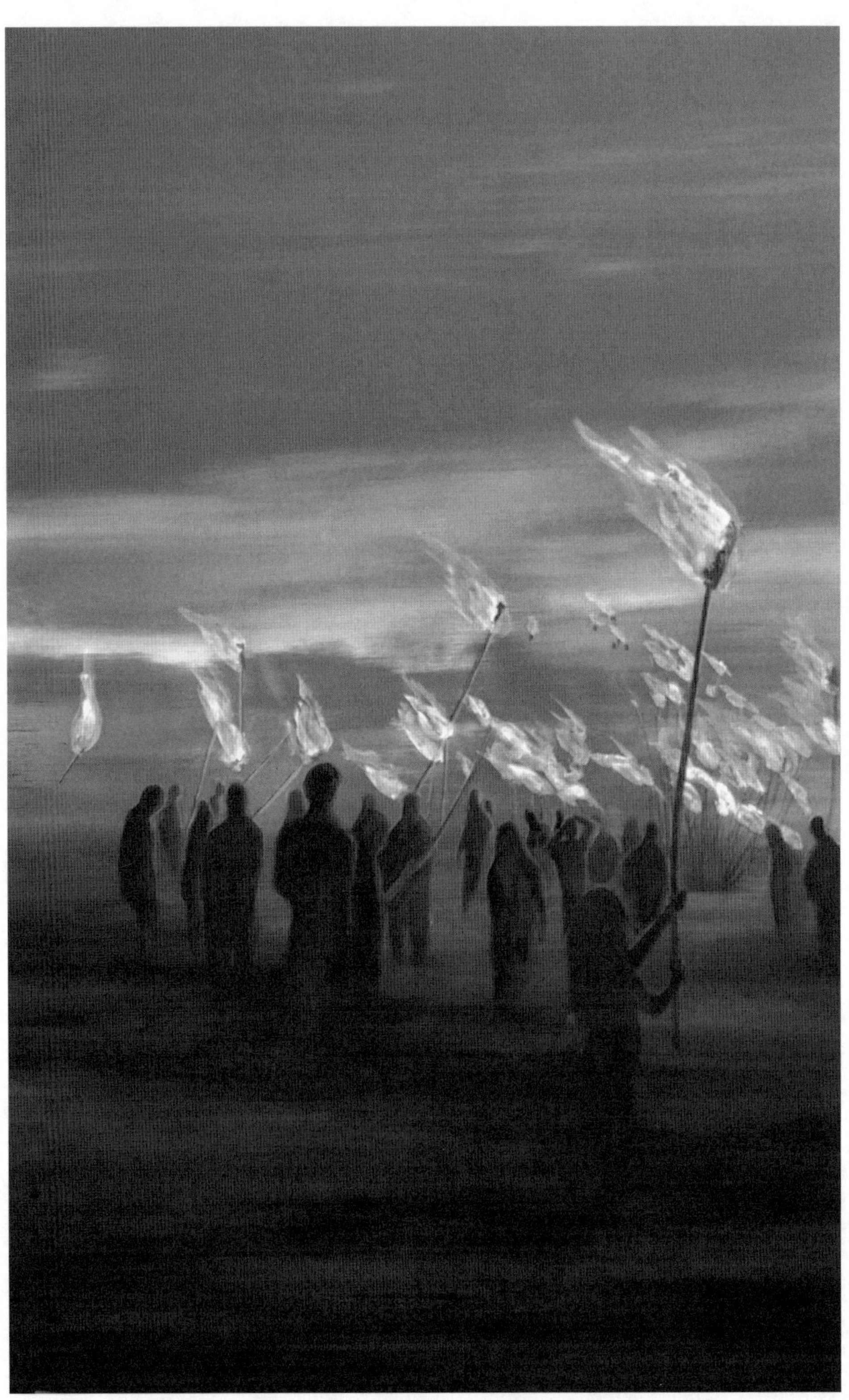

CONTRIBUTORS

Note: Now that YETI has an actual web site (one that's moved beyond technologies available in 1994), thanks to internet genius Marcus Estes, we plan to keep readers abreast of recent developments from past, present and future contributors. We'll also have a web log, news, exclusive mp3s and opportunities for you to buy things from us there: yetipublishing.com

KEVIN ARROW is a widely exhibited visual artist. He lives and works in Miami, and invites questions and comments to arrowfuentes@hotmail.com . . . **MARTIN BEELER** lives in Brooklyn . . . **BLOODNINJA** is currently seeking refuge from Scientology elders (it's a long story) on the outskirts of a village in one of those Nordic countries that does really violent things to their vowels. She (or he) only asks is that you pray for him (or her) . . . **MEREDITH BROSNAN** was born in Dublin fifty years ago. He emigrated to America in 1984. He lives in New York City with his wife Shana and their two beautiful cats, Milo and Bella. Meredith's novel *Mr. Dynamite* was published by Dalkey Archive Press in 2004. He's the former bass player in (and a contributing lyricist to) Peacocks Penny Arcade: myspace.com/peacockspennyarcade . . . **SAUL CHERNICK** (b.1975) has exhibited internationally in galleries, museums, and cultural institutions including the Aldrich Museum of Contemporary Art, the Bronx Museum of Art, The Arad Museum of Art, and the Max Protetch Gallery. He received an MFA from the Mason Gross School of the Arts at Rutgers University, and a BFA at the Rhode Island School of Design. He lives in Brooklyn with his wife, Edith . . . **LORI D** likes to make things by hand: things like quilts, pictures, biscuits, films, booklets, miniature sweaters, and animation . . . **ERIK DAVIS** posts regularly at techgnosis.com. His last book was *The Visionary State: A Journey through California's Spiritual Landscape*, which includes lots of pretty pictures. He plays a Martin OM-21 in a variety of tunings and likes to take long walks on short piers . . . **GREGG EINHORN** is a graphic designer and illustrator; he lives in Santa Monica, but is considering moving somewhere with considerably less traffic. His work can be seen at betweenhereandthere.com . . . **FRANCESCA GRANATA** is completing a Ph.D. in fashion history and theory at Central Saint Martins, in London, and is a research fellow at the Metropolitan Museum of Art's Costume Institute. She lives in New York City and edits *Fashion Projects* (fashionprojects.org) . . . **ALAN GRISWOLD** was born in Knoxville, Tennessee in 1974. He currently lives in Los Angeles, where he runs a company called Monkey Deux. He sometimes still draws . . . **CHRIS MARTIN** is the author of *American Music*, a collection of poems that were awarded the Hayden Carruth Prize. He is furthermore a rapper, teacher, and itinerant philosopher. You can find him in Brooklyn … **HISHAM MAYET** is a founding member of the Sublime Frequencies collective and a Seattle-based ethnographic archivist in various media … **MIKE McGONIGAL** is the author of a book on My Bloody Valentine's *Loveless* published by Continuum ($33\frac{1}{3}$). A collection culled from Mike's old 'zine *Chemical Imbalance* will be published next summer, while his *'Buked & Scorned: The Yeti Guide to Sanctified Blues & Gritty Gospel* will arrive at the end of this year. Today, Mike is most psyched how the *Life is a Problem* LP he worked on for Mississippi Records turned out, and is helping to compile a sequel … **SCOTT MEYERS** is an artist living and working in New York City. He spends his time drawing, pushing through the streets, taking photographs and creating a mess in the kitchen. You can see what he's up to at kaleidoscott.com … **KEVIN SAMPSELL** publishes fiction, book reviews, and essays in a variety of publications. He lives in Portland, Oregon where he runs the small press, Future Tense Books. His latest book of short fiction is *Creamy Bullets* (Chiasmus Press) … **SCOTT SEWARD** is a hospital custodian who lives on an island with Maria, Rufus, Cyrus, and Catcher. In 2007, his essay on Divine Styler was featured in the book *Marooned*. From 1999 to 2006, he wrote frequently about music for the *Village Voice*; he now writes monthly for *Decibel* magazine. His blog *Pie.Metal.Love.* can be found at skotrok.blogspot.com … **DIMITRI SIMAKIS** is a dude's dude. He gets his inspiration from the guiding powers, the Sun and Moon (represented by the Lion and the Unicorn). Dimitri sees the Lion as golden yellow, ruling through strength and dominating all, constantly chasing the Unicorn, silver white, who rules through harmony and strength of cooperation. Seldom does he allow the Lion to catch his prey, yet when he does, it is the Sun and not the Moon that is obscured. Needless to say, this led Dimitri to cast an I Ching hexagram, in which the three coins gave him the power of a "Hsu" (Waiting/Nourishment). Thus, Dimitri went up into the mountains where he awaited the "conversation and knowledge of the Holy Guardian angel." There he has remained: creating monster trucks, mythical beasts, and big-name money rappers to plague and vex us. He is Ever Waiting for the sign to come and make us holy again … **JUSTIN TAYLOR** is the editor of *The Apocalypse Reader* (Thunder's Mouth), a collection of 34 stories about the end of the world; and *Come Back, Donald Barthelme* (McSweeney's), a celebration of the author's life and work. He has written for *Paste, The Believer*, and numerous other magazines. His piece "Fort Smith, Arkansas—A Monologue" was cited as a Notable Essay in *Best American Essays 2007*. He lives in Brooklyn. Point your computer his way at justindtaylor. net … **JASON TRAEGER** grew up punk on the U.S. West Coast. He made music for many years, did stand-up comedy for fewer years, and is now a painter living in Portland, Oregon. ❧

ADVERTISEMENTS

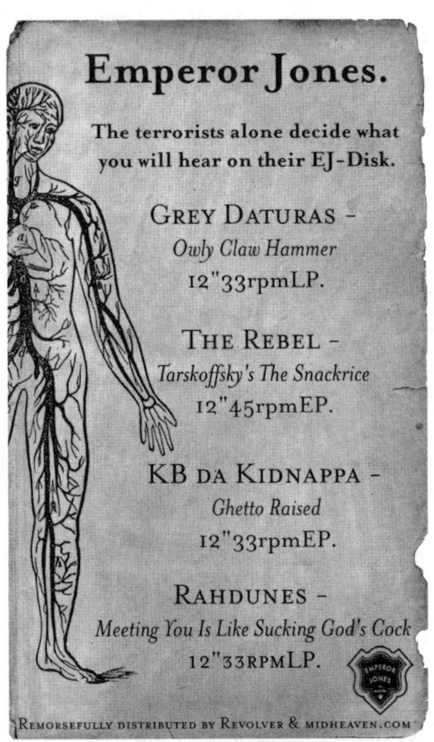

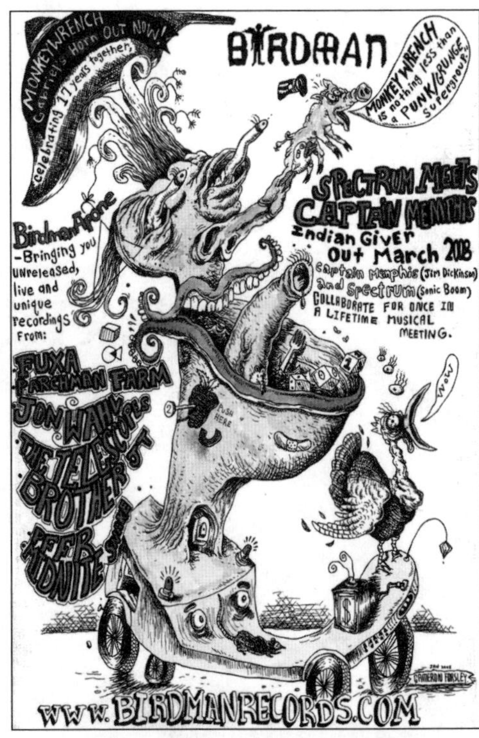

THESE RELEASES AVAILABLE NOW FROM GNOMONSONG

VETIVER
- *You May Be Blue/Been So Long (Neighbors Remix)* 12-inch (GONG-10)
- Upcoming: *Thing of The Past* LP/CD in May & EP in August

JANA HUNTER
- *There's No Home* LP/CD (GONG-06)
- *Carrion EP* CD (GONG-05)
- *Blank Unstaring Heirs of Doom* CD (GONG-01)
- Upcoming: Touring Europe with Phosphorescent in the spring

www.gnomonsong.com for news, tourdates, and more

MICHAEL HURLEY
- *Ancestral Swamp* LP/CD (GONG-07)
- Upcoming: Recording tracks for *Tea Song EP*

PAPERCUTS
- *Can't Go Back* LP/CD (GONG-04)
- Upcoming: Recording in the spring

RIO EN MEDIO
- *Bride of Dynamite* CD (GONG-03)

FEATHERS
- *Feathers* CD (GONG-02)

distributed by Revolver USA
www.midheaven.com

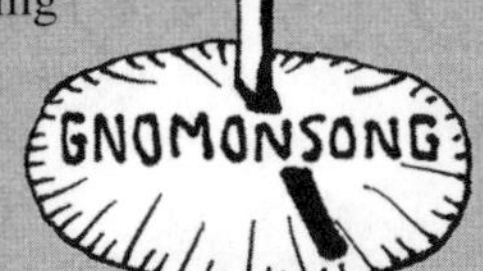

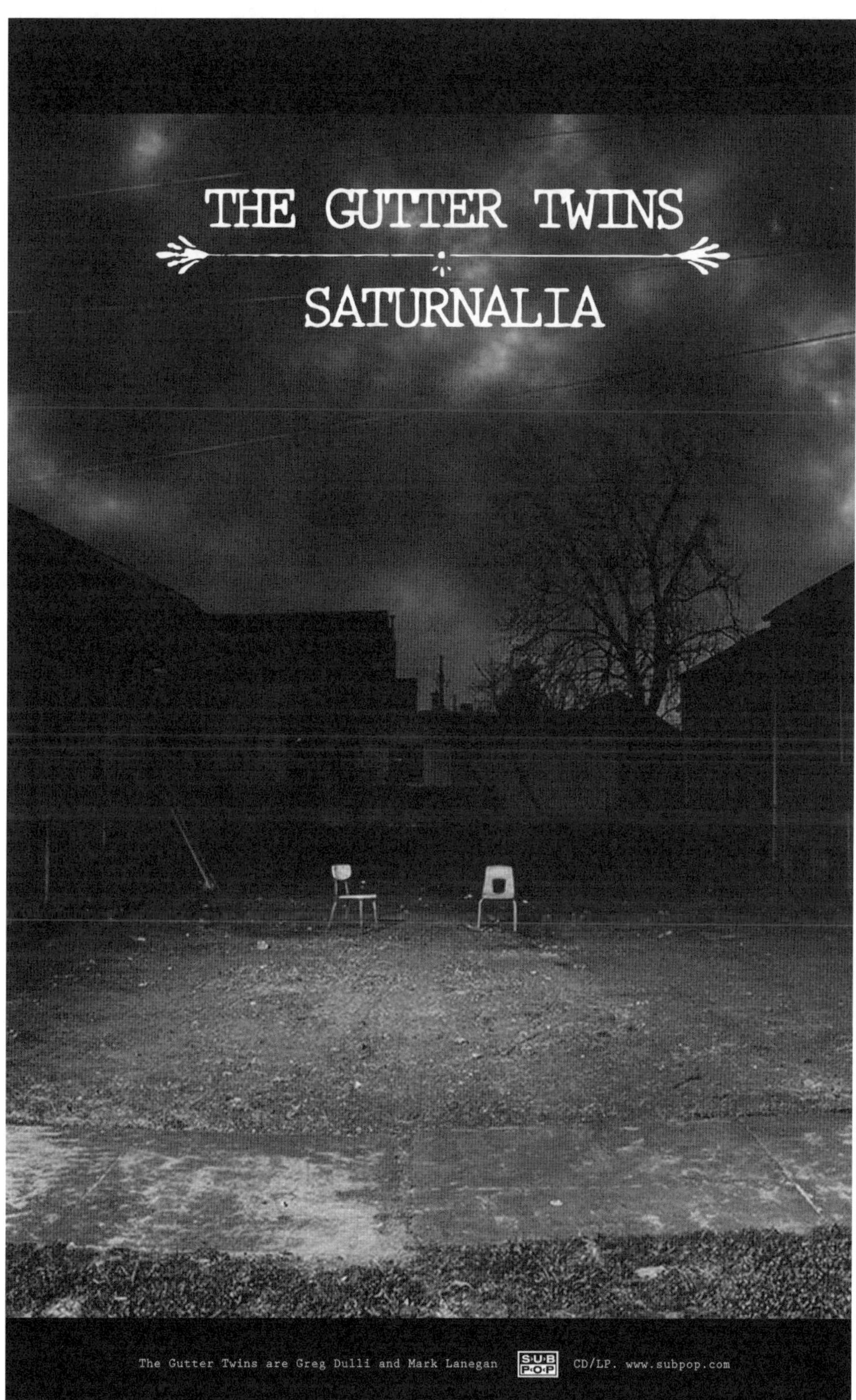

THE GUTTER TWINS
SATURNALIA
The Gutter Twins are Greg Dulli and Mark Lanegan   S·U·B P·O·P   CD/LP. www.subpop.com

NEW IN THE SERIES:

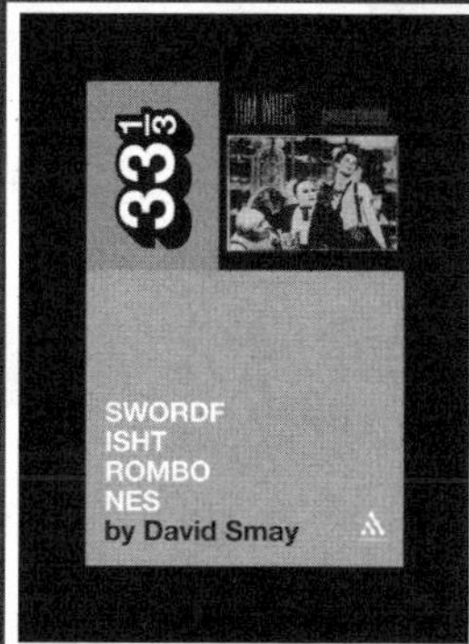

Tom Waits' Swordfishtrombones
by David Smay

David Smay unwraps the vinegar pleasures of Swordfishtrombones and creates a freewheeling portrait of an American genius. This is the story of a man who reinvented himself and changed the musical landscape forever, a love story built on exotic percussion and phantom landscapes.

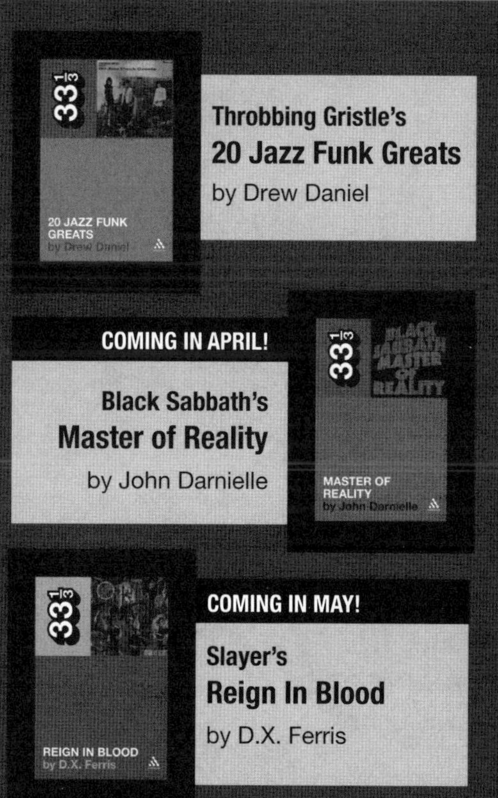

Throbbing Gristle's
20 Jazz Funk Greats
by Drew Daniel

COMING IN APRIL!

Black Sabbath's
Master of Reality
by John Darnielle

COMING IN MAY!

Slayer's
Reign In Blood
by D.X. Ferris

ALSO AVAILABLE IN THE 33 1/3 SERIES:

Nick Drake's
Pink Moon
by Amanda Petrusich

Belle & Sebastian's
If You're Feeling Sinister
by Scott Plagenhoef

My Bloody Valentine's
Loveless
by Mike McGonigal

Neutral Milk Hotel's
In the Aeroplane Over the Sea
by Kim Cooper

Led Zeppelin's
Led Zeppelin IV
by Erik Davis

James Brown's
Live at the Apollo
by Douglas Wolk

Steely Dan's
Aja
by Don Breithaupt

Magnetic Fields'
69 Love Songs
by L. D. Beghtol

Sonic Youth's
Daydream Nation
by Matthew Stearns

Celine Dion's
Let's Talk About Love
by Carl Wilson

FOR MORE INFORMATION:
1-800-561-7704
www.33third.blogspot.com

continuum

books from **yeti**

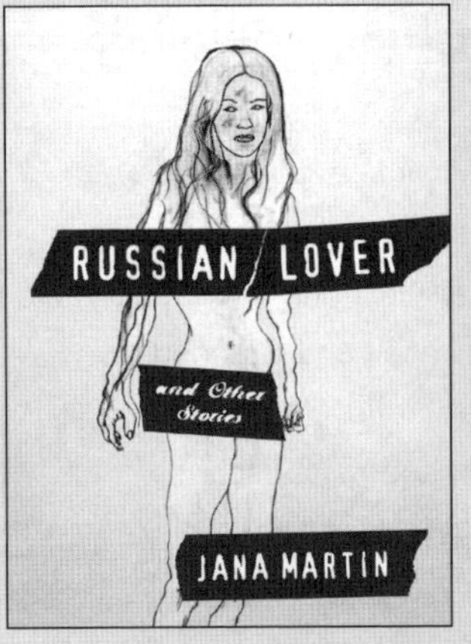

JANA MARTIN
Russian Lover and other stories

"Joining the ranks of female fiction writers such as Amy Hempel and A.M. Homes."—**Bust**

LUC SANTE
Kill All Your Darlings

"Tough in his thinking, empathic in his analysis, and liberated in expression, Sante selects barbed details, tunes in to danger and suspense, and dispenses wry humor and sure insight."—**Booklist**

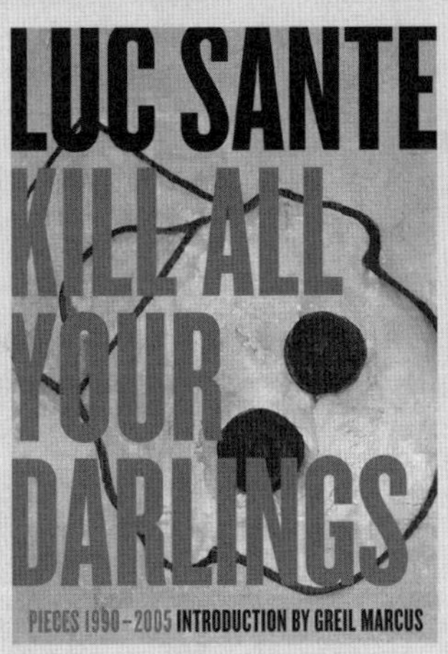

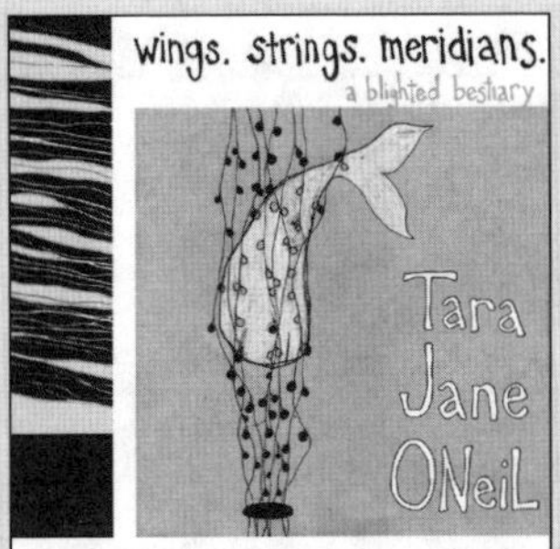

TARA JANE O'NEIL
Wings. Strings. Meridians.

Art and music together in one beautiful six-inch-square package. 96 pages of paintings and drawings, plus a CD of live songs, home recordings and film scores.

Yeti books are published in association with Verse Chorus Press. yetipublishing.com

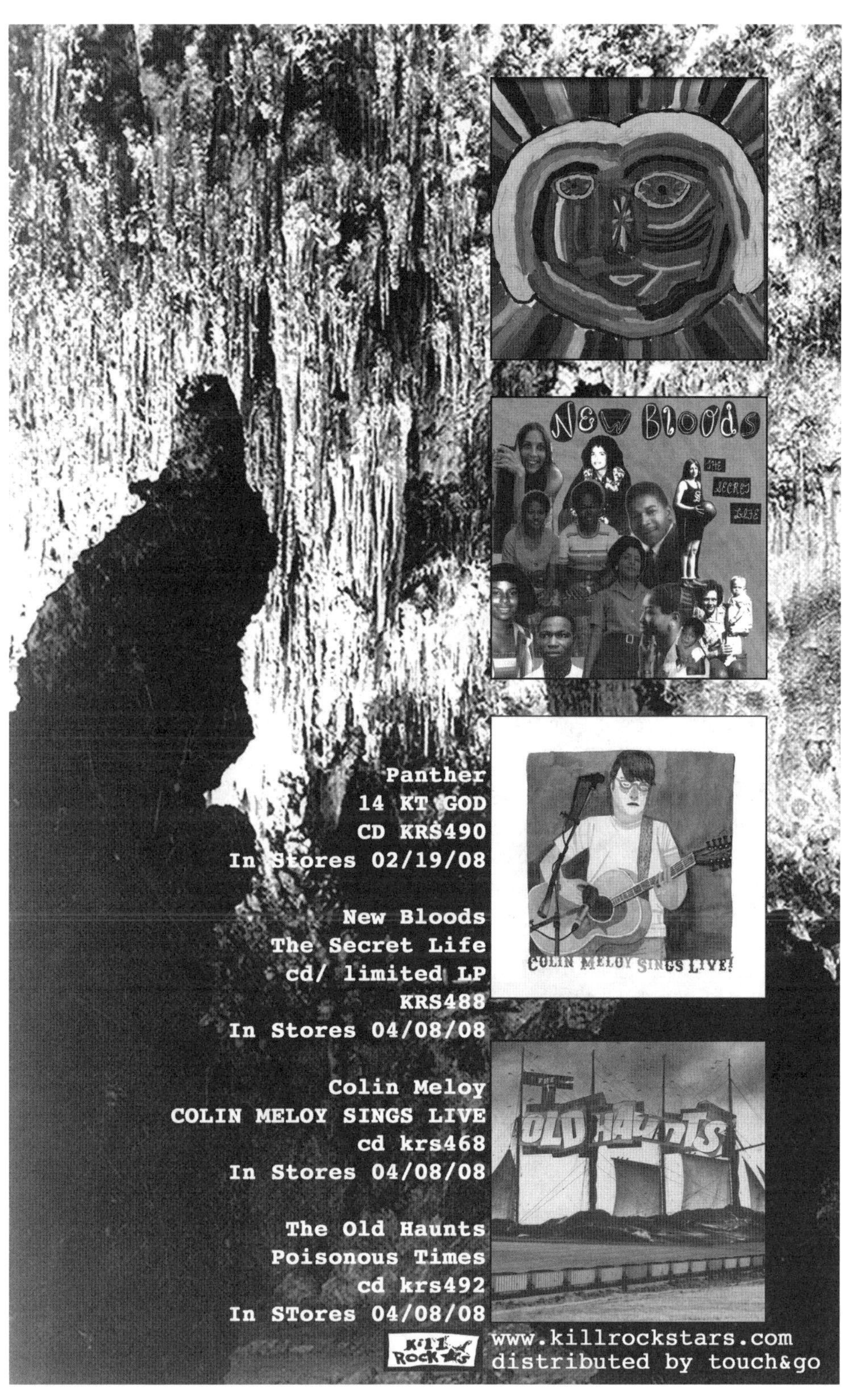
Panther
14 KT GOD
CD KRS490
In Stores 02/19/08

New Bloods
The Secret Life
cd/ limited LP
KRS488
In Stores 04/08/08

Colin Meloy
COLIN MELOY SINGS LIVE
cd krs468
In Stores 04/08/08

The Old Haunts
Poisonous Times
cd krs492
In STores 04/08/08

www.killrockstars.com
distributed by touch&go

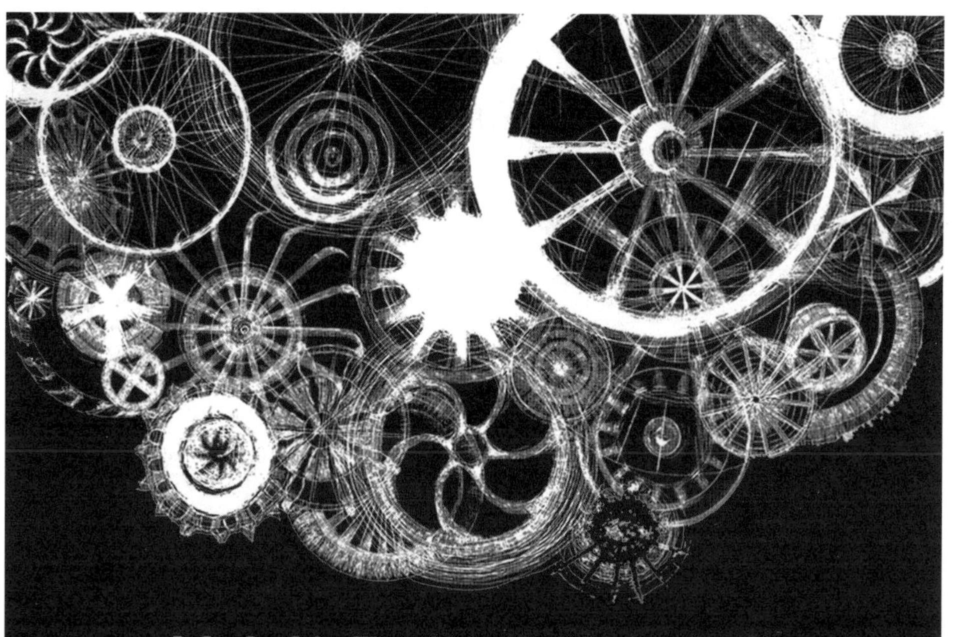

MIKE WEXLER
SUN WHEEL
debut album CD|LP

UPCOMING

HALL OF FAME First Came Love, Then Came the Tree... LP
Extremely limited re-issue plus bonus live CDr
(The 1999 album available on vinyl for the first time)

BLACK TAJ Beyonder CD

SON OF EARTH tba LP

CDs, LPs and more from P.G.Six, Hall of Fame, Metabolismus, Oakley Hall, Theo Angell, Black Taj, Ivanovich

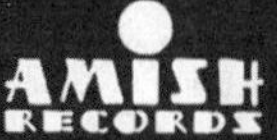

www.myspace.com/mikewexler
www.myspace.com/amishrecords
www.amishrecords.com

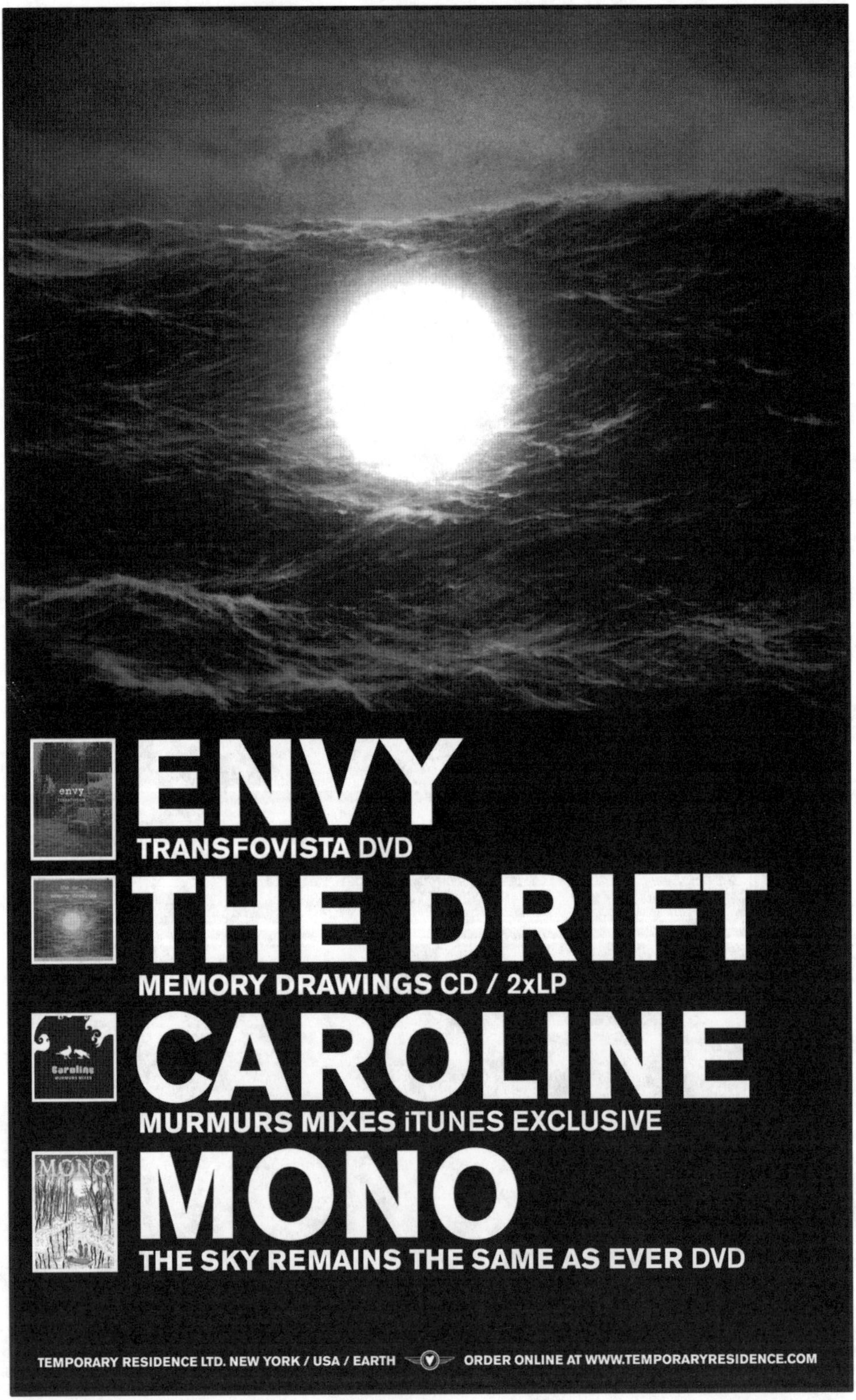

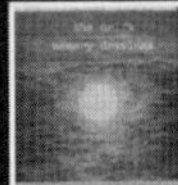
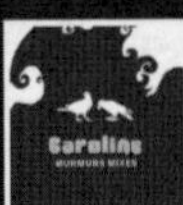
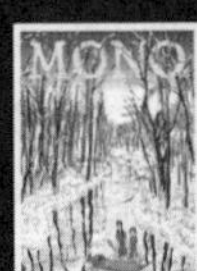

ENVY
TRANSFOVISTA DVD
THE DRIFT
MEMORY DRAWINGS CD / 2xLP
CAROLINE
MURMURS MIXES iTUNES EXCLUSIVE
MONO
THE SKY REMAINS THE SAME AS EVER DVD

TEMPORARY RESIDENCE LTD. NEW YORK / USA / EARTH   ORDER ONLINE AT WWW.TEMPORARYRESIDENCE.COM

EL PERRO DEL MAR

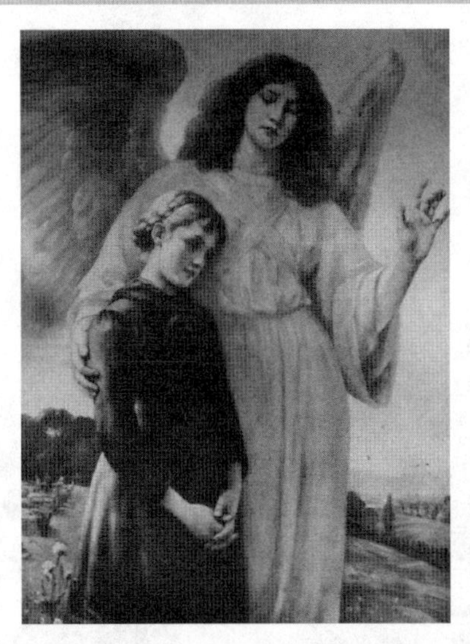

FROM THE VALLEY TO THE STARS

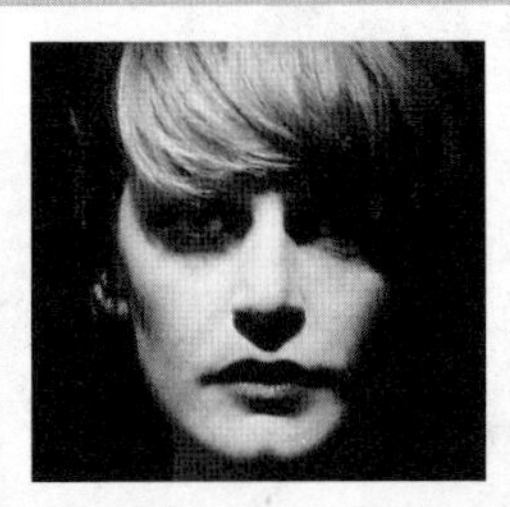

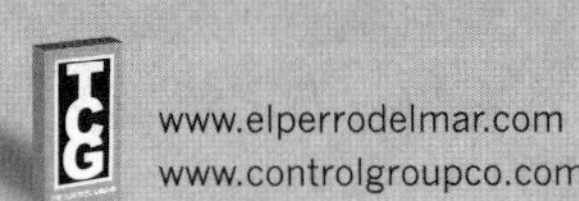

D+ "On Purposes: 1997 – 2007"
A collection of rarities and hits from the loose-folk power trio of Bret
Lunsford, Phil Elvrum and Karl Blau. Sparse double-edged ballads that
sing woe, hope or humor depending on when you hear them. Limited
release of 1000, the numbered hand-screened jackets will feature
artwork from Olympia's splendid Nikki McClure.

Khaela Maricich "Look For It In The Sky, It Will Always Be There"
Khaela's first album, originally released in 2001, hints at the mega-stardom soon to
follow. It sounds like some kind of ragtime sung sweetly with only the distant breath of
an accordion or ukulele as the vehicle. The words alone are so substantial you could eat
them with soup.

Jesus Chords "Kelp Bong"
Knw-Yr-Own's newest band, releasing their third album, the Jesus
Chords have a punk-skewed brand of outlaw country that speaks to the
hard times of the working class. "The working man's 'Workingman's
Dead'!" First 500 with hand-screened with glow in the dark ink.

Also, keep you ear to the ground for a reissue of
Karl Blau's first cd-r "Shell Collection" on gorgeous colored
vinyl, D+'s new album "What Is Doubt For?", and
"Grw-Yr-Own" a charming compilation of music for little
folks. . . coming soon!

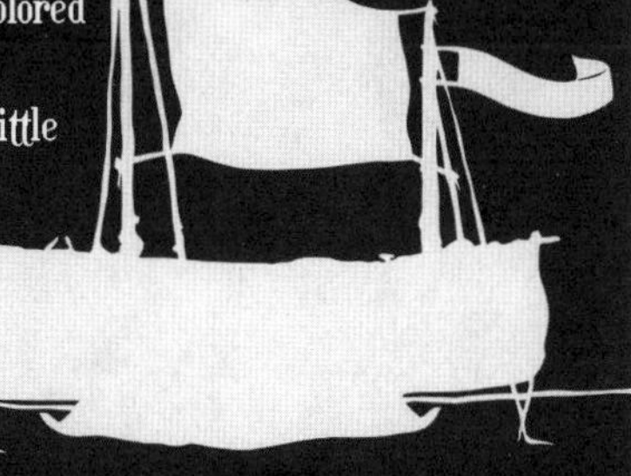

Knw-Yr-Own Records: hauling songs out of the Pacific Northwest since 1987

CAKESHOP
152 LUDLOW STREET NYC
CAKESHOP
152 LUDLOW STREET NYC
CAKESHOP
152 LUDLOW STREET NYC
CAKESHOP
152 LUDLOW STREET NY
CAKES
152 LUDL
CAKESHOP
152 LUDLOW STREET NYC
ALL WORLD. COME VISIT. NEW RELEASES ON CAPE SHOK RECORDS!
KIRSTEN KETSJER THE ROCK BAND+AIR WAVES+HOLOGRAM+MORE!

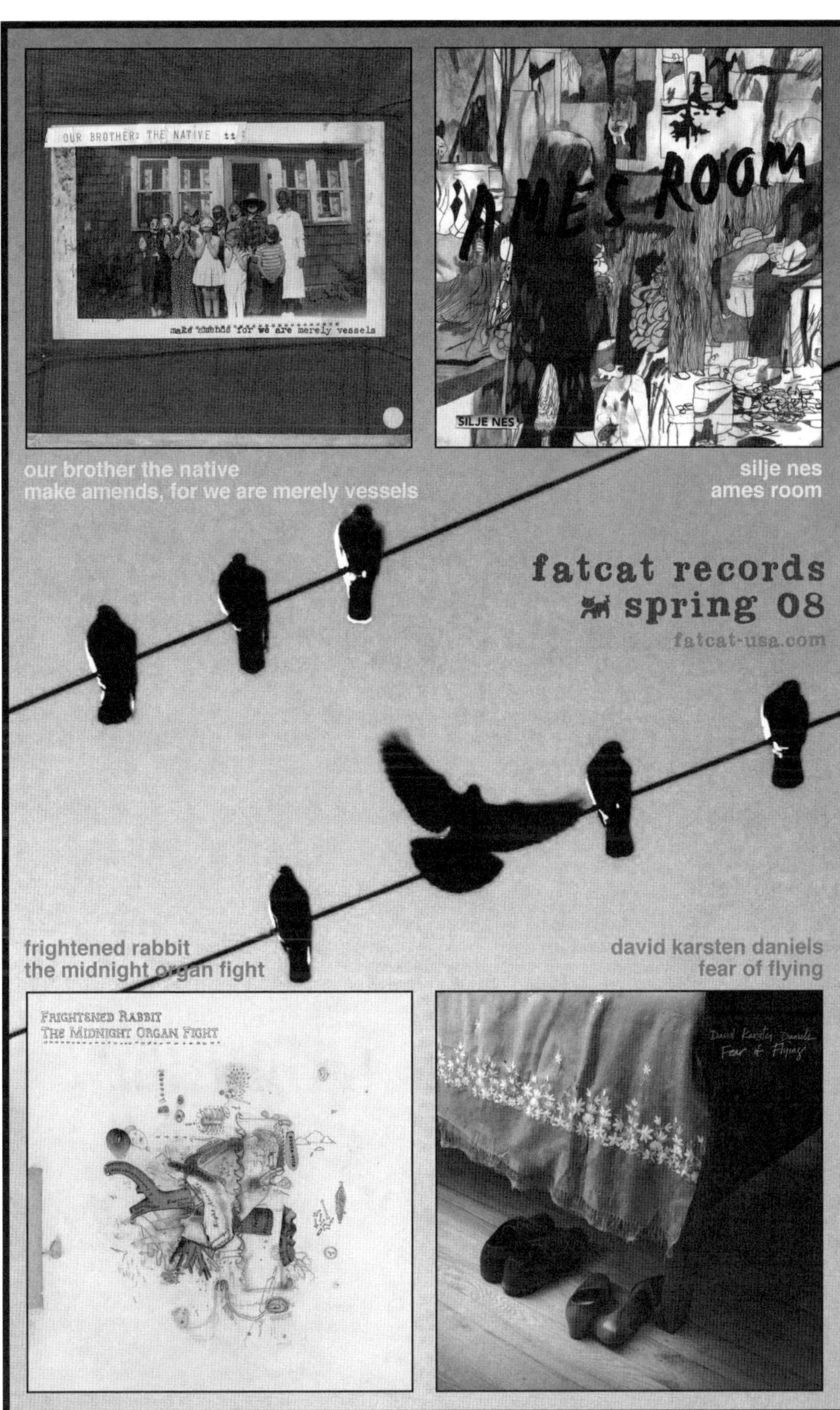
our brother the native
make amends, for we are merely vessels

silje nes
ames room

fatcat records
spring 08
fatcat-usa.com

frightened rabbit
the midnight organ fight

david karsten daniels
fear of flying

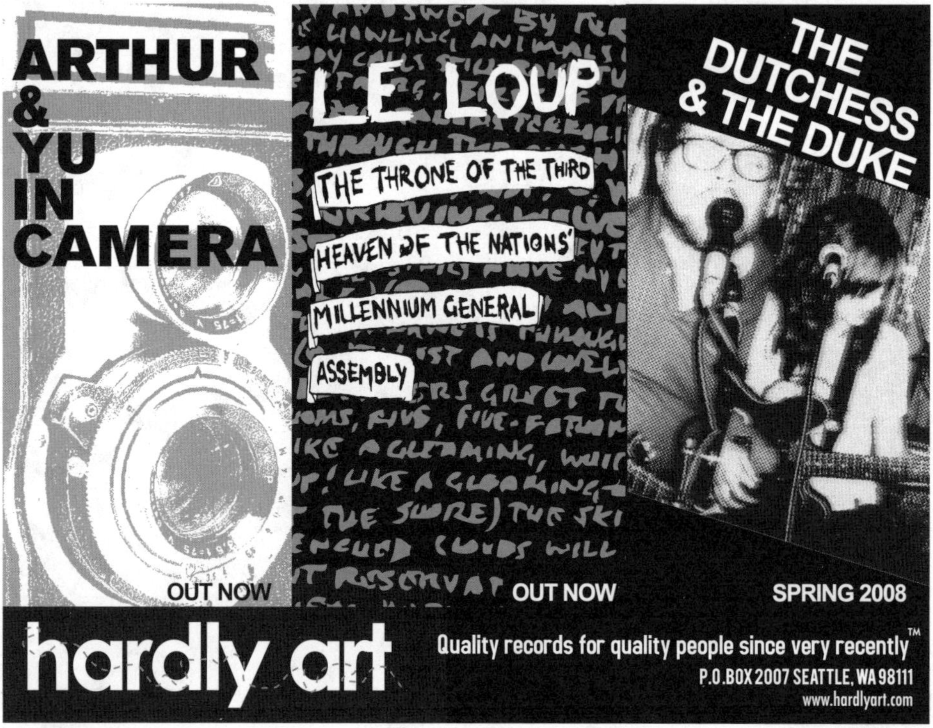

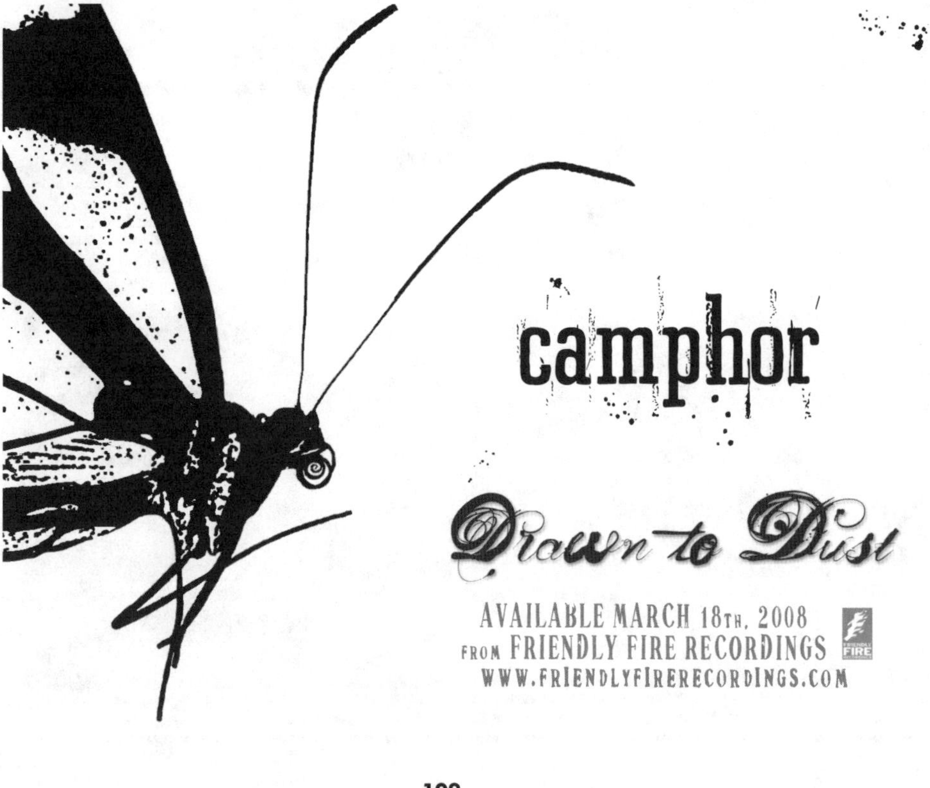

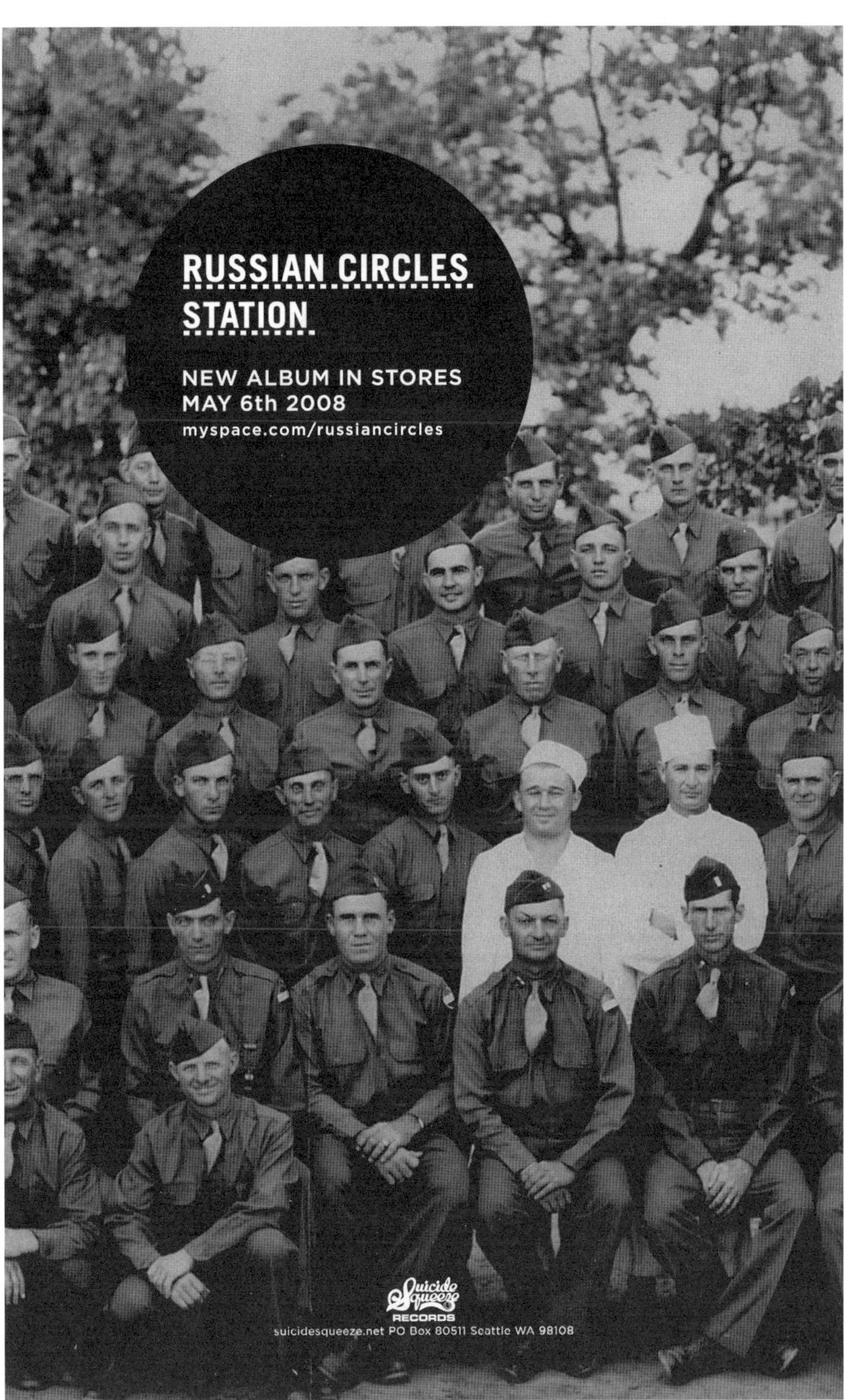

RUSSIAN CIRCLES
STATION
NEW ALBUM IN STORES
MAY 6th 2008
myspace.com/russiancircles
Suicide Squeeze
RECORDS
suicidesqueeze.net PO Box 80511 Seattle WA 98108

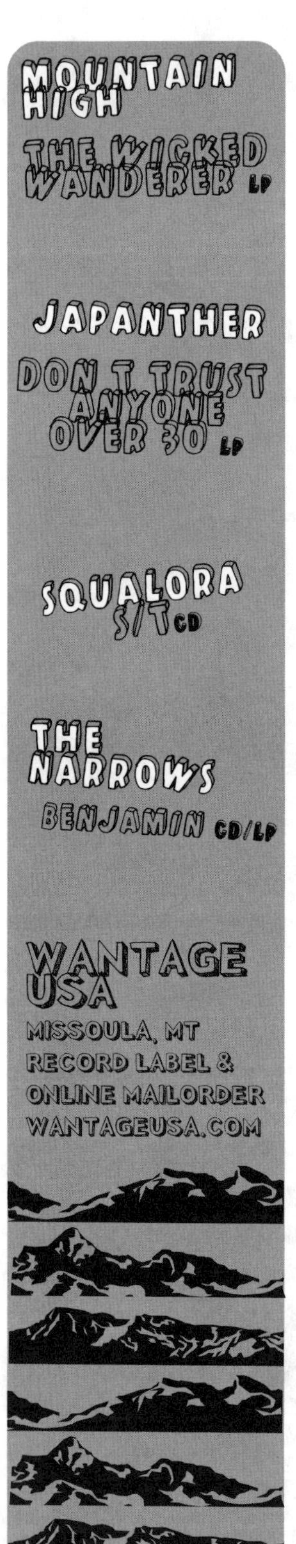

MOUNTAIN HIGH
THE WICKED WANDERER LP

JAPANTHER
DON'T TRUST ANYONE OVER 30 LP

SQUALORA
S/T CD

THE NARROWS
BENJAMIN CD/LP

WANTAGE USA
MISSOULA, MT
RECORD LABEL &
ONLINE MAILORDER
WANTAGEUSA.COM

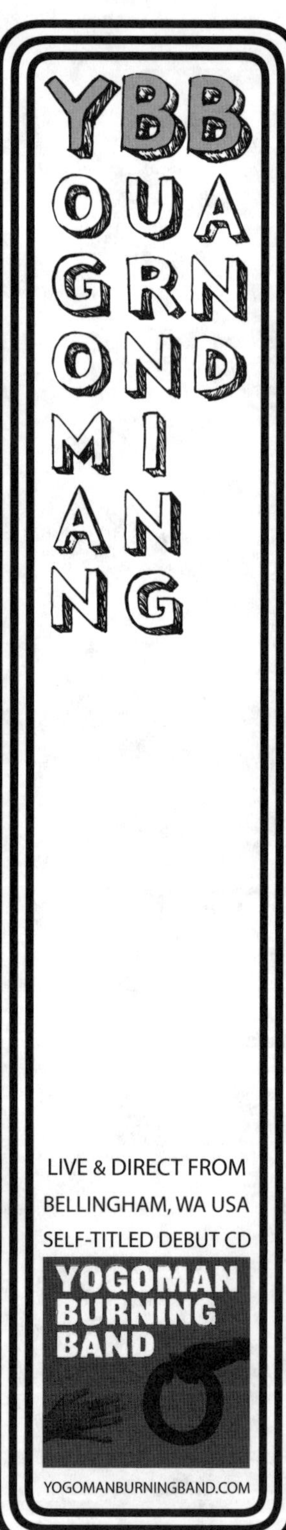

YBB
YOGOMAN
OUR GRAND
BURNING
MANING
LIVE & DIRECT FROM
BELLINGHAM, WA USA
SELF-TITLED DEBUT CD
YOGOMAN
BURNING
BAND
YOGOMANBURNINGBAND.COM

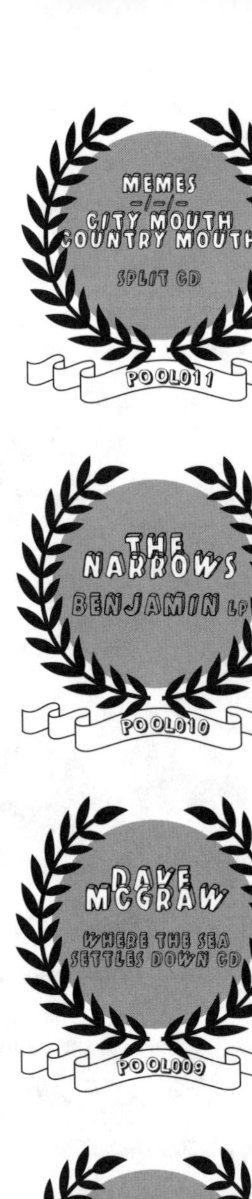

MEMES
-/-/-
CITY MOUTH
COUNTRY MOUTH
SPLIT CD
POOL011

THE NARROWS
BENJAMIN LP
POOL010

DAVE McGRAW
WHERE THE SEA
SETTLES DOWN CD
POOL009

JORDAN RAIN
(YOGOMAN)
STREET LIGHTS CD
POOL008

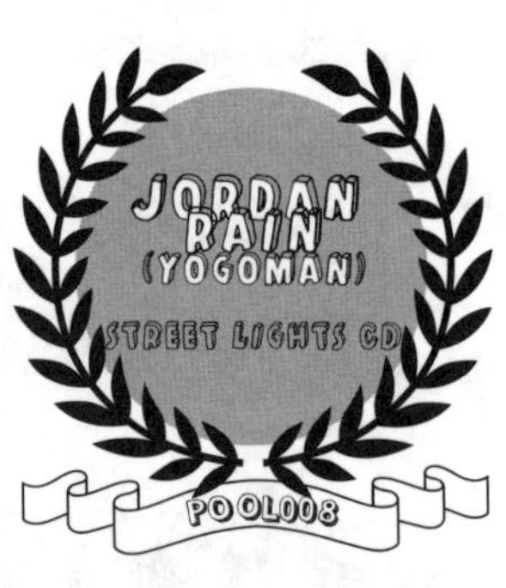

POOL OR POND
RECORD LABEL &
ONLINE MAILORDER
POOLORPOND.NET
CATCH & RELEASE

IDA
LOVERS PRAYERS

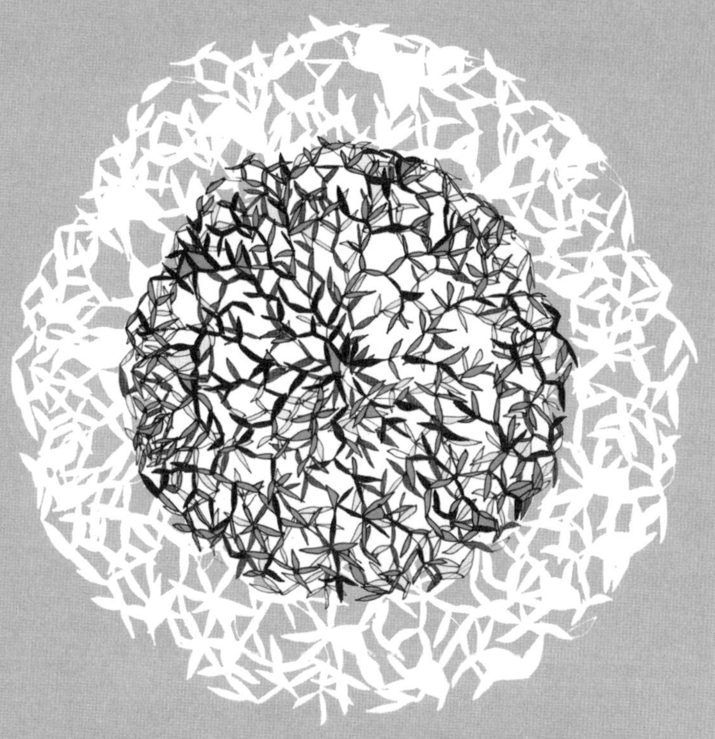

CD/2xLP with Bonus Tracks
www.idamusic.com

BURNT TOAST VINYL 2008

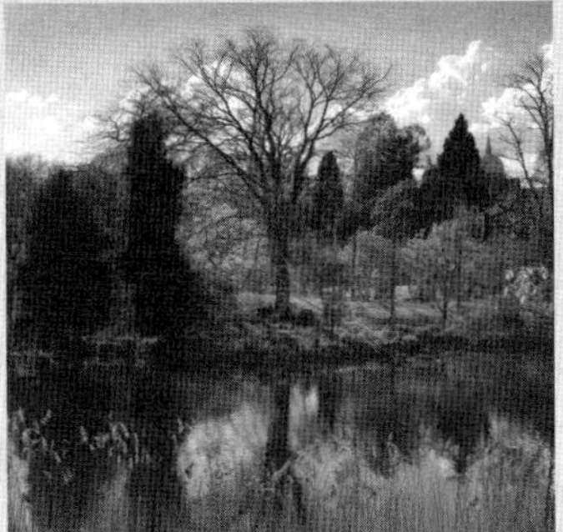

EFTERKLANG : ONE-SIDED LP

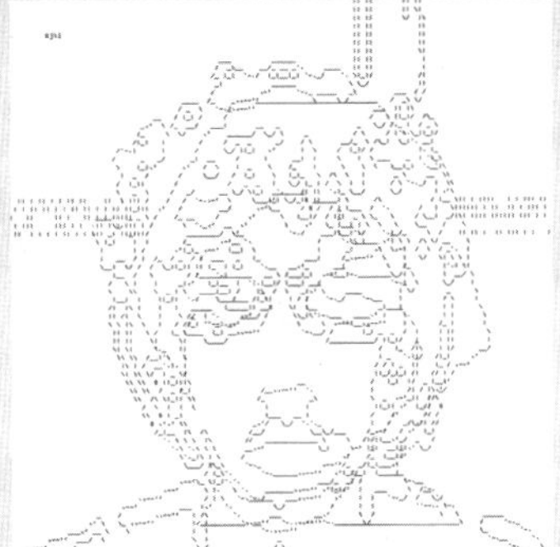

EMPEROR X : THE BLYTHE
ARCHIVES VOLUME ONE LP

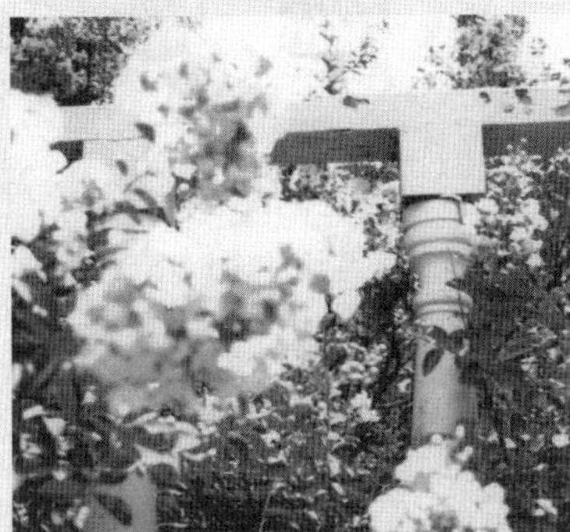

UNWED SAILOR : LITTLE WARS CD/2XLP
ON TOUR THROUGHOUT 2008!

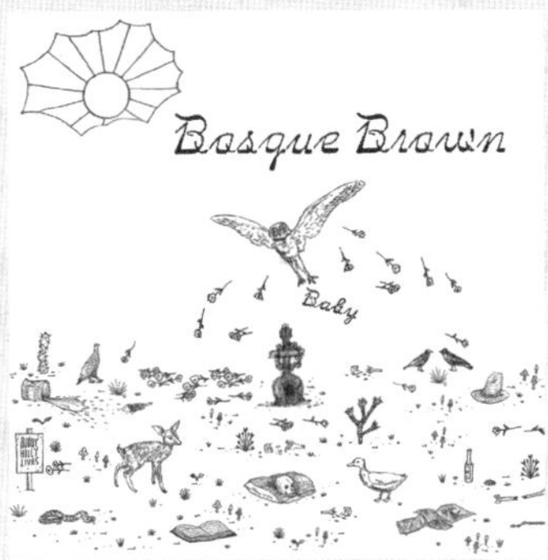

BOSQUE BROWN : BABY CD/LP

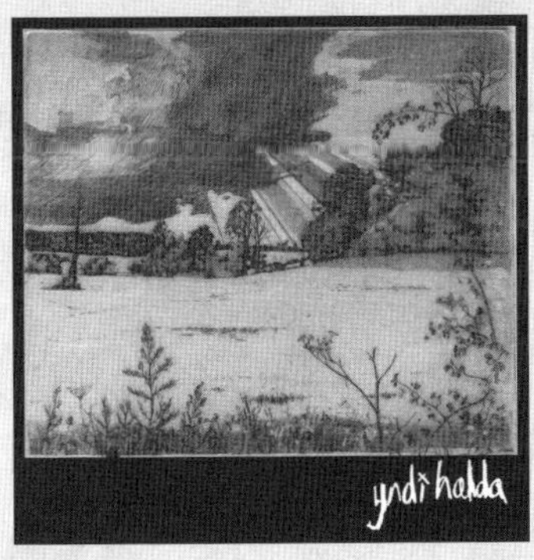

YNDI HALDA : ENJOY ETERNAL BLISS CD/2XLP
AMERICAN TOUR, AUGUST 2008!

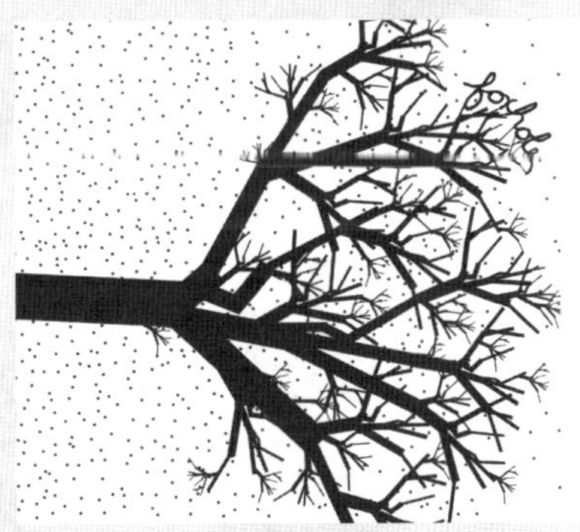

FOXHOLE : WE THE WINTERING TREE CD/2XLP

ONE-SIDED LPS FROM BOSQUE BROWN, JUNE PANIC, AND ISOLATION YEARS NOW,
3/4HADBEENELIMINATED, STEVEN R. SMITH, AND BIRCHVILLE CAT MOTEL SOON

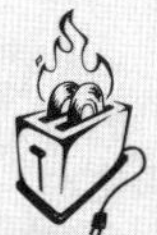

What-the-Heck Fest

July 18th, 19th & 20th, 2008

Anacortes, Washington

Mirah

Calvin Johnson

the Jesus Chords

the Bryan Elliott Band

Karl Blau

Mount Eerie   D+   Ô Paon

Khaela Maricich

...and many more

What-the-Heck Fest is an annual celebration of music, art and community that takes place on beautiful Fidalgo Island. Each year the festival occurs in conjunction with Shipwreck Day, a flea market, featuring 8 city blocks in downtown Anacortes packed full of good junk, antiques, collectibles, tools and all kinds of treasures.

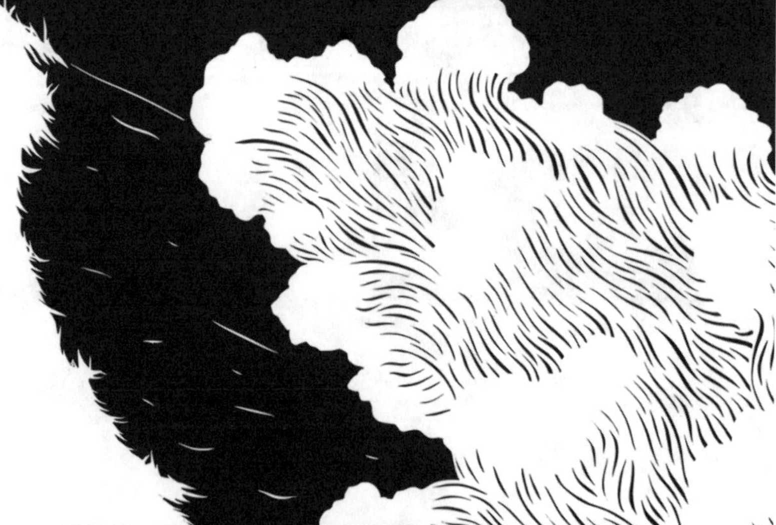

Tickets and info: www.whattheheckfest.com

www.knw-yr-own.com   www.krecs.com   www.departmentofsafety.com

Always WELL worth the wait..

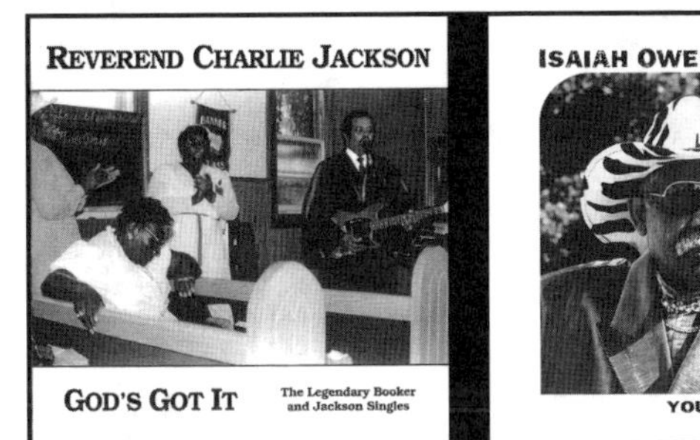

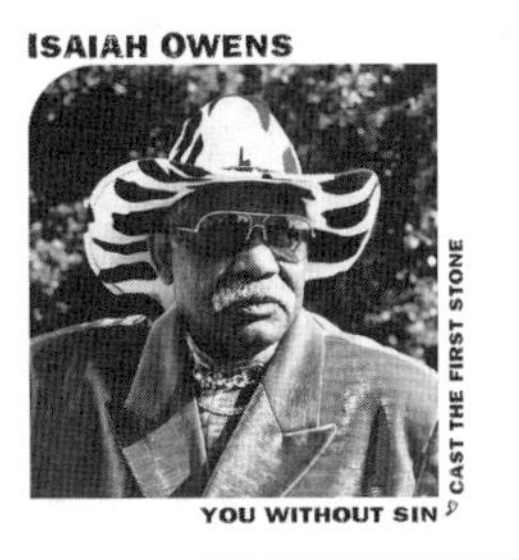

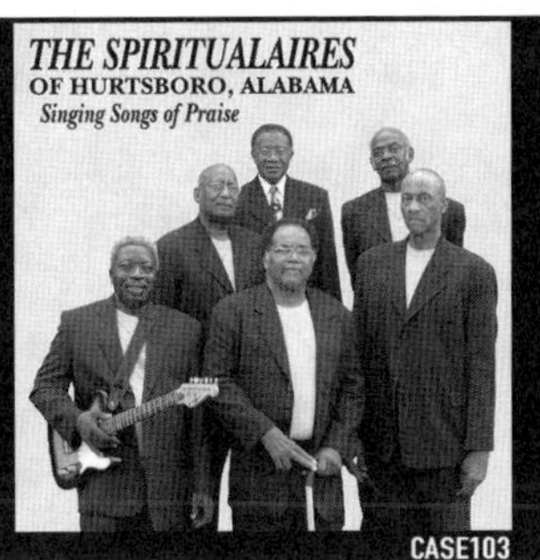

and YES, CASE104 is coming in 2008, being the Elder Utah Smith book+CD project. Hallelujah!

CaseQuarter   www.aumfidelity.com/casequarter.html

>>> a pair of exclusive treats on the Yeti 5 CD !

Premier jazz album productions, unabated..

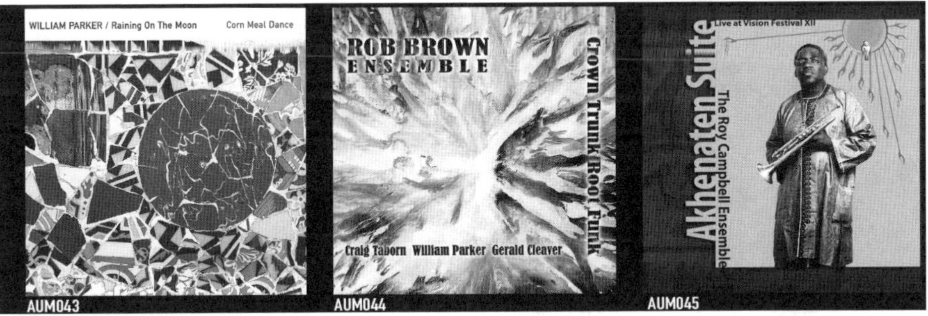

further forthcoming in 2008 are Eri Yamamoto projects both Duo and Trio;
the Double Sunrise Over Neptune orchestra; William Parker Quartet;
the new David S. Ware group; yet more..

www.aumfidelity.com
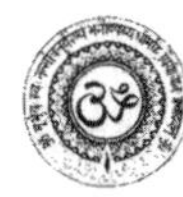
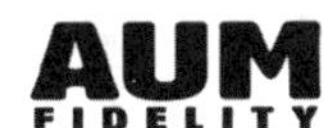

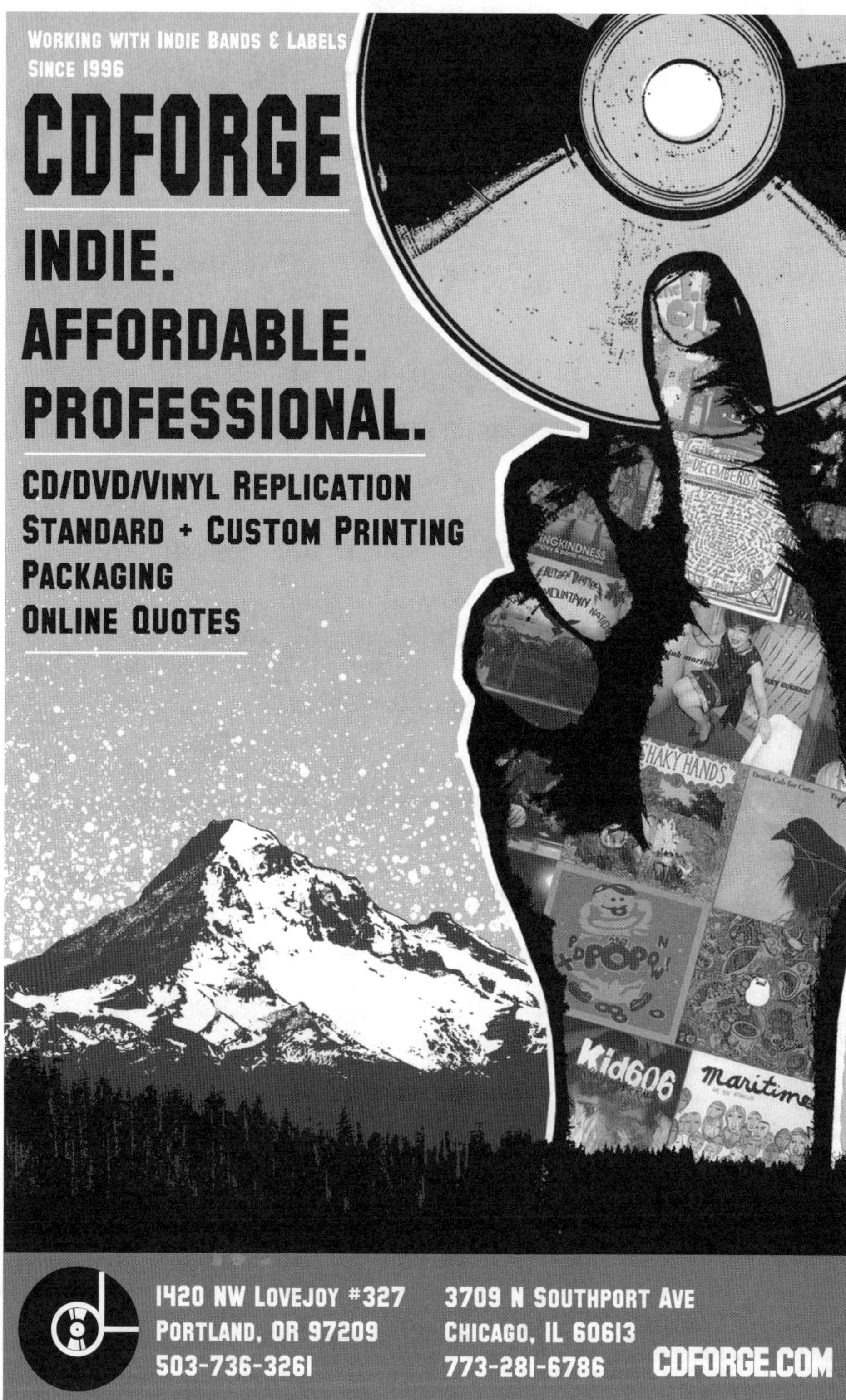
WORKING WITH INDIE BANDS & LABELS SINCE 1996

CDFORGE

INDIE.
AFFORDABLE.
PROFESSIONAL.

CD/DVD/Vinyl Replication
Standard + Custom Printing
Packaging
Online Quotes

1420 NW Lovejoy #327
Portland, OR 97209
503-736-3261

3709 N Southport Ave
Chicago, IL 60613
773-281-6786

CDFORGE.COM

SCRAM, a journal of unpopular culture, is on hiatus while its editrix* creates offbeat bus tours of unknown Los Angeles.

YETI readers will benefit from a special offer on Scram back issues if they send an email with the subject line "Borage" to scram@scrammagazine.com

SHOULD they wish to ride the Esotouric bus at discount, an email (subj. line "Brittlestar") sent to tours@esotouric.com will prove effective.

www.scrammagazine.com
www.esotouric.com

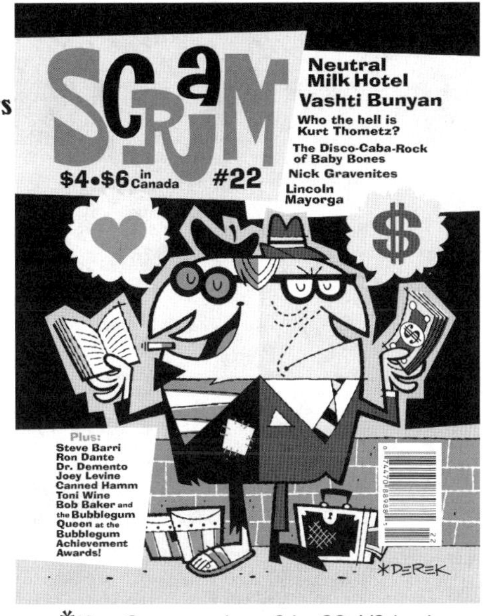

*Kim Cooper, author of the 33 1/3 book on Neutral Milk Hotel and co-editor of "Lost in the Grooves" & "Bubblegum Music is the Naked Truth."

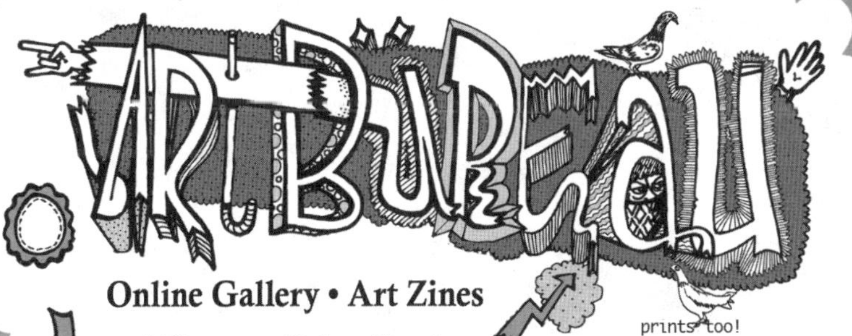

Online Gallery • Art Zines

44flavours, Kelsey Brookes, Catalina Estrada, Eyeformation, Katy Horan, Linzie Hunter, Inksecticid, Stuart Kolakovic, Mulheres Barbadas, Piktorama, Brad Strain, Daria Tessler, Junichi Tsuneoka, Bubi Au Yeung, Someguy from 1,000 Journals & Bomb It!—the movie.

artbureau.etsy.com

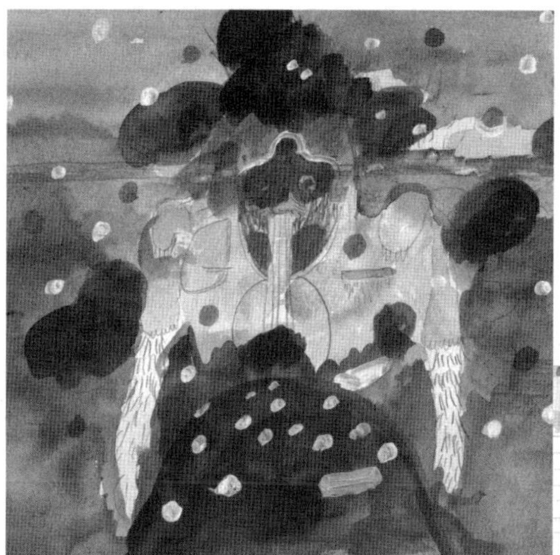

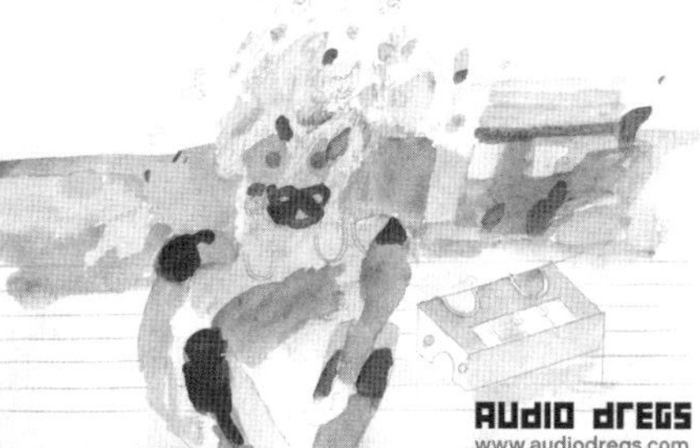

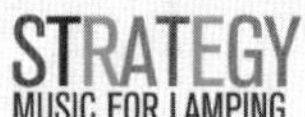

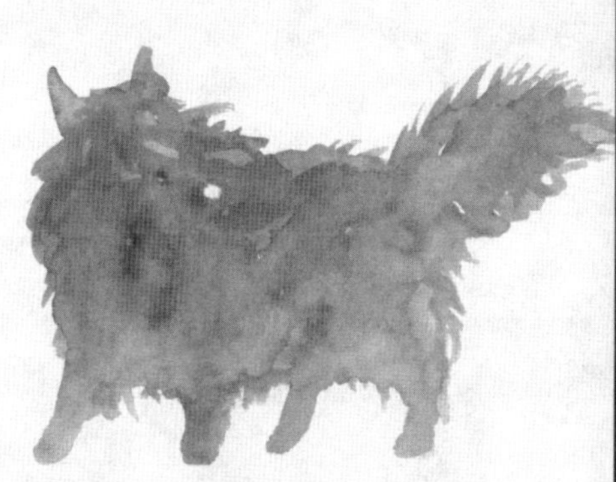

"Music for Lamping contains six years' worth of music that can roughly be called ambient - perhaps "meditative" is a better word. All of this music combines my interest in blurring/expanding/clouding processes--such as granular synthesis, vocoding, and bucket-brigade delay--with happenstance sound sources, such as field recordings or a favorite record sitting around the studio. The earliest music dates to a 2002 CD that was never released, entitled Strategy At Beacon Rock, which was intended as a 'gentle' or 'atmospheric' treatment of plundered audio. The material from 2004 onwards dates to a period of soundwalks in my neighborhood of Northwest Portland (a perfect strolling zone). Taken altogether, these pieces form a traceable thread through my work where I use my usual raw materials to reach a more liquid, spontaneous end result."
-Paul Dickow (Strategy)

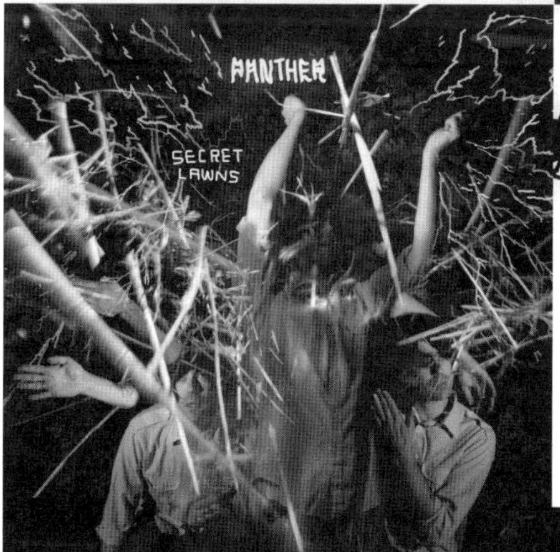

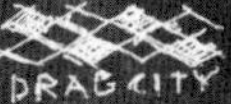

SINGER

UNHISTORIES

New CD & Deluxe LP available from Drag City
www.dragcity.com
DRAG CITY

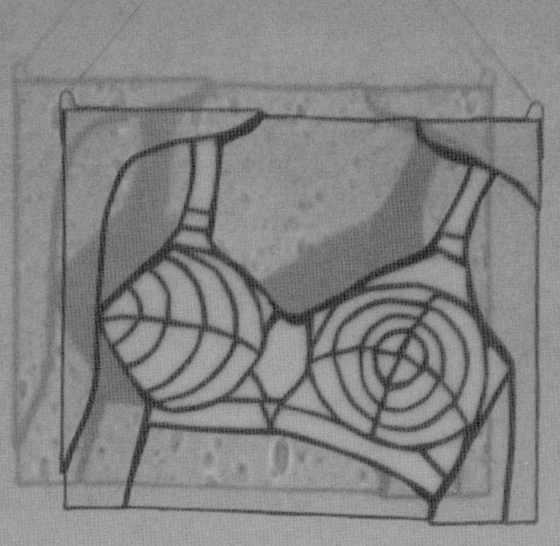

Stained glass by Mimi Lipson
(hangings, windows, functional objects):

http://www.mimilipson.com
215/880-3035
mimilipson@gmail.com

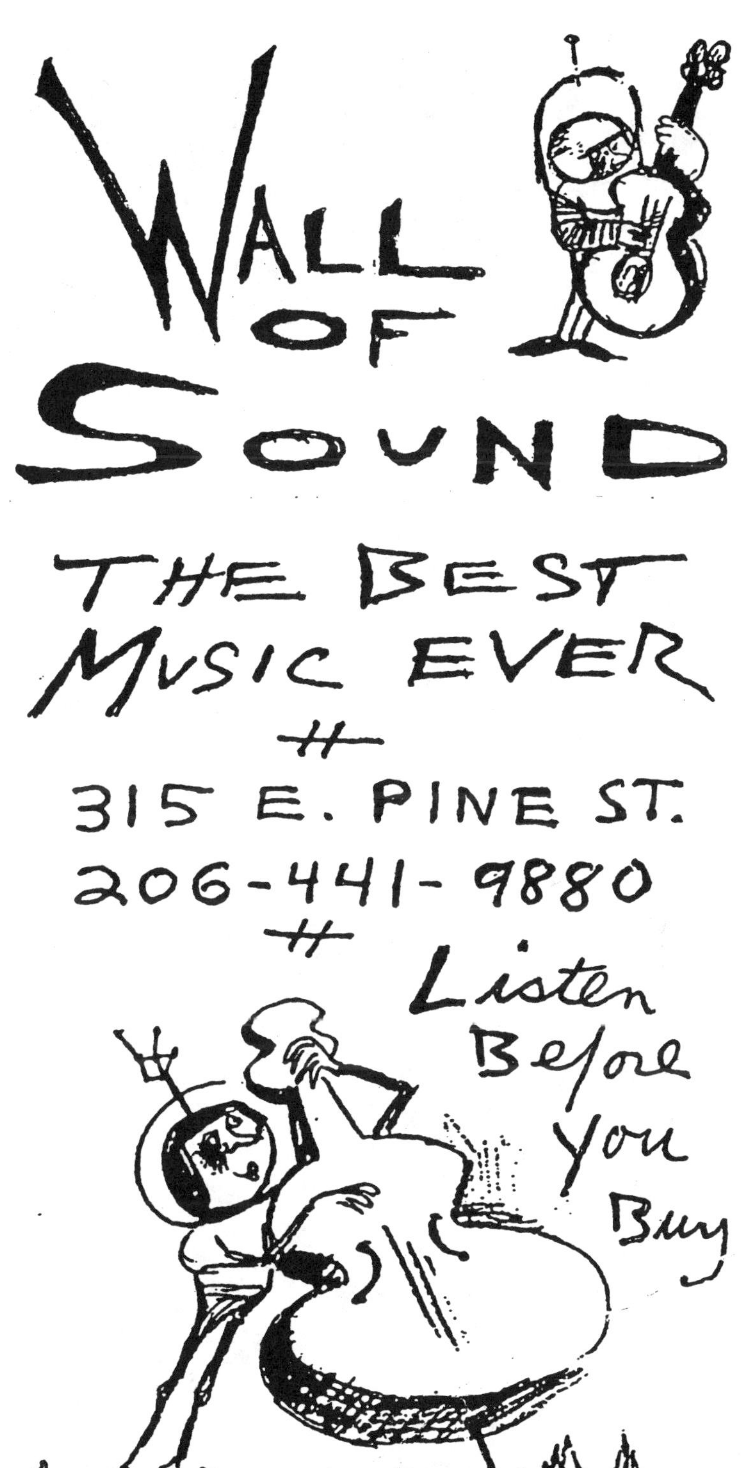

WALL OF SOUND
THE BEST MUSIC EVER
#
315 E. PINE ST.
206-441-9880
#
Listen Before you Buy
WOSOUND.COM

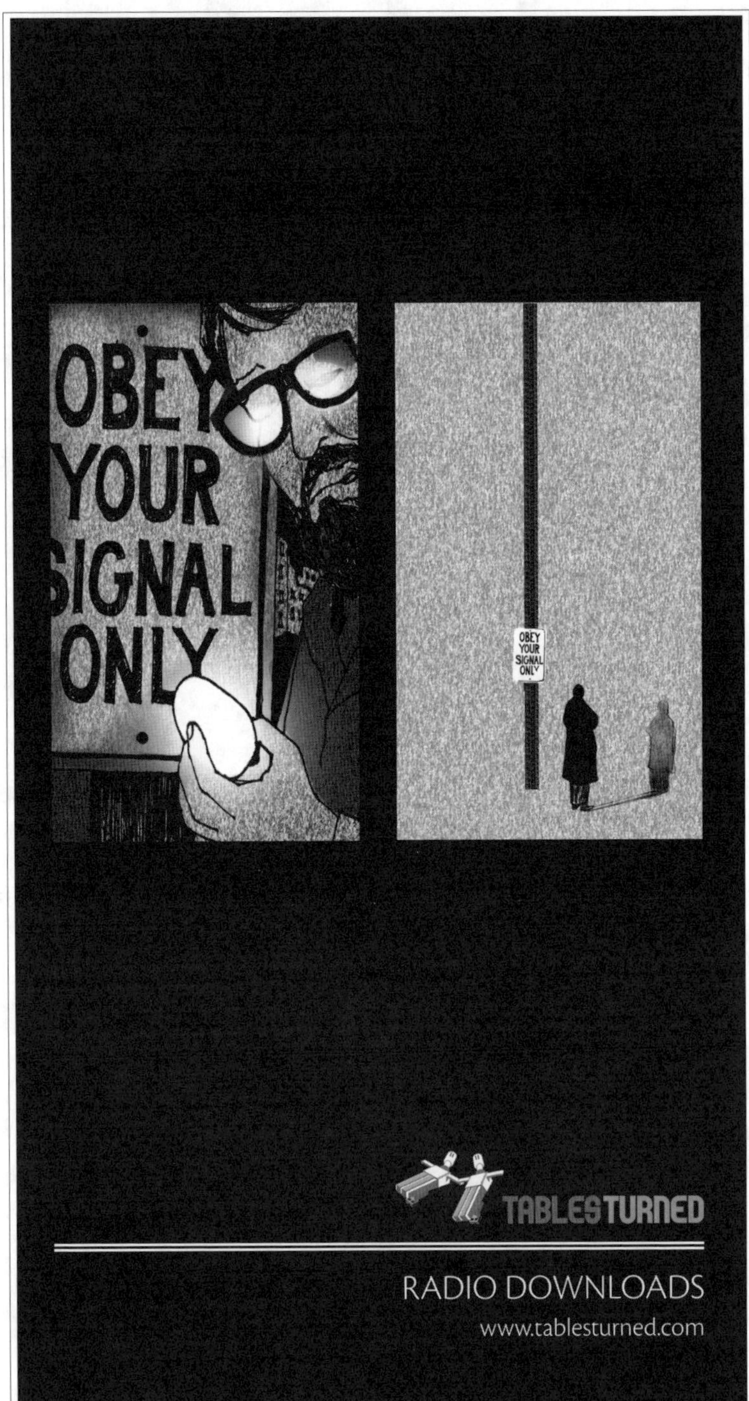

OBEY
YOUR
SIGNAL
ONLY

OBEY
YOUR
SIGNAL
ONLY

TABLESTURNED

RADIO DOWNLOADS
www.tablesturned.com

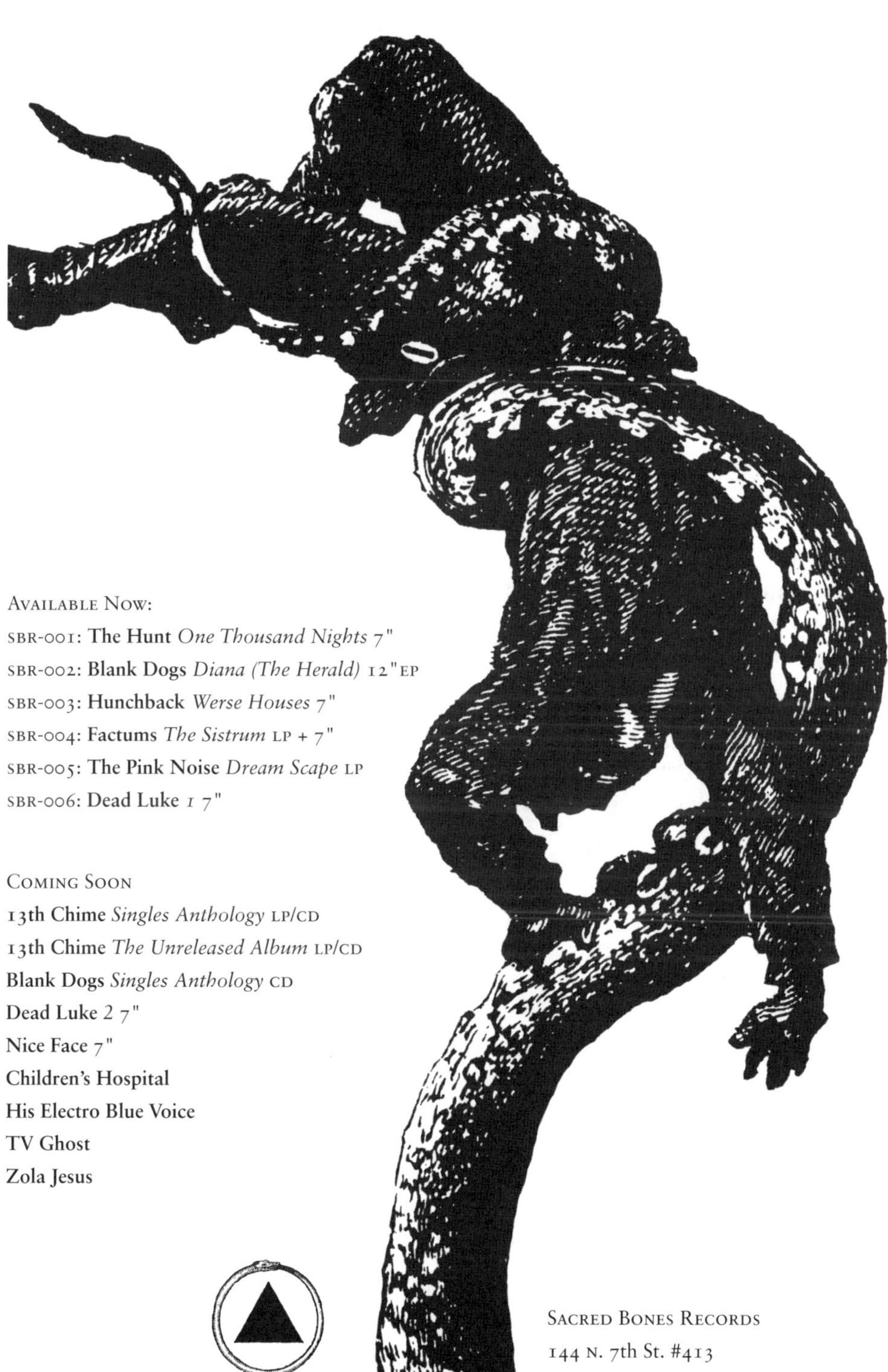

THE YETI FIVE CD

It's an Unfriendly World

ILLUSTRATION BY JEFF MANGUM

With the fifth *YETI* compilation disc, we have endeavored to provide the listener with eighty minutes of recession-proof entertainment. Hopefully, the recession doesn't become a depression; we can't vouch for the thing being fully *depression*-proof, with the arguable exception of a few numbers at the very end.

Let us pray that the manner in which W. and his cronies have gutted and Enronned the entire nation (if not quite a bit of the globe) will not too soon lead to dustbowls, soup kitchens and worse . . . Actually, it might better serve us to hope that our future robot/corporate/Saudi warlords will show enough benevolence to allow us one day of rest a month—enough time to go check out that hot new band, catch up on celebrity snapshots with MSPaint doodles on them, and tend to our festering work sores. Then again, I've probably watched one too many dystopic sci-fi- flicks, and everything's going to be just fine. Really!

This eighty-minute disc was compiled by Mike McGonigal and mastered by Tim Stollenwerk in late January, 2008. Many thanks to Aaron and Eric from Mississippi Records for help with the vinyl transfers—and of course, to everyone who contributed music. As usual, a lot of great music didn't make it on due to the constraints of both time and space. Check the *YETI* website for some of those goodies to appear throughout the year, though: we just figured out the Internets are good for some stuff other than emails—who knew?

1. SPIRITUALAIRES: "Be Ready When He Comes"—This song was recorded in the studios of WBIL 580-AM Tuskegee, Alabama, sometime in 2004 during the Spiritualaires' (who are from nearby Hurtsboro) weekly 30-minute gospel radio broadcast. Kevin Nutt, their label person and gospel expert, explains: "The lead singer here is not a member of the Spiritualaires but a DJ at the station, Sylvester McPherson, who often MCs local gospel programs as well. The nature of the Spiritualaires show is that friends and acquaintances of the group often drift in and out of the studio during the broadcast and even join in on the singing."

The quartet's relatively loose style is closer to the moaning roots of gospel

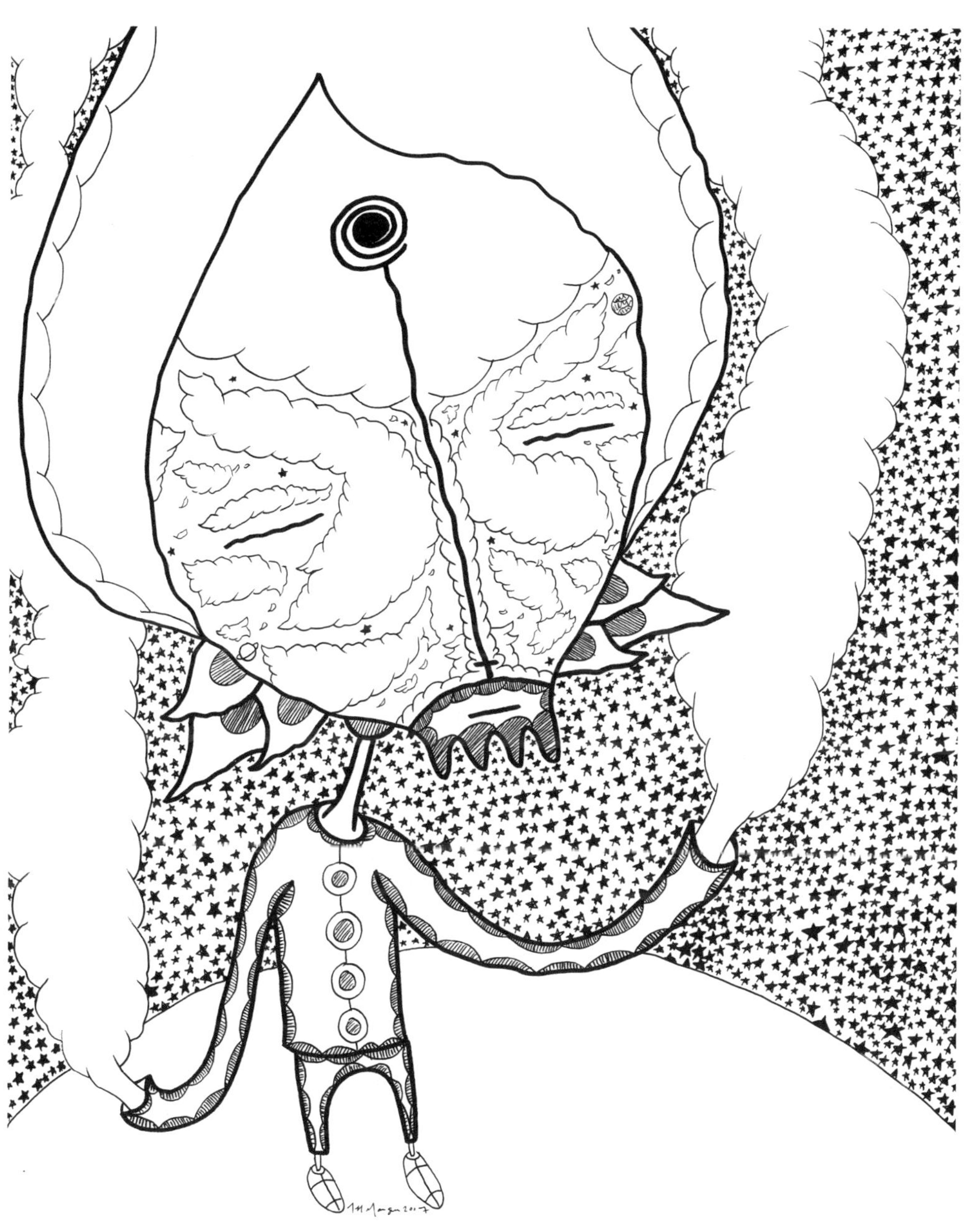

spirituals than your typical Golden Age-era hard shouting or jubilee-style group. The Spiritualaires do hail from the Golden Age. They've been together since 1948, regularly producing radio broadcasts for almost forty years—and they just released their first album, *Singing Songs of Praise* (CaseQuarter) last year! The album was culled from those broadcasts and was among our favorite records of '07.

2. SADOUM OULED AIDA "Untitled"—This recording was made by Hisham Mayet in Nouakchott, Mauritania in 2006. For more on this great artist, check out Hisham's travel journal in this issue. If you like the track, we strongly suggest hunting down the *Group Doueh* and *Group Inerane* LPs released by Sublime Frequencies in the last two years; both are amazing. And for the best interview we know of with Hisham, go to blastitude.com.

3. PHOAMING EDISON "Sheba"—Phoaming Edison is the solo recording alias of James Kavoussi, one of the leaders of New York's long-running and most awesome art-rock band Fly Ashtray. Speaking of art rock, this here is a cover of a song by none other than Mike Oldfield. It's taken from the Phoaming Edison album *A Long Day And a Bad Sandwich*, which was recorded between April and August of 2006, and which will hopefully soon exist beyond CD-R status.

4. RADIO SUMATRA "Outtake #1"—Alan Bishop writes that these *Radio Sumatra* outtakes were "recorded and edited in real time by me in August 2004," and adds that these particular tracks (which we've peppered throughout this disc) "were recorded in Medan, Sumatra."

5. ATLAS SOUND "It's Fair Fair Game Inside"—Atlas Sound is the solo project of Deerhunter's Bradford Cox. He's recently expanded the group to include some of our very favorite people: Brian Foote from Nudge; Honey Owens from Valet, Nudge, Jackie O and World; and Adam Forkner of White Rainbow, Yume Bitsu, Jackie O and World. Bradford explains that the song "is actually kind of a Sparks cover." He elaborates thusly: "Here's the story: I recorded it when I was staying at my friends Karen's house in LA. She has this electric piano K.K. Barrett of the Screamers gave her. I went to In-N-Out Burger and got a milkshake. Then I went to Amoeba and bought the Sparks' [1975] *Indiscreet* LP for $2 and then I went back to Karen's house and smoked all this pot and put on the record and was really stoned and got hypnotized by this one part of the song "Happy Hunting Ground" so I mic'd the electric piano and covered thirty seconds of it. And then I looped the electric piano, because I was high as shit. It's stupid and funny and short."

6. DEAN AND BRITTA "Tugboat (live)"— It's naturally a pleasure to get a swell Dean & Britta song on here, especially as the song in question is "Tugboat," from Galaxie 500's first single on Aurora Records in 1988 (one of the top three review copy records I've ever been sent). This live version was recorded by Uelie Steinmann at El Lokal, Zürich on December 2, 2007. Dean Wareham describes Mr. Steinmann as "a highly trained and very talkative Swiss engineer," and says the song was recorded "on a recent tour, with Anthony LaMarca (drums) and Ben Freeman (Roland XP-30)" backing himself and partner Britta Phillips.

7. AKRON /FAMILY "Small Shape (live)"—Akron/Family were kind enough to send us a song that's never appeared elsewhere. Miles Seaton says that this slowly gestating number was "recorded at Tonic on July 15th, 2005 by Michael Lopez." He adds that "at that time, Akron/Family was Dana Janssen, Seth Olinsky, Miles Seaton, and Ryan Vanderhoof, with guest whistling by Ossian Foley." The guest whistling really makes it, as I'm sure you will agree.

8. ANGLIN BROTHERS "It's An Unfriendly World"—This song was recorded on Saturday, November 12th, 1938 and originally released as a 78 on Vocalion. The Anglins were born in Franklin, Tennessee and reared in Athens, Alabama. They recorded initially as the Anglin Twins (Jack & Jim Anglin, born three years apart) and then as the Anglin Twins & Red (that would be the "twins" with their older brother Red) before cutting their final sides as the Anglin Brothers. Brother duos were hugely important in early country music—the Stanleys, Delmores, Monroes and Louvins among the most prominent (and sublime). Today the Anglins are best known for spawning the 1940s duo Johnnie & Jack (featuring brother Jack) and thence, indirectly, the career of Kitty Wells. Although the brothers cut a total of 34 songs together, only 14 were ever released. There is a 1979 collection that compiles those commercial releases, an LP called *The South's Favorite Trio* on Old Homestead Records (OHS #122). Thankfully, plans are in the works for a reissue.

According to the Alabama Music Hall of Fame website, the Anglins came from a family of eight boys and two girls. In 1930, the Anglin family moved to Nashville. There, in 1933, they formed

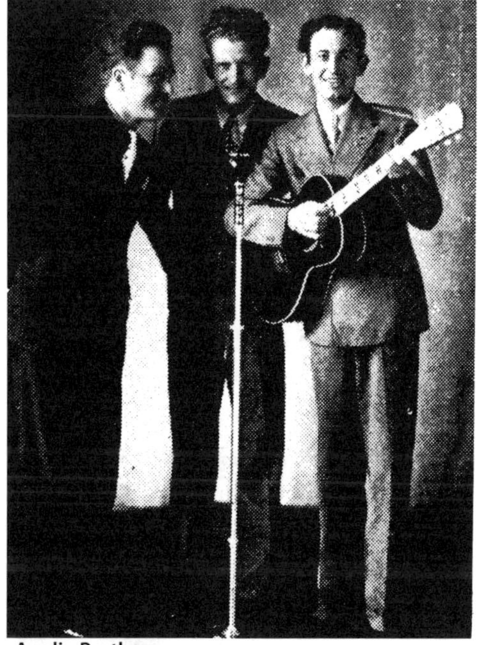
Anglin Brothers

a vocal trio, with Jack playing guitar and Jim on string bass. Red had the best voice so he was the lead vocalist. The Anglins had a popular radio show in Nashville, but as it was unpaid they moved to Birmingham at the recommendation of their friends the Delmores, and later they bounced around various cities across the South—Memphis, New Orleans, and then Atlanta—holding down radio jobs. Red became one of the first men drafted in World War II, and was injured during the Allied invasion of France. He returned home shell-shocked, and was never involved in commercial music-making again; he died in the mid-'70s. According to the *All Music Guide,* Jim Anglin became one of the great country songwriters of the 1940s and '50s, "composing key items in the repertoires of Roy Acuff and later Kitty Wells." Brother Jack found the greatest success of the three when he formed a duo with his brother-in-law Johnnie Wright in the early '40s. That group, Johnnie & Jack, had numerous hits for RCA until 1963, when Jack was killed in a car crash.

9. DEERHOOF "Forbidden Fruits (live)"—Greg from Deerhoof writes that this recording is from a show at a venue called The Garage in London. "I don't really remember the date of the show; it was probably December 2005. But there's no need to put any details like that in the CD, if that's why you're asking—I'd be happy for it to just say 'The Forbidden Fruits Live Version,'" which is pretty much what we did, OK. The song originally appeared on the band's 2003 release *Apple O'* (Kill Rock Stars), while this version was released on *YETI*'s only LP, the compilation record we put together for the first Halleluwah Festivall in Portland, OR in 2006. (If you want one, I think we're down to our last twenty or so copies.)

10. RADIO SUMATRA "Outtake #2"

11. TRIPTYCH MYTH/COOPER-MOORE "Distance"—We asked label dude Steve Joerg for information on this track and he had this to say: "Triptych Myth is the band, composed of Cooper-Moore on piano and sometimes other instruments, Tom Abbs on bass, and Chad Taylor on drums. The group largely and wisely features Cooper-Moore's gorgeous compositions, along with some of Tom's and Chad's, and some free improv for very good measure. They've recorded two albums, including a live one that shows them in their formative stage and an exquisite studio recording that fully lives up to its title and shows them fully arrived as an impeccable unit in the annals of music. This latter album is *The Beautiful*, released on AUM Fidelity in 2005." Now, that bit might sound like an unpaid advertisement (unlike most sampler CDs, labels don't pay to be on a YETI disc), but we agree with what he has to say there, which makes it editorial. (Right? Isn't that the difference? We don't want a repeat of the *Rolling Stone*/Camel debacle here…)

"This track," Joerg continues, "is from the session for that album and though I myself would have been very happy to include it on *The Beautiful*—and indeed wanted it to be so—it was not. "The Distance" is a four minute experiment of Cooper-Moore's. He spoke to Tom and Chad about what he was looking/ aiming for in this composition. Then, each of them went back into the studio and played alone for four minutes—unheard by the other two members. Each of their tracks was then layered together; we did this in the studio, all on the same day."

JEFF MANGUM'S FAVORITE 78s

Here is a special section of the disc curated by Jeff Mangum, legendary musician and visual artist. We're very psyched and grateful to present these tunes. Jeff entrusted us with the actual 78s, mailing them from his home in the upper regions of Northern America. These aren't necessarily his alltime favorite 78s, but rather some 78s he likes a lot and which (as far as either of us knows) have never been issued on CD or LP. Hopefully Jeff will one day compile his own anthology of 78s in the vein of the *Secret Museum of Mankind* series Pat Conte put together for Yazoo, or Ian Nagoski's *Black Mirror* comp on Dust to Digital.

When we initially spoke of this project, this is what Jeff had to say: "I have about five 78s which I think are pretty special: all female vocals and perhaps a little too pretty for your taste—hard to say, although I know you love all kinds of sounds. But anyway, what if I sent them to you, as you probably know a pretty decent mastering person, and if you like them, maybe you could include one or two or five on your CD (a couple of Marika Papagikas, a female choir from Central Asia, and a poppier track from Ceylon)?"

We do like the songs, so here they are:

12. MARIKA PAPAGIKA "Sometime You Might Love Me"—Marika was born in 1890 on the island of Kos. She moved to the United States in 1913 and began recording in 1918. Her husband Gus accompanied her on most of her early recordings on the cymbalum, a Greek kind of hammered dulcimer. They bought a nightclub but lost it in the Great Crash of 1929, which also ended the market for her recordings (though she recorded again briefly in the late '30s). As *Wikipedia* succinctly puts it, "Marika died in New York in 1943; it has been said that she died of disappointment."

13. ALEXANDRA POTSKHERSHVILI "Suliko"—Jeff writes that we should "make sure to include the Russian side I suggest, as the flip was already included in the *Secret Museum*." Written by Akaki Tsereteli (1840-1915), this Georgian folk song was widely reputed to be a personal favorite of the Great Leader and Teacher. The first verse translates loosely as: "I looked for the grave of my beloved / Grief tormented my heart (x2) / It is not easy for the heart without love / Where are you? Answer, Suliko!" So, yeah—sounds pretty Russian to us!

14. UNKNOWN "?"—Sorry, we've got nothing on this one. It's clearly Asian, and likely from the 1930s. The label for this side has been printed to the right here. If anyone can identify it for us, we'll gladly post that info on our web site.

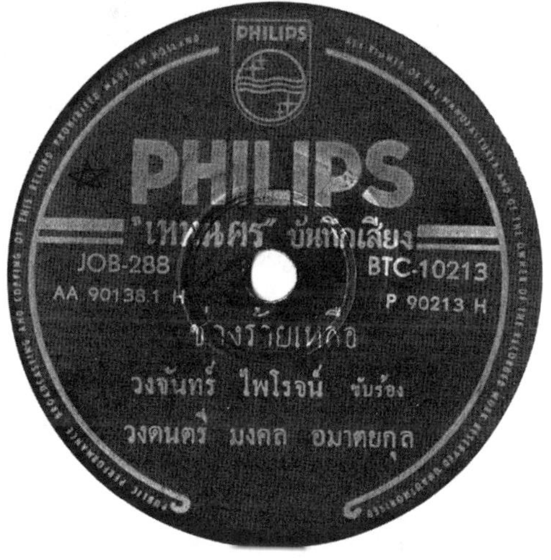

15. MARIKA PAPAGIKA "I Want to Hold You Tight in My Arms"—Received opinion among 78 geeks is that the only Papagika tracks worth hearing are her rebetika ones. After giving these an earful, we disagree. Rebetika (sometimes spelled rembetika) Is often referred to as "the Greek blues." A great introduction to this music can be found in the Rounder CD *Women of Rembetika*. It's packed with beautiful songs that were part of the "Greek underworld tradition." Apparently, these women were allowed far greater freedom within the Greek mafia than outside of it; a "Rembetisse" was a free spirit. Papagika's best-known song from that era translates as "I'll Smash the Glasses"; the song's first line is "I'll get drunk and smash the glasses for what you said to me"—so you pretty well know what you're in for from the start.

16. RADIO SUMATRA "Outtake #3"

17. D+ "Clever Knot"—Minimalist indie-popsters D+ are led by singer/guitarist Bret Lunsford, previously a member of the slightly influential Olympia, WA-based trio Beat Happening. Around 1995, Lunsford befriended drummer Phil Elverum (Mt. Eerie, the Microphones) who soon joined Lunsford in the band. With the addi-

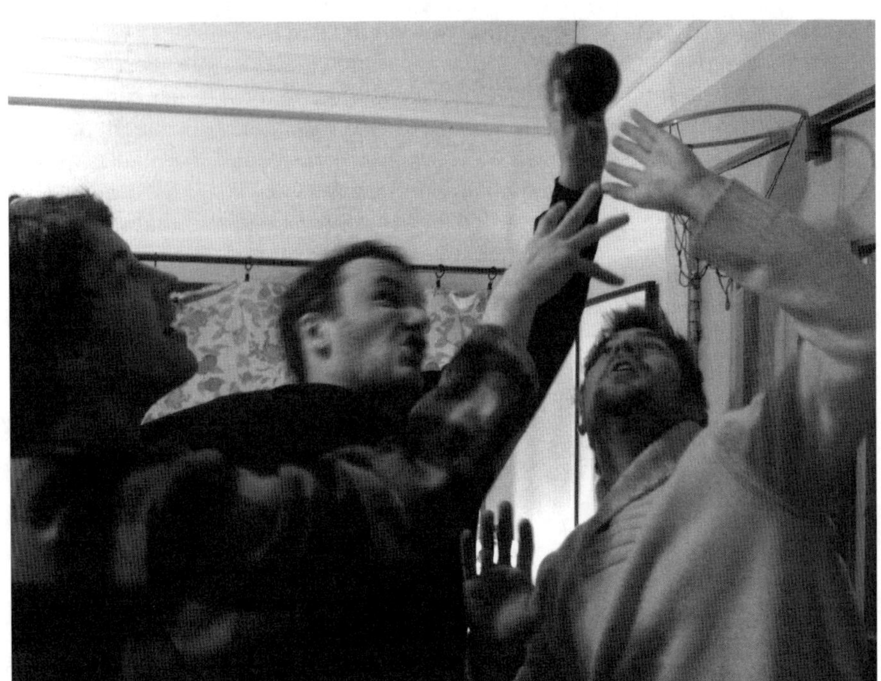

D+ (Photo by Maddy Crowe)

tion of bassist/singer Karl Blau, the group's line-up was complete (as they say). Their self-titled debut appeared in 1997, and their imminent release *D+: On Purpose (1997-2007)*, on Knw-Yr-Own Records, is a super swell compilation of rarities and hits. And the summer of '08 will see the release of their sixth album, *What Is Doubt For?*

"Clever Knot" was first released in a vinyl, letterpress-cover, limited edition of 300 on 2007's *No Mystery* via the label PW Elverum & Suns. Originally composed as a spoken number by Bret, listeners were spared this fate when Phil made up organ music for it. Phil sings, accompanied by Karl. It was engineered and produced by D+ in Anacortes during the dark months of 2006. Its title began as a sleep-deprived joke about the stupid names people give to their boats; its sister song is "Fiendish Plot."

18. MT. EERIE "Blue Light (instrumental)"—Phil Elverum writes that this song "was recorded by me at the Department of Safety in Anacortes, WA," and adds that it's "the music to a song called "Blue Light On The Floor" that I never sang the singing for. I have recorded a few versions of this song and the one I'm going to end up releasing is coming out in a few months on a new Mt. Eerie EP called *Black Wooden Ceiling Opening* which is six songs recorded with this small 'hardcore' band I had for a tour in November of 2006. Amazing Norwegian drummer, Jason Anderson on guitar. Weird attempts at 'extreme' music." Look for more from Phil in *YETI* 6.

19. A HAWK AND A HACKSAW WITH THE HUN HANGAR ENSEMBLE "Vereb / The Sparrow (live)"—Jeremy Barnes, who started A Hawk And A Hacksaw as a more-or-less solo project, has really expanded the group in the last year or so, especially since he's begun to collaborate with the Hun Hangar Ensemble. Of all the folks comprising that alleged micro-trend of Eastern European-influenced indie rock, A Hawk And A Hacksaw's always struck us as the most compelling, and the least schtick-y. Perhaps that stems from this kind of music already being quite a big influence on his former band Neutral Milk Hotel? That might be part of it.

"Vereb / The Sparrow" is from a festival the group played in Krems, Austria in July of 2007. The musicians on the track are: Heather Trost on violin and vocals; Jeremy Barnes on accordion, drums and vocals; Zsolt Kurtosi on upright bass; and Daniel Szabo on the cimbalom.

20. IRON & WINE "Wolves (Song of the Shepherd's Dog) (live)"—This song was recorded on October 29, 2007 at the Queens Hall in Edinburgh, Scotland. Extra thanks to Sam, AJ and Howard Greynolds for this version, which differs quite a bit from the recorded one.

21. RADIO SUMATRA "Outtake #4"—This is the last excerpt on the CD; hope you liked these little outtakes, and were not too terribly confused by their intrusion here. Me, I love the SF *Radio* series. But then I've spent much of my life confused already—perhaps because of that, (allegedly) puzzling and abrupt things often have a calming effect on me.

22. SHAWN DAVID McMILLEN "Texarkana 1971"—Mr. McMillen is from East Texas—specifically Dow Chemical's company town Lake Jackson, a planned community built in the early '40s. Lake Jackson is renowned for two things: outsiders always get hopelessly lost in its crazily winding streets, and then there's the high rate of cancer. Due *perhaps* to all that chemical exposure, the city earned the title "Cancer Capital of America."

Shawn moved to Houston at the age of 16, joined bands you've never heard of, and couch-surfed. In the early '90s, he befriended Tom and Christina Carter of Charalambides. He's collaborated with members of that band ever since—today he plays in Tom Carter's own act the Friday Group. Shawn's released one solo record, *Catfish*, and one disc with Ash Castles on the Ghost Coast, the band he and his girlfriend Heather Leigh Murray started back in the 1990s. More recently, he too moved to Austin and started another band called Iron Kite. Shawn also plays in Rubble with King Coffey (the nicest person to stay in the Butthole Surfers through their various incarnations).

I love this song; it's got a lot going on inside of it. That has to be the best use of harmonica we've heard in some time. This song will be featured on *Imaginational Anthem Vol. 3* (Tompkins Square Records), out later in '08.

23. A.C. & BLIND MAMIE FOREHAND "Honey in the Rock"—This number was recorded by the blind husband-and-wife team in a makeshift recording booth in Memphis, Tennessee in 1927. Guitarist A.C. Forehand was born in Columbus, Georgia, probably in 1890. He lost his sight in 1904 and his first wife, Mamie, said to have been born in 1895, was also blind (presumably from birth). During the 1920 census, the couple resided in Birmingham, Alabama. A.C. gave his occupation as "none."

On February 25th, 1927, they recorded two songs, "Mother's Prayer" and "I'm So Glad Today." A.C. (whose name might more commonly be spelled "Asey") played guitar and harmonica, while his wife, who they called "Blind Mamie Forehand" on the studio card (though it's unknown whether that's what she called herself) accompanied him on the service bell. Three days later, Mamie made two recordings under her own name: "Honey In The Rock," written by the composer F.A. Graves, and the Forehands' take on "Wouldn't Mind Dying If Dying Was All." She sang on those tunes while A.C. accompanied her on guitar. Mamie died in the '30s, and A.C. later remarried, to an organist active in the Church of God in Christ. He passed away in 1972 and was buried in Memphis, in a grave without a marker.

24. MARY PRICE "Dark Was the Night"—This dramatic field recording was made in the mid 1950s by Frederic Ramsey Jr. It's included here to show the hymn that Bind Willie Johnson's song was based on, and as an example of one person singing both the "lead" and "choral" parts of a lining hymn—and also because it sounds great. Do-it-yourself Mobys might have fun combining this and the next track.

25. BLIND WILLIE JOHNSON "Dark Was the Night, Cold Was the Ground"— Since there's an article in this issue about this song, I am not sure what else I can say about it. I know that I fiddled a lot with its placement on the disc. Somehow it seemed cheesy to end with this song (not that the piece itself is cheesy, of course). It's just that this is exactly what you'd expect, to have the song play out the end of the disc, as if credits would roll atop it. The problem with placing it anywhere else is that another track would have to follow it. And, apparently, it's impossible to follow Blind Willie Johnson and not have your musical ass handed to you.

WHAT'S ON THAT CD?
(Cliffs Notes Version)

1. SPIRITUALAIRES, Be Ready When He Comes — **2. SADOUM OULED AIDA,** Untitled — **3. PHOAMING EDISON,** Sheba — **4. RADIO SUMATRA,** Outtake #1 — **5. ATLAS SOUND,** It's Fair Fair Game Inside — **6. DEAN AND BRITTA,** Tugboat (live) — **7. AKRON/FAMILY,** Small Shape (live) — **8. ANGLIN BROTHERS,** It's An Unfriendly World — **9. DEERHOOF,** Forbidden Fruits (live) — **10. RADIO SUMATRA,** Outtake #2 — **11. TRIPTYCH MYTH/COOPER-MOORE,** Distance — **12. MARIKA PAPAGIKA,** Sometime You Might Love Me — **13. ALEXANDRA POTSKHERSHVILI,** Suliko — **14. UNKNOWN,** ? — **15. MARIKA PAPAGIKA,** I Want to Hold You Tight in My Arms — **16. RADIO SUMATRA,** Outtake #3 — **17. D+,** Clever Knot — **18. MT EERIE,** Blue Light (instrumental) — **19. A HAWK AND A HACKSAW,** Vereb / the Sparrow (live) — **20. IRON & WINE,** Wolves (Song of the Shepherd's Dog) (live) — **21. RADIO SUMATRA,** Outtake #4 — **22. SHAWN DAVID McMILLEN,** Texarkana 1971 — **23. A.C. & BLIND MAMIE FOREHAND,** Honey in the Rock — **24. MARY PRICE,** Dark was the Night — **25. BLIND WILLIE JOHNSON,** Dark Was the Night, Cold was the Ground